Essentials

W9-BLD-153

of **PSYCHOLOGICAL ASSESSMENT** Series

Everything you need to know to administer, score, and interpret the major psychological tests.

I'd like to order the following
ESSENTIALS OF PSYCHOLOGICAL ASSESSMENT:

All titles are $34.95* each

- ❏ WAIS®-III Assessment / 0471-28295-2
- ❏ WISC-III® and WPPSI-R® Assessment / 0471-34501-6
- ❏ WJ III® Cognitive Abilities Assessment / 0471-34466-4
- ❏ Cross-Battery Assessment / 0471-38264-7
- ❏ Cognitive Assessment with KAIT & Other Kaufman Measures / 0471-38317-1
- ❏ Nonverbal Assessment / 0471-38318-X
- ❏ PAI® Assessment / 0471-08463-8
- ❏ CAS Assessment / 0471-29015-7
- ❏ MMPI-2™ Assessment / 0471-34533-4
- ❏ Myers-Briggs Type Indicator® Assessment / 0471-33239-9
- ❏ Rorschach® Assessment / 0471-33146-5
- ❏ Millon™ Inventories Assessment, Second Edition / 0471-21891-X
- ❏ TAT and Other Storytelling Techniques / 0471-39469-6
- ❏ MMPI-A™ Assessment / 0471-39815-2
- ❏ NEPSY® Assessment / 0471-32690-9
- ❏ Neuropsychological Assessment / 0471-40522-1
- ❏ WJ III® Tests of Achievement Assessment / 0471-33059-0
- ❏ Individual Achievement Assessment / 0471-32432-9
- ❏ WMS®-III Assessment / 0471-38080-6
- ❏ Behavioral Assessment / 0471-35367-1
- ❏ Forensic Assessment / 0471-33186-4
- ❏ Bayley Scales of Infant Development—II Assessment / 0471-32651-8
- ❏ Career Interest Assessment / 0471-35365-5
- ❏ WPPSI™-III Assessment / 0471-28895-0
- ❏ 16PF® Assessment / 0471-23424-9
- ❏ Assessment Report Writing / 0471-39487-4
- ❏ Stanford-Binet Intelligence Scales (SB5) Assessment / 0471-22404-9
- ❏ WISC®-IV Assessment / 0471-47691-9
- ❏ KABC-II Assessment / 0471-66733-1
- ❏ WIAT®-II and KTEA-II Assessment / 0471-70706-6

Please complete the order form on the back

TO ORDER BY PHONE, CALL TOLL FREE 1-877-762-2974
To order online: www.wiley.com/essentials
To order by mail refer to order form on next page

WILEY

Essentials

of PSYCHOLOGICAL ASSESSMENT Series

Order Form

Please send this order form with your payment (credit card or check) to:

    John Wiley & Sons, Inc.
    Attn: J. Knott
    111 River Street
    Hoboken, NJ 07030-5774

Name _____

Affiliation _____

Address _____

City/State/Zip _____

Phone _____

E-mail _____

❑ Please add me to your e-mailing list

Quantity of Book(s) ordered _____ x $34.95* each

Shipping charges:	Surface	2-Day	1-Day	
First Item	$5.00	$10.50	$17.50	**Total $_____**
Each additional item	$3.00	$3.00	$4.00	

For orders greater than 15 items, please contact Customer Care at 1-877-762-2974.

Payment Method: ❑ Check ❑ Credit Card (*All orders subject to credit approval*)
                     ❑ MasterCard ❑ Visa ❑ American Express

Card Number _____ Exp. Date_____

Signature _____

                               * Prices subject to change.

TO ORDER BY PHONE, CALL TOLL FREE 1-877-762-2974
To order online: www.wiley.com/essentials

WILEY

Essentials of WIAT®-II and KTEA-II Assessment

Essentials of Psychological Assessment Series

Series Editors, Alan S. Kaufman and Nadeen L. Kaufman

Essentials

of WIAT®-II and

KTEA-II Assessment

Elizabeth O. Lichtenberger

Donna R. Smith

John Wiley & Sons, Inc.

To my sisters,
Laura and Lesley

*You have both been an inspiration to me as I've watched you
conquer great challenges and persevere through difficulties in your lives.
I am very proud of all you have achieved.*

With love from your big sister,
Liz

To the grandkids—

*Ryan, Kevin, T. J., Emily, Caroline, Sean,
Grant, Brayden, Luke, and Brylee.
You put a song in my heart and a smile on my face.*

I love you.
Grandma

CONTENTS

SERIES PREFACE

I n the *Essentials of Psychological Assessment* series, we have attempted to provide the reader with books that will deliver key practical information in the most efficient and accessible style. The series features instruments in a variety of domains, such as cognition, personality, education, and neuropsychology. For the experienced clinician, books in the series will offer a concise yet thorough way to master utilization of the continuously evolving supply of new and revised instruments, as well as a convenient method for keeping up to date on the tried-and-true measures. The novice will find here a prioritized assembly of all the information and techniques that must be at one's fingertips to begin the complicated process of individual psychological diagnosis.

Wherever feasible, visual shortcuts to highlight key points are utilized alongside systematic, step-by-step guidelines. Chapters are focused and succinct. Topics are targeted for an easy understanding of the essentials of administration, scoring, interpretation, and clinical application. Theory and research are continually woven into the fabric of each book but always to enhance clinical inference, never to sidetrack or overwhelm. We have long been advocates of what has been called "intelligent" testing—the notion that a profile of test scores is meaningless unless it is brought to life by the clinical observations and astute detective work of knowledgeable examiners. Test profiles must be used to make a difference in the child's or adult's life, or why bother to test? We want this series to help our readers become the best intelligent testers they can be.

In *Essentials of WIAT®-II and KTEA-II Assessment,* the authors have attempted to provide readers with succinct, straightforward, theory-based methods for competent clinical interpretation and application of the second editions of two widely used tests of individual achievement. Both the WIAT-II and KTEA-II are normed for children, adolescents, and adults from Pre-Kindergarten through college. This book helps ease the transition of examiners who have been longtime users of the first editions of these tests, and provides a solid foundation for new examiners, who are first discovering the abundance of information that can be gathered from these two individual assessment instruments. Both of these tests of achievement tap the important domains of academic ability required for assessment of learning disabilities. This book thoroughly integrates theory, research, clinical history, and clinical inference, with sets of guidelines that enable the examiner to give, and then systematically interpret and apply, these thoroughly revised and restandardized instruments.

Alan S. Kaufman, PhD, and Nadeen L. Kaufman, EdD, Series Editors
Yale University School of Medicine

One

OVERVIEW

O ver the past few years there have been many changes affecting those who administer standardized achievement tests. New, individually administered tests of achievement have been developed and older instruments have been revised or renormed. The academic assessment of individuals from preschool to post high school has increased over the past years due to requirements set forth by states for determining eligibility for services for learning disabilities. Individual achievement tests once used to be primarily norm-based comparisons with peers, but now serve the purpose of analyzing academic strengths and weaknesses via comparisons with conormed (or linked) individual tests of ability. In addition, the focus of academic assessment has been broadened to include not only reading decoding, spelling, and arithmetic, but also reading comprehension, arithmetic reasoning, arithmetic computation, listening comprehension, oral expression, and written expression (Smith, 2001).

These changes in the field of individual academic assessment have led professionals to search for resources that would help them remain current on the most recent instruments. Resources covering topics such as how to administer, score, and interpret frequently used tests of achievement, and how to apply these tests' data in clinical situations, need to frequently be updated. Thus, in 2001, Douglas K. Smith published a book in the *Essentials* series titled *Essentials of Individual Achievement Assessment,* which devoted chapters to four widely used, individually administered tests of achievement.[1] Smith's volume was the inspiration for writing this book, which focuses on the recent second editions of two of the instruments written about in *Essentials of Individual Achievement Assessment:* the Wechsler Individual Achievement Test (WIAT) and Kaufman Test of Educational Achievement (K-TEA). Because both of these instruments are widely used

---

[1] Another widely used achievement test, the Woodcock Johnson—Third Edition (WJ III) is the topic of its own book in the *Essentials* series, *Essentials of WJ III Tests of Achievement Assessment* (Mather, Wendling, & Woodcock, 2001).

achievement tests in school psychology and related fields, the second editions of the WIAT and of the K-TEA are deserving of a complete, up-to-date book devoted to their administration, scoring, interpretation, and to the clinical applications of the tests. *Essentials of WIAT-II and KTEA-II Assessment* provides that up-to-date information and includes rich information beyond what is available in the tests' manuals. An entire chapter is devoted to illustrative case reports, to exemplify how the results of the WIAT-II and KTEA-II can be integrated with an entire battery of tests to yield a thorough understanding of a student's academic functioning. In a chapter devoted to clinical applications of the tests, the following topics are discussed: the integration of KTEA-II and WIAT-II with their respective conormed tests of cognitive ability, focusing on the conceptual and theoretical links between tests, and the assessment of special populations, including specific learning disabilities and Attention-Deficit/Hyperactivity Disorder (ADHD).

PURPOSES AND USES OF ACHIEVEMENT TESTS

The WIAT-II and KTEA-II are used for many reasons, including diagnosing achievement, identifying processing, analyzing errors, program planning, measuring academic progress, evaluating interventions or programs, making placement decisions, and research. Some pertinent applications of these tests are described in the following pages.

Diagnosing Achievement

The WIAT-II and KTEA-II provide an analysis of a student's academic strengths and weaknesses in reading, mathematics, written language, and oral language. In addition, the reading-related subtests of these tests allow for the investigation of related factors that may affect reading achievement, such as Phonological Awareness and Naming Facility (Rapid Automatized Naming, or RAN) on the KTEA-II and the phonemic/phonological awareness and automaticity sections of Word Reading on the WIAT-II.

Identifying Processes

Pairwise comparisons of subtests on both the WIAT-II and KTEA-II allow examiners to better understand how students take in information (Reading Comprehension versus Listening Comprehension) and express their ideas (Written Expression versus Oral Expression).

Analyzing Errors

The KTEA-II provides a detailed quantitative summary of the types or patterns of errors a student makes on subtests in each of the achievement domains (Reading, Math, Written Language, and Oral Language), as well as for Phonological Awareness and Nonsense Word Decoding. Tracking error patterns can help examiners plan appropriate remedial instruction specifically targeting the difficulties a student displays, and the KTEA-II ASSIST software offers instructional strategies to help examiners design appropriate interventions based on a student's error pattern.

The WIAT-II provides a way to qualitatively examine a student's errors, called skills analysis. Each subtest includes sets of items that measure a specific skill or set of skills. The information yielded from analyzing the student's errors through the skills analysis can then be used in the design of an instructional plan or specific intervention for a student. The WIAT-II Scoring Assistant provides a summary by subtest of a student's performance at the individual as well as aggregate skill levels.

Program Planning

The norm-referenced scores, along with the error and skills analysis information, indicate a student's approximate instructional level. These results can help facilitate decisions regarding appropriate educational placement as well as appropriate accommodations or curricular adjustments. The information can also assist in the development of an Individualized Education Program (IEP) based on a student's needs. For young adults, the results can help inform decisions regarding appropriate vocational training or General Equivalency Diploma (GED) preparation.

Measuring Academic Progress

The two parallel forms of the KTEA-II allow an examiner to measure a student's academic progress while ensuring that changes in performance are not due to the student's familiarity with the battery content. Academic progress can also be measured on the WIAT-II with a retest, taking into consideration any potential practice effect.

Evaluating Interventions or Programs

The WIAT-II and KTEA-II can provide information about the effectiveness of specific academic interventions or programs. For example, administering one or more of the composites could demonstrate the effectiveness of a new reading program within a classroom or examine the relative performance levels between classrooms using different math programs.

Making Placement Decisions

The WIAT-II and KTEA-II can provide normative data to aid in placement decisions regarding new student admissions or transfers from other educational settings.

Research

The WIAT-II and the KTEA-II Comprehensive Form are reliable, valid measures of academic achievement suitable for use in many research designs. Indeed, a brief search of the literature via PsycInfo yielded hundreds of articles that utilized the WIAT and the K-TEA. The two parallel forms of the KTEA-II make it an ideal instrument for longitudinal studies or research on intervention effectiveness using pre- and post test designs.

The WIAT-II Abbreviated form and KTEA-II Brief Form are also reliable, valid measures of academic achievement that are ideal for research designs that call for a screening measure of achievement. The brevity of the WIAT-II Abbreviated Form and KTEA-II Brief Form make them useful in estimating the educational achievement of large numbers of prisoners, patients in hospitals, military recruits, applicants to industry training programs, or juvenile delinquents awaiting court hearings, where administering long tests may be impractical.

Screening

The WIAT-II Abbreviated Form and the KTEA-II Brief Form are intended for screening examinees on their global skills in mathematics, reading, and written language. The results of the screening may be used to determine the need for follow-up testing.

SELECTING AN ACHIEVEMENT TEST

Selecting the appropriate achievement test to use in a specific situation depends on a number of factors.[2] The test should be reliable, valid, and used only for the

---

[2] Portions of this section were adapted from Chapter One of *Essentials of Individual Achievement Assessment* (Smith, 2001).

purposes for which it was developed. The Code of Fair Testing Practices in Education (Joint Committee on Testing Practices, 1988) outlines the responsibilities of both test developers and test users. Key components of the *Code* are outlined in Rapid Reference 1.1.

The first factor to consider in selecting an achievement test is the purpose of the testing. Discern whether a comprehensive measure (covering the areas of achievement specified in the Individuals with Disabilities Improvement Act of 2004 (P.L. 108-446)) is needed or whether a less specific screening measure is appropriate. Another issue is whether an ability-achievement discrepancy will need to be examined. Although P.L. 108-446 recently removed the requirement of demonstrating an achievement-ability discrepancy from determining eligibility for learning disabilities services, states still have the option to include this discrepancy if they choose. For this purpose, using achievement tests with co-normed or linked ability tests is best. To gather diagnostic information and information about level of skill development, you should use a test with skills analysis procedures.

The second factor to consider in selecting an achievement test is whether a particular test can answer the specific questions asked in the referral concerns. The specificity of the referral questions will help guide the test selection. For example, if the referral concern is about a child's reading fluency, the test you select should have a subtest or subtests that directly assess that domain.

The third factor to consider in selecting an achievement test is how familiar an examiner is with a certain test. Familiarity with a test and experience scoring and interpreting it is ethically necessary to utilize it in an assessment. If you plan to use a new test in an assessment, you should ensure that you have enough time to get proper training and experience with the instrument before using it.

The fourth factor to consider in selecting an achievement test is whether the test's standardization is appropriate. Consider how recent the test's norms are. Most recent major tests of academic achievement are well standardized, but you should still review the manual to evaluate the normative group. See if students with disabilities were included in the standardization sample (which is important when assessing a student suspected of having a learning disability). Ensure that appropriate stratification variables were used in the standardization sample.

The fifth factor to consider in selecting an achievement test is the strength of the psychometric properties of a test. Consider whether the test's data have adequately demonstrated its reliability and validity. A test's internal consistency, test-retest reliability, correlations with other achievement tests and tests of cognitive ability should all be examined. Additionally consider the floor and ceiling of a test across age levels. Some tests have poor floors at the youngest age levels for the

≡ Rapid Reference 1.1

Excerpts from the Code of Fair Testing Practices in Education

Selecting Appropriate Tests

1. First define the purpose for testing and the population to be tested. Then, select a test for that purpose and that population based on a thorough review of the available information.

2. Investigate potentially useful sources of information, in addition to test scores, to corroborate the information provided by tests.

3. Read the materials provided by test developers and avoid using tests for which unclear or incomplete information is provided.

4. Become familiar with how and when the test was developed and tried out.

5. Read independent evaluations of a test and of possible alternative measures. Look for evidence required to support the claims of test developers.

6. Examine specimen sets, disclosed tests or samples of questions, directions, answer sheets, manuals, and score reports before selecting a test.

7. Ascertain whether the test content and norms group(s) or comparison group(s) are appropriate for the intended test takers.

8. Select and use only those tests for which the skills needed to administer the test and interpret scores correctly are available.

Interpreting Scores

1. Obtain information about the scale used for reporting scores, the characteristics of any norms or comparison group(s), and the limitations of the scores.

2. Interpret scores taking into account any major differences between the norms or comparison groups and the actual test takers. Also take into account any differences in test administration practices or familiarity with the specific questions in the test.

3. Avoid using tests for purposes not specifically recommended by the test developer unless evidence is obtained to support the intended use.

4. Explain how any passing scores were set and gather evidence to support the appropriateness of the scores.

5. Obtain evidence to help show that the test is meeting its intended purpose(s).

Striving for Fairness

1. Evaluate the procedures used by test developers to avoid potentially insensitive content or language.

2. Review the performance of test takers of different races, gender, and ethnic backgrounds when samples of sufficient size are available. Evaluate the extent to which performance differences may have been caused by inappropriate characteristics of the test.

3. When necessary and feasible, use appropriately modified forms of tests or administration procedures for test takers with handicapping conditions. Interpret standard norms with care in the light of the modifications that were made.

Informing Test Takers

1. Provide test takers or their parents/guardians with information about rights test takers may have to obtain copies of tests and completed answer sheets, retake tests, have tests rescored, or cancel scores.

2. Tell test takers or their parents/guardians how long scores will be kept on file and indicate to whom and under what circumstances test scores will or will not be released.

3. Describe the procedures that test takers or their parents/guardians may use to register complaints and have problems resolved.

Note. The *Code* was developed in 1988 by the Joint Committee of Testing Practices, a cooperative effort of several professional organizations that has as its aim the advancement, in the public interest, of the quality of testing practices. The Joint Committee was initiated by the American Educational Research Association (AERA), the American Psychological Association (APA), and the National Council on Measurement in Education (NCME). In addition to these three groups, the American Association for Counseling and Development/Association for Measurement and Evaluation in Counseling and Development, and the American Speech-Language-Hearing Association also now sponsor the Joint Committee.

children with the lowest skills and other tests have poor ceilings at the oldest age levels for the children with the highest skill levels. You can judge the adequacy of the floors and ceilings by examining the standard score range of the subtests and composites for the age range of the student you are assessing.

In chapters 2 and 3 of this book we review what we feel are the strengths and weaknesses of the WIAT-II and KTEA-II, respectively. We encourage examiners to carefully review the test they select to administer, whether WIAT-II, KTEA-II, or another achievement test, to ensure that it can adequately assess the unique concerns of the student for whom the evaluation is being conducted. Rapid Reference 1.2 summarizes the key points to consider in test selection.

ADMINISTERING STANDARDIZED ACHIEVEMENT TESTS

The WIAT-II and KTEA-II are standardized tests, meaning that they measure a student's performance on tasks that are administered and scored under known conditions that remain constant from time to time and person to person. Standardized testing allows examiners to directly compare the performance of one student to the performance of many other students of the same age who were tested in the same way. Strict adherence to the rules allows examiners to know

≋ Rapid Reference 1.2

Summary of Key Points to Consider in Test Selection

Consider the purpose of the assessment and what type of test(s) it demands

- Comprehensive assessment
- Screening assessment
- Ability-achievement discrepancy analysis
- Skills analysis

Consider your experience with the assessment instrument you are planning to administer

- Administration (extensive, some, or no experience)
- Scoring (extensive, some, or no experience)
- Interpretation (extensive, some, or no experience)

Consider the adequacy of the test's standardization

- Are norms recent?
- Was the standardization sample appropriate?
- Were students with learning disabilities included?
- Was the norm sample appropriately stratified according to age, gender, geographic region, ethnicity, and socioeconomic status?

Consider the psychometric qualities of the test

- Is the test's reliability adequate (internal consistency and test-retest reliability)?
- Is the test's validity adequate (correlations with other achievement tests, correlations with ability tests)?
- Does the test have an adequate floor for the age of the student you are assessing?
- Does the test have an adequate ceiling for the age of the student you are assessing?

that the scores obtained from the child they tested are comparable to those obtained from the normative group. Violating the rules of standardized administration renders norms of limited value. Being completely familiar with the test, its materials, and the administration procedures allows examiners to conduct a valid assessment in a manner that feels natural, comfortable, and personal, not mechanical. The specific administration procedures for the WIAT-II are discussed in Chapter 2 and those for the KTEA-II are discussed in Chapter 3.

Testing Environment

Achievement testing, like most standardized testing, should take place in a quiet room that is free of distractions. The table and chairs that are used during the assessment should be of appropriate size for the student being assessed. That is, if you are assessing a preschooler, the table and chairs used should ideally be similar to those that you would find in a preschool classroom. However, if you are assessing an adolescent, adult-size table and chairs are appropriate. The seating arrangement should allow the examiner to see both sides of the easel and to write responses and scores discretely on the record form (out of plain view of the examinee). Many examiners find the best seating arrangement is to be at a right angle from the examinee, but others prefer to sit directly across from the examinee. The test's stimulus easel can be used to shield the record form from the student's view, but if you prefer you can use a clipboard to keep the record form out of view. Most importantly, you should sit wherever it is most comfortable for you and that allows you easy access to all of the components of the assessment instrument.

Establishing Rapport

In order to ensure that the most valid results are yielded from a testing, you need to create the best possible environment for the examinee. Perhaps more important than the physical aspects of the testing environment discussed previously is the relationship between the examiner and the student. In many cases the examiner will be a virtual stranger to the student being assessed. Thus, the process of establishing rapport is a key component in setting the stage for an optimal assessment.

Rapport can be defined as a relationship of mutual trust and/or emotional affinity. Such a relationship typically takes time to develop. To foster the development of positive rapport, you need to plan on a few minutes of relaxed time with the student before diving into the assessment procedures. Some individuals are "slow to warm up" to new acquaintances, whereas others are friendly and comfortable with new people from the get-go. Assume that most students you meet will need time before being able to comfortably relate to you.

You can help a student feel more comfortable through your style of speech and your topics of conversation. Adapt your language (vocabulary and style) to the student's age and ability level (i.e., don't talk to a 4-year-old like you would a teenager, and vice versa). Use a friendly tone of voice and show genuine personal interest and responsiveness. For shy children, rather than opening up immediately with conversation, try an ice-breaking activity such as drawing a picture or playing with an age-appropriate toy. This quiet interaction with concrete materials may provide an opening to elicit conversation about them.

In most instances it is best not to have a parent, teacher, or other person be present during the assessment, as it can affect the test results in unknown ways. However, when a child is having extreme difficulty separating, it can be useful to permit another adult's presence in the initial rapport-building phase of the assessment, to help the child ease into the testing situation. Once the child's anxiety has decreased, or at least once the child has become interested in playing or drawing with you, encourage the student to begin the assessment without the adult present.

Maintaining rapport requires diligent effort throughout an assessment. Watch students for signs of fatigue, disinterest, and frustration. These signs are clues that you need to increase your feedback, give a break, or suggest a reward for completing tasks. Using good eye contact will help you show interest and enthusiasm for the student's efforts. Use your clinical judgment about how much encouragement a child needs for their efforts. Some children will need more pats on the back than others. Always praise students for their efforts, not the correctness of their responses.

SUMMARY INFORMATION ABOUT THE TESTS AND THEIR PUBLISHERS

The WIAT-II and the WIAT-II Abbreviated are published by Harcourt Assessment, Inc. under the brand of PsychCorp. The KTEA-II Comprehensive Form and KTEA-II Brief Form are published by American Guidance Service (AGS). In Rapid References 1.3 and 1.4, we provide a summary of important information about both the WIAT-II, WIAT-II Abbreviated, KTEA-II Comprehensive Form, and KTEA-II Brief Form. These Rapid References provide information on the following topics: test author, publisher, publication date, what the test measures, age range covered by the test, administration time, qualification of examiners, and test price.

≋ Rapid Reference 1.3

Wechsler Individual Achievement Test–Second Edition

Author	WIAT-II: The Psychological Corporation
	WIAT-II Abbreviated: The Psychological Corporation
Publication date	2001
What the test measures	WIAT-II measures the following achievement domains: Reading, Mathematics, Written Language, and Oral Language
	WIAT-II Abbreviated measures the following achievement skills: Spelling, Word Reading, and Numerical Operations
Age range	4–85 years
Administration time	PreK–Kindergarten 45 min
	Grades 1–6 90 min
	Grades 7–16 90–120 min
	WIAT-II Abbreviated: 10–20 min
Qualification of examiners	Examiners must have a master's degree in psychology, education, or a related field, with relevant training in assessment or certification by a professional organization recognized by the publisher
Publisher	Harcourt Assessment, Inc.
	19500 Bulverde Road
	San Antonio, TX 78259
	800-211-8378
	http://harcourtassessment.com
Price *(retrieved from harcourtassessment.com in January 2005)*	WIAT-II Kit: $399
	Includes Stimulus Book 1, Stimulus Book 2, Record Form (pkg. of 25), Response Booklet (pkg. of 25), Examiner's Manual, Scoring Normative Supplement for Grades PreK–12, Scoring and Normative Supplement for College Students and Adults, Word Cards, audiotape, and bag.
	WIAT-II Abbreviated Kit: $165
	Includes Manual, 25 Combination Record Forms/Response Booklets, and 2 Word Cards in a bag.
	WIAT-II Scoring Assistant Software: $199
	CD-ROM Windows or Macintosh

≡Rapid Reference 1.4

Kaufman Test of Educational Achievement–Second Edition

Authors	Alan S. Kaufman and Nadeen L. Kaufman
Publication date	KTEA-II Comprehensive Form: 2004
	KTEA-II Brief Form: 2005
What the test measures	The following achievement domains are measured in both the Comprehensive and Brief Forms: Reading, Mathematics, and Written Language. The Comprehensive Form measures an additional fourth domain: Oral Language
Age range	4:6–25 (Comprehensive Form)
	4:6–90+ (Brief Form)
Administration time	Comprehensive Form—(PreK–K) 25 min; (Grades 1–2) 50 min; (Grades 3+) 70 min;
	Brief Form—(4:6–90 years) 20–30 min
Qualification of examiners	Examiner must have completed graduate training in measurement, guidance, individual psychological assessment, or special appraisal methods appropriate for an individual achievement test
Publisher	AGS Publishing
	4201 Woodland Road
	Circle Pines, MN
	55014-1796
	800-328-2560
	http://www.agsnet.com
Price *(retrieved from www.agsnet.com in January 2005)*	KTEA-II Comprehensive Form A or B Kit: $299.99 Includes 2 Easels, Manual, Norms Book, Form A Record Forms (25), Form A Student Response Booklets (25), Form A Error Analysis Booklets (25), 2 each of 3 Form A WE Booklets, all necessary stimulus materials, Form A Administration CD, puppet, and tote bag
	KTEA-II Comprehensive Computer ASSIST™: $99.99
	CD-ROM Macintosh and Windows
	KTEA-II Brief Form Kit: $149.99
	Includes 1 easel, 1 manual, 25 record forms, 25 response booklets

Two

WIAT-II

DESCRIPTION OF THE WIAT-II

The Wechsler Individual Achievement Test–Second Edition (WIAT-II; The Psychological Corporation, 2002) consists of two forms: the comprehensive battery and the WIAT-II abbreviated form. The comprehensive battery, consisting of nine subtests and requiring 60 to 90 minutes to administer, is the focus of this chapter. The WIAT-II Abbreviated (WIAT-II-A; The Psychological Corporation, 2001) consists of three subtests (Word Reading, Spelling, and Numerical Operations) that are taken directly from the comprehensive battery. The abbreviated battery, which takes approximately 10 to 15 minutes to administer, can be given alone or administered as a screener to show when a more comprehensive assessment is indicated. The WIAT-II-A is also designed to be a brief assessment of targeted skills for providing a second or alternate measure of achievement, or for monitoring academic progress as a result of intervention. In addition to scores for each of the three subtests, the abbreviated form also yields a composite score as a general indicator of academic achievement. Normative data were derived using the WIAT-II standardization sample. If the two tests are given close in time the three subtests do not need to be readministered, and scores can be incorporated into the comprehensive battery report. The comprehensive form of the WIAT-II covers the age range 4:0 to 85 years and prekindergarten (PreK) to grade 16, and results can be reported using either age- or grade-based scores. The abbreviated form offers similar scores but covers the age range 6 to 85 years and kindergarten through grade 16.

History and Development

The first edition of the WIAT was published in 1992 (WIAT; The Psychological Corporation, 1992) as a measure of academic achievement of students in grades kindergarten through 12, and aged 5:0 years to 19:11 years, and was the only individually administered achievement test directly linked with the Wechsler intelligence scales (e.g., Wechsler Preschool and Primary Scale of Intelligence–Revised [WPPSI-R], Wechsler Intelligence Scales for Children–Third Edition [WISC-III], and Wechsler Adult Intelligence Scale–Revised [WAIS-R]). The WIAT provided comprehensive coverage of the areas of learning disability specified in the Education for All Handicapped Children Act of 1975 (P.L. 94-142): oral expression, listening comprehension, written expression, basic reading skill, reading comprehension, mathematics calculation, and mathematics reasoning. Because of the link between the WIAT and the Wechsler intelligence scales, clinicians were able to identify when a student demonstrated a discrepancy between achievement and ability.

Changes from WIAT to WIAT-II

Although the basic structure of the revision retains specific features from the first edition of the WIAT, including domain coverage and linkage with the most current editions of the Wechsler intelligence scales, the WIAT-II incorporates several modifications. These include: the addition of a new subtest (Pseudoword Decoding), the revision of content in all subtests, the extension of the age range down to age 4:0 years and up to age 85 years, improved scoring capabilities, including the computerized WIAT-II Scoring Assistant, and the expansion of the ability-achievement discrepancy tables. A significant change from WIAT to WIAT-II occurred through the strengthening of the link between assessment and instruction/intervention. The unique skill analysis feature of the WIAT was expanded by including an evaluation of both product (e.g., writing sample) and process (e.g., word fluency), qualitative observation checklists, the inclusion of various scoring options (e.g., word reading automaticity), and a quick inventory of a student's skills produced by the WIAT-II Scoring Assistant. Rapid Reference 2.1 illustrates major subtest differences between the WIAT and the WIAT-II.

The comprehensive battery is composed of the following subtests: Word Reading, Pseudoword Decoding, Reading Comprehension, Numerical Operations, Math Reasoning, Spelling, Written Expression, Listening Comprehension, and Oral Expression. The subtests yield four composite scores—Reading, Mathematics, Written Language, and Oral Language—along with a Total Achievement score. For children aged 4:0 to 4:11, or in PreK, subtest scores are reported only for Word Reading, Math Reasoning, Listening Comprehension, and Oral Expression, and the only composite score is for Oral Language. For children aged 5:0 to 5:11, or in kindergarten, all of the subtest scores are reported except Pseudoword Decoding, Reading Comprehension, and Written Expression; therefore,

Rapid Reference 2.1

Subtest Differences between WIAT and WIAT-II

WIAT Subtest	Measures	WIAT-II Subtest	Measures
Basic Reading	• Accuracy of word recognition	Word Reading	• Letter identification • Phonological awareness • Alphabet principle (letter-sound recognition) • Accuracy of word recognition • Automaticity of word recognition
		Pseudoword Decoding	• Phonological decoding • Accuracy of word attack
Reading Comprehension	• Literal comprehension • Inferential comprehension	Reading Comprehension	• Literal comprehension • Inferential comprehension • Lexical comprehension • Reading rate • Oral reading accuracy • Oral reading fluency • Oral reading comprehension • Word recognition in context
Numerical Operations	• Number writing • Calculation using basic operations • Calculation using fractions, decimals, algebra	Numerical Operations	• Counting • One-to-one correspondence • Number identification and writing • Calculation using basic operations • Calculation using fractions, decimals, algebra

(continued)

WIAT Subtest	Measures	WIAT-II Subtest	Measures
Math Reasoning	• Quantitative concepts • Problem solving • Money, time, and measurement • Geometry • Reading and interpreting charts and graphs • Statistics	Math Reasoning	• Quantitative concepts • Multistep problem solving • Money, time, and measurement • Geometry • Reading and interpreting charts and graphs • Statistics and probability • Estimation • Identifying patterns
Spelling	• Alphabet principle • Written spelling of regular and irregular words from dictation • Written spelling of homonyms (integration of spelling and lexical comprehension)	Spelling	• Alphabet principle • Written spelling of regular and irregular words from dictation • Written spelling of homonyms (integration of spelling and lexical comprehension)
Written Expression	• Descriptive writing (evaluated on extension and elaboration, grammar and usage, ideas and development, organization, unity and coherence, and sentence structure and variety) • Narrative writing (evaluated on the same criteria as descriptive writing)	Written Expression	• Timed alphabet writing • Written word fluency • Sentence combining • Sentence generation • Written responses to verbal and visual cues • Descriptive writing (evaluated on organization, vocabulary, and mechanics) • Persuasive writing (evaluated on organization, vocabulary, theme development, and mechanics) • Writing fluency

WIAT Subtest	Measures	WIAT-II Subtest	Measures
Listening Comprehension	• Receptive vocabulary • Listening-literal comprehension • Listening-inferential comprehension	Listening Comprehension	• Receptive vocabulary • Expressive vocabulary • Listening-inferential comprehension
Oral Expression	• Expressive vocabulary • Giving directions • Explaining steps in sequential tasks	Oral Expression	• Verbal word fluency • Auditory short-term recall for contextual information • Story generation • Giving directions • Explaining steps in sequential tasks

composite scores are only available for Mathematics and Oral Language. Standard scores with a mean of 100 and a standard deviation of 15 are reported for each subtest and composite and are derived from both age- and grade-based norms. Other derived scores include normal curve equivalents (NCEs), stanines, percentile ranks, quartile-based scores, decile-based scores, grade equivalents, and age equivalents. Each of the Mathematics, Written Language, and Oral Language composite scores is based on the two subtests comprising the composite. The Reading composite is based on three contributing subtests. The composition of the composites is found in Rapid Reference 2.2, and a description of the WIAT-II subtests, task demands, and optional measures is provided in Rapid Reference 2.3.

STANDARDIZATION AND PSYCHOMETRIC PROPERTIES OF THE WIAT-II

Standardization

The WIAT-II standardization sample consisted of the age-based sample of students aged 4 to 19 ($N = 2,950$), the grade-based sample of students from grades PreK to 12 ($N = 3,600$), and the college and adult sample representing grades 13 to 16 ($N = 707$) that was drawn from both 2- and 4-year colleges, and ages 17 to 89 years ($N = 500$). Of the 3,600 participants in the grade-based sample for PreK

≡Rapid Reference 2.2

Subtests Comprising the WIAT-II Composites

Composites	Subtests
Reading	Word Reading Pseudoword Decoding Reading Comprehension
Mathematics	Numerical Operations Math Reasoning
Oral Language	Listening Comprehension Oral Expression
Written Language	Spelling Written Expression

≡ Rapid Reference 2.3

Description of the WIAT-II Subtests, Task Demands, and Optional Measures

Subtest	Description	Tasks[a]	Optional Measures
Word Reading	• Assesses emerging literacy (phonological awareness, phonemic awareness) and word recognition of regular and irregular words	• Name alphabet letters • Identify and generate rhyming words • Identify the beginning and ending sounds of words • Match sounds with letters and letter combinations • Read aloud from a graded word list	• Automaticity of word reading • Self-corrections • Qualitative behavioral observations
Pseudoword Decoding	• Assesses the ability to apply phonetic decoding skills to the reading of nonsense words	• Read aloud a list of nonsense words designed to mimic the phonetic structure of words in the English language	• Informal error analysis
Reading Comprehension	• Assesses word knowledge and reasoning in reading sentences and short passages	• Match a written word with its representative picture • Read aloud graded sentences containing target words (word recognition in context) and answer content questions • Read silently graded passages (narrative, informative, and functional) and answer content questions	• Detailed skills analysis • Quartile-based reading speed score • Reading rate (expressed as the relationship between speed and accuracy) • Quartile-based Target Word reading accuracy score • Qualitative behavioral observations

(continued)

Subtest	Description	Tasks[a]	Optional Measures
Numerical Operations	• Evaluates the ability to use numbers and mathematical calculation to solve number problems	• Identify and write numbers • Number counting using 1:1 correspondence • Solve written calculation problems using addition, subtraction, multiplication, and division • Solve written calculation problems using decimals, fractions, and algebra	• Detailed skills analysis • Qualitative behavioral observations • Error analysis
Math Reasoning	• Evaluates the ability to reason mathematically	• Count with 1:1 correspondence • Identify geometric shapes • Solve single- and multistep word problems • Interpret graphs • Identify patterns • Solve problems related to probability and statistics	• Detailed skills analysis • Qualitative behavioral observations • Error analysis
Spelling	• Assesses the ability to write dictated letters, letter combinations, and words	• Write a dictated letter or letter combination • Use word knowledge to correctly spell and write a dictated word used in the context of a sentence	• Detailed error analysis • Qualitative behavioral observations

Subtest	Description	Tasks[a]	Optional Measures
Written Expression	• Measures writing skills at all levels of language (i.e., subword, word, and text levels)	• Timed alphabet writing • Timed written word fluency • Combine sentences • Generate sentences • Compose a rough-draft paragraph in response to a prompt • Compose a rough-draft persuasive essay in response to a prompt	• Holistic writing score for paragraph and essay • Decile-based alphabet writing score • Quartile-based written word fluency score • Quartile-based writing fluency score based on word count
Listening Comprehension	• Assesses word knowledge and the ability to listen for details	• Select the picture that matches a verbally presented word or sentence • Generate a word that matches a picture and a verbal description	
Oral Expression	• Evaluates oral language skills at the word and text levels of language	• Timed verbal word fluency • Sentence repetition • Generate verbal stories from visual cues • Generate verbal directions from visual or verbal cues	• Quartile-based verbal fluency score

[a]Tasks may be grade-specific.

through twelfth grade, 2,171 individuals were also included in the age-based sample. Data were collected during the 1999–2000 and 2000–2001 school years and are representative of the U.S. population as reported in the October 1998 census. In order to obtain continuous grade-based normative data, students in PreK through eighth grade were further divided into Fall and Spring sampling groups. A stratified random sampling plan included representative proportions of individuals in each sampling group according to the demographic variables of grade, age, sex, race/ethnicity, geographic region, and parent/self education level. Grades PreK to 12 students enrolled in both private and public schools were included. Students who received special education services in school settings were not excluded from participation. As a result, 8 to 10 percent of the standardization sample at each grade and age level consists of students classified by their schools as having a learning disability, a speech or language impairment, an emotional disturbance, mild mental impairment, an Attention-Deficit Disorder, or a mild hearing impairment. In addition, approximately 3 percent of the sample at each grade level consisted of students in gifted and talented programs. The college sample was drawn from participants enrolled in public or private school settings. Participants who received disability services were not excluded from participation. As a result, 5 percent of the college standardization sample consisted of students classified as having a learning disability or an Attention-Deficit Disorder.

The match between the two school-age samples and the U.S. population is quite close, especially for the grades PreK to 8 and the ages 5 to 14 groups. The greatest disparity is on the geographic region variable, with the West and South slightly overrepresented and the Northeast slightly underrepresented. Detailed information on the standardization sample is presented in the administration manual. The match for college students and adults was also close in regard to age and race/ethnicity. The adult sample was also matched closely on geographic region and self education level. The college sample had slight overrepresentation of Hispanics, and the adult sample had a slight underrepresentation of individuals from the Northeast region. A small amount of case weighting was used to produce an adult standardization sample that was more closely representative of the U.S. population. The weighted sample was used solely to derive adult demographic and normative information. The college and adult samples are described in detail in the Supplement for College Students and Adults.

The WIAT-II linking samples were originally developed from a subset of standardization participants who were administered one of three Wechsler intelligence scales: WPPSI-R, WISC-III, or the WAIS-III. With the revision of the WPPSI and the WISC, new linking studies were conducted. The final linking samples consisted of 1,116 participants, including 208 aged 4:0 to 7:3 children who were given the WPPSI-III, 550 children aged 6:0 to 16:11, who were given the WISC-IV, and 358 participants aged 16 to 85, who were administered the WAIS-III. A description of the WPPSI-III linking sample is found on pages 99 to 101 of the *WPPSI-III Technical and Interpretive Manual* (The Psychological Corporation, 2002), and the updated ability-achievement discrepancy tables are reported in Appendix C. Standardization of the new WISC-IV included a linking sample of 550 children aged 6 to 16, which is described on pages 61 and 69 to 70 of the *WISC-IV Technical and Interpretive Manual* (The Psychological Corporation, 2003), and updated ability-achievement discrepancy tables are found in Appendix B of the *Manual*.

Reliability

Split-half reliability coefficient procedures, as used with the Wechsler intelligence scales, were used for the WIAT-II as a measure of internal consistency. PreK to grade 12 mean split-half reliability coefficients for the subtests range from .80 (Listening Comprehension) to .97 (Word Reading, Pseudoword Decoding), and for the composites from .89 (Oral Language) to .98 (Reading). The Total Composite mean coefficient was .98. The Reading subtest and composite reliability coefficients are significantly higher than on the original WIAT.

Mean test-retest correlations for the subtests for ages 6 to 19 range from .85 (Written Expression) to .98 (Word Reading), while correlations for the composites range from .92 (Oral Language) to .97 (Reading). The Total Composite mean coefficient was .98. With the exception of the Listening Comprehension subtest, very small practice effects were observed, with test-retest scores differing by 2 to 3 standard-score points. Reliability coefficients for the WIAT and WIAT-II age-based samples are compared in Rapid Reference 2.4. Rapid Reference 2.5 reports the average reliability coefficients for the college and adult sample.

The Reading Comprehension, Written Expression, and Oral Language subtests are somewhat subjective to score, so interscorer agreement was evaluated. High levels of agreement in scoring responses were reported, with average interscorer reliability coefficients of .94 on Reading Comprehension, .85 on Written Expression, and .96 for Oral Expression.

Validity

Several studies were conducted to provide evidence of construct-, content-, and criterion-related validity. Content representativeness of the WIAT-II subtests

≣Rapid Reference 2.4

Average Age-Based Reliability Coefficients of the WIAT and WIAT-II Composites for Student Sample Ages 4–19

WIAT Composites	Split-Half	Test-Retest	WIAT-II Composites	Split-Half	Test-Retest
Reading	.95	.93	Reading	.98	.97
Mathematics	.92	.91	Mathematics	.95	.95
Writing	.90	.94	Written Language	.94	.94
Language	.90	.78	Oral Language	.89	.92
Total Composite	.97	.96	Total Composite	.98	.98

Note: Data are from Tables 5.1 and 5.11 of the WIAT Manual (The Psychological Corporation, 1992) and Tables 6.1 and 6.9 of the WIAT-II Administration Manual (The Psychological Corporation, 2002).

≣Rapid Reference 2.5

Average Reliability Coefficients of the WIAT-II Composites for Adults Ages 17–85

WIAT-II Composites	Split-Half	Test-Retest
Reading	.98	.93
Mathematics	.96	.95
Written Language	.92	.75
Oral Language	.88	.84
Total Composite	.98	.96

Note: Data are from Tables 2.1 and 2.5 of the WIAT-II Supplement for College Students and Adults (The Psychological Corporation, 2002).

was examined continuously during test development by aligning test items to curriculum objectives as specified in the Individuals with Disabilities Education Act Amendments of 1997 (IDEA). These curriculum objectives, in turn, defined the scope of the subtests, and were evaluated by comparison with school textbooks, other achievement tests and diagnostic instruments, emerging curricular trends, various state standards, opinions of nationally recognized experts and teacher surveys. Details of the process used for selecting and developing each subtest and its items are presented in Chapter 5 of the WIAT-II administration manual.

Evidence for construct validity was obtained through analysis of WIAT-II subtest intercorrelation scores and correlations between WIAT-II and the IQ scores of the Wechsler intelligence scales. The patterns of correlations confirm the expected relations between subtests and the domains they comprise. For example, the updated correlation studies reported in Table 5.15 of the *WISC-IV Technical and Interpretive Manual* show that the highest composite correlations are between FSIQ and Reading and Mathematics on WIAT-II, and the lowest composite correlation is between the PSI (Processing Speed Index) on WISC-IV and the WIAT-II Oral Expression. The correlation studies indicate that the Math Reasoning, Listening Comprehension, and Reading Comprehension subtests require a higher level of cognitive skill than the other WIAT-II subtests.

Criterion-related validity studies include correlation studies with other individually administered achievement tests: the WIAT, the Process Assessment of the Learner-Test Battery for Reading and Writing (PAL-RW; Berninger, 2001), the Wide Range Achievement Test–Third Edition (WRAT3; Wilkinson, 1993), the Differential Ability Scales (DAS; Elliott, 1990), and the Peabody Picture Vocabulary Test–Third Edition (PPVT-III; Dunn & Dunn, 1997). For college students, a correlation study with the Woodcock-Johnson Psycho-Educational Battery–Revised, Tests of Achievement (WJ-R; Woodcock & Johnson, 1989) is reported in Table 2.6 of the college and adult manual. Studies also compared WIAT-II to group-administered achievement tests, school grades, and the Academic Competence Evaluation Scales (ACES: DiPerna & Elliott, 2000). Results are reported in the administration manual and indicate that the WIAT-II is a valid measure of achievement.

Test performance by individuals belonging to special groups also provided evidence of the validity of the WIAT-II. Clinical studies, which are reported in the administration manual, included students in gifted programs ($N = 123$), as well as individuals with mental retardation ($N = 39$), with emotional disturbance ($N = 85$), with learning disabilities in reading ($N = 162$), with learning disabilities not specific to reading ($N = 81$), with ADHD ($N = 178$), with comorbid ADHD and LD ($N = 51$), with mild hearing impairments ($N = 31$), and with speech and/or language impairment ($N = 49$). Study data with clinical groups show expected patterns of mean standard scores and illustrate that the WIAT-II subtests are effective in the identification process for large percentages of individuals with these disabilities.

HOW TO ADMINISTER THE WIAT-II

As with any other standardized test, the WIAT-II examiner should follow closely the test administration instructions contained in the administration manual and within the stimulus booklets. Although the test is relatively easy to administer, it is imperative that the examiner become familiar with test directions prior to administration. Deviation from the standard procedures could reduce the reliability and validity of test results (American Psychological Association, 1999). In order to obtain a Total Achievement score, all subtests must be administered; however, WIAT-II was designed in such a way that individual subtests can be selected for administration to assess an identified area of need, to identify specific achievement deficits, or to answer specific referral questions. The Don't Forget insert lists the order of subtest administration. Chapter 3 of the administration manual describes a number of testing considerations, including suitability of the test, administration time, and materials needed. Information is also provided about the appropriate physical setting, ways to establish and maintain rapport, and issues related to testing examinees with physical or language impairments. The WIAT-II uses an easel format, with items presented on the student's side of the easel and administration instructions, items, and in some cases, scoring information on the examiner's side. In general, subtests should be administered in the sequence indicated by the stimulus booklet and the record form, because this is the order used in the standardization of the test. When giving only selected subtests, the sequence should also follow the prescribed order.

> **DON'T FORGET**
> ....
>
> **Order of
> Subtest Administration**
>
> 1. Word Reading
> 2. Numerical Operations
> 3. Reading Comprehension
> 4. Spelling
> 5. Pseudoword Decoding
> 6. Math Reasoning
> 7. Written Expression
> 8. Listening Comprehension
> 9. Oral Expression

Test materials consist of two easel-bound stimulus booklets, an administration manual, a Scoring and Normative Supplement for grades PreK to 12 (scoring manual), a record form, a response booklet, a Pseudoword card, a Word Reading card, and a Pseudoword audiotape, which should only be used by the examiner for scoring purposes. When testing college students and adults, the examiner would use the Supplement for College Students and Adults for administration and scoring (college and adult manual). In addition, the examiner must supply blank white paper (for the math subtests) and a pencil without an eraser (for the Math Reasoning, Spelling, Numerical Operations, and Written Expression subtests). If testing children in grades K or 1, you will need eight pennies for the Numerical Operations subtest. Some items require timing using a stopwatch or a clock that has a second hand. It is recommended that the examiner use a clipboard to hold the record form open to the appropriate section when recording responses. A tape recorder may also be used to facilitate recording and scoring the verbatim responses for Oral Expression and Pseudoword Decoding.

Prior to beginning administration, you should complete the demographic information on the front of the record form. Care should be taken when calculating the chronological age of the examinee. Space is provided to record general behavioral observations once testing is complete; however, subtest-specific behavioral observations—called Qualitative Observations—are recorded following the administration of the Word Reading, Numerical Operations, Reading Comprehension, Spelling, and Math Reasoning subtests.

Starting, Reversing, Discontinuing, and Stopping

The administration rules are listed by subtest. To facilitate administration, the start points, reverse rules, discontinue rules, and stop points of each subtest are provided using the icons in the record form and on the examiner's page of the stimulus booklets (see Figure 2.1). Because of the unique administration rules for Reading Comprehension, start points, reverse rule, discontinue rule, and stop points will be discussed for this subtest in the subtest administration section.

Discontinue Rule   **Stop Point**

Start Point   **Reverse Rule**

Figure 2.1 Icons for WIAT-II discontinue rule, stop point, start point, and reverse rule

Start Point

The start point is determined by the examinee's current grade level. If you are testing a student who has completed a grade but not yet started the next, start at the level of the completed grade. If you are testing an adult, start at the grade level of the last grade completed. If you have reason to believe that the examinee's skills are significantly below grade level, with the exception of Reading Comprehension and Written Expression, you may begin at the start point for the previous grade.

Reverse Rule

Reverse rules help ensure that the most appropriate items are administered to an examinee. Seven of the WIAT-II subtests have a basal requirement: Word Reading, Numerical Operations, Reading Comprehension, Spelling, Math Reasoning, Listening Comprehension (where there are actually three separate basal requirements), and the Sentence Repetition section of Oral Expression. If the examinee establishes basal by correctly responding to the first three items following the start point, award 1 point for each preceding, unadministered item. For example, a 5th-grade student would start with item 81 on Word Reading. If correct responses were given for items 81, 82, and 83, then credit would be awarded for items 1 to 80. The reverse rule for all of these subtests, except Reading Comprehension, requires that if the examinee scores 0 points on any of the first three items administered, you proceed backward from the start point (i.e., reverse order) until you can establish the basal level with three consecutive, correct responses. Once a basal is established, award 1 point for each preceding, unadministered item and proceed forward with the subtest items until the discontinue criterion is met. On occasion, an examinee may not be able to establish a basal level. In this case, once the discontinue criteria is met, credit is given for correctly answered, administered items.

Discontinue Rule

Subtest administration is stopped when the discontinue criterion is met. Discontinue rules apply to items administered in forward or reverse order. The criterion applies when the examinee scores 0 on a specified number of consecutive items. If you are unsure how to score a response and cannot determine quickly whether to discontinue, administer additional items until you are certain that the discontinue rule has been met. Once testing is completed and items have been scored, apply the discontinue rule. In other words, if a correct response was given on an item that would not have been administered had the discontinue rule been applied immediately, no credit is given.

Stop Point

Only two WIAT-II subtests have stop points rather than a discontinue rule: Reading Comprehension and Written Expression. These subtests are stopped when all of the items for a grade level have been administered. All other subtests end when the discontinue criterion has been met. Rapid Reference 2.6 summarizes the start points, reverse rules, discontinue rules, and stop points for the subtests.

Recording Responses

You will be able to score responses during administration for Word Reading, Numerical Operations, Math Reasoning, and Listening Comprehension; however, it is still important to record responses for error analysis. Reading Comprehension, Pseudoword Decoding, and Oral Expression require recording of responses verbatim for scoring once administration is completed. Writing responses on the record form can be supplemented or replaced by tape recording responses. Recorded responses should be preserved or transcribed to the record form. Examinees respond in the response booklet for the Spelling and Written Expression subtests. In order to conduct error analysis, a pencil without an eraser should be provided. Qualitative behavioral observations are recorded on the record form after each subtest is administered.

Timing

Exact timing requirements occur on many sections of Written Expression: a 15-second limit on Alphabet Writing (PreK to 2), a 1-minute limit on Word Fluency (grades 3 to 16), a 10-minute limit on Paragraph Writing (grades 3 to 6), and a 15-minute limit on Essay Writing (grades 7 to 16). Exact timing is also required on the Word Fluency section (all grades) of Oral Expression. Word Reading has

---

DON'T FORGET

When to Use a Stopwatch

Written Expression
- 15-second limit on Alphabet Writing
- 1-minute limit on Word Fluency
- 10-minute limit on Paragraph Writing
- 15-minute limit on Essay Writing

Oral Expression
- 1-minute limit on Word Fluency

≡ Rapid Reference 2.6

Summary of Subtest Start Points, Reverse Rules, Discontinue Rules, and Stop Points

Subtest	Start Points		Reverse Rule	Discontinue Rule	Start Points	
	Grade	Start Item			Grade	Stop After
Word Reading	PreK–K	1	Score of 0 on any of the first 3 items given; administer the preceding items in reverse order until 3 consecutive scores of 1.	After 7 consecutive scores of 0		
	1	22				
	2	34				
	3	48 Letter A				
	4	72 Letter B				
	5	81 Letter C				
	6	84 Letter D				
	7–8	93 Letter E				
	9–16	96 Letter F				
	Adults	Last grade completed				
Numerical Operations	PreK	Don't administer	Score of 0 on any of the first 3 items given; administer the preceding items in reverse order until 3 consecutive scores of 1.	After 6 consecutive scores of 0		
	K–1	1 Letter A				
	2–4	8 Letter B				
	5–8	13 Letter C				
	9–16	15 Letter D				
	Adults	Last grade completed				

Reading Comprehension				
	PreK–K	Don't Administer		
	1	1	1	Item 27
	2	10	2	Item 44
	3	20	3	Item 54
	4	34	4	Item 69
	5	55	5	Item 85
	6	59	6	Item 93
	7–8	75	7	Item 107
	9–12	94	8	Item 114
	13–16	108	9–12	Item 127
	Adults	Last grade completed	13–16	Item 140

Grade 1–8: Score of 0 on all of the grade-specific basal items given, go back 3 start points and continue by following the administration rules of the new grade level.

Grades 9–12: Score 0 on all of the grade-specific basal items given, administer items 75–114.

Grades 13–16: Score 0 on all of the grade-specific basal items given, administer items 94–127.

an optional timing element, where responses that take more than 3 seconds are marked to indicate lack of automaticity. Reading Comprehension has an optional reading speed component that requires the recording of elapsed time when the examinee is silently reading passages.

Repeating, Prompting, Querying

Except where specifically prohibited, directions and questions can be repeated following an examinee request or when the examinee does not seem to understand. Requests for repetition should be noted on the record form, and frequent requests should be recorded next to Behavioral Observations on the first page. Prompts can also be provided when an examinee hesitates or does not provide a response. An appropriate prompt would be *Just try it once more,* or *Try it a little longer.* If an examinee requests help in providing a response, say *I want to see how well you can do it yourself.* Queries such as *Tell me more about that* are appropriate when an examinee provides an incomplete or ambiguous response. Do not query a clearly incorrect response. If after a query is provided, a response improves from a 1-point to a 2-point, or from a 0-point to a 1-point, the higher score should be awarded. Prompts (P) and queries (Q) should be recorded on the record form.

Subtest-by-Subtest Rules of Administration

Word Reading

The first 47 items of Word Reading, which are typically administered to children in grades PreK to 2, measure emerging literacy skills of phonological and phonemic awareness and require the use of Stimulus Booklet 1. Examinees are asked to name all of the letters of the alphabet, identify and generate rhyming words, identify beginning and ending sounds of words, blend sounds into words, and match sounds to letters. Correct responses can be scored on the record form during administration. Incorrect responses should be recorded verbatim. Item responses are scored correct (1) or incorrect (0).

Beginning with Item 48, examinees are asked to read aloud words from a separate word card. To assist you in monitoring the frequency of self-corrections or delayed responses, space is provided to place a check mark beside the item in columns on the record form marked SC (self-corrections) and >3". In some cases, both columns may be marked. A box is provided on the record form at the end of the subtest to record the total number of checkmarks, and the information can be used to rate the frequency of the behaviors using the Word Reading Qualita-

≡ Rapid Reference 2.7

Key Administration Points for Word Reading

Materials: Stimulus Booklet 1, Word Card, Record Form

1. Begin at the grade-determined start point. If you have reason to believe that the examinee's word reading skills are significantly below grade placement level, you may start at the previous grade level.

2. Direct the examinee to read across the word card. Establish a basal with 3 consecutive correct responses. Remember to give credit for previous, un-administered items.

3. Record incorrect responses verbatim. Use some form of notation to indicate how the examinee pronounced the word.

4. The circled letters on the word card indicate start points, as identified on the record form.

5. Measuring automaticity of word reading is strongly recommended. Do not use a stopwatch to determine if the 3-second limit was met. Use your watch or a clock with a second hand or count, *one, one thousand, two, one thousand, three, one thousand.*

6. Discontinue after seven consecutive scores of 0.

7. You may "test the limits" for examinees who have a very low score by administering items in reverse order, beginning with Item 47, to identify prereading skills. Performance will not change the score for the subtest, but can provide useful information for instructional planning.

8. After administration of the subtest, complete the Qualitative Observations checklist by rating the frequency of target behaviors.

tive Observations. Credit is awarded when a word is read correctly even if pronunciation did not occur within 3 seconds. (See Rapid Reference 2.7.)

Numerical Operations

This subtest evaluates the ability to identify and write numbers, to count, using 1:1 correspondence, and to solve written calculation problems and simple equations involving the basic operations of addition, subtraction, multiplication, and division. Items include the use of fractions, decimals, exponents, negative integers, square root, basic algebraic equations, and basic geometry. Administration is straightforward, but the examinee's work must be monitored unobtrusively to determine whether basal and discontinue rules have been met. Some individuals may be distressed because they are not provided a pencil with an eraser. When this occurs, you may say *I would like you to show all of your work. If you make a mistake or change your mind, mark through it, and continue on.* If the requirement creates a sig-

≡ Rapid Reference 2.8

Key Administration Points for Numerical Operations

Materials: Stimulus Booklet 1, Record Form, Response Booklet, blank paper, pencil without eraser, 8 pennies (Grades K–1 only)

1. Begin at the grade-determined start point. The letters A–D on the response booklet indicate start points. If you have reason to believe that the examinee's calculation skills are significantly below grade placement level, you may start at the previous grade level.

2. Monitor examinee responses so you can apply the basal and discontinue rules. Establish a basal with 3 consecutive correct responses. Remember to give credit for previous, unadministered items.

3. Provide a pencil without an eraser.

4. If an examinee is spending an inordinate amount of time on a single item, encourage moving on to the next problem.

5. Discontinue after six consecutive scores of 0.

6. If you cannot read a response, you may ask the examinee to read the response aloud. Write the response and circle it on the booklet next to the examinee's written response to remind you that an oral response was given.

7. Do not penalize when a fraction is correct but not expressed in simplest or lowest terms. Fractions that are expressed in correct decimal form also receive credit.

8. After administration of the subtest, complete the Qualitative Observations checklist by rating the frequency of target behaviors.

nificant problem for the examinee, provide an eraser, but carefully observe how calculations are done. Item responses are scored correct (1) or incorrect (0).

Note that the record form includes the skill that is measured next to each item. This information, along with the Qualitative Observations that you complete after subtest administration, will be used when interpreting test results. (See Rapid Reference 2.8.)

Reading Comprehension

The Reading Comprehension subtest measures the ability to understand what has been read and to respond by verbally answering questions about the passage. The specific comprehension skills are listed in Table 7.2 in the WIAT-II administration manual. This subtest may be initially difficult to administer because of its complexity. Unlike all of the other subtests, Reading Comprehension is divided into grade-specific item sets and scores are determined by the level of difficulty of items (using item response theory [IRT] methodology) within a set. There is considerable overlap between item sets; sets include items that are below the assigned grade reading level, items on level, and items that are above the assigned grade reading level. As a result, when the reverse rule must be applied, it is possible to measure a broad range of reading levels relatively quickly. Items are composed of sentences that must be read aloud by the examinee and passages that can be read aloud or silently. The optional reading speed score, however, is based only on silent reading of passages. After each sentence or passage is read, comprehension questions are asked. Questions assigned to a passage are not in order of difficulty. Responses are scored 2, 1, or 0, depending on the quality of the response, and guidelines for scoring are included in Stimulus Booklet 1 and the scoring manual. Responses that require a query are marked with (Q). Target words, which are printed in bold type on the record form, are embedded in the sentence items. Oral reading of the sentence items provides an added opportunity to informally assess reading fluency, and the reading aloud of target words, where context is provided, can be compared to reading words from a list on Word Reading. The Target Word items are shaded on the record form as a reminder that the score is not included when calculating the Reading Comprehension subtest raw score.

In order to be representative of the types of reading materials used in the classroom, passages are narrative, informational, or functional. Comprehension questions measure both lower- and higher-order critical thinking skills, such as summarizing the main idea, recognizing stated detail, understanding both stated and implied cause and effect, and using context to determine meaning. Reading speed can only be obtained for students who stay within their grade-appropriate item set, and this optional score should be calculated only if the examinee is actively engaged in reading the passage. The reading speed score will be used in conjunction with the reading accuracy score to describe Reading Rate, using the Reading Rate graph on the record form.

Reading Comprehension Start and Stop Points   The start points for Reading Comprehension are determined by the grade level of the examinee. If the examinee is known to be reading significantly below grade placement, the reverse rule can be applied immediately. Once the appropriate item set has been identified, administer all of the items within that item set. Do not continue on to the next item set even if the examinee is performing well. A full range of standard scores, from approximately 40 to 160, is available for each item set.

Reading Comprehension Reverse Rule   The purpose of the reverse rule is to quickly route the examinee to the appropriate set of items. The grade-specific basal items

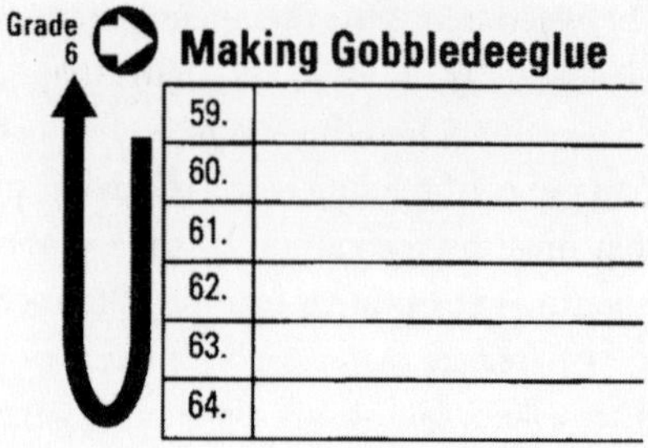

Figure 2.2 Icon for WIAT-II Reading Comprehension reverse items

for each item set are noted on the record form with a reverse icon in the left margin (see Figure 2.2).

If the examinee scores 0 points on all the grade-specific basal items, apply the reverse rule. The reverse rule states that administration of the grade-assigned item set is discontinued and testing resumes with the item set that is 3 start points lower. When the reverse rule is applied, administer items in forward sequence, beginning with the first item of the new item set, until the stop point for the new item set is reached. See the Don't Forget box for start points, basal items, and reversal item sets for Reading Comprehension.

On rare occasions an examinee may be able to answer one of the easier items

DON'T FORGET

Reverse Points for Reading Comprehension

Grade-Specific Item Set Start Points	Basal Items with Scores of 0	Reverse to New Item Set
Grade 2: Item 10	Items 10–14	Grade 1: Administer Items 1–27
Grade 3: Item 20	Items 20–25	Grade 1: Administer Items 1–27
Grade 4: Item 34	Items 34–39	Grade 1: Administer Items 1–27
Grade 5: Item 55	Items 55–58	Grade 2: Administer Items 10–44
Grade 6: Item 59	Items 59–64	Grade 3: Administer Items 20–54
Grade 7: Item 75	Items 75–80	Grade 4: Administer Items 34–69
Grade 8: Item 75	Items 75–80	Grade 4: Administer Items 34–69
Grades 9–12: Item 94	Items 94–98	Administer Items 75–114
Grades 13–16: Item 108	Items 108–112	Administer Items 94–127

correctly while scoring 0 points on all of the other basal items. You may use your clinical judgment to determine if the reverse rule should still be applied. In the case of examinees who are reading 4 or more years below grade placement, the basal requirement for the reversed item set may not be met. When this occurs, continue administering items in the new item set until you are certain that the examinee is unable to read sentences or passages in the set. The reverse rule can only be applied once. You cannot reverse a second time, even if the basal requirement is unmet. In this case, the score for the subtest will be very low but appropriate as a comparison of the examinee's abilities to age or grade peers.

The grade 1 item set begins with reading readiness items that are appropriate for students in that grade; however, for students in grade 3 or grade 4 who must reverse to the grade 1 item set, adequate performance on those items may result in an overestimation of their reading *comprehension* skills. In these cases, especially if performance on the Word Reading subtest was adequate, use your clinical judgment to determine whether administering the grade 2 item set will provide a more adequate measure of the examinee's reading comprehension skills.

Three total raw scores can be calculated in the space provided following each item set on the record form. *Credit is not given for previous item sets.* The Reading Comprehension total raw score, which is based on the total correct responses on comprehension items, must be converted to a weighted raw score before a standard score can be obtained. Use Table B.1 (grade-based) or Table E.1 (age-based) in the scoring manual to convert the total raw score to the weighted raw score. This is the point at which items are assigned different weights, based on level of difficulty for an examinee in that grade or at that age. The optional Target Words total raw score is based on the total correctly read target words in the item set. The optional Reading Speed total raw score is determined by adding together the elapsed time for reading all of the passages within the item set. These two scores should be converted to quartile-based scores by using the Supplemental Score Conversion Worksheet at the end of the record form. Target Words and Reading Speed scores cannot be obtained if the reverse rule was applied during administration. The Qualitative Observations checklist can be completed after subtest administration. (See Figures 2.3 and 2.4, and Rapid Reference 2.9.)

Spelling

The Spelling subtest measures the ability to spell dictated letters, letter blends, and words. Scoring is dichotomous. The inclusion of homonyms, which appear in bold type on the record form, requires that the examinee use context clues, provided in dictated sentences, to spell the appropriate form of the word. Errors on homonyms are more frequent in examinees identified with learning disabilities.

	Reading Comprehension Total Raw Score	max = 60	
Grade 3	Target Words Total Raw Score	max = 25	Grade 3
	Reading Speed Total Raw Score	__ + __ + __ + __	

Figure 2.3 Sample of the WIAT-II Grade 3 Reading Comprehension scoring box

Source: Wechsler Individual Achievement Test–Second Edition. Copyright © 2002 by Harcourt Assessment, Inc. Reproduced with permission. All rights reserved.

Supplemental Score Conversion Worksheet

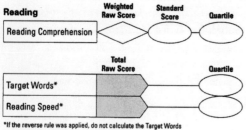

*If the reverse rule was applied, do not calculate the Target Words and Reading Speed supplemental scores.

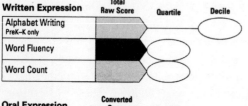

1. Transfer the weighted raw score and total raw scores to the appropriate spaces. Transfer the Written Expression Word Fluency quartile and the Oral Expression converted score from the subtest pages to the appropriate spaces.

2. Use Appendix B (grade-based) or E (age-based) to obtain the supplemental scores.

3. Reading Comprehension *only*: For examinees in *Grades 1–12* or *college*, use Table C.1 to convert the weighted raw score to a *grade-based* standard score. Use Table B.2 to convert the standard score to a quartile. Use Tables B.3 and B.4 to convert the Target Words and Reading Speed total raw scores to quartiles. Record the scores in the appropriate spaces.

   For *adult* examinees, use Table F.1 to convert the weighted raw score to an *age-based* standard score. Use Table E.2 to convert the standard score to a quartile. Use Tables E.3 and E.4 to convert the Target Words and Reading Speed total raw scores to quartiles. Record the scores in the appropriate spaces.

4. Oral Expression *only*: Divide the converted score by 2 and record the score in the appropriate space.

5. Transfer the supplemental scores to the Summary Report on the front of this record form.

Figure 2.4 Sample of the WIAT-II Supplemental Score Conversion Worksheet

Source: Wechsler Individual Achievement Test–Second Edition. Copyright © 2002 by Harcourt Assessment, Inc. Reproduced with permission. All rights reserved.

≡Rapid Reference 2.9

Key Administration Points for Reading Comprehension

Materials: Stimulus Booklet I, Record Form, stopwatch

1. The examinee's grade level determines which item set is administered. All of the items in the item set must be administered.

2. Do *not* give credit for previous, unadministered item sets. The subtest raw score is based only on performance on the items in the administered item set.

3. A basal must be established for an item set. If the examinee scores 0 points on all of the basal items, discontinue administration of that item set and reverse to the item set that is 3 *start points* lower. When the reverse rule is applied, administer items in forward sequence, beginning with the first item of the new item set, until the stop point for the new item set is reached.

4. The reverse rule can only be applied *once*. If the examinee is unable to establish basal on the reverse item set, continue administration of items until it is clear that the examinee cannot read either the sentences or the passages. Use your professional judgment to discontinue when appropriate. If the subtest is discontinued prematurely, assign a score of (0) to the balance of the items within the item set.

5. The raw score for Target Words is calculated by adding together the total number of target words read correctly in the item set. The Target Word items are shaded on the record form. The raw score is converted to a quartile-based score using the Supplemental Score Conversion Worksheet on the record form and Appendix B (grade-based) or Appendix E (age-based) in the scoring manual.

6. For examinees who read the passages silently, note elapsed time for each passage on the record form. The cumulative elapsed time for all the passages within an item set will determine the optional Reading Speed score. The raw score for speed is converted to a quartile-based score using the Supplemental Score Conversion Worksheet on the record form and Appendix B (grade-based) or Appendix E (age-based) in the scoring manual.

7. The Reading Speed quartile-based score is used to calculate Reading Rate by comparing it to the quartile-based score for Reading Comprehension, which represents reading accuracy. Use Appendix B (grade-based) or Appendix E (age-based) of the scoring manual to convert the Reading Comprehension score to a quartile-based score, then plot the two quartile-based scores on the Reading Rate graph that is provided on the record form. If you are using the Scoring Assistant, the graph will be created for you once the scores are calculated.

≡Rapid Reference 2.10

Key Administration Points for Spelling

Materials: Stimulus Booklet 1, Record Form, Response Booklet, pencil without eraser

1. Begin at the grade-determined start point. If you have reason to believe that the examinee's spelling skills are significantly below grade placement level, you may start at the previous grade level.
2. Monitor examinee responses so you can apply the basal and discontinue rules. Establish a basal with 3 consecutive correct responses. Remember to give credit for previous, unadministered items.
3. Spelling words and sentences can be repeated upon request. If the examinee does not begin writing after about 10 seconds, repeat the item. After another 10 seconds, go on to the next item if no response is written.
4. Provide a pencil without an eraser.
5. Discontinue after six consecutive scores of 0.
6. If you cannot read a response, you may ask the examinee to rewrite or spell the response aloud. Write the response and circle it on the booklet next to the examinee's written response to remind you that an oral response was given. Credit is given for correct oral responses.
7. Correct placement of the apostrophe is required for credit on contractions.
8. Homonyms are noted in **bold type** on the record form to assist with error analysis, completing the Qualitative Observation checklist, and the interpretation of subtest results.

Words and sentences can be repeated at the request of the examinee or when a response is not forthcoming after about 10 seconds. Although federal law does not identify spelling as one of the seven areas of a learning disability, performance on this subtest is important in the diagnosis of a reading and/or writing disability, specifically, dyslexia and/or dysgraphia. The Qualitative Observations checklist should be completed after subtest administration. (See Rapid Reference 2.10.)

Pseudoword Decoding

Pseudoword Decoding assesses the ability to apply phonetic decoding skills to nonwords. Nonsense words are a purer measure of decoding because previous experience or exposure to a word is limited. They are designed to be representative of the phonetic structure of words in the English language. Because this subtest requires that the examiner know the correct pronunciation of the nonsense

≡Rapid Reference 2.11

Key Administration Points for Pseudoword Decoding

Materials: Stimulus Booklet 1, Record Form, Pseudoword card, Pseudoword audiotape (for examiner's use only)

1. Before you administer this subtest, listen carefully to the Pseudoword audiotape to familiarize yourself with the correct pronunciation of the nonsense words.
2. Everyone begins with the first item, so there is no basal to establish. The words are listed in order of difficulty, but it is not unusual to see uneven performance, with incorrect responses interspersed with correct ones.
3. Be sure that the examinee understands that words are read going across rather than down the card.
4. If a response is not given in about 5 seconds, direct the examinee to go on to the next word.
5. Record incorrect responses verbatim. Use some form of notation to indicate how the examinee pronounced the word. Some examiners find it helpful, especially when words are read quickly, to use a tape recorder.
6. Discontinue after seven consecutive scores of 0.
7. A Pseudoword Decoding Qualitative Observations checklist is not included on the record form. Note when the examinee laboriously sounds out words, self-corrects errors, loses his or her place when reading words, makes accent errors, or adds, omits, or transposes syllables when reading words.

words, an audiotape is provided. The tape is not used in subtest administration. Incorrect responses should be recorded verbatim so that error analysis can be conducted, and you may use a tape recorder. The examinee will read from a separate word card. If an immediate response is not given after about 5 seconds, direct the examinee to the next word. Once you become familiar with the correct pronunciations, you will be able to score this subtest during administration. Incorrect responses are scored 0 points; correct responses earn 1 point. (See Rapid Reference 2.11.)

Math Reasoning

In Stimulus Booklet 2, the Math Reasoning subtest presents a series of visual and/or verbal prompts that evaluate the ability to reason mathematically. Items include asking the examinee to count, identify geometric shapes, and solve single- and multi-step word problems. Items relate to telling time, using money, and measuring; solving problems with whole numbers, fractions, and decimals; and interpreting charts and graphs, identifying mathematical patterns, and using statistics and probability. Blank paper and a pencil without an eraser should be provided. Correct responses are scored (1), incorrect responses are scored (0). If the examinee is not actively engaged in solving a problem, move on to the next item after about 1 minute. Items can be repeated upon examinee request. Charts and graphs are read to the student as part of the item to control for reading problems. Closely observe the strategies the examinee uses when solving problems to assist with the completion of the Qualitative Observations checklist. (See Rapid Reference 2.12.)

≡Rapid Reference 2.12

Key Administration Points for Math Reasoning

Materials: Stimulus Booklet 2, Record Form, blank paper, pencil without eraser

1. Begin at the grade-determined start point. If you have reason to believe that the examinee's math reasoning skills are significantly below grade placement level, you may start at the previous grade level.

2. Establish a basal with 3 consecutive correct responses. Remember to give credit for previous, unadministered items.

3. Inform the examinee that the blank paper may be used for calculation. Save the paper for error analysis.

4. Provide a pencil without an eraser.

5. Allow the examinee about 1 minute to respond after an item is read. Unless he or she is actively working on the item, go on to the next item. Items can be repeated upon request.

6. For those items that require the examinee to point to a response, sit so that you can see which picture is selected.

7. Alternate correct responses are listed on the record form and in the stimulus booklet. The examinee is not penalized if fractions are not expressed in simplest or lowest terms.

8. Discontinue after six consecutive scores of 0.

9. After administration of the subtest, complete the Qualitative Observations checklist by rating the frequency of target behaviors.

10. You may "test the limits" after standardized administration for an examinee when you observe that an incorrect response is based on a calculation or a procedural error. Provide a calculator, and determine if the examinee can correct the response. Another approach is to ask the examinee to work through a problem or problems aloud. This can help identify where the solution process is breaking down. Performance will not change the score for the subtest, but can provide useful information for instructional planning.

Written Expression

The Written Expression subtest on the WIAT-II evaluates the *process* of writing, not just the *product*. There are several advantages to this approach. First, this approach is more likely to produce some kind of writing to evaluate from individuals who are reluctant to write. Second, it allows for the evaluation of writing at all levels of language (i.e., subword, word, and text levels) for the purposes of identifying where the writing process breaks down, so as to target instruction for students with writing difficulties. This approach also allows for the assessment of writing in developmentally appropriate ways. As a result, the Written Expression subtest can be used to assess individuals in pre-kindergarten through college. There are five sections to this subtest: Alphabet Writing, Word Fluency, Sentences, Paragraph, and Essay. Specific sections and items are administered, based on the grade of the examinee, and all sections except Sentences have a timing requirement. Refer to the Don't Forget insert for a listing of items by grade level. Children in PreK–Kindergarten will be administered a single item, timed alphabet writing, which will yield a decile-based score. Performance on this item, although highly predictive of whether a child is at risk for developing a writing disorder, should not be used as the sole criteria for the disorder. Examinees will write responses in the response booklet using a pencil without an eraser. Some examinees will prefer a mechanical pencil that maintains a sharp point for the writing

DON'T FORGET

Items Administered by Grade Level for Written Expression

Grade	Items Administered
PreK–K	Item 1. Alphabet Writing
Grade 1	Item 1. Alphabet Writing Item 2. Word Fluency Items 3–5. Sentences
Grade 2	Item 1. Alphabet Writing Item 2. Word Fluency Items 3–7. Sentences
Grades 3–6	Item 2. Word Fluency Items 3–8. Sentences Item 9. Paragraph
Grades 7–16	Item 10. Word Fluency Items 11–15. Sentences Item 16 or 17. Essay

tasks. An alternate prompt is available for the Paragraph and the Essay sections. Use Prompt B if Prompt A is spoiled or if you are conducting a reevaluation. The Paragraph and the Essay items can be scored analytically, by using the scoring rubric on the record form, or holistically, by following the directions in the scoring manual. Less time is required for holistic scoring, but you will not be able to get a standard score for the subtest. When testing an individual whose writing abilities are very significantly below grade placement, you must first administer the grade-appropriate items in order to obtain a standard score for the subtest. Then, you can "test the limits" by administering the paragraph item, following the scoring rules and evaluating performance qualitatively for purposes of guiding instruction/intervention. For students in grade 6 who are older than 12 years of age you must use grade-based norms, as there is no age-based normative data for out-of-age-range individuals. (See Rapid Reference 2.13.)

Listening Comprehension

This subtest evaluates the ability to listen for details in order to identify a word or sentence and to generate words that match pictures paired with a verbal description. It is divided into three sections: Receptive Vocabulary, Sentence Comprehension, and Expressive Vocabulary; the Total Raw Score is based on the sum of the scores for the sections. Each section has its own start point, reverse rule, and discontinue rule. Allow about 10 seconds for the examinee to respond before moving to the next item. Any prompt can be repeated once at the examinee's request. Receptive Vocabulary requires a single word response. You should record responses verbatim on the Expressive Vocabulary section. Items are scored correct (1) or incorrect (0), and you should be able to score items during administration. (See Rapid Reference 2.14.)

Oral Expression

This subtest was designed to screen for individuals who may have underlying language-based deficits that require more comprehensive language assessment. Oral Expression measures the general ability to use oral language to communicate effectively. There are four sections: Sentence Repetition, Word Fluency, Visual Passage Retell, and Giving Directions, and you must record verbatim or tape record and transcribe each response for scoring. With the exception of Sentence Repetition, which is administered only to PreK–3, all sections are administered to all examinees. For students who are 9 years of age and in grade 3, there are separate, age-based norms tables on pages 244–245 of the scoring manual that should be used to calculate the Oral Expression standard score. For the Sentence Repetition section, a sentence can only be presented once. If the examinee does not respond

≡Rapid Reference 2.13

Key Administration Points for Written Expression

Materials: Stimulus Booklet 2, Record Form, Response Booklet, blank paper, pencil without eraser, stopwatch

1. The examinee's grade determines which items are administered. If you do not administer the correct item set, you will not obtain a standard score for the subtest. There is no discontinue rule; rather, all of the items for the specified grade level must be administered.

2. On Alphabet Writing, you may need to show the examinee what you mean by lowercase letters by pointing to the sample lowercase "a" on the response booklet. If necessary, you may substitute another term that may be more familiar to the student.

3. If an examinee is actively engaged in writing the alphabet, you can record the exact place he or she is working when 15 seconds have elapsed, and then let the examinee continue writing. The Alphabet Writing score is based on performance within the time limit; however, useful instructional information may be provided by "testing the limits." Emphasize in your instructions that letters should be written *as quickly and as carefully as you can*. If the examinee is not working quickly, you can prompt with *Remember to work as quickly and as carefully as you can*.

4. Children in PreK–K will not have a standard score for Written Expression nor a composite score for Written Language. They will receive a decile-based score that compares their performance to age- or grade-mates.

5. Word Fluency requires exact timing with a stopwatch. Because this is a fluency task, if an examinee begins writing "pizza," prompt with *Write a different word than pizza*, or include that instruction in your directions. Credit is not given for "pizza."

6. A dictionary or spelling tool cannot be used. If the examinee asks for help with spelling, respond with *Spell the word the best you can*. At examinee's request, you can read unfamiliar words in the stimulus book.

after about 10 seconds, go to the next item. Do not emphasize individual words or phrases, and read at a normal rate. The Word Fluency section is timed using a stopwatch. The idea behind Visual Passage Retell is to determine if the examinee can use visual cues to reproduce a sequential, meaningful story. Begin this section by modeling storytelling through the sample story. Use your voice to make the story interesting. The Giving Directions section asks the examinee to provide a step-by-step explanation of how to do specific tasks. The first item provides visual cues; the second does not. (See Rapid Reference 2.15.)

≡ Rapid Reference 2.14

Key Administration Points for Listening Comprehension

Materials: Stimulus Booklet 2, Record Form

1. Each of the 3 sections has its own start point, reverse rule, and discontinue rule. If you believe that an examinee's vocabulary is below grade level, you may begin with the first item in each section.

2. Begin the Receptive Vocabulary section at the grade-specific start point. Position yourself where you can see where the examinee points. If no response is provided after about 10 seconds, proceed to the next item.

3. Prompts may be repeated once at the examinee's request.

4. Continue administration with the Sentence Comprehension and Expressive Vocabulary sections.

5. Incorrect responses for Expressive Vocabulary should be recorded verbatim. If the examinee answers with more than one word, remind him or her of the one-word requirement. Responses that require a query are noted in the Stimulus Booklet.

6. Correct responses for Expressive Vocabulary items are listed in the Stimulus Booklet.

≡ Rapid Reference 2.15

Key Administration Points for Oral Expression

Materials: Stimulus Booklet 2, Record Form

1. Administer Sentence Repetition items only to children in grades PreK–3 where they are developmentally appropriate. Note the different grade level start points and the reverse rule.

2. All examinees take all of the Word Fluency, Visual Passage Retell, and the Giving Directions items. You present the items for Visual Passage Retell and the first item for Giving Directions by showing the examinee a picture in Stimulus Booklet 2.

3. Allow about 10 seconds for the examinee to begin responding, then go on to the next item or section. Instructions and items can be repeated upon examinee request on all sections except Sentence Repetition.

4. If the examinee includes verbatim the Word Fluency sample items *bear* or *goat*, or the sample items *run* or *ride in a car*, in his or her response, do not provide correction or credit. Record responses for later scoring. For Word Fluency B, a variation of the prompt (e.g., *ride a horse*) can be credited.

HOW TO SCORE THE WIAT-II

Because of their straightforward, dichotomous nature, many subtests or parts of subtests can be scored during administration. Typically, correct responses are summed to calculate the subtest raw score, which is then converted to a standard score using the C.1 Tables (grade-based) and the F.1 Tables (age-based) from the WIAT-II scoring manual. For Written Expression and Oral Expression, sections of the subtest are converted to a quartile-based score prior to calculating the subtest raw score. For Reading Comprehension, the sum of correct responses is converted to a weighted raw score prior to being converted to a standard score. To make this process easier, a Total Raw Score Conversion Worksheet is provided at the end of the record form (see Figure 2.5). After each subtest total raw score is obtained, transfer the number to the worksheet. At the same time, provide the data for the Supplemental Score Conversion Worksheet. By using the worksheets, you can convert all of the subtest raw scores to derived scores in a single step. A variety of scores are reported for WIAT-II (these scores are listed and defined in Rapid Reference 2.16). Generally the standard score will be used when comparing performance on one subtest to another, one composite to another, and in comparing WIAT-II results to another test (e.g., the Wechsler intelligence scales). We assume that achievement is distributed on a normal curve with the majority of individuals scoring within +/−1 standard deviation (SD) of the mean.

Total Raw Score Conversion Worksheet

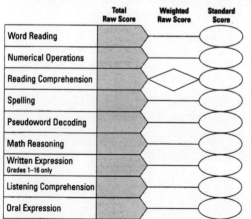

1. Determine whether you will use grade-based or age-based scores.

2. Transfer the total raw scores for each subtest to the Total Raw Score column.

3. Reading Comprehension *only*: Use Table B.1 or E.1 to convert the total raw score to a weighted raw score. To obtain the weighted raw score, find the total raw score and read across the table to the column for the appropriate item set administered. Record the score in the appropriate space.

4. Use Appendix C (grade-based) or F (age-based) to obtain the standard scores for each total raw score and weighted raw score. Refer to the examinee's age or grade to locate the appropriate page of Table C.1 or F.1. Record the scores in the Standard Score column.

5. Transfer the standard scores to the Summary Report on the front of this record form.

Figure 2.5 Total raw score conversion worksheet from WIAT-II Record Form

≡Rapid Reference 2.16

Types of Scores Yielded from the WIAT-II

Type of Score	Use in WIAT-II
Raw score	The sum of points awarded for each individual subtest (raw score) is converted to a norm-referenced score (e.g., standard score, quartile score, decile score). Raw scores should never be used to compare performance across subtests or composites, or between tests.
Weighted raw score	The raw score on Reading Comprehension is converted to a weighted raw score prior to conversion to a standard score. This score assigns different weights to items based on the age or grade of the examinee and the level of difficulty of the items for that group.
Standard score	A normalized transformation of a distribution of raw scores with a mean of 100 and a standard deviation of 15, used to compare an individual's performance to others. Scores range from 40 to 160. Use Tables C.1 (grade-based) and F.1 (age-based) to convert raw scores to standard scores. Grade-based standard scores are reported for Fall, Winter, and Spring for Grades PreK–8. Age-based standard scores are reported in 4-month intervals for ages 4:0–13:11, and in annual intervals for ages 14–19, and by 5 age bands for adults: ages 17–19, ages 20–25, ages 26–35, ages 36–50, and ages 51–85. Standard scores are also used to directly compare WIAT-II performance to scores on the Wechsler intelligence scales.
Decile-based score	The derived decile-based score on Alphabet Writing (WL), which represents the distribution of percentile ranks divided into 10 equal parts, is calculated using Tables B.5 (grade-based) or E.5 (age-based). The lowest decile-based score is 10, and includes scores between 0% and 10%; the highest decile-based score is 100, and includes scores between 90% and 100%.
Quartile-based score	Derived quartile-based scores are calculated using Appendix B (grade-based) or E (age-based) for Target Words (RC), Reading Speed (RC), Word Fluency (WE), Paragraph Word Count (WE), Paragraph Spelling Errors (WE), Paragraph Punctuation Errors (WE), Essay Word Count (WE), Essay Spelling Errors (WE), Essay Punctuation Errors (WE), and Word Fluency (OE), and for converting the Reading Comprehension standard score to a quartile score when calculating Reading Rate. Quartile scores represent the distribution of percentile ranks divided into 4 equal parts (e.g., the lower

Type of Score	Use in WIAT-II
Quartile-based score (*continued*)	25% corresponds to a quartile score of 1). For Word Fluency (WE and OE) and Paragraph Spelling and Punctuation Errors (WE) and Essay Spelling and Punctuation Errors (WE) a quartile score of 0 is provided to identify the lowest 5% of scores.
Percentile rank	Indicates the percentage of individuals in the standardization sample at a given age or grade who obtained scores less than or equal to a given raw score. Percentile ranks range from 1 to 99. Caution should be used when comparing student performance using percentile rank, because they do not form an equal-increment scale and tend to cluster near the median of 50. Use Table D.3 (grade-based) or Table G.3 (age-based) to convert WIAT-II standard scores to percentile ranks.
Normal curve equivalents	NCEs typically are used to quantify the academic progress of groups of children. Scores range from 1 to 99, with a mean of 50 and a standard deviation of 21.06, and express equally spaced units along the normal curve. WIAT-II standard scores can be converted to grade-based NCE scores using Table D.3 or to age-based NCE scores using Table G.3.
Stanine	A stanine ("standard nine") is the score that results from conversion of an age-based or a grade-based standard score to a 9-point scale. Stanines are normalized scores ranging from 1 to 9 with a mean of 5 and a standard deviation of 2. The use of stanines can help prevent overinterpretation of small differences in scores. Use Table D.3 (grade-based) or Table G.3 (age-based).
Grade equivalent	A grade equivalent indicates the school grade and month of that grade for which a given total raw score is average or typical. Grade equivalent scores have significant limitations for interpretation and should not be used to compare performance across subtests or to demonstrate student progress. Table D.4 presents the WIAT-II grade equivalents.
Age equivalent	An age equivalent indicates the age, in years and months, at which a given raw score is average or typical. These scores have the same limitations as grade equivalents and should be used very cautiously. Table G.4 reports the age equivalent scores.

Note: Adapted from the *WIAT-II Administration Manual* (The Psychological Corporation, 2002). All tables referenced in this Rapid Reference box refer to tables in the *WIAT-II Scoring Manual*.

Thus, about 66 percent of examinees will score in the range of 85 to 115. Less than 3 percent will score below 70 or above 130.

Written Expression and Oral Expression Scoring Keys

Scoring is more complex for two subtests: Written Expression and Oral Expression, because examinees in different grades take different sections, and individual sections scores are converted prior to calculating the total raw score. The Don't Forget box lists the Written Expression items that should be administered according to grade level and the sections that contribute to the total raw score.

Scoring the Alphabet Writing Section of Written Expression

The Alphabet Writing score is based on the number of correctly formed and sequenced letters that are written in 15 seconds. Refer to Appendix A.2 of the WIAT-II scoring manual for comprehensive scoring guidelines and examples of scored responses. The accompanying Don't Forget insert provides a scoring sample for Alphabet Writing. It is common for examiners to be too lenient when scoring this item, so follow the scoring rules carefully. Sequencing is scored so that the examinee will receive the most possible credit for correctly formed letters. For grades PreK–K, the raw score for Alphabet Writing is transferred to the Supplemental Score Conversion Worksheet where it is converted to a decile-based score. For grades 1 to 2, the raw score is written in the Item 1 box beside Alphabet Writing on the record form. The maximum raw score is 25 because credit is not given for writing the letter *a*.

Scoring the Word Fluency Section of Written Expression

The scoring criteria for both Word Fluency items are described and illustrated in Appendix A.2 of the WIAT-II scoring manual. To be correct, a response must meet the specified category and be a distinct object or action—not variations of an object or action. A score of 2 points is given for a correct, multisyllable word, and 1 point is awarded for a single-syllable word. A response is not penalized for spelling as long as the word can be determined. Since these items evaluate fluency, credit is not given when the examinee writes the sample provided (e.g., *pizza*).

Scoring the Sentences Section of Written Expression

Each item in the Sentences section is scored 2, 1, or 0, depending on the quality of the response. Appendix A.2 in the scoring manual provides numerous samples to guide your scoring. Only those errors that are specified are scored. If a response is not represented in the scoring samples, determine the appropriate score by choosing the most comparable example. A 2-point response typically is one

DON'T FORGET

Scoring Alphabet Writing

The examinee printed the letters *a, b, d, c, f, e, g*. A score of 4 is based on:

1. The last letter completed at the 15-second limit was the letter *g*. Scoring will be based on all 7 of the letters written.
2. No credit is given for the letter *a*.
3. The letter *b* receives credit because it is both written correctly and in the correct sequence.
4. The letter *d* does not receive credit because it is formed incorrectly. If it had been formed correctly, it still would not receive credit because it is out of sequence.
5. The letter *c* restores the sequence and is correctly formed and receives credit.
6. The letter *f* receives credit because it follows *c* in sequence (in this way the examinee is not penalized twice for the sequence error) and is correctly formed.
7. The letter *e* does not receive credit because it is formed incorrectly. If it had been formed correctly, it still would not receive credit because it is out of sequence.
8. The letter *g* receives credit because it restores the sequence and is formed correctly.

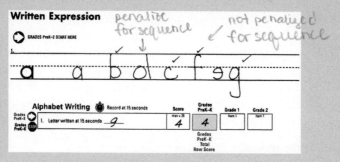

that is well-written, maintains the meaning of the original sentences, follows specific item directions (i.e., write a sentence about this picture), and does not contain the specified spelling, capitalization, or punctuation errors. A response may be awarded 1 point when no more than one of each type of the listed errors occurs, or when some information is missing but the original meaning does not change. A sentence fragment or a sentence that significantly alters the original meaning is scored 0. After the sentence items are scored, the points are totaled and recorded by grade in the Item 2 box provided on the record form.

Scoring the Paragraph Section of Written Expression

Individuals in grades 3 to 6 will write a paragraph in response to a verbal prompt. The writing sample can be scored holistically by following the scoring criteria in Table 4.1 of the administration manual and by consulting the examples in Appendix A.2 of the scoring manual, but the holistic score cannot be used to obtain a standard score for the Written Expression subtest. The rubric for analytic scoring is in the record form, and guidelines for scoring, with examples, are provided in Appendix A.2 of the scoring manual. The scoring rubric includes three evaluation categories: Mechanics, which includes spelling and punctuation; Organization, which addresses sentence structure and content; and Vocabulary. Subtotal scores for each category are recorded on the record form. The subtotal scores from all of the administered sections will be summed for the total raw score for the subtest. All paragraph writing samples are scored, but samples with six or fewer words are penalized through the Mechanics score by recording a quartile score of 0 instead of counting spelling errors, and then recording another quartile score of 0 instead of counting punctuation errors. The Multiple Spellings score is obtained; the Mechanics subtotal score is the sum of the two quartile scores, which is zero, and the Multiple Spellings score. If the paragraph contains seven or more words, then those spelling and punctuation errors that are specified on pages 37–39 in the scoring manual are counted, and the totals are converted to quartile-based scores using Table B.8 (grade-based) or Table E.8 (age-based). Not all types of punctuation errors are penalized, because only those errors that were most discriminating between students with and students without writing disorders in the standardization clinical studies are included. Because subjectivity is involved in scoring, you are encouraged to follow the scoring guidelines carefully and refer to the paragraph samples on pages 41–56 of the WIAT-II scoring manual for guidance.

Scoring the Essay Section of Written Expression

Examinees in grades 7 to 16 and all adults will write a persuasive essay that will be scored on mechanics, organization, theme development, and vocabulary. There is a minimum word count of at least 24 words; the score on Mechanics is penalized in the same way as on Paragraph writing when the requirement is unmet. The mechanics rules for the essay differ from those on the paragraph and are described on pages 57–62 of the scoring manual. Examples of scored essays follow on pages 64–86. Additional samples of adult writing are found on pages 65–82 of the college and adult manual. The sum of the quartile-based scores for spelling errors and for punctuation errors along with the multiple spellings score will provide the Mechanics subtotal score. The total raw score for the essay will be composed of the subtotal scores from Mechanics, Organization, Theme Development, and Vocabulary. If other types of errors, other than those specified and scored, occur in the essay writing, you can include the information qualitatively when describing the student's writing abilities. To obtain the Written Expression total raw score, add together the scores from the grade-specific sections. (See Figure 2.6.)

Scoring Oral Expression

The Oral Expression subtest is similar to Written Expression in scoring because the total raw score for the subtest is comprised of subtotal scores from grade-specific sections. For children in grades PreK to 3, scores will be awarded dichotomously for Sentence Repetition. For all other grades, the first section to administer and score is Word Fluency. The scoring rules and examples are in Appendix A.3 of the WIAT-II scoring manual and are similar to those on Written Expression Word Fluency. Add the total number of points earned for Word Fluency A and Word Fluency B, and record the sum in the space provided on the record form. Use Table B.13 (grade-based) or Table E.12 (age-based) in the WIAT-II scoring manual to convert the Word Fluency score. The purpose of the converted score is to assign the appropriate weight to Word Fluency when calculating the Oral Expression total raw score. The Visual Passage Retell section is scored using the rubric on the record form. Scoring rules and examples can be found on pages 88–100 in the scoring manual. In similar fashion, the Giving Direction section is scored using the rubric on the record form by following the scoring rules and examples on pages 101–114 in the scoring manual. The Oral Expression total raw score is composed of the Sentence Repetition subtotal raw score (only for grades PreK to 3), the Visual Passage Retell subtotal raw score, the Word Fluency converted score, and the Giving Directions subtotal raw score. When comparing performance on the Oral Expression Word Fluency to the Written Expression Word Fluency, use the quartile-based scores that are calculated on the Supplemental Score Conversion Worksheet.

Computer Scoring Procedures

Several software configurations are available for the optional computer scoring of WIAT-II. The Scoring Assistant can be used alone or in combination with WPPSI-III, WISC-IV, or WAIS-III. The software platform is the same for all of the Wechsler scales, so once an individual's file is set up, you will only add new test data. Provision is made for comparing ability and achievement, and results from both the WIAT-II and a Wechsler IQ test can be included in a single report. Raw

Paragraph

⏱ Stop at 10 minutes

9. Scoring Rubric

Mechanics

☐ Word count ≤ 6
If checked, Quartiles for A and B = 0

	Score	Quartile
A. Spelling Errors	No. of Errors / Use Table B.8 E.8	
B. Punctuation Errors	No. of Errors / Use Table B.3 E.3	
C. Multiple Spellings	0	1

Organization

A. Sentence Structure	0	1	2
B. Paragraph has at least two sentences	0	1	2
C. Paragraph uses linking expressions	0	1	2
D. Paragraph has examples	0	1	2
E. Paragraph is unified. It does not veer from the topic	0	1	
F. The sentences follow in a logical order, one idea links to another	0	1	

Vocabulary

A. Words are varied	0	1	2	3
B. Any unusual expressions that capture the reader's interest and add spark to the writing	0	1	2	

Grades 3–6 🛑

Word Count for Paragraph (optional)

Holistic Score _____ (optional)

Figure 2.6 Scoring rubric for Written Expression paragraph from WIAT-II Record Form

score data is entered using the *Assessments* button on the far left side of the screen and the *Raw Scores* tab at the top of the screen. (See Figure 2.7.)

Enter the raw score for each section of subtests. The most common examiner error occurs when quartile scores are entered rather than raw scores. Use the pull-down menu to identify the item set administered for Reading Comprehension. You will receive an alert message if the reversal rule was applied and the administered item set does not match the grade level of the examinee, and quartile scores will not be calculated for Reading Comprehension, Target Words, and Reading Speed. A standard score for the subtest will still be reported. If the word count for the Written Expression paragraph or essay does not meet the minimum requirement, enter the number of words that were produced next to Essay/Paragraph Word Count. The program will automatically score the Mechanics section correctly, even if you have entered the number of spelling and punctuation errors. One of the most valuable features of the computer scoring is the Error Analysis. The information in the Don't Forget insert will guide you through the process of computer-scored error analysis. Another

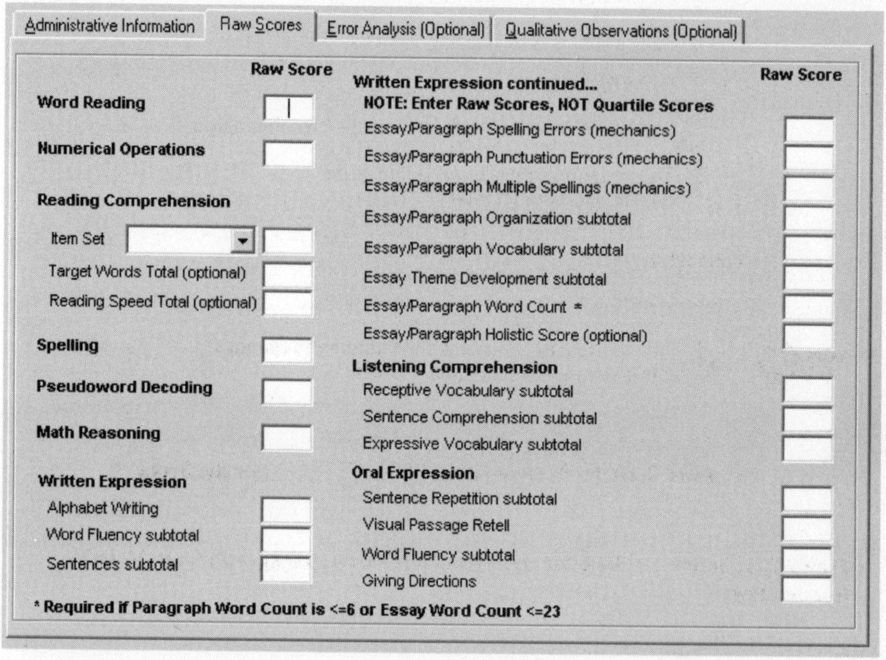

Administrative Information	Raw Scores	Error Analysis (Optional)	Qualitative Observations (Optional)

	Raw Score	**Written Expression continued...**	**Raw Score**
Word Reading		NOTE: Enter Raw Scores, NOT Quartile Scores	
		Essay/Paragraph Spelling Errors (mechanics)	
Numerical Operations		Essay/Paragraph Punctuation Errors (mechanics)	
		Essay/Paragraph Multiple Spellings (mechanics)	
Reading Comprehension		Essay/Paragraph Organization subtotal	
		Essay/Paragraph Vocabulary subtotal	
Item Set		Essay Theme Development subtotal	
Target Words Total (optional)		Essay/Paragraph Word Count *	
Reading Speed Total (optional)		Essay/Paragraph Holistic Score (optional)	
Spelling		**Listening Comprehension**	
Pseudoword Decoding		Receptive Vocabulary subtotal	
		Sentence Comprehension subtotal	
Math Reasoning		Expressive Vocabulary subtotal	
Written Expression		**Oral Expression**	
Alphabet Writing		Sentence Repetition subtotal	
Word Fluency subtotal		Visual Passage Retell	
Sentences subtotal		Word Fluency subtotal	
		Giving Directions	

* Required if Paragraph Word Count is <=6 or Essay Word Count <=23

Figure 2.7   Screen for reporting raw scores using Scoring Assistant

DON'T FORGET

Steps to Follow for the Computer-Scored Error Analysis

1. Click on the *Error Analysis* tab.
2. Use the pull-down menu to select a subtest.
3. Fill the *Beginning Item #* and the *Ending Item #* boxes to indicate the items that were administered.
4. Click the button for *Create Set.*
5. The item numbers administered will immediately appear in the box below *Administered Items.* Use the cursor to highlight the number for any missed item.
6. Click on the › symbol and the numbers for the missed items will appear in the box below *Zero Scored Items.* You can correct your entry by using the ‹ or the « buttons and reentering information.
7. Return to the pull-down menu and select the next subtest for analysis. Repeat the process for any subtest where you wish to have error analysis data.

feature of the WIAT-II Scoring Assistant is the computer scoring for the Qualitative Observations checklists (the accompanying Don't Forget box explains how to enter data for the Qualitative Observations).

DON'T FORGET

Steps to Follow for the Computer-Scored Qualitative Observations

1. Click on the *Qualitative Observations* tab.
2. Use the pull-down menu to select a subtest.
3. The observations specific to the selected subtest will appear. Use the pull-down menu beside each observation to select and highlight your frequency rating.
4. Return to the pull-down menu for selecting a subtest and repeat the process for all subtests with Qualitative Observation information.

Once the assessment data are entered, select the *Reports* button. Select the examinee, check the box next to WIAT-II under the *Assessment Type* column, then select *Next.* On the WIAT-II Options page, you will determine the content of your report. If you want to include the Error Analysis and Qualitative Observations, you must place a checkmark under *Additional Report Information.* The *Ability Score Type* section provides the space to enter IQ information if you have selected the *Parent/Client Summary* report type. Select *Preview* at the bottom of the screen and you will be taken to the actual report. The report can be printed by using your *File* menu and selecting *Print.* Figure 2.8 shows a sample WIAT-II Scoring report.

Individual Performance Summary Report

Wechsler Individual Achievement Test®
Second Edition

Examinee: Casey W.
Grade: 8   Sex: Male
Examiner: John Jones
Summary Report

Date Tested: 11/20/2004
Date of Birth: 1/5/1990
Age: 14 years 10 months
Age Based Scores

WIAT-II Subtests	Standard Score	Composite Standard Score	Confidence Interval 95%	Percentile	Age Equivalent	Grade Equivalent	Other NCE
Reading							
Word Reading	88		81- 95	21	12:0	6:8	33
Reading Comprehension	65		59- 71	1	9:0	3:5	1
Pseudoword Decoding	85		79- 91	16	9:4	3:2	29
Composite Score (Sum of Subtest SS)	238	77	73- 81	6			18
Mathematics							
Numerical Operations	102		96- 108	55	14:0	9:4	53
Math Reasoning	87		79- 95	19	12:0	6:8	32
Composite Score (Sum of Subtest SS)	189	93	88- 98	32			40
Written Language							
Spelling	89		82- 96	23	11:8	6:5	35
Written Expression	83		72- 94	13	10:8	5:5	26
Composite Score (Sum of Subtest SS)	172	85	78- 92	16			29
Oral Language							
Listening Comprehension	101		88- 114	53	14:0	8:8	51
Oral Expression	115		104- 126	84	>19:11	>12:9	71
Composite Score (Sum of Subtest SS)	216	109	99- 119	73			63
Total Composite Score (Sum of All Subtest Standard Scores)		86	82- 90	18			30

Supplemental Scores	Raw Score	Quartile	Decile
Reading			
Reading Comprehension	65*	1**	
Target Words	23	1**	
Reading Speed	615	1**	
Written Expression			
Alphabet Writing			
Word Fluency	16	3	
Word Count	62	1	
Holistic Score (Paragraph or Essay)			
Oral Expression			
Word Fluency	38	4	

Reading Rate**

Comprehension / Speed grid

1 - Far below average to below average
2 - Below average to average
3 - Average to above average
4 - Above average to far above average

*Represents standard score. **Represents quartile scores using grade based normative data.

Figure 2.8 Sample WIAT-II scoring report

**Wechsler Individual Achievement Test®
Second Edition**

Word Reading Subtest

Error Analysis

Skill	Item Numbers	Errors	% Correct
Matching Alphabet Letters	1, 2, 3		100%
Identifying Alphabet Letters	4, 5, 6, 7, 8, 9, 10, 11, 12, 13, 14, 15, 16, 17, 18, 19, 20, 21, 22, 23, 24, 25, 26, 27, 28, 29		100%
Identifying Rhyming Words	30, 31, 32, 33		100%
Identifying Beginning Sounds	34, 35, 36		100%
Identifying Ending Sounds	37, 38		100%
Blending Phonemes into Words	39, 40, 41		100%
Matching sound to symbol	42, 43, 44, 45, 46, 47		100%
Recognizing words	48, 49, 50, 51, 52, 53, 54, 55, 56, 57, 58, 59, 60, 61, 62, 63, 64, 65, 66, 67, 68, 69, 70, 71, 72, 73, 74, 75, 76, 77, 78, 79, 80, 81, 82, 83, 84, 85, 86, 87, 88, 89, 90, 91, 92, 93, 94, 95, 96, 97, 98, 99, 100, 101, 102, 103, 104, 105, 106, 107, 108, 109, 110, 111, 112, 113, 114, 115, 116, 117, 118, 119, 120, 121, 122, 123, 124, 125, 126, 127, 128, 129, 130, 131	98, 100, 105, 106, 107, 111, 112, 113, 114, 115, 118, 119, 120, 123, 124, 126, 127, 128, 129, 130, 131	75%

Observations
On the Word Reading subtest:

Often	Pronounces words automatically
	Self-corrects errors
Seldom	Laboriously "sounds out" words
	Makes accent errors
	Adds, omits, or transposes syllables when reading words

Reading Comprehension Subtest

Error Analysis

Skill	Item Numbers	Errors	% Correct
Recognizing Stated Detail	75, 77, 89, 100, 103, 107, 109, 111	89, 107	75%
Recognizing Implied Detail	98, 102, 106, 114	102, 106, 114	25%
Predicting Events and Outcomes	110, 112	110, 112	0%
Drawing Conclusions	76, 92, 97	76, 92	33%
Using Context to Determine Word Meaning	80, 83, 85, 88, 93, 94, 104, 108	93, 108	75%
Recognizing Stated Cause and Effect	87, 90	90	50%
Recognizing Implied Cause and Effect	82, 105	105	50%
Identifying Main Idea	91	91	0%
Making Inferences	78, 79, 95, 96	79, 95, 96	25%

Figure 2.8 (continued)

Individual Performance Summary Report

Observations

On the Reading Comprehension subtest:

Always	Reads passage silently when given a choice
Often	Makes self-corrections when reading
	Uses context clues when decoding unknown words
	Uses phonetic decoding skills when decoding unknown words
Seldom	Refers back to reading passage in order to answer questions
	Reads sentences fluently
Never	Reads passage aloud when given a choice

Math Reasoning Subtest

Error Analysis

Skill	Item Numbers	Errors	% Correct
Count with 1:1 correspondence and use sum to compare quantities	1, 2, 3, 8, 11		100%
Order numbers	12, 14, 15, 19, 32		100%
Identify, compare and contrast shapes, solids, lines, angles	4, 5		100%
Identify the results of rotations and reflections	45, 51	51	50%
Recall and apply basic addition and subtraction facts and procedures	9, 13, 26, 31, 35	35	80%
Recall and apply basic multiplication and division facts and procedures	38, 39, 48, 49, 58	58	80%
Use fraction words to name parts of a whole object or set	29, 40, 46, 53	40	75%
Compare and order fractions	47	47	0%
Relate fractions to decimals	57	57	0%
Solve addition and subtraction problems using fractions and decimals	43, 55	43, 55	0%
Extend pictorial patterns	17, 18		100%
Use patterns to make predictions or generalizations	50		100%
Use patterns to skip count	23, 37		100%
Use attributes such as length, weight, or capacity to compare and order objects	16		100%
Select and use appropriate formulas to solve problems involving length, area, capacity, and weight	41		100%
Tell time and use time to compare and order events	22, 28, 52		100%
Use calendar to compare and order events	21, 33		100%
Multi-step problems	26, 35, 39, 44, 49, 54, 58	35, 54, 58	57%
Use grids and graphs to make comparisons, draw conclusions, or answer questions	6, 7, 10, 24, 25, 36, 42, 59	59	88%
Use words and numbers to describe the values of individual coins	20, 27		100%
Determine the value of a collection of coins	30		100%
Apply calculation skills using decimals to solve problems involving money	44, 54	54	50%
Use theoretical and experimental probability to draw conclusions, answer questions, and make predictions	34, 56	56	50%

Observations

On the Math Reasoning subtest:

Always	Disregards component(s) of word-problem that is not required for solution
Often	Uses paper and pencil to complete problem
	Organizes work on scratch paper to facilitate problem-solving
	Breaks multi-step problem into smaller units to obtain solution
	Uses correct operation(s) to compute solution

Figure 2.8 (*continued*)

Individual Performance Summary Report

Observations
On the Math Reasoning subtest:

Often	Employs use of an effective strategy (i.e., working backwards, drawing pictures, systematic guessing, or making a
Never	Uses concrete aids (e.g., fingers) for computation
	Uses repeated addition as a substitute for multiplication when problem-solving
	Uses repeated subtraction as a substitute for division when problem-solving

Numerical Operations Subtest

Error Analysis

Skill	Item Numbers	Errors	% Correct
Number discrimination	1, 2		100%
Identifying missing number in rote counting	3		100%
Writing single and double digit numbers	4, 5		100%
Counting to 8 by rote	6		100%
Writing number to correspond with rote counting	7		100%
Addition - basic facts	8, 9, 11		100%
Subtraction - basic facts	10, 12		100%
Addition - multi-digits - no renaming	13		100%
Subtraction - multi-digits - no regrouping	14		100%
Addition - multi-digits - with renaming	15, 17, 27		100%
Subtraction - multi-digits - with regrouping	16, 18, 19		100%
Subtraction - with regrouping using decimals	20, 31		100%
Multiplication - basic facts	21, 22		100%
Multiplication - multi-digit and single digit	23		100%
Division - basic facts	24		100%
Division - using single digit divisor - no regrouping	25		100%
Division - using single digit divisor - with regrouping	26		100%
Addition - using single digit decimals	28		100%
Subtraction of simple fractions with common denominators	29		100%
Subtraction of simple fractions with different denominators	30		100%
Multiplication - multi-digits	32		100%
Multiplication - simple fractions	33		100%
Division - using multi-digits - with regrouping	34		100%
Calculating with exponents	35, 36		100%
Multiplication - using decimals	37		100%
Calculating square root	38	38	0%
Addition of negative integers	39		100%
Calculating percent	40	40	0%
Division - using simple fractions	41	41	0%
Solving simple algebraic equations	42, 43	42, 43	0%
Multiplication of simple fractions and whole numbers	45	45	0%
Calculation of pi	44	44	0%

Observations
On the Numerical Operations subtest:

Always	Uses place value correctly during calculation so as to avoid "spatial" errors
Often	Demonstrates automatized math facts when completing computations
Seldom	Makes sequential errors in procedures for multi-step calculation
Never	Writes incorrectly formed or reversed numerals
	Uses fingers/aids for counting or calculating
	Follows sequential procedures correctly, but makes math fact errors

Figure 2.8 (*continued*)

Individual Performance Summary Report

Wechsler Individual Achievement Test®
Second Edition

Listening Comprehension Subtest

Error Analysis

Skill	Item Numbers	Errors	% Correct
Receptive Vocabulary	1, 2, 3, 4, 5, 6, 7, 8, 9, 10, 11, 12, 13, 14, 15, 16	12, 14, 15, 16	75%
Sentence Comprehension	17, 18, 19, 20, 21, 22, 23, 24, 25, 26	23, 25	80%
Expressive Vocabulary	27, 28, 29, 30, 31, 32, 33, 34, 35, 36, 37, 38, 39, 40, 41	39, 40, 41	80%

Spelling Subtest

Error Analysis

Skill	Item Numbers	Errors	% Correct
Initial single consonant sound	2, 4, 5		100%
Ending single consonant sound	6		100%
Initial single vowel sound	3		100%
Initial consonant blend	7, 8		100%
Ending blend/digraph	10, 12, 33		100%
Diphthong	11		100%
Combination of phonemes in word	9		100%
High frequency words	13, 14, 15, 16, 17, 19		100%
"y" ending as "long e" sound	18		100%
Contractions	27		100%
Silent letter at onset of word	24		100%
Silent letter in medial position of word	21, 31, 32, 34, 35, 36	35, 36	67%
"soft c or g followed by e" spelling rule	23, 37, 39	37, 39	33%
Homonyms	19, 21, 24, 30, 37, 38, 39	37, 38, 39	57%
"gh" sounding like "f" sound	28		100%
Sight words	20, 26		100%
"ed" suffix	22, 32		100%
"less" suffix	25		100%
"ing" suffix	29		100%
"ment" suffix	40	40	0%

Observations
On the Spelling subtest:

Often	Writes the incorrect homonym (words shown in bold type)
	Makes spelling errors in medial position of words
	Spells phonetically
Seldom	Makes spelling errors at the ending of words
	Writes and rewrites a word several ways to determine which "looks" right
	Self-corrects errors
	Omits suffixes that mark tense or part of speech markers (i.e., -ed, -ing, -ly)
Never	Has difficulty with single consonant letter/sound relationships
	Makes spelling errors on contractions
	Has difficulty with consonant letter cluster/sound relationships
	Makes spelling errors at the beginning of words

Figure 2.8 (*continued*)

HOW TO INTERPRET THE WIAT-II

Introduction to Interpretation

Both quantitative and qualitative information should be considered when interpreting test results. The norm-referenced scores obtained on the WIAT-II represent the individual's performance in comparison to others of the same age or in the same grade. It is recommended that when achievement is compared to ability (i.e., IQ), age-based norms should be used to quantify student performance on the achievement measure. However, with WIAT-II as well as other measures of academic achievement, there are times when age-based scores can be misleading. For example, when a student has been retained in a grade, comparing him or her to age mates assumes that the equivalent instructional opportunity has been provided. In such a case, the individual might have lower scores because some skills have not been taught. For this reason, it is important to review both age-based and grade-based scores for students with a history of grade retention. When talking with teachers, it also makes more sense to discuss where a student performs in relation to others in the same grade. It is also recommended that you use the confidence interval information for each subtest and composite found in the WIAT-II scoring manual (Tables D.1 or G.1 for subtest standard scores and in Tables D.2 or G.2 for composites). A 90 percent or 95 percent level of confidence can be selected. A confidence interval allows you to report a score within a range. For example, if the confidence interval is ±4 at the 90 percent level, then an achieved standard score of 92 would fall within a range of 88 to 96.

Subtest Score Comparisons

One of the first steps in interpreting test results is to compare scores and behaviors across the subtests that contribute to a composite. This step is especially important in the area of reading, because differences and similarities in scores for the three subtests, which measure different sets of reading skills, can be diagnostic of distinct types of reading disorders, can help determine the degree of intervention needed, and can provide critical information to direct instruction. Not all reading problems have the same etiology, respond to the same treatment, or have the same prognosis (Berninger, 2005). A pervasive problem across the reading subtests, for example, could be indicative of dyslexia. The International Dyslexia Association (IDA) defines dyslexia as a specific learning disability characterized by unexpected difficulty in accuracy and rate of decoding, word reading, text reading, and in spelling (Lyon, Shaywitz, & Shaywitz, 2003). Further, the reading subtests were designed to measure both low-level and high-level skills at all levels of language (subword, word, and text), as recommended by Virginia Berninger from the University of Washington (Berninger, 1998). Low-level skills must be learned to a level of automaticity to free up mental energy and effort to work on higher-level skills. According to Samuels (1988), the goal for fluency in reading must be "beyond accuracy to automaticity." In other words, the goal of an efficient reader is to spend as little energy as possible on the low-level skill of reading words accurately so that whatever is left over can be spent on comprehension (high-level skill). Another strong influence on the development of the reading subtests was the report of the National Reading Panel (2000). A more in-depth discussion is found in Chapter 2 of the administration manual. A brief summary of using reading subtest results to inform decisionmaking related to diagnosis and intervention planning is presented in Rapid Reference 2.17.

Comparing an individual's performance on the Numerical Operations and the Math Reasoning subtests helps identify whether difficulties in math are specific to calculation or to using math skills to solve real problems. Items on these subtests closely align with state standards and were significantly influenced by the National Council of Teachers of Mathematics (2000).

Performance on the Spelling subtest should be compared to performance on the Mechanics section of the Paragraph or Essay writing in Written Expression to determine if spelling skills can be generalized to a writing activity. It is important to compare Spelling performance to the Word Reading and Pseudoword Decoding subtests, as individuals with certain types of reading disorders, dyslexia, for example, by definition have trouble with both encoding (spelling) and decoding (Lyon, Shaywitz, & Shaywitz, 2003). Spelling performance should also be viewed in light of handwriting performance. Berninger and colleagues report (1998) that children with dual disabilities in handwriting and spelling are more impaired than those with either spelling or handwriting problems, and respond more slowly to early intervention. Finally, compare Listening Comprehension performance to that on Oral Expression to investigate if language difficulties are specific to certain tasks (i.e., expressive vocabulary but not receptive vocabulary), and to identify if the individual understands what has been said, but may not possess the expressive language skills to communicate effectively with others.

Comparing Subtest Scores

One way to develop a profile of an individual's academic strengths and weaknesses is to compare performance across subtests. This can be accomplished by comparing pairs of subtests to each other or by comparing a specific subtest to the mean of a group of subtests. Making the comparison is not as simple as determining that one score is greater than the other. Rather, two conditions must be

Reading Subtest Results and Research-Based Implications for Diagnosis and Suggestions for Intervention Planning

Subtest	Diagnostic Implications	Suggestions for Intervention Planning
Word Reading: letter identification	Excellent school-entry predictor of how well children learn to read during the first 2 years of instruction (National Reading Panel, 2000).	An appropriate measure for selecting students for differing levels of intervention (Adams, 1990; Lennon & Slesinski, 1999).
Word Reading: phonemic and phonological awareness	Delays are often found in children with developmental reading disabilities (Alexander, Andersen, Heilman, Voeller, & Torgesen, 1991). Early assessment of skills prior to formal reading instruction is a reliable predictor of later reading achievement (Torgesen, Wagner, & Rashotte, 1994).	The development of efficient word-recognition skills is associated with improved reading comprehension (Stanovich, 1985). Students benefit from explicit, systematic, instruction, including such activities as phoneme identification, phoneme blending, phoneme deletion, phoneme substitution (National Reading Panel, 2000), because instruction improves a student's skill in decoding new words. Games such as *Find the Hidden, Say the Missing, Say the Word Without*, and *Substitute* are effective drill and practice activities (Berninger & Abbott, 2003). Henry (2003) and Masterson, Apel, and Wasowicz (2002) provide instructional techniques to help students in upper elementary, middle school and high school learn to read and spell longer and more morphologically, orthographically, and phonologically complex words.

Word Reading: automaticity	Inefficient word recognition skills are associated with poor reading comprehension (Stanovich, 1985; Berninger, 1998). Laborious decoding may require all available cognitive resources and thereby leave little or no resources available for comprehending what has been read (Berninger, 1998). Additional testing using rapid automatic naming tasks could provide additional evidence for automaticity deficits.	Automaticity can be taught through extended practice (Samuels, 1988), but competent reading requires skills that extend beyond the single-word level to contextual reading. This skill can best be acquired by practicing reading in which the words are in a meaningful context (National Reading Panel, 2000).
Pseudoword Decoding	Measures whether the phonological decoding mechanism is developing in an age-appropriate manner (Berninger, 2001). Difficulty in reading aloud well-spelled nonsense words is a singularly powerful indicator of a specific reading disability (Rack, Snowling, and Olson, 1992). Dyslexic children showed significant impairment in all reading skills involving word reading, phonological decoding, and oral text reading (Berninger & O'Donnell, 2005).	Practice in applying the alphabet principle with activities built around *Talking Letters* can improve a student's skill in decoding new words (Berninger, 2001).

(continued)

Subtest	Diagnostic Implications	Suggestions for Intervention Planning
Reading Comprehension: Oral Reading of Sentences	Fluency of oral reading is a necessary skill for reading comprehension (Kuhn & Stahl, 2000). Informal procedures can be used in the classroom to assess fluency and monitor progress: informal reading inventories (Johnson, Kress, & Pikulski, 1987), miscue analysis (Goodman & Burke, 1972), running records (Clay, 1972), and reading speed calculations (Hasboruck & Tindal, 1992).	Explicit instruction directs student's conscious attention to implicit linguistic knowledge in order to develop both automatic word reading and fluent oral reading of passages, and nonautomatic application of strategies and construction of meaning (Berninger; Nagy et al., 2003). Techniques such as "folding-in" where new information is interspersed within materials that is already known (Roberts, Turco, & Shapiro, 1991), guided repeated oral reading, and previewing are effective teaching strategies to improve fluency (Elliott, DiPerna, & Shapiro, 2001).
Reading Comprehension: Reading Rate	Lovett (1987) identified two subtypes of reading disability: *accuracy* disability (deficits in both speed and word recognition) and *rate* disability (no deficit in word recognition but slow reading speed). Students with a *double deficit* (problems with both rate and accuracy) are at highest risk.	See fluency activities.
Reading Comprehension: Content Comprehension	Additional assessment of executive functions can evaluate the role played by working memory in reading comprehension (Altemeier; Jones, Abbot, & Berninger, in press).	Students benefit from explicit instruction in comprehension strategies (National Reading Panel, 2000), including: use of prereading activities to activate students' prior knowledge, use of goal-directed strategies that reinforce the student's successful reading, use of post-reading activities to help students remember the essential information, direct instruction of specific skills, modeling of the skill (reciprocal teaching activities), guided practice, and evaluation of the effectiveness of the strategy (Elliott, DiPerna & Shapiro, 2001).

| Reading Comprehension: Vocabulary | When poor performance on vocabulary items is paired with low verbal comprehension ability, consider a comprehensive language evaluation. | Bryant, Ugel, Thompson, and Hamff (1999) identify two effective interventions to build vocabulary: *semantic mapping and semantic feature analysis*. The National Reading Panel (2002) reported that: (1) computer-assisted vocabulary instruction shows positive learning gains, (2) vocabulary instruction leads to gains in comprehension, (3) vocabulary can be learned incidentally, but repeated exposure to vocabulary items is important for learning gains, (4) preinstruction of vocabulary words prior to reading can facilitate both vocabulary acquisition and comprehension, and (5) restructuring of the text materials or procedures facilitates acquisition and comprehension (e.g., substituting easy for hard words). |

met before a difference between two scores can be called a discrepancy. The following steps guide you through the process of comparing subtests.

Step 1. Calculate the standard scores for the selected subtests by using Tables C.1 (grade-based) or F.1 (age-based) in the WIAT-II scoring manual.

Step 2. To determine if a difference between the standard scores of any 2 subtests is *statistically significant* consult Tables K.9, K.10 (grade-based) or Table K.11 (age-based) in the WIAT-II scoring manual. (See page 149 of the administration manual for a discussion of statistical significance.) First, determine the level of significance you will use. The shaded area of the table reports scores at the .15 level of significance, and the unshaded area reports scores at the .05 level. To compare two subtests, select the column for one subtest and the row for the other subtest on the chart. The number found at the intersection of the column and the row is the difference required for statistical significance. The number should be rounded off. For example, in order for the difference between Word Reading and Reading Comprehension to be statistically significant at the .05 level of significance, there must be a 9.76 (round to 10) point difference. In this example, if the difference is less than 10, there is no discrepancy between the two scores. If the difference is 10 or greater, then the second condition must be met.

Step 3. A difference can be statistically significant but common. In order to establish that a discrepancy exists between two scores, you must also determine that the difference is unusual or rare. Use Table K.12 (the Base Rate table) in the WIAT-II scoring manual to find the percentage of individuals in the standardization sample with a difference of that magnitude. Notice that the standardization samples are divided into grade and age groupings. Identify the score for the difference between the two subtests in the Scatter column, then read across the table until you find the column for the group you want to use from standardization. The number that appears at the intersection is the *base rate* or the frequency rate. In our example, the 10-point difference that was statistically significant for Word Reading and Reading Comprehension occurred in 99.8 percent of the grades 1 to 12 fall standardization sample (see Table K.9 at the .05 level of significance). The difference is not unusual—in fact, it is quite common. Generally speaking, a difference is considered rare when it occurs in no more than 10 to 15 percent of the population. In this case the difference was statistically significant but it was not unusual; therefore, it is not a discrepancy. Once you have established that a discrepancy exists between two subtests possible explanations for the discrepancy should be considered. Rapid Reference 2.3 can be helpful in explaining discrepancies.

Subtest scatter is another way to identify intraindividual differences. In the WIAT-II scoring manual, Tables K.6 and K.7 (grade-based) and Table K.8 (age-based) identify the required size of the difference between a subtest and the mean of either all nine subtests, or the selected six subtests, or the selected four subtests at the .05 and .15 significance levels. The cumulative percentage of individuals in the selected standardization sample with a difference of the identified magnitude is also provided, in order to establish whether the difference is unusual. To illustrate, you have a difference of 15 points between the standard score on Math Reasoning and the mean of the scores on all nine of the subtests. At the .15 level of significance, the difference must be at least 9.75 (round to 10 points) in order to be statistically significant. By reading across the table, you note that 10 percent of the standardization sample had a difference of 14.78 (round to 15) points. The difference is both statistically significant and unusual; therefore, it represents a discrepancy. It is also important to consider if there is restricted range with any of the subtests. Rapid Reference 2.18 reports by age the lowest possible score for each subtest, based on a raw score of 0. Rapid Reference 2.19 reports by age the highest possible score, based on the maximum raw score for each subtest. When discrepancies occur between the subtests that contribute to a composite score, the individual subtest scores should be used instead of the composite to calculate an ability-achievement discrepancy because the individual's deficits could be hidden if using only the composite.

Composite Score Comparisons

The same procedure is followed when comparing one composite score to another. Remember that the difference between two composite standard scores must be both statistically significant and unusual in order to be a discrepancy. In the WIAT-II scoring manual, Tables K.1 and K.2 (grade-based) and Table K.3 (age-based) present the data for the different standardization samples. You can select the data by a specific grade or age or you can use the average of all grades (the last row on the tables) or the average of all ages. For most cases, the average values are sufficient for the purpose of assessing the significance of differences between composite scores. Base rates for composite score differences are found in Table K.4 (grade-based) and Table K.5 (age-based).

Rapid Reference 2.18

Effective Range of Subtest Scores by Age (Based on Raw score of 0)[a]

Age	WR	NO	RC	SP	PD	MR	WE	LC	OE
4:0–4:3	84	—	—	—	—	70	—	70	72
4:4–4:7	82	—	—	—	—	68	—	68	69
4:8–4:11	80	—	—	—	—	66	—	66	66
5:0–5:3	77	69	—	85	—	63	—	63	64
5:4–5:7	75	65	—	81	—	61	—	61	61
5:8–5:11	69	61	—	77	—	59	—	58	59
6:0–6:3	64	58	64	73	90	56	76	55	56
6:4–6:7	58	54	61	69	88	54	74	52	54
6:8–6:11	53	49	58	65	86	50	72	49	51
7:0–7:3	47	45	56	60	84	46	71	47	48
7:4–7:7	42	40	53	56	82	42	69	44	45
7:8–7:11	41	40	50	52	80	41	67	43	43
8:0–8:3	41	40	46	48	77	41	65	41	42
8:4–8:7	40	40	43	44	75	40	63	40	40
8:8–8:11	40	40	42	43	73	40	60	40	40
9:0–9:3	40	40	41	41	71	40	58	40	48/40[b]
9:4–9:7	40	40	40	40	69	40	55	40	48/40[b]
9:8–9:11	40	40	40	40	68	40	54	40	48/40[b]
10:0–10:3	40	40	40	40	67	40	52	40	47
10:4–10:7	40	40	40	40	66	40	51	40	47
10:8–10:11	40	40	40	40	65	40	50	40	47
11:0–11:3	40	40	40	40	63	40	48	40	46
11:4–11:7	40	40	40	40	62	40	47	40	46
11:8–11:11	40	40	40	40	61	40	46	40	45
12:0–12:3	40	40	40	40	61	40	46	40	45
12:4–12:7	40	40	40	40	60	40	45	40	44
12:8–12:11	40	40	40	40	59	40	44	40	44
13:0–13:3	40	40	40	40	59	40	44	40	44
13:4–13:7	40	40	40	40	58	40	43	40	44
13:8–13:11	40	40	40	40	57	40	42	40	43
14:0–14:11	40	40	40	40	56	40	41	40	42
15:0–15:11	40	40	40	40	53	40	40	40	40
16:0–16:11	40	40	40	40	53	40	40	40	40
17:0–17:11	40	40	40	40	50	40	40	40	40

Source: Data are from Table F.1 of the *WIAT-II Scoring Manual* (The Psychological Corporation, 2002).
Note: WR = Word Reading; NO = Numerical Operations; RC = Reading Comprehension; SP = Spelling; PD = Pseudoword Decoding; MR = Math Reasoning; WE = Written Expression; LC = Listening Comprehension; OE = Oral Expression.
[a]Shaded cells indicate standard scores that are 2 standard deviations or more below the mean.
[b]Score for 9-year-old examinee in grade 3.

≡Rapid Reference 2.19

Effective Range of Subtest Scores by Age
(Based on Maximum Score for Subtest)[a]

Age	WR	NO	RC	SP	PD	MR	WE	LC	OE
4:0–4:3	160	—	—	—	—	160	—	160	160
4:4–4:7	160	—	—	—	—	160	—	160	160
4:8–4:11	160	—	—	—	—	160	—	160	160
5:0–5:3	160	160	—	160	—	160	—	160	160
5:4–5:7	160	160	—	160	—	160	—	160	160
5:8–5:11	160	160	—	160	—	160	—	160	160
6:0–6:3	160	160	160	160	154	160	160	160	160
6:4–6:7	160	160	160	160	150	160	160	160	160
6:8–6:11	159	160	160	160	146	160	160	160	160
7:0–7:3	159	160	160	160	143	160	160	160	160
7:4–7:7	158	160	160	160	139	160	160	160	160
7:8–7:11	154	160	160	160	137	160	160	159	160
8:0–8:3	149	160	160	160	134	160	160	158	160
8:4–8:7	145	160	160	160	132	160	160	157	160
8:8–8:11	144	160	160	159	130	160	160	155	160
9:0–9:3	143	160	160	158	129	160	160	153	160
9:4–9:7	142	160	160	157	127	160	160	151	160
9:8–9:11	141	160	160	154	126	158	160	149	160
10:0–10:3	141	160	160	152	125	157	160	148	160
10:4–10:7	140	160	160	149	124	155	160	146	160
10:8–10:11	139	160	160	148	123	152	160	144	160
11:0–11:3	137	160	160	147	123	149	160	143	160
11:4–11:7	136	160	160	146	122	146	160	141	160
11:8–11:11	135	157	159	144	122	143	160	139	160
12:0–12:3	134	155	157	143	121	140	160	138	160
12:4–12:7	133	152	156	139	121	137	160	136	160
12:8–12:11	133	148	155	140	121	135	160	135	160
13:0–13:3	132	143	154	138	121	132	160	133	160
13:4–13:7	132	139	153	137	121	130	160	132	160
13:8–13:11	131	137	152	136	121	129	159	131	160
14:0–14:11	128	132	152	133	120	128	135	130	160
15:0–15:11	126	130	151	133	119	128	156	127	160
16:0–16:11	120	128	150	132	119	126	152	125	160
17:0–17:11	120	124	147	130	118	124	148	123	160

Source: Data are from Table F.1 of the *WIAT-II Scoring Manual* (The Psychological Corporation, 2002).
Note: WR = Word Reading; NO = Numerical Operations; RC = Reading Comprehension; SP = Spelling; PD = Pseudoword Decoding; MR = Math Reasoning; WE = Written Expression; LC = Listening Comprehension; OE = Oral Expression.
[a]Shaded cells indicate standard scores that are 2 standard deviations or more below the mean.

In response to requests from test users, the publisher of the WIAT-II produced Basic Reading Composite Standard Scores in 2002. This composite is comprised of the Word Reading and Pseudoword Decoding subtests. Caution should be used when interpreting any composite score, as discrepancies between contributing subtests and the skills they measure could be masked. The Pseudoword Decoding subtest has a natural floor for young students that can affect the Basic Reading composite below grade 3. Decoding skills in the early grades develop at different rates, depending in part on instruction received. The lowest scores on decoding (raw scores of 0 to 1) can produce standard scores as high as 86 in grade 1, whereas similar raw scores at grade 3 yield standard scores of 72 to 73. Consequently, the Basic Reading composite score may overestimate reading achievement for students in grades 1 to 2 who perform poorly on the Pseudoword Decoding subtest. Rapid Reference 2.20 reports the Basic Reading Composite scores.

Moving Beyond the Scores

Subtest and composite scores by themselves provide limited information about intervention. To develop an appropriate IEP for a student, more detailed information is necessary. For example:

1. Which skills or sets of skills have been learned and which have not?
2. What strategies did the student employ to demonstrate the skill?
3. Under what conditions was success achieved? Under what conditions did failure occur? At what level of independence was the student able to perform?

The Role of Qualitative Data

Qualitative information can be obtained by recording general behavioral observations during testing and through the use of the Qualitative Observations checklists and error and skills analyses. A qualitative analysis helps clarify why an individual might achieve a set of scores. Investigate whether test behaviors are typical of the individual's performance by talking with teachers, parents, or others who are familiar with the examinee. Determine if there are mitigating circumstances such as illness or anxiety that might have affected test performance. Note if test behaviors are consistent from one subtest to another. Pay close attention to comments that an examinee may make regarding his or her academic interests, strengths, and weaknesses. Record the use of problem-solving strategies. For

Rapid Reference 2.20

Basic Reading Composite Scores

Standard Score	Sum of Standard Scores Grade-Based	Sum of Standard Scores Age-Based	Standard Score	Sum of Standard Scores Grade-Based	Sum of Standard Scores Age-Based	Standard Score	Sum of Standard Scores Grade-Based	Sum of Standard Scores Age-Based
40			80	162–163	163–164	121	239–240	240–241
41	90	90	81	164–165	165–166	122	241–242	242–243
42	91–92	91–92	82	166–167	167–168	123	243–244	244–245
43	93–94	93–94	83	168–169	169	124	245–246	246–247
44	95	95–96	84	170–171	170–171	125	247–248	248–249
45	96–97	97–98	85	172–173	172–173	126	249–250	250–251
46	98–99	99	86	174	174–175	127	251–252	252–253
47	100–101	100–101	87	175–176	176–177	128	253	254–255
48	102–103	102–103	88	177–178	178–179	129	254–255	256
49	104–105	104–105	89	179–180	180–181	130	256–257	257
50	106–108	106–108	90	181–182	182–183	131	258	258
51	109–110	109–110	91	183–184	184–185	132	259	259
52	111	111	92	185–186	186	133	260–261	260–261
53	112	112–113	93	187–188	187–188	134	262–264	262–264
54	113–114	114–115	94	189–190	189–190	135	265–267	265–267
55	115–116	116	95	191	191–192	136	268–269	268–270
56	117–118	117–118	96	192–193	193–194	137	270	271–272
57	119–120	119–120	97	194–195	195–196	138	271–272	273–274
58	121–122	121–122	98	196–197	197–198	139	273–274	275
59	123–124	123–124	99	198–199	199	140	275–276	276–277

(continued)

| | **Sum of Standard Scores** | |
Standard Score	Grade-Based	Age-Based
60	125–126	125–126
61	127	127–128
62	128–129	129–130
63	130–131	131–132
64	132–133	133–134
65	134–135	135
66	136–137	136–137
67	138–139	138–139
68	140–141	140–141
69	142–143	142–143
70	144	144–145
71	145–146	146–147
72	147–148	148–149
73	149–150	150–151
74	151–152	152
75	153–154	153–154
76	155–156	155–156
77	157–158	157–158
78	159	159–160
79	160–161	161–162

| | **Sum of Standard Scores** | |
Standard Score	Grade-Based	Age-Based
100	200–201	200–201
101	202–203	202–203
102	204–205	204–205
103	206	206–207
104	207–208	208–209
105	209–210	210–211
106	211–212	212–213
107	213–214	214–215
108	215–216	216–217
109	217–218	218–219
110	219–220	220–221
111	221	222
112	222–223	223–224
113	224–225	225–226
114	226–227	227–228
115	228–229	229
116	230–231	230–231
117	232–233	232–234
118	234–235	235–236
119	236–237	237–238
120	238	239

| | **Sum of Standard Scores** | |
Standard Score	Grade-Based	Age-Based
141	277–278	278–279
142	279–280	280–281
143	281–282	282–283
144	283–284	284
145	285	285
146	286	286
147	287	287
148	288	288
149	289	289
150	290–291	290–291
151	292–293	293–294
152	294–296	295–298
153	297–299	299–301
154	300–302	302–304
155	303–304	305–306
156	305–306	307–308
157	307–308	309
158	309	310–311
159	310	312–313
160		314

Sum the Grade-based or Aged-based Standard scores for the Word Reading and Pseudoword Decoding subtests. Using Table 1, convert the sum to the Basic Reading Composite standard score.

example, an examinee that uses subvocalization when writing a spelling word is probably using a different strategy than an examinee who writes a word with various spellings and comments that "that doesn't look right." Observations are important because they provide information that can serve as a cross-check on the validity of the examinee's scores (Glutting, Oakland, & Konold, 1994).

Skills Analysis

Skills analysis is particularly useful when developing an instructional or intervention plan. WIAT-II subtests have been grouped into academic domains to measure various components of a construct. Each subtest measures a unique set of skills, and within subtests there are more specific skill sets. The quickest way to conduct a skills analysis is by using the Scoring Assistant, but Chapter 7 of the WIAT-II administration manual includes several tables that delineate the skills or sets of skills matched to items within a subtest. Table 7.1 lists the Word Reading skills, and Table 7.2 identifies the skills for Reading Comprehension. The Numerical Operations skills, found in Table 7.3, and the Math Reasoning skills, located in Table 7.4, also appear beside the items on the record form. You may notice that Table 7.4 for Math Reasoning has several item numbers printed in **bold** type. The items that require multistep solution are singled out because many students with math disabilities perform differently, depending on the requirement for multistep solution. You can use the skills tables to identify specific skill deficits or to develop a profile of individual strengths and weaknesses. Since skills are evaluated by a small number of items, one way to double-check your findings is to go over them with the examinee's teacher prior to including them in an intervention plan (see Caution box).

CAUTION

The Skills Analysis evaluates skills with a small number of items; thus, findings must be confirmed with other data. Such data may include teacher's reports, performance on school tests, performance on homework, or performance on other standardized tests.

Error Analysis

Two sources of information will be helpful when conducting error analysis. First, you must pay close attention to student performance by watching the examinee as unobtrusively as possible during subtests such as Numerical Operations, Spelling, and Written Expression. Observe how the examinee approaches the task. Is an error the result of carelessness, inattentiveness, or lack of effort? Does the examinee use self-monitoring by checking his or her work, by rereading what has been written, or by rechecking a passage prior to answering a comprehension question? Does frustration set in once errors begin to occur? Does the examinee seek out your encouragement and approval? You should also review responses to determine where the problemsolving process may break down. Because examinees are required to write their responses with a pencil without an eraser you can more easily identify how errors were made on written responses. Additional insight can be gained through testing the limits by asking the examinee to work a problem or spell a word aloud after the subtest has been administered following standardized procedure. Special attention should be paid to how the examinee decodes unfamiliar words when reading from a list on Word Reading and Pseudoword Decoding, in comparison to reading words in the context of a sentence on Reading Comprehension. Are errors more likely to occur with the decoding of vowels in general or only vowels with the long sound? Do errors occur primarily when decoding or spelling irregular words? On Oral Expression, is the individual able to provide step-by-step directions when a visual prompt is provided but not when one is missing? By understanding why an error occurs or under what conditions an individual achieves success, an individualized intervention plan can be developed. Knowing that a student's spelling problem is related to morphology (i.e., word form, such as root word, suffix, prefix) rather than phonology (sound-symbol relationship) can direct the teacher to provide explicit, systematic instruction in that area. Berninger developed an error coding scheme for the WIAT-II Spelling subtest with links to research-based intervention. Eight error types are described in Rapid Reference 2.21. Just as early identification and intervention for reading problems are more likely to produce favorable outcomes for students, early intervention for at-risk spellers is more likely than later intervention to result in improved spelling (Berninger et al., 1998). In other words, error analysis is an effective way to link assessment results to instructional planning. To guide you in this process, Rapid Reference 2.22 provides sample error types with examples for Math. Two excellent resources to help you identify intervention/instructional strategies based on error types are *Teaching Mathematics to the Learned Disabled* (Bley & Thornton, 1989) and *Spelling Development, Disability, and Instruction* (Moats, 1995). The *SPELL (Spelling Performance Evaluation for Language & Literacy)* is a software program (Masterson, Apel, & Wasowicz, 2002) that provides more in-depth analysis of spelling errors and yields customized learning objectives.

≡Rapid Reference 2.21

Coding Spelling Errors with Links to Intervention

Error Type 1: Phonological Processing Problems

These errors indicate that the student does not have precise phonological representation of all the phonemes in a spoken word that is being translated into its written form. Mixed phonological errors are the most indicative of serious phonological processing problems.

Examples: deleted phonemes (*pinsiss* for princess), added phonemes (*abpsent* for absent), transposed phonemes (*rust* for ruts), substituted phonemes (*bug* for dug), and mixed phonological errors (*vamlee* for family).

Intervention: phonological awareness training with feedback.[a]

Error Type 2: Phonological-Orthographic Processing Problems

These errors may be implausible given the conventional phoneme-spelling correspondences and their alternations in English.

Examples: fich (fish), *lorchj* (large), *ridn* (riding), *sithed* (sight).

Intervention: teach the alphabet principle and its alternations in the direction of phonemes to one- or two-letter spelling units.[a]

Error Type 3: Word-Specific Orthographic Processing Problems

These errors occur when a spelling is plausible for a conventional phoneme-spelling correspondence in English, but not appropriate for a specific word context. Errors include spelling a schwa and silent letters (which can only be spelled correctly by memorizing for a specific word context).

Examples: cairful (careful), *monkee* (monkey), *briet* (bright), *seperately* (separately), *sentance* (sentence), and *anser* (answer)

Intervention: combine teaching alphabet principle and its alternations in the direction of phonemes to one- or two-letter spelling unit with word-specific training by spelling target word in dictated sentence.[a]

Error Type 4: Morphological Processing Problems

These include errors in inflectional suffixes or stem changes in tense, errors with prefixes, derivational suffixes, and not maintaining the stem morpheme.

Examples: adcite (excite), *inpolite* (impolite), and *religous* (religious), *nashunal* (national) and *bomming* (bombing).

Intervention: combine morphological awareness training with word-specific training by spelling target word in dictated sentence.[a]

Error Type 5: Spelling Conventions (Rules)

Errors related to doubling final consonant of closed syllables, changing *y* to *i* when adding morpheme, forming a contraction, twinning for *l, s,* or *f* in final position, and final e for soft *c* or soft *g.*

(continued)

Examples: acomodate (accommodate), *begining* (beginning), and *busyer* (busier) and *woulden't* (wouldn't), and *kised* (kissed), and *dans* (dance).

Intervention: systematically and explicitly teach spelling rules[a] (see Masterson, Apel, & Wasowicz, 2002, for strategies).

Error Type 6: Phonological/Orthographic/Morphological Confusions

Errors in spelling a homonym or homograph.

Examples: too (two), *him* (hymn) and He *red* (read) the book.

Intervention: spelling targeted words in dictated sentences so that sentence context must be taken into account.

Error Type 7: Prealphabetic Principle State of Spelling Development

Errors that occur in early development of representing speech in writing.

Examples: utody (train), *bz* (bees).

Intervention: phonological awareness and alphabetic principle training.[a]

Error Type 8: Letter Production Errors

Errors including letter reversals, letter inversions, and letter transpositions.

Examples: maq (map), *me* (we), *tow* (two).

Intervention: combine Handwriting Lessons and alphabetic principle training.[a]

[a]Intervention data adapted from Berninger, V. (1998). *Process assessment of the learner (PAL): Guides for Intervention.* San Antonio, TX: Psychological Corporation.

USING WIAT-II WITH THE WECHSLER INTELLIGENCE SCALES

Assessment of both achievement and ability for the purposes of documenting discrepancies was a cornerstone in the Education for All Handicapped Children Act of 1975 (P.L. 94-142) and in the Individuals with Disabilities Education Act (IDEA) Amendments of 1997. Even though IDEA 2004 no longer requires an ability-achievement discrepancy as the sole criteria for a learning disability, this does not mean that conducting the analysis is a waste of time. An ability-achievement discrepancy is still relevant; it's just not diagnostic. It is important to know whether a gap exists between reasonable expectations for the student and actual skill acquisition. However, there are causes of an ability-achievement gap other than a learning disability, and some students with a learning disability will not show a gap between the two. In other words, an ability-achievement gap can be useful is describing a student's performance rather than in diagnosing LD. When conducting an ability-achievement discrepancy analysis using WIAT-II, the following steps should be followed.

Step 1: It is recommended that an achievement test should be used with a conormed or linked ability test for purposes of an ability-achievement discrepancy analysis. WIAT-II is linked to WPPSI-III, WISC-IV, and WAIS-III. For each

≡ Rapid Reference 2.22

Sample Error Types with Examples for Math Subtests

Error Type	Examples
Computational error related to basic facts.	$8 \times 5 = 45$ $4 + 5 + 6 = 14$
Computational error related to the process of continually switching direction in space that is required for paper and pencil calculation.	Student works bottom to top on subtraction problem. Student works multiplication problem from left to right.
Computation error related to the sequential steps required for multistep problem solution.	*Johnny spent a quarter, a dime, and a nickel on a toy. How much change would he receive from $1.00?* Student adds .25 + .10 + .05 but fails to subtract the total from 1.00.
Computational error related to inattention to the sign.	$80 - 56 = 136$ $19 \times 5 = 24$
Selects an incorrect process (add, subtract, multiply, divide) for problem solution (may be related to inability to translate math vocabulary into math process).	*How many would be left? Which is more? What is the average score?*
Includes irrelevant information when setting up the problem prior to calculation.	*Susie went to the library 4 times this month. On the first trip she checked out 2 books, on the second trip she checked out 3 books, on the third trip she returned 2 books, and on the fourth trip she checked out 4 books. How many books did she check out from the library this month?* Student adds 2 + 3 + 4, then, subtracts 2 from the total.
Calculation error due to misalignment of digits when solving multi digit problems (generally in multiplication and division problems).	$\begin{array}{r} 19 \\ \times\,22 \\ \hline 38 \\ 38 \\ \hline 76 \end{array}$
Difficulty drawing conclusions, which may appear as inability to continue patterns.	*Finish this pattern: 2, 4, 6, ____.* Student responds with 12.

of the pairings, a linking sample was collected during standardization, so that a stratified sample representing the appropriate ages would be administered in both tests. The linking samples, which are described in the ability scale manuals, are nationally representative in terms of age, sex, ethnicity, geographic region, and parent or self education level. Based on another linking study, discrepancy information is available for comparing WIAT-II to the Differential Ability Scales (DAS; Elliott, 1990). Those tables can be obtained by contacting PsychCorp. Alternate ability measures that are not statistically linked to WIAT-II should be used with extreme caution. Formulas for their use are found on pages 154–157 of the WIAT-II administration manual.

Step 2: Determine which ability score will be used in the discrepancy analysis. In most cases, the full-scale IQ is the best overall representation of an individual's general intellectual abilities. There are times, however, when a different score may be more appropriate. In January 2005 PsychCorp posted the WISC-IV Technical Report #4: General Abilities Index, which contains GAI scores and information about their use on their website (www.PsychCorp.com). In general, the use of the GAI should be reserved for those cases where working memory performance is discrepant from verbal comprehension performance and/or processing speed performance is discrepant from perceptual reasoning performance (remember that the differences must be both statistically significant and unusual). It is also appropriate to compare FSIQ to GAI. This comparison can be helpful in intervention planning. Tables 2 and 3 of the technical report provide the necessary data to determine if a discrepancy exists between the two composite scores.

Step 3: Next, you must determine the method for the discrepancy analysis. The two most common methods are the models for simple-difference and the predicated-achievement. The simple-difference method requires that a WIAT-II standard score (either subtest or composite) be subtracted from the selected ability or IQ score. This method is easy to use and widely employed but, as Braden and Weiss (1988) showed, the correlation between the two scores is ignored, and can thereby result in errors of classification (see Caution insert). The accuracy of discrepancy analysis is enhanced when the correlation between ability and achievement is taken into account. In the predicted-achievement model the ability score is used in a regression equation to predict the expected achievement score. To be more specific, the IQ score is used to predict an achievement score; then, the actual achievement score is subtracted from the predicted score. A discussion of the two methods is found on pages 154–157 of the WIAT-II administration manual. The tables in the WIAT-II scoring manual compare performance using WISC-III. For comparisons between WIAT-II and WISC-IV, consult Appendix B of the *WISC-IV Technical and Interpretive Manual* (use Tables B.4 and B.5 for statistical significance, and Tables B.6 to B.8 for the base rates when using the predicted-achievement method; use Tables B.9 and B.10 for statistical significance, and Tables B.11 to B.13 for the base rates when using the simple-difference method). With the recent revision of IDEA (P.L. 108-446), the

CAUTION

The predicted-achievement model is preferred over the simple-difference method in comparing scores from ability and achievement tests, as it is a more psychometrically sound method.

door is open to other ways of identifying individuals with a learning disability other than sole use of an ability-achievement discrepancy (a more in-depth discussion of this topic is provided in Chapter 4 of this book, which discusses Clinical Applications). Use of the WIAT-II continues to be appropriate for the following reasons:

1. Using WIAT-II with WISC-IV as part of a process-focused assessment battery supports the identification of hallmark processing deficits (e.g., verbal working memory) paired with low reading and spelling achievement, which many researchers (Berninger, 2005) believe are necessary to the diagnosis of reading disability.
2. Using WIAT-II with the new WISC-IV Integrated supports a broader-based *process approach* to assessment. The use of the Qualitative Observations, skills analysis, and error analysis on the WIAT-II will have even greater value within this model of evaluation.
3. WIAT-II is recommended as a useful instrument in an alternative three-tier assessment model as described in Berninger, Stage, Smith, and Hildebrand (2001) and outlined in "Research-Supported Differential Diagnosis of Specific Learning Disabilities," a chapter in *WISC-IV Clinical Use and Interpretation* (Prifitera, Saklofske, Weiss, & Rolfhus, 2005).

STRENGTHS AND WEAKNESSES OF THE WIAT-II

Rapid Reference 2.23 lists strengths and weaknesses of the WIAT-II in the following areas: test development, administration and scoring, reliability and validity, standardization, and interpretation. Overall, the test development, standardization, and psychometric properties of the WIAT-II are excellent. The administration and scoring procedures for the majority of the subtests are straightforward—however, the Reading Comprehension and Written Expression

Strengths and Weaknesses of the WIAT-II

Test Development

Strengths	Weaknesses
• Item development based on current research, state standards, use of curriculum consultants, and disability experts	• Limited ceiling at higher age and grade levels for gifted individuals for some subtests
• Large number of items for very young children in preschool and kindergarten that measure emerging literacy, numeracy, writing, and oral language	• Restricted range of scores for Pseudoword Decoding subtest
• Engaging, full-color artwork and graphics	
• Addition of the Pseudoword Decoding subtest as a purer measure of word attack/decoding	
• Numerous optional scores can be obtained	
• Updated linkage with WPPSI-III, WISC-IV, and WAIS-III	
• Basic Reading composite score combines Word Reading and Pseudoword Decoding as a measure of word level	

Standardization

Strengths	Weaknesses
• Size of PreK–12 standardization sample (300 per grade level except for grades PreK, 9–12	• Small adult sample size ($N = 707$ for college sample; $N = 515$ for adult ages 17–85 sample)
• Inclusion of students receiving special education services at every grade level (8%–10%). Inclusion of gifted individuals at every grade level (3%)	• Use of case-weighting procedures for the WAIS-III linking sample to adjust the standard deviation
• Demographic details provided on the linking samples with ability measures	
• Linked to *Process Assessment of the Learner Test Battery for Reading and Writing* (Berninger, 2001)	

Reliability and Validity	
Strengths	**Weaknesses**
• High split-half reliabilities for composites (range from .89 to .98 with a total achievement reliability of .98) and for subtests (range from .80 to .97) • High test-retest coefficients for composites (range from .92 to .97 with a total achievement coefficient of .98) and for subtests (range from .85 to .98) • High interrater reliability coefficients across ages for Reading Comprehension (overall .94), Written Expression (overall .85), and Oral Expression (overall .96) subtests • Strong evidence for face validity based on use of state standards, curriculum guides, and advisory panels • Correlation studies with measures of ability, group achievement tests, other achievement tests, and grades show evidence of construct validity • Large number of clinical studies with special groups (study groups included gifted students and individuals with mental retardation, with emotional disturbance, with learning disabilities in reading, with learning disabilities not specific to reading, with ADHD, with comorbid ADHD and LD, with hearing impairments, and with speech and/or language impairments).	• Standard Errors of Measurement (SEM) high for Oral Language composite (5.01) as well as for some ages for some subtests • Limited number of students in test-retest reliability study (children younger than 6 were not included and $N = 76$ for college and adult sample) • Small sample sizes on some validity studies ($N = 36$ on WIAT-II/WRAT-III; $N = 27$ on WIAT-II/DAS) • Small sample sizes for clinical group studies ($N = 39$ for group with MR; $N = 31$ for group with Hearing Impairment) • Limited number of correlation studies with other individually administered achievement tests (included WIAT, PAL-RW, WRAT-III, DAS, PPVT-III, and WJ-R (college and adult sample only). Studies using WJ-III and K-TEA and studies with language measures such as CELF 4 and PLS-4 would be helpful.

(continued)

subtests are more complex to administer and to score. The addition of the Pseudoword Decoding subtest, the extension of the age range to include both younger and older individuals, and the provision for a user-friendly Scoring Assistant that can facilitate the skills and error analysis process make the WIAT-II a useful tool in the comprehensive evaluation of academic achievement.

Administration and Scoring

Strengths	Weaknesses
• Directions for administration included in the Stimulus Booklets	• Complex administration procedures for Reading Comprehension
• User-friendly layout of record form	• Complex scoring procedures for Written Expression requires practice
• Clearly marked start and stop points based on grade	
• Consistent reverse rule on majority of subtests	• There are no age-based norms for students 13 years of age and older for Paragraph Writing
• Dichotomous scoring of most subtests	• Oral Expression norms table for 9-year-olds is easy to miss in the scoring manual (on pages 244–245).
• Option of an easy-to-use scoring assistant for calculation of scores, skills analysis, and discrepancy analysis	• The quartile and decile scores are less familiar to many examiners than standard scores (Mean = 100; SD = 15) and percentile ranks. Therefore, examiners, parents, and teachers may have more difficulty meaningfully interpreting the quartile and decile scores.
• Large number of Written Expression scoring examples provided in the scoring manual	
• Large number of Oral Expression scoring examples provided in the scoring manual	
• Both age and grade norms provided with fall, winter, spring norms for grades PreK–8	

Interpretation	
Strengths	**Weaknesses**
• Optional scores provide additional information on some subtests • Skills analysis procedures provide the opportunity for a more in-depth level of interpretation • Error analysis procedures facilitate linking results to intervention planning • Linkage to Wechsler scales allows ability-achievement discrepancy analysis across age groups • WIAT-II Administration manual includes chapter on interpretation process and suggestions for intervention planning	• Insufficient ceiling for high-scoring 13–19-year-olds for some subtests (see Rapid Reference 2.20) • Optional scores for Reading Comprehension cannot be calculated if the reverse rule was applied • Skills analysis is time consuming to complete without the WIAT-II Scoring Assistant • Results of skills analysis offer only percent of items correct but no normative comparisons are available. Thus, it is difficult to judge whether earning a particular percent correct in a skill area is an "Average," "Below Average," or "Above Average" level of skill compared to a student's peers. • Some skills in the Skills Analysis are only measured by one or two items (e.g., some skills measured by Numerical Operations subtest and by Math Reasoning subtest), making it difficult to draw hypotheses about a particular skill.

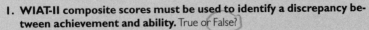

TEST YOURSELF

1. **WIAT-II composite scores must be used to identify a discrepancy between achievement and ability.** True or False?

2. **Which of the following should be followed in order to determine the correct start point for Reading Comprehension?**
   (a) Students who have been retained in a grade should start at the grade level immediately preceding their assigned grade level.
   (b) Students who score 0 points on all of the basal items at their assigned grade level must reverse to the previous grade start point.
   (c) Students who score 0 points on all of the basal items at their assigned grade level must reverse to the item set 3 start points lower.
   (d) The examiner can select the start point based on the examinee's performance on Word Reading.

3. **The WIAT-II is linked to the WPPSI-III, the WISC-IV, and the WAIS-III.** True or False?

4. **The Oral Expression subtest was designed to identify individuals with language disorders.** True or False?   *screening tool*

5. **What is the purpose of the Qualitative Observations checklists that follow subtest administration?**
   (a) They provide additional information about how an examinee performs a task that can be helpful when designing effective intervention/instruction plans.
   (b) They identify problem-solving strategies employed by the examinee.
   (c) They compare an individual's performance to others of the same age or at the same grade level with a standard score.
   (d) a and b
   (e) a, b, and c

6. **In order for the difference between two composite scores to be a discrepancy, the difference must be statistically significant and unusual.** True or False?

7. **The timed alphabet writing task on Written Expression is only administered to children in PreK to kindergarten.** True or False?   *Grade 2*

8. **Which of the following subtests have timing elements that require the use of a stopwatch?**
   (a) Word Reading
   (b) Numerical Operations
   (c) Oral Expression
   (d) Pseudoword Decoding

9. **If the examinee chooses to read the Reading Comprehension passages aloud, the reading speed score cannot be calculated.** True or False?

10. Quartile-based scores can be used to

(a) compare an individual's performance on the Written Expression Word Fluency task to the Oral Expression Word Fluency task.

(b) identify preschool children who are at risk for developing a writing disorder.

(c) identify a discrepancy between achievement and ability.

(d) determine if the discontinue criterion has been met.

Answers: 1. False, both subtest and composite scores can be used to identify a discrepancy; 2. c; 3. True; 4. False, it was designed to screen for possible language disorders and to identify those individuals who should be referred for more comprehensive assessment; 5. d; 6. True; 7. False; it is administered to Grades PreK to 2; 8. c; 9. True; 10. a

Three

KTEA-II

DESCRIPTION OF THE KTEA-II

The Kaufman Test of Educational Achievement–Second Edition (KTEA-II; Kaufman & Kaufman, 2004) was developed to assess the academic achievement of children and adolescents ages 4:6 through 25. The KTEA-II has two versions: the Brief Form and the Comprehensive Form (the Comprehensive Form is composed of two independent, parallel forms, A and B). The Brief Form assesses three academic domains (reading, math, and written expression), and the Comprehensive Form assesses an additional fourth domain (oral language). Although the Brief and Comprehensive Forms tap three of the same academic domains, there is no overlap in items between the two forms of the test. This chapter reviews the content of the KTEA-II Comprehensive and Brief Forms.

History and Development

Over a 4-year period, beginning in 1981, Drs. Alan and Nadeen Kaufman developed the first edition of the Kaufman Test of Educational Achievement (K-TEA). During those years, items were developed and tried out in 1981, 1982, and 1983. The K-TEA was standardized in both the spring and fall of 1983. The normative groups were composed of 1,409 students in the spring and 1,067 students in the fall. Upon completion of the standardization, the K-TEA was published in 1985. Then in the mid-1990s, American Guidance Service, publisher of the K-TEA, restandardized the original K-TEA to match the 1994 U.S. Bureau of the Census estimates of the population. No changes were made to the items and scales of the K-TEA during the restandardization, but the norms were thoroughly updated. The renorming project involved four achievement batteries: the K-TEA, the Peabody Individual Achievement Test–Revised (PIAT-R), Key-Math–Revised (KeyMath-R), and the Woodcock Reading Mastery Tests–Revised (WRMT-R). The instruments all measured one or more domains of academic achievement. During the renorming, each student was administered one of the primary batteries along with subtests from the other instruments. Thus, each of the primary batteries was administered to approximately one-fifth of the standardization sample (with 3,429 total participants in the Age-Norm sample and 3,184 total participants in Grade-Norm sample). The renorming of the K-TEA was finalized with the publication of the K-TEA/Normative Update (K-TEA/NU) by Drs. Kaufman in 1997.

Because professionals in school psychology and related fields used the K-TEA and K-TEA/NU so frequently, the test authors decided to revise the test, beginning in 1995. Indeed, studies of test usage have shown that both the K-TEA and the K-TEA/NU are used frequently in educational and clinical settings (Archer, Maruish, Imhof, & Piotrowski, 1991; Hammill, Fowler, Bryant, & Dunn, 1992; Hutton, Dubes, & Muir, 1992; Laurent & Swerdlik, 1992; Stinnett, Havey, & Oehler-Stinnett, 1994; Wilson & Reschley, 1996). To ensure that the KTEA-II provided the most useful and practical information to clinicians, the Kaufmans developed their plan for the second edition based on current research and clinical practice. Four main goals were identified for the revision of the K-TEA, which are outlined in Rapid Reference 3.1.

Chapter 5 of the *KTEA-II Comprehensive Form Manual* (Kaufman & Kaufman, 2004a) discusses the content development for each subtest in depth. Generally, the first step in the development of each subtest was to define at a conceptual level which skills should be measured for a particular academic domain. Both literature reviews and expert opinion were used to determine what should be measured within each academic domain. The original K-TEA items were reviewed to determine which item formats should be retained and which should be modified. Since four new achievement areas were added in the KTEA-II, expert advisors contributed suggestions for content and item formats for written expression, oral expression, listening comprehension, and reading-related skills. Part of the content development of the subtests involved making sure that certain skills were systemat-

=== Rapid Reference 3.1

Goals of the KTEA-II Revision

- Improve the measurement of the achievement domains measured by the original K-TEA
- Add content that is appropriate for preschool and college-age students
- Add subtests to assess written and oral expression, listening comprehension, and reading-related skills
- Make error analysis more informative through the systematic representation of skills and, on some subtests, a more fine-grained approach to classifying errors

ically represented. Developing subtests in this manner helped to make error analysis more informative and also allowed a more fine-grained approach to classifying errors on some subtests.

Changes from K-TEA to KTEA-II

The Comprehensive Form of the K-TEA was modified in a number of ways to create the KTEA-II: The age range assessed was increased from 6:0 to 18:11 on the K-TEA to 4:6 to 25:11 on the KTEA-II, the number of academic domains

---

DON'T FORGET
....

Changes from the K-TEA to the KTEA-II Comprehensive Form

Increased Age Range	
KTEA Age Range: 6:0 to 18:11	KTEA-II Age Range: 4:6 to 25:11

Increased Number of Academic Domains Measured	
K-TEA Composites: Reading Mathematics	KTEA-II Composites: *Domain Composites* 　Reading 　Mathematics 　Written Language 　Oral Language *Reading-Related Composites* 　Sound-Symbol 　Decoding 　Oral Fluency 　Reading Fluency

Modified Existing Subtests and Added New Subtests	
Number of K-TEA Subtests: 5	Number of KTEA-II Subtests: 14

Note: Subtests of the K-TEA and KTEA-II are listed in Rapid Reference 3.2.

assessed increased from two on the K-TEA to eight on the KTEA-II, and several new subtests were added to assess abilities related to learning disabilities (five K-TEA subtests were retained and modified and nine new subtests were added to the KTEA-II Comprehensive Form). The Don't Forget box reminds readers of these changes from the K-TEA to the KTEA-II and Rapid Reference 3.2 describes the KTEA-II subtests that were retained from the K-TEA, as well as those that are new to the KTEA-II.

Like the Comprehensive Form, the KTEA-II Brief Form has also been modified from its original structure. The changes mainly involved modifying subtests to integrate several types of items, so as to provide more thorough skill coverage. The *KTEA-II Brief Form Manual* (Kaufman & Kaufman, 2005) lists the following as the key changes in the subtests.

- The *Writing* subtest replaces the Spelling subtest, providing a much broader measure of the examinee's skill in written expression (including spelling, sentence structure, grammar, capitalization, and punctuation). The K-TEA NU Spelling subtest and KTEA-II Writing subtest correlate .68, reflecting the moderate differences in what these subtests measure.
- The *Reading* subtest has been expanded into two distinct parts: Recognition and Comprehension. The Recognition part retains letter and word recognition, which were part of the original K-TEA Brief, but the Comprehension part presents passage comprehension items along with the "following directions" item type. The K-TEA NU and KTEA-II Reading subtests correlate .81, which demonstrates the similarities between the original and revised versions of this subtest.
- The *Math* subtest includes the same types of items as the original version, but computation and application items are interspersed throughout the subtest, and new, colored illustrations replace the original ones. The K-TEA NU and KTEA-II Math subtests correlate .88, which demonstrates the strong similarities between the original and revised versions of this subtest.

Despite the many changes in the revision of the K-TEA Comprehensive Form, the original version correlates very highly with the KTEA-II Comprehensive Form. For example, in a sample of 68 children in grades 2 to 6, the K-TEA Battery Composite and the KTEA-II Comprehensive Achievement Composite correlated .94, and the correlation between these two composites for 62 seventh-through eleventh-grade children was .88. These correlations are quite strong, despite the fact that the KTEA-II Comprehensive Achievement Composite

Rapid Reference 3.2

Brief description of KTEA-II Comprehensive Form subtests

Reading Subtest	Range	Description
Letter and Word Recognition	Ages 4:6–25:11	The student identifies letters and pronounces words of gradually increasing difficulty. Most words are irregular, to ensure that the subtest measures word recognition (reading vocabulary) rather than decoding ability.
Reading Comprehension	Grade 1–age 25:11	For the easiest items, the student reads a word and points to its corresponding picture. In following items, the student reads a simple instruction and responds by performing the action. In later items, the student reads passages of increasing difficulty and answers literal or inferential questions about them. Finally, the student rearranges five sentences into a coherent paragraph, and then answers questions about the paragraph.
Phonological Awareness	Grades 1–6	The student responds orally to items that require manipulation of sounds. Tasks include rhyming, matching sounds, blending sounds, segmenting sounds, and deleting sounds.
Nonsense Word Decoding	Grade 1–age 25:11	The student applies phonics and structural analysis skills to decode invented words of increasing difficulty.
Word Reading Fluency	Grade 3–age 25:11	The student reads isolated words as quickly as possible for one minute.
Decoding Fluency	Grade 3–age 25:11	The student applies decoding skills to pronounce as many nonsense words as possible in one minute.
Associational Fluency	Ages 4:6–25:11	The student says as many words as possible in thirty seconds that belong to a semantic category or have a specified beginning sound.

		The student names objects, colors, and letters as quickly as possible.
Naming Facility (RAN)	Ages 4:6–25:11	

Math Subtest	Range	Description
Math Concepts and Applications	Ages 4:6–25:11	The student responds orally to test items that focus on the application of mathematical principles to real-life situations. Skill categories include number concepts, operation concepts, rational numbers, measurement, shape and space, data investigations, and higher math concepts.
Math Computation	Grade K–age 25:11	The student computes solutions to math problems printed in a student response booklet. Skills assessed include addition, subtraction, multiplication, and division operations; fractions and decimals; square roots, exponents, signed numbers, and algebra.

Written Language Subtest	Range	Description
Written Expression	Ages 4:6–25:11	Kindergarten and pre-kindergarten children trace and copy letters and write letters from dictation. At grades 1 and higher, the student completes writing tasks in the context of an age-appropriate storybook format. Tasks at those levels include writing sentences from dictation, adding punctuation and capitalization, filling in missing words, completing sentences, combining sentences, writing compound and complex sentences, and, starting at Spring of grade 1, writing an essay based on the story the student helped complete.
Spelling	Grade 1–age 25:11	The student writes words dictated by the examiner from a steeply graded word list. Words were selected to match acquired spelling skills at each grade level, and for their potential for error analysis. Early items require students to write single letters that represent sounds. The remaining items require students to spell orthographically regular and irregular words of increasing complexity.

(continued)

Oral Language Subtest	Range	Description
Listening Comprehension	Ages 4:6–25:11	The student listens to passages played on a CD and then responds orally to questions asked by the examiner. Questions measure literal and inferential comprehension.
Oral Expression	Ages 4:6–25:11	The student performs specific speaking tasks in the context of a real-life scenario. Tasks assess pragmatics, syntax, semantics, and grammar.

Note: Five of the 14 KTEA-II Comprehensive Form subtests were retained and expanded from the K-TEA, including: Math Concepts and Applications (originally called Mathematics Applications), Letter and Word Recognition (originally called Reading Decoding), Spelling, Reading Comprehension, and Math Computation (originally called Mathematics Computation). Subtest descriptions are from Table 1.1 of *KTEA-II Comprehensive Form Manual* (Kaufman & Kaufman, 2004a).

contains subtests that were not part of the K-TEA Battery Composite (i.e., Written Expression and Listening Comprehension).

The two K-TEA composites also correlated very highly with their like-named composites on the KTEA-II Comprehensive. For example, the correlations between the K-TEA and KTEA-II Reading Composites were .88 and .86 for grades 2 to 6 and grades 7 to 11, respectively. The correlations between the K-TEA and KTEA-II Mathematics Composites were .85 and .93 for grades 2 to 6 and grades 7 to 11, respectively. Similar to the relationships found between the composites, the five K-TEA subtests correlated strongly with their KTEA-II counterparts. For grades 2 to 6 the correlations between K-TEA and KTEA-II Comprehensive Form subtests ranged from .77 for Reading Comprehension and Math Computations to .85 for Spelling. For grades 7 to 11, correlations between K-TEA and KTEA-II subtests ranged from .68 for Reading Comprehension to .91 for Math Computation. Rapid Reference 3.3 provides the correlations between K-TEA and KTEA-II subtests of the same name.

≡Rapid Reference 3.3

Correlations between K-TEA and KTEA-II Comprehensive Form Subtests of the Same Name and Composites of the Same Name

Subtest or Composite	Adjusted r	
	Grades 2–6 (N = 68)	Grades 7–11 (N = 62)
Letter & Word Recognition	.84	.87
Reading Comprehension	.77	.68
Math Concepts and Applications	.83	.82
Math Computation	.77	.91
Spelling	.85	.86
Reading Composite	.88	.86
Mathematics Composite	.85	.93
Comprehensive Achievement Composite	.94	.88

Note: All values are corrected for the variability of the norm group, based on the standard deviation obtained on the KTEA-II, using the variability correction of Cohen, J., Cohen, P., West, S. G., & Aiken, L. S. (2003, p. 58). Coefficients are from Tables 7.15 and 7.16 of the KTEA-II Comprehensive Form Manual (Kaufman & Kaufman, 2004a).

Scales and Composites of the KTEA-II

The KTEA-II Comprehensive Form has 14 subtests, which are grouped into four domain composites and four Reading-Related composites. The four KTEA-II Comprehensive domain composites are Reading, Mathematics, Written Language, and Oral Language, and the four Reading-Related composites are Sound-Symbol, Decoding, Oral Fluency, and Reading Fluency. The composition of the KTEA-II Comprehensive varies slightly according to grade level (or age). For example, for grade 1 through age 25, six of the eight subtests contribute to the Comprehensive Achievement Composite, but for ages 4:6 through kindergarten, four of the eight subtests come together to yield the Comprehensive Achievement Composite (Figure 3.1 details which subtests contribute to the Comprehensive Achievement Composite and which to the domain composites).

For children in Pre-Kindergarten (Pre-K is defined as children who have not yet begun kindergarten), the KTEA-II Comprehensive yields two domain composites: Written Language and Oral Language. Although no math domain composite is calculated at the Pre-K level, Math Concepts and Applications (a math subtest) is administered to these children. In addition, three reading-related subtests are administered to Pre-K children: Letter and Word Recognition, Associational Fluency, and Naming Facility. One Reading-Related Composite may be calculated for Pre-K children: Oral Fluency. Seven total subtests can be administered to children at the Pre-K level.

For kindergarteners, the KTEA-II Comprehensive yields three domain composites: Math, Written Language, and Oral Language. No Reading domain composite is obtained for kindergarteners, but three reading-related subtests are administered: Letter and Word Recognition, Associational Fluency, and Naming Facility. Similar to Pre-K children, one Reading-Related Composite may be calculated for kindergarteners: Oral Fluency. At the kindergarten level, eight subtests can be administered in total.

For children and adolescents in grades 1 through 12 and above, the four aforementioned domain composites are calculated based upon scores yielded from eight KTEA-II Comprehensive subtests. From grade 1 to 12+, two of the reading-related composites are calculated for the entire age range: Decoding and Oral Fluency. However, Sound Symbol is calculated only from grades 1 through 6, and Reading Fluency is calculated only from grades 3 through 12 and above. Rapid Reference 3.4 lists which of the reading-related subtests contribute to the four reading-related composites.

The KTEA-II Brief Form offers three subtests for children, adolescents, and adults, spanning the age range from 4:6 to 90. Although these subtests are paral-

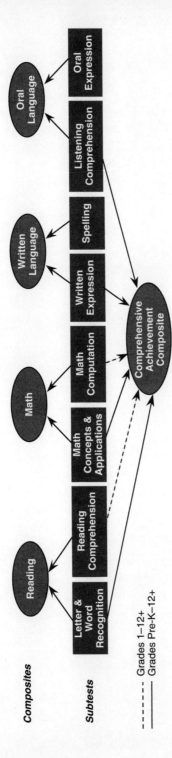

Figure 3.1 Structure of the KTEA-II Comprehensive Form

Note: The ages at which subtests may first be administered vary from PreK to grade 1. Five subtests are administered beginning at the PreK level: Letter and Word Recognition, Math Concepts and Applications, Written Expression, Listening Comprehension, and Oral Expression. One subtest, Math Computation, is first administered at the kindergarten level, and two subtests are first administered at the grade 1 level: Reading Comprehension and Spelling. At the PreK level, two domain composites can be obtained: Written Language and Oral Language. At the kindergarten level, three domain composites can be obtained: Math, Written Language, and Oral Language. From grade 1 on, all four domain composites can be obtained.

≡ Rapid Reference 3.4

Composites Formed by the KTEA-II Comprehensive Form Reading-Related Subtests

Subtests	Sound Symbol (Grades 1–6)	KTEA-II Reading-Related Composites		
		Decoding (Grades 1–12+)	Oral Fluency (Pre-K–Grade 12+)	Reading Fluency (Grades 3–12+)
Phonological Awareness (Grades 1–6)	X			
Nonsense Word Decoding (Grades 1–12+)	X	X		
Letter and Word Recognition (Grades Pre-K–12+)		X		
Associational Fluency (Grades Pre-K–12+)			X	
Naming Facility (RAN) (Grades Pre-K–12+)			X	
Word Recognition Fluency (Grades 3–12+)				X
Decoding Fluency (Grades 3–12+)				X

lel to those in the Comprehensive Form, the Brief Form contains a completely different set of items than the Comprehensive Form. One global score is yielded from the Brief Form subtests: the Brief Achievement Composite. For Pre-K children that composite is comprised of only the Reading and Math subtests, but for children in kindergarten through those in grade 12 and above, the Brief Achievement Composite is derived from all three subtests. The Brief Form subtests are described in the section on subtests that follows.

Subtests

The KTEA-II Comprehensive and Brief Forms provide much flexibility for examiners. If only one particular domain of academic functioning is of concern, examiners may choose to administer a single subtest or any combination of subtests in that domain in order to assess a student's academic achievement. If multiple domains need to be measured, then all of the age-appropriate subtests can be administered to obtain the desired composite score(s). Brief descriptions of each of the KTEA-II Comprehensive Form subtests are given in Rapid Reference 3.2, which is organized by content area. The age range for each subtest varies, so the table indicates the age and grade range at which each subtest may be administered. Regardless of whether grade or age norms are being used, examiners should use student's grade level to guide selection of subtests.

The subtests of the KTEA-II Brief Form cover content that is similar to that of the Comprehensive Form, but the item sets are different. Descriptions of each of the three Brief Form subtests follow:

1. *Reading*. Part 1 contains 27 recognition items. In these items the examinee identifies letters and pronounces words of gradually increasing difficulty. Most words are irregular, to ensure that the subtest measures word recognition (reading vocabulary) more than decoding ability. Part 2 contains 46 comprehension items. Some of these items require an examinee to read a simple instruction and then do what the instruction says. Other items require examinees to read passages of increasing difficulty and answer a literal or inferential question about them.

2. *Math*. In the 67 Math items, examinees respond orally to items that focus on the application of mathematical principles to real-life situations. The examinee is also required to work on computation items by writing solutions to math problems printed in the Response Booklet. A variety of mathematical skills are assessed from addition and subtraction to higher level skills, such as square roots, exponents, and algebra.

3. *Writing*. The 46 writing items vary according to age. Children who are kindergarten and younger are required to copy letters and write letters

from dictation. Students or adults from grade 1 on complete writing tasks in the context of an age-appropriate newsletter format. Tasks at those levels involve adding punctuation and capitalization, filling in missing words, completing sentences, combining sentences, and writing complex sentences. The examinees also spell regular and irregular words dictated by the examiner.

STANDARDIZATION AND PSYCHOMETRIC PROPERTIES OF THE KTEA-II

This section of the chapter describes the standardization samples of the KTEA-II Comprehensive and Brief Forms and reliability and validity information about the tests.

Standardization

The KTEA-II Comprehensive Form was standardized with an age-norm sample of 3,000 examinees ages 4:6 through 25, and a grade-norm sample of 2,400 students in kindergarten through grade 12. For each grade level, the sample size ranged from 140 to 220 students (with more examinees contributing to the earlier grades). For each age level, the sample sizes ranged from 100 to 220 students (with the exception of age 19, which had a sample of only 80 examinees). The KTEA-II Comprehensive Form contains two parallel forms, so approximately half of the norm sample was administered Form A and the other half was administered Form B. The standardization sample was chosen to closely match the U.S. population. Thus, on the variables of gender, ethnicity, parental education, geographic region, and special education or gifted placement the standardization sample closely corresponded to data from the 2001 Current Population Survey of the Bureau of the Census.

Similar to the Comprehensive Form, the KTEA-II Brief Form was standardized on a large representative sample that closely corresponded to the 2001 Current Population Survey of the Bureau of the Census. The Brief Form normative sample matched the U.S. population on the variables of gender, education level of examinee or parent, race/ethnicity, and geographic region. The grade-norm sample consisted of 1,645 students from kindergarten through grade 12. The number of students sampled from each grade ranged from 75 to 90 for grades 9 to 12, to 110 to 125 for grades 3 to 8, and 210 students were sampled for grades 1 and 2. The size of the Brief Form total age sample ($N = 2,495$) was larger than that of the grade sample. At each age, for children under age 15, the samples included 100 to 210 children. For ages 15 to 25, the samples included 75 to 150 children, and the adult samples over age 25 (to age 90) included 50 to 60 individuals for each age group.

Reliability

The internal-consistency reliability of the KTEA-II Comprehensive is strong for both Forms A and B. The average internal-consistency reliability value across grades and forms for the Comprehensive Achievement Composite was .97. The averages for the Reading, Math, and Decoding composites were .96, .96, and .97, respectively. The average reliability value for the Written Language Composite and Sound-Symbol Composite was .93. For Oral Language and Oral Fluency composites, the average reliabilities were .87 and .85, respectively. Reliability values based on age groups were very similar to what was reported for the reliability values found with the grade-level samples. Table 3.1 presents the internal consistency reliability values of the KTEA-II Comprehensive Form subtests and composites averaged across forms.

The KTEA-II Brief Form also had strong average internal-reliability values. For the individual subtests scored via Grade Norms (grades K to 12) the average reliability values were .94, .90, and .86 for the Reading, Math, and Writing subtests, respectively. For the individual subtests scored via Age Norms (ages 4:6 to 90) the values were .95, .91, and .90 for the Reading, Math, and Writing subtests, respectively. The split-half reliability value for the Brief Achievement Composite was .96 for both the Grade and Age norms.

Alternate-form reliability values were calculated by administering the two forms of the KTEA-II Comprehensive to a sample of 221 children. The forms were administered approximately 3½ to 4 weeks apart, on average. Similar to the internal-consistency reliability values, the values for the alternate-form reliability were also high. The Comprehensive Achievement Composites showed very high consistency across time and forms (low to mid .90s). The Reading, Math, Written Language, Decoding, and Reading Fluency composites have alternate-form reliabilities in the high .80s to mid .90s. These strong values indicate that the alternate forms of the KTEA-II will be useful for reducing practice effects when the test is administered more than once. Table 3.2 shows the alternate form reliability values.

For the KTEA-II Brief Form, test-retest reliability was examined by administering the test twice within a 2 to 8 week period (mean interval 3.7 weeks) to 327 students. Across the Grade-Norm and Age-Norm samples, the average adjusted

Table 3.1 Average Split-Half Reliability Coefficients for KTEA-II Comprehensive Form and Brief Form Subtests and Composites

KTEA-II Subtest/Composite	Mean Grade-Level Reliability	Mean Age-Level Reliability
Letter & Word Recognition	.96	.97
Reading Comprehension	.93	.93
Reading Composite	**.96**	**.97**
Math Concepts & Applications	.92	.93
Math Computation	.93	.94
Mathematics Composite	**.96**	**.96**
Written Expression	.85	.87
Spelling	.93	.94
Written Language Composite	**.93**	**.94**
Listening Comprehension	.85	.85
Oral Expression	.78	.79
Oral Language Composite	**.87**	**.87**
Phonological Awareness	.86	.88
Nonsense Word Decoding	.94	.94
Sound-Symbol Composite	**.93**	**.93**
Decoding Composite	**.97**	**.97**
Associational Fluency	.73	.72
Naming Facility (RAN)	.89	.89
Oral Fluency Composite	**.85**	**.87**
Comprehensive Achievement	**.97**	**.97**
Reading (Brief Form)	.94	.95
Math (Brief Form)	.90	.91
Writing (Brief Form)	.86	.90
Brief Achievement Composite	**.96**	**.96**

Note: From Tables 7.1 and 7.2 of the *KTEA-II Comprehensive Form Manual* (Kaufman & Kaufman, 2004a), and Tables 6.1 and 6.2 of the *KTEA-II Brief Form Manual* (Kaufman & Kaufman, 2005). All reliabilities are based on the standard deviation of scores for both forms combined. Reliabilities of composites were computed using the formula provided by Nunnally (1978). Mean grade-level values and mean age-level values were calculated using Fisher's z transformation.

Table 3.2 Alternate-Form Reliability Coefficients for Subtests and Composites

KTEA-II Subtest/Composite	Pre-Kindergarten to Grade 1		Grade 2 to Grade 6		Grade 7 to Grade 12	
	N	r^a	N	r^a	N	r^a
Letter & Word Recognition	62	.97	83	.85	79	.89
Reading Comprehension	27	.88	83	.76	79	.80
Reading Composite	**27**	**.94**	**83**	**.87**	**79**	**.89**
Math Concepts & Applications	62	.84	80	.84	79	.89
Math Computation	45	.86	80	.87	79	.90
Mathematics Composite	**45**	**.87**	**80**	**.90**	**79**	**.94**
Written Expression	62	.79	83	.82	79	.79
Spelling	27	.87	80	.91	79	.88
Written Language Composite	**27**	**.85**	**80**	**.90**	**79**	**.90**
Listening Comprehension	62	.50	80	.56	79	.73
Oral Expression	62	.62	80	.54	79	.58
Oral Language Composite	**62**	**.64**	**80**	**.68**	**79**	**.81**
Phonological Awareness	60	.77	83	.58		
Nonsense Word Decoding	27	.74	83	.90	79	.89
Sound-Symbol Composite	**27**	**.84**	**83**	**.80**		
Word Recognition Fluency			61	.89	79	.87
Decoding Fluency			63	.92	78	.88
Reading Fluency			**61**	**.95**	**78**	**.91**
Decoding Composite	**27**	**.90**	**83**	**.92**	**79**	**.93**
Associational Fluency	61	.47	80	.55	73	.64
Naming Facility (RAN)	54	.65	75	.76	71	.76
Oral Fluency Composite	**54**	**.59**	**75**	**.67**	**70**	**.78**
Comprehensive Achievement	**62**	**.92**	**80**	**.94**	**79**	**.95**

Note: From Table 7.5 of the *KTEA-II Comprehensive Form Manual* (Kaufman & Kaufman, 2004a). KTEA-II scores are based on age norms.

[a]All reliability coefficients were corrected for the variability of the norm group, based on the standard deviation obtained on the first testing, using the variability correction of Cohen et al. (2003).

test-retest reliabilities were as follows: Reading = .93, Math = .90, Writing = .81, and Brief Achievement Composite = .94.

Validity

The validity of the KTEA-II was demonstrated via multiple methods. Intercorrelations between the subtests and composites were calculated to show the relationships between the academic domains. Factor analyses were conducted to show that the structure of the test was empirically grounded. Correlations with other instruments were also conducted to evaluate the construct validity of the test. Finally, special population studies were conducted to show the efficacy of applying the KTEA-II to the assessment of children with learning disabilities, mental retardation, Attention/Deficit Hyperactivity Disorder, and of children with other special qualities such as deafness or giftedness. The results of these special studies are detailed in the chapter in this book on Clinical Applications.

Confirmatory factor analysis was conducted to investigate the relationships between the KTEA-II Comprehensive Form subtests and composites in a systematic manner. The factor analysis proceeded in a stepwise fashion, with the eight primary subtests yielding a final model composed of four factors. The final model had good fit statistics and all subtests had high loadings on their factors. The results of the factor analysis are shown in Figure 3.2.

The KTEA-II Comprehensive and Brief forms were administered along with other tests of achievement and cognitive ability during standardization. In addition to the results of the correlational data already reported with the original K-TEA (see Rapid Reference 3.4), correlations were calculated between the KTEA-II Comprehensive and Brief Forms. In a sample of 1,318 students administered both the Comprehensive and Brief Forms, the correlations were .85, .86, .78, and .89 for Reading, Math, Writing, and Achievement Composite, respectively. Further correlations were calculated between the KTEA-II Comprehensive Form and the following achievement tests: WIAT-II, Woodcock-Johnson Tests of Achievement, Third Edition (WJ III ACH; Woodcock, McGrew, & Maher, 2001), the Peabody Individual Achievement Test–Revised, Normative Update (PIAT-R/NU; Markwardt, 1998), and the Oral and Written Language Scales (OWLS; Carrow-Woolfolk, 1996). A summary of the KTEA-II Comprehensive Form correlational studies with the WIAT-II and WJ III are provided in Table 3.3 (for grades 1 to 5 and grades 6 to 11). The results of the studies with the WIAT-II and WJ III are very similar to those found with the original K-TEA. That is, most correlations between like-named composites were in the mid- to high-.80s, and correlations between most of the total achievement scores

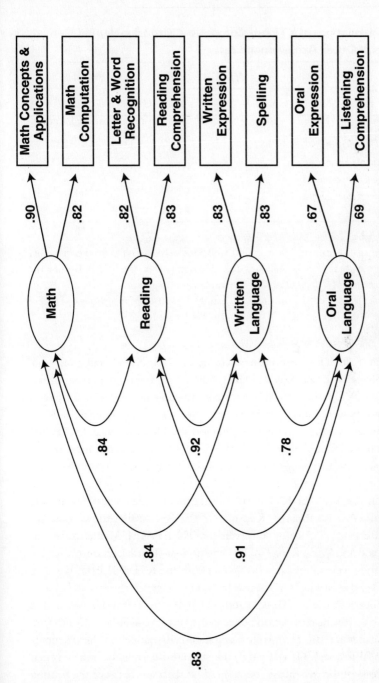

Figure 3.2 Results of Confirmatory Factor Analysis of Eight KTEA-II Comprehensive Form subtests

Source: Figure is adapted from Figure 7.1 of the *KTEA-II Comprehensive Form Manual* (Kaufman & Kaufman, 2004a).

Note: Results are based on the complete norm sample (age norms) at grade 1 and above (*n* = 2,560). Factors are shown in the ovals on the left, and subtests are in rectangles on the right. The numbers represent factor intercorrelations or factor loadings.

Table 3.3 Correlations of KTEA-II Composites with Like-Named Composites of Other Achievement Tests

	WIAT-II		WJ III	
KTEA-II Composite	Grades 1–5	Grades 6–11	Grades 1–5	Grades 6–10
Reading Composite	.85	.85	.82	.76
Mathematics Composite	.82	.87	.87	.87
Written Language Composite	.87	.87	.92	.84
Oral Language Composite	.52	.70	.71	.74
Comprehensive Achievement Composite	.89	.90	.84	.89

Note: Data are from Tables 7.17, 7.18, 7.19, and 7.20 of the *KTEA-II Comprehensive Form Manual* (Kaufman & Kaufman, 2004a). All correlations were corrected for the variability of the norm group, based on the standard deviation obtained on the KTEA-II using the variability correction of Cohen et al. (2003). Sample sizes for grades 1–5 were $N = 82$ for the WIAT-II study and $N = 33$ for the WJ III study. Sample sizes for grades 6–11 were $N = 89$ for the WIAT-II study and $N = 47$ for the WJ III study.

hovered around .90. The correlations with the PIAT-R/NU overall composite score were .86 for both grades K to 5 and grades 6 to 9. For domain composites, the PIAT-R/NU's highest correlations were for reading, ranging from .89 to .78; lower correlations were found for mathematics and spelling (ranging from .67 to .70). The OWLS has three subtests; the highest correlation with the KTEA-II was between the tests of Written Expression (.75); the instruments' measures of Oral Expression and Listening Comprehension correlated only at a modest level (in the .40s).

Correlations between the KTEA-II Brief Form and other achievement tests were also examined (Kaufman & Kaufman, 2005). Specifically, the Woodcock–Johnson–Third Edition Tests of Achievement (WJ III ACH; Mather & Woodcock, 2001) and the Wide Range Achievement Test–Third Edition (WRAT3; Wilkinson, 1993) were administered together with the KTEA-II Brief Form to samples of 25 and 80 students, respectively. (Table 3.4 details these correlations.) Correlations between the WJ III ACH and KTEA-II Brief Form subtests ranged from .74 to .79, with the correlation between the Brief Achievement Composite and WJ III Academic Skills composite being slightly higher (.89). When comparing the WRAT3 to the KTEA-II Brief, the strongest correlation was between Reading subtests of the two measures (.84); the weakest was between the Writing subtest of the KTEA-II Brief and the Spelling subtest of the WRAT3 (.64). As the

Table 3.4 Correlations of KTEA-II Brief Form with Other Achievement Test Composites

KTEA-II Brief Subtests/Composite	WRAT3	WJ III ACH
Reading	.84	.78
Mathematics	.75	.74
Writing	.64[a]	.79
Brief Achievement Composite		.89

Note: Data are from Tables 6.19 and 6.15 of the *KTEA-II Brief Form Manual* (Kaufman & Kaufman, 2005). All correlations were corrected for the variability of the norm group, based on the standard deviation obtained on the KTEA-II using the variability correction of Cohen et al. (2003). Sample sizes were $N = 80$ for the WRAT3 study and $N = 25$ for the WJ III ACH study. Data on the WRAT3 are for ages 7–19 and data for the WJ III ACH are for ages 7–16. WJ III correlations are based on the following: Broad Reading, Broad Math, Broad Written Language, and Academic Skills.

[a] This is the correlation between WRAT3 Spelling and KTEA-II Brief Writing.

KTEA-II Brief Writing subtest measures more than simply spelling ability, the lower correlation is not surprising.

In addition to the correlational data showing the relationships between the KTEA-II and other tests of academic achievement, the *KTEA-II Comprehensive Form Manual* provides data showing the correlations between the KTEA-II and three tests of cognitive ability: the KABC-II, Wechsler Intelligence Scale for Children–Third Edition (WISC-III; Wechsler, 1991) and the Woodcock-Johnson Tests of Cognitive Abilities, Third Edition (WJ III COG; Woodcock, McGrew, & Mather, 2001). A very large sample ($N = 2,520$) was used in the study with the KABC-II, as this test was conormed with the KTEA-II. Sample sizes were 97 and 51 for the studies with the WISC-III and WJ III COG, respectively.

The KTEA-II Comprehensive Achievement Composite correlates .79 with the KABC-II Fluid Crystallized Index (FCI), .74 with the KABC-II Mental Processing Index (MPI), and .69 with the KABC-II Nonverbal Index (NVI) for the total sample. Very similar correlations were found between the Comprehensive Achievement Composite and global cognitive scores on the WISC-III and WJ III COG. The Comprehensive Achievement Composite correlated .79 with the WISC-III Full Scale IQ (FSIQ) and .82 with the WJ III COG General Intellectual Ability (GIA). For all three tests of cognitive ability, the KTEA-II's Reading Composite and Mathematics Composites had the strongest relationship to overall cognitive ability. Correlations with the Reading Composite were .74, .69, and .72 for the KABC-II FCI, WISC-III FSIQ, and WJ III GIA, respectively. Correlations with the Mathematics Composite were .71, .65, and .76 for the KABC-II FCI, WISC-III FSIQ, and WJ III GIA, respectively. The other academic domains measured by the KTEA-II did not correlate as strongly with overall cognitive ability. For example, Written Language and Oral Language correlated .66 and .67, respectively, with the KABC-II FCI. A summary of KTEA-II and KABC-II correlations is provided in Table 3.5.

Correlational data were also analyzed for KTEA-II Brief Form and three mea-

Table 3.5 KTEA-II Composites Correlations with KABC-II Global Scales (ages 4½–18 years)

KTEA-II Composite	KABC-II Global Scale		
	FCI	MPI	NVI
Reading			
Ages 4½–6	.67	.68	.57
Ages 7–18	.74	.68	.61
Total sample	.74	.69	.61
Math			
Ages 4½–6	.70	.71	.65
Ages 7–18	.71	.68	.67
Total sample	.71	.68	.67
Written Language			
Ages 4½–6	.67	.70	.56
Ages 7–18	.66	.62	.56
Total sample	.66	.63	.56
Oral Language			
Ages 4½–6	.62	.57	.52
Ages 7–18	.67	.61	.56
Total sample	.67	.60	.55
Comprehensive Achievement			
Ages 4½–6	.75	.73	.65
Ages 7–18	.80	.74	.70
Total sample	.79	.74	.69

Note: FCI = Fluid Crystallized Index; MPI = Mental Processing Index; NVI = Nonverbal Index. All correlations were corrected for the variability of the norm group, based on the standard deviation obtained on the KTEA-II, using the variability correction of Cohen et al. (2003). Data are adapted from Table 7.25 and Appendix J of the *KTEA-II Comprehensive Form Manual* (Kaufman & Kaufman, 2004a).

Table 3.6 KTEA-II Brief Form Correlations with Measures of Global Cognitive Ability

Measure of Global Cognitive Ability	N	KTEA-II Brief Form			
		Reading	Math	Writing	Brief Achievement Composite
KABC-II FCI	1,266	.65	.63	.60	.70
KABC-II MPI	1,266	.61	.63	.60	.70
KBIT-2 IQ Composite	747	.74	.71	.54	.78
WASI Full Scale IQ-4	142	.73	.65	.48	.71

Note: FCI = Fluid Crystallized Index; MPI = Mental Processing Index. Data are from Tables 6.20–6.31 of the *KTEA-II Brief Form Manual* (Kaufman & Kaufman, 2005). All correlations were corrected for the variability of the norm group, based on the standard deviation obtained on the KTEA-II using the variability correction of Cohen et al. (2003). The WASI FSIQ is based on 4 subtests: Vocabulary, Block Design, Similarities, and Matrix Reasoning.

sures of cognitive ability: the KABC-II, the Kaufman Brief Intelligence Test–Second Edition (KBIT-2; Kaufman & Kaufman, 2004c), and the Wechsler Abbreviated Scale of Intelligence (WASI; The Psychological Corporation, 1999). Patterns of correlation between the KTEA-II Brief Form and the measures of cognitive ability were similar to what was found on the Comprehensive Form. That is, the KTEA-II Brief Form Reading and Math subtests correlated more strongly with global cognitive ability than did the Writing subtest (see Table 3.6). The Brief Achievement Composite correlated most strongly with the KBIT-2 IQ Composite ($r = .78$) and correlated about equally with the WASI FSIQ (.71) and the KABC-II FCI (.70).

HOW TO ADMINISTER THE KTEA-II

As with any standardized test, when administering the KTEA-II you should follow closely the test administration instructions contained in the test manual and easels. Chapter 2 of both the *KTEA-II Comprehensive Form Manual* (Kaufman & Kaufman, 2004a) and the *KTEA-II Brief Form Manual* (Kaufman & Kaufman, 2005) review the general administration procedures and the test easels list specific administration directions.

The KTEA-II Comprehensive Form offers much flexibility to examiners in

CAUTION

If you depart from the suggested subtest administration sequence, you must always:

1. Administer Letter and Word Recognition before Reading Comprehension.
2. Administer Word Recognition Fluency and Nonsense Word Decoding before Decoding Fluency.

CAUTION

Remember that the last subtests listed in the Record Form, Associational Fluency, and Naming Facility (RAN) must be administered intermittently throughout the battery. Thus, do not wait until the end of the battery to administer them (see Rapid Reference 3.5 for a suggested administration order).

terms of the subtests that can be administered and the order in which they are administered. The entire battery may be administered or you may choose to administer only select composites or subtests. Once you have decided whether the KTEA-II Brief Form battery or a complete or partial KTEA-II Comprehensive Form battery will be administered, then you need to determine the sequence of the subtests. The easels and record form provide the suggested administration order, but you may select a different administration order if you prefer (see Caution insert). For the KTEA-II Comprehensive, if you choose to follow the sequence of subtests presented in the record form and easels, you must plan to administer two subtests out of easel order: Associational Fluency (13th subtest) and Naming Facility (14th subtest). These two subtests are administered together in four separate "task pairs," which include one Fluency task and one Naming Facility task as a pair. You should administer each pair intermittently among the other subtests. A suggested order for interspersing these task pairs with the other subtests is presented in Rapid Reference 3.5. The accompanying Caution box reminds you not to wait until the end of the battery to administer the Associational Fluency and Naming Facility tasks.

Starting and Discontinuing Subtests

Like most standardized tests of individual achievement, the KTEA-II items are ordered by difficulty, with the easiest items first. Grade-based starting points are listed in the record form and on the first page of a subtest's directions in the easel. If you have knowledge or suspicion based on clinical judgment that the child you are testing will benefit from an earlier or later start point, you may select a different start point.

If you have started administering a subtest from a starting point other than

≡ Rapid Reference 3.5

Suggested Subtest Administration Order When Administering Associational Fluency and Naming Facility

Subtest Number	Subtest	Grade Range for Administration
1	Phonological Awareness	K–6
2	Letter and Word Recognition	PreK–12+
13 & 14	Associational Fluency and Naming Facility (RAN): Task Pair 1	PreK–12+
3	Math Concepts and Applications	PreK–12+
13 & 14	Associational Fluency and Naming Facility (RAN): Task Pair 2	PreK–12+
4	Nonsense Word Decoding	1–12+
5	Math Computation	K–12+
13 & 14	Associational Fluency and Naming Facility (RAN): Task Pair 3	1–12+
6	Reading Comprehension	1–12+
7	Written Expression	Pre-K–12+
14	Associational Fluency: Task 4	1–12+
8	Spelling	1–12+
9	Listening Comprehension	Pre-K–12+
10	Oral Expression	Pre-K–12+
11	Word Recognition Fluency	3–12+
12	Decoding Fluency	3–12+

Note: Associational Fluency and Naming Facility (RAN) Task Pairs must be given out of easel order, and should be administered intermittently among other subtests. Subtests may be administered in alternative orders as well. "PreK" refers to children aged 4:6 or older who have not yet entered kindergarten. "Grade 12+" indicates that the subtests can be administered up to the top of the age range (age 25:11).

item 1, you must make sure that the examinee is able to achieve a basal. That is, the examinee must demonstrate proficiency on the task by getting the first few items correct in order to achieve the basal. If the examinee does not meet the basal criterion, then you must drop back to the preceding start point. The basal rules are listed in the record form as well as on the first page of the directions for a subtest in the easel. Some subtests on the KTEA-II do not have traditional basal rules because the items are grouped into item sets (see Figure 3.3). These Com-

6. Reading Comprehension

Range: Grades 1–12+

Basal: If starting at Set B, must pass first 3 items or drop back to item 1. If Starting at Set C or above, must pass at least 2 items in the first passage administered, or drop back one start point as needed.

Discontinue: at stop point (■) for set if there are at least 4 failures and 4 passes in a set or pair of sets; or after 5 consecutive failures

Note: Mark skill categories only for items within the set or pair of sets

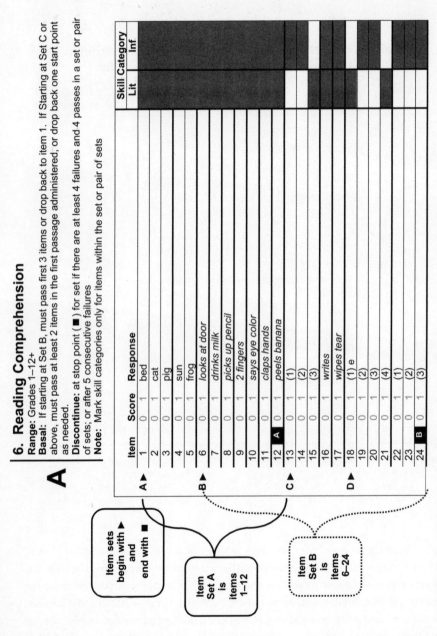

Figure 3.3 Example of Item Sets on Reading Comprehension of the KTEA-II Comprehensive Record Form

DON'T FORGET

Start Points, Basal Rules, and Discontinue Rules for Reading Comprehension, Listening Comprehension, and Oral Expression

Subtest	Start Point	Basal	Discontinue
Reading Comprehension	Determined by raw score on Letter and Word Recognition (see Start Point Table on record form or easel)	If start point is Set B, examinee must pass first 3 items. If start point is Set C or above, examinee must pass 2 items in the first passage administered.	Discontinue at a stop point for a set IF there are at least four failures and four passes in a set or pair of sets OR if there are five consecutive failures.
Listening Comprehension	Determined by grade (see Start Point Table on record form or easel)	Must pass at least 2 items in the first passage administered	
Oral Expression	Determined by grade (see Start Point Table on record form or easel)	At least four preliminary scores of 1 in the first set	

prehensive Form subtests with item sets include Reading Comprehension, Listening Comprehension, and Oral Expression. The Writing subtest on the KTEA-II Brief Form also is administered with item sets. The Don't Forget box describes the administration procedures for these subtests that do not have traditional basal rules. Figure 3.4 exemplifies the basal and discontinue rules for a student administered Reading Comprehension.

Sample and Teaching Items

Unlike many cognitive tests, such as the KABC-II, very few KTEA-II subtests include sample or teaching items. These items are intended to communicate the nature of the task by allowing the examiner to give feedback and explain the task further in order to teach the task. Three KTEA-II Comprehensive Form subtests include either sample or teaching items: Phonological Awareness, Nonsense Word Decoding, and Oral Expression. Sample items or teaching items are indi-

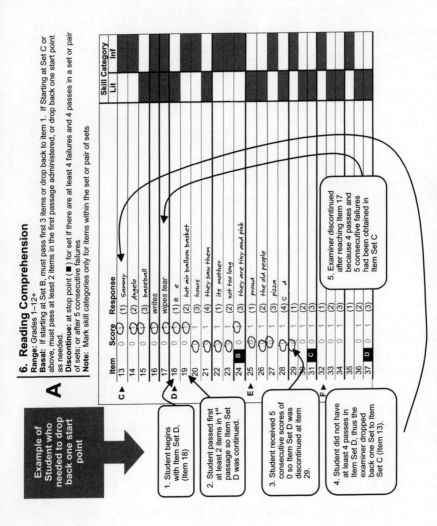

Figure 3.4 Example of how the discontinue and basal rules are implemented and recorded on Reading Comprehension of the KTEA-II Comprehensive Record Form

cated on the record form by an apple icon. Each of the five sections of Phono-logical Awareness has one or two sets of sample items. The first two scored items on Nonsense Word Decoding are teaching items and the third and sixth items on Oral Expression are teaching items.

Recording Responses

Accurately recording responses during administration of KTEA-II subtests is very important—especially if you intend to conduct error analysis after scoring the subtests is complete. On 3 of the 14 Comprehensive Form subtests, the ex-aminees write their responses themselves (i.e., Written Expression, Spelling, and Math Computation), requiring no recording on the examiner's part until scoring is conducted. Phonological Awareness and Math Concepts and Applications re-quire simple recording of either a zero for incorrect or a one for correct, or recording a one-word response. Reading Comprehension and Listening Com-prehension require that the gist of the examinee's responses are recorded with as much detail as possible, but Oral Expression and Associational Fluency require that an examinee's responses are recorded verbatim (and may be recorded via a tape recorder). Letter and Word Recognition and Nonsense Word Decoding re-quire careful listening in order to correctly record the child's responses. Mis-pronunciations on these two subtests should be recorded using the phoneme key provided on the record form, or write the student's response phonetically. Re-cording responses either by the phonetic key or by phonetically spelling the child's response takes some practice. Chapter 4 of the *KTEA-II Comprehensive Form Manual* (Kaufman & Kaufman, 2004a) describes in more detail how to record re-sponses for use with the error analysis system.

Timing

Most subtests on the KTEA-II are not timed. However, four of the Reading-Related subtests do require timing. Specifically, for Word Recognition Fluency, Decoding Fluency, and Associational Fluency, the student's performance within the specific time is the basis of the score. For Naming Facility (RAN), the time taken by the student to complete each trial is converted to a point score.

Querying

Occasionally, examinees' responses may be missing an essential detail or qualifier to be 100 percent correct. These instances will most commonly occur during

Reading Comprehension and Listening Comprehension, and will require you to query the examinee to clarify his or her response. Specific queries are listed right in the easel, and when querying is done, a notation should be made on the record form (e.g., "Q"). Occasionally students give multiple responses and it is unclear which response is the final answer. In such instances you should ask the examinee which is the intended response.

Subtest-by-Subtest Notes on Administration

This section highlights pertinent information for administering each of the KTEA-II subtests, and points out common errors in administration. Subtests are listed in the order in which they appear in the KTEA-II Comprehensive Form easels. Because administrative procedures for the Brief Form are very similar to those of the Comprehensive Form, we review notes on administration of the Brief Form subtests under the sections on the related Comprehensive Form subtests to reduce redundancy. The Don't Forget box reminds you where to look for administrative information on the Brief Form subtests.

Phonological Awareness
Phonological Awareness has five sections: (1) Rhyming, (2) Sound Matching, (3) Blending, (4) Segmenting, and (5) Deleting Sounds. All five sections are adminis-

DON'T FORGET

Where in This Chapter to Look for Administrative Information on KTEA-II Brief Form Subtests

Brief Form Subtest	Look under the following subsection in "Subtest-by-Subtest Notes on Administration"
Reading (Part 1)	Letter and Word Recognition
Reading (Part 2)	Reading Comprehension
Math (concepts and applications items)	Math Concepts and Applications
Math (computation items)	Math Computation
Writing	Written Expression

Note: Although the KTEA-II Brief and Comprehensive Forms are similar in general content and administrative procedures, they do not have overlapping items.

tered to children in kindergarten, but only Sections 1, 4, and 5 are administered to children in first through sixth grades. Beginning in Section 3, this subtest requires use of Pepper, the dog puppet, as well as the KTEA-II Easel 1 for administration. The CD that accompanies this subtest is very useful for ensuring that you understand how to properly administer Section 3 (Blending) and Section 5 (Deleting Sounds). Most children find Pepper quite engaging, but some are distracted and seem to more easily go off task when it is their turn to make Pepper talk. With such children, remind them to stay on task, but suggest that they can have a few minutes to "play with Pepper" after the task is over (a nice, built-in reward of the task). Occasionally children may struggle with trying to make Pepper's mouth move. Encourage these children to focus on segmenting the word properly and worry less about getting Pepper to move his mouth.

Since this task is purely auditory (except for Section 2, which has pictorial stimuli, too), ensure that the child is paying attention prior to beginning an item. If necessary, you may repeat an item during the task.

Letter and Word Recognition

The key to properly administering Letter and Word Recognition from the Comprehensive Form and Reading Part 1 from the Brief Form is having knowledge of the proper pronunciation of all the stimulus words. If you are unsure of how a word should be pronounced, you will undoubtedly struggle with whether an examinee correctly pronounced it, and will therefore not know whether to continue. This problem is less of an issue when testing younger children, but when assessing older children and adolescents, they may be administered the highest levels of words, which are quite challenging. Thus, before administering the subtest, listen to the CD provided with the test kit to hear the correct pronunciations of the most difficult words.

Most of the stimulus words are presented six to a page, and examinees should be allowed to attempt to pronounce all words on a page, even if they have met the discontinue rule before reaching the sixth word on a page. Such administration methods will continue to foster good rapport. Sometimes children will pronounce words in disconnected pieces, but to receive credit, a child must pronounce words as a connected, relatively smooth whole. Thus, they should be instructed to "Say it all together" if they pronounce a word in disconnected pieces and then stop.

Math Concepts and Applications

On the Comprehensive Form, an entire subtest is devoted to assessing mathematical concepts and applications; on the Brief Form, items measuring math concepts and applications are interspersed among computation items in a single subtest. Regardless of whether you are administering the Comprehensive or Brief Form, you will find that some children require more concrete ways to process the problems in Math Concepts and Applications, and such children will more often count with their fingers or use the pictures to aid them in coming up with a response. Fingers are an acceptable tool for problem solving during math computation and application items, but calculators are not. On the Brief Form, paper and pencil are allowed for all Math subtest items. However, prior to item 34 on the Comprehensive Form subtest, children are not allowed to use paper and pencil; however, beginning with item 34 children should be offered paper and pencil should they wish to use them. In the latter half of the subtest there are several word problems; although the word problems are printed on the easel for the examinee to see, you should read each of these problems aloud to the examinee.

Nonsense Word Decoding

Similar to Letter and Word Recognition, the key to properly administering Nonsense Word Decoding is having knowledge of the proper pronunciation of all the stimulus words. Thus, it is crucial to listen to the CD provided with the test kit that demonstrates how the words should be pronounced. Most of the stimulus words are presented six on an easel page. To maintain rapport and minimize frustration for children, it is best to administer an entire easel page (all six words), even if a child has discontinued before reading the sixth word. However, only the words read before the discontinue rule was met should be counted toward the final raw score. As the nonsense words become more challenging, some children will get stuck on a particular word with which they are struggling. In such cases, you should encourage children to try the next one so that the test continues without multiple, lengthy delays.

Nonsense Word Decoding is one of the few KTEA-II subtests that allows teaching of the task. On items 1 and 2, you are to tell the student the correct answer if they respond incorrectly (you are reminded that they are teaching items, with the apple icons on the record form). Before you administer this subtest, it is advisable to practice how to record children's responses (whether you choose to do so using the phonemic key on the record form or another method). At times children will rapidly read the words, requiring you to increase your pace for recording their responses. In addition to recording the responses to specific items, you may record what the student's general approach to pronouncing the nonsense words was by marking one of three boxes at the bottom of the record form (letter-by-letter, chunking, or whole word). However, if a child doesn't use the same general approach to most of the items, checking these "Response Style" boxes will not be that useful.

Math Computation

The Student Response Booklet and a pencil with an eraser are needed to administer the Math Computation subtest on the Comprehensive Form and the computation items of the Brief Form's Math subtest. The Student Response Booklet should be folded so that the examinee can only see the page that he or she is currently working on. Some children will impulsively turn the page to see what comes next, but encourage such children not to worry about the next problems, and rather just focus on finishing the page in front of them. Children may work out problems by counting on their fingers or by writing notes on the paper, but may not use calculators. If necessary, remind children that it is okay to erase. Children with disabilities that cause difficulty with writing should be allowed to respond orally.

It is important to observe children closely as they solve the problems. Some children with fill the entire square with scratch notes, and it may be unclear which number is their final response. If you are uncertain about which number the child intended as their final answer, ask the child to circle his or her final response before the next item has been started. As you are observing the child work out the problems make notes about repeated erasures, verbal mediation of the problems, or other notable behaviors.

Reading Comprehension

To determine the starting point on the Comprehensive Form's Reading Comprehension subtest, you must first administer Letter and Word Recognition, then enter the child's raw score on that subtest into the "Start Point Table" on page 12 of the KTEA-II record form or on the first page of the Reading Comprehension subtest in the easel. Items 1 to 5 require that examinees point to a picture of a word that they read, and items 6 to 12 require the examinee to read a command and do what it says (e.g., "Stand up"). On items 6 to 12, some examinees may require you to encourage them to pretend or make believe in response to the command that they read (The first six items of Reading Part 2 of the Brief Form are also "command" items). Items 13 to 87 of Reading Comprehension and Items 7 to 25 of the Brief Form's Reading Part 2 subtest require the examinee to read a paragraph and answer questions about what he or she read. Examinees may read the paragraphs and questions silently or aloud, but are not penalized if they make mistakes while they read aloud. However, such mistakes while reading aloud are noteworthy, especially if they are made frequently. In the remaining few items of Reading Comprehension on the Comprehensive Form, examinees must read a series of sentences and decide the correct order of the sentences (items 88 and 90). Examinees are allowed to use paper and pencil to organize the sentence numbers for these two items if they wish. While reading the paragraphs or questions, examinees sometimes ask for clarification of a term or help to read a particular word. In such cases, you should not give them help, but rather encourage them to just try their best.

Some of the passage questions are multiple choice and require only recording a letter response (e.g., a, b, c, d). However, other questions are open-ended—in such cases, the examinee's responses should be recorded verbatim. Generally, querying is not necessary for most responses, but if the examinee provides multiple responses and you are unsure which is their intended final response, ask for clarification.

Written Expression

Although there are many similarities in the skills tapped in the Comprehensive Form's Written Expression subtest and the Brief Form's Writing subtest, there are some important differences in administration, so we discuss each subtest in turn in this section. For the Comprehensive Form, examinees' responses to items on the Written Expression subtest are recorded in the appropriate Written Expression Booklet (grades 1 to 12) or in the Student Response Booklet (Pre-K and kindergarten). The first easel page of Written Expression lists which of the booklets examinees should use, based upon their grade level. (The Caution box reminds examiners of an important point for administering to students in grade 1.) The booklets, *Pam and Don's Adventure, The Little Duck's Friend, Kyra's Dragon, The Amazing Scrapbook, A Day on the Set,* and *The News at Six* each tell a story, with the goal of engaging the student in the writing tasks. Thus, when presenting the subtest, the examiner's directions written in the easel emphasize the fact that the booklets are stories. Before administering any level of Written Expression, you should familiarize yourself with the response booklet so that you know where to point to the words as you read them and so that you know where the student should write his or her response to each item (indicated by numbers printed in small boxes). The last item for each of the stories requires the examinee to write a summary of the story (items 30, 49, and 60 in Form A, and items 31, 48, and 58 in Form B). For each of these

CAUTION

If administering Written Expression to children in the spring of grade 1, Booklet 2 must be tentatively scored at the midpoint (after item 23 in Form A and item 24 in Form B) in order to decide whether the student should continue to the end. If you are uncertain about whether the preliminary score is adequate to necessitate administration of the rest of Level 2, it is best to err on the side of caution and continue with the test.

items the examinees are given 5 to 10 minutes to write their summary; thus, you will need a watch or clock to time these final items.

In Written Expression on the Comprehensive Form you are allowed to repeat story segments or item instructions if necessary. As

> **DON'T FORGET**
>
> ....
>
> Spelling is not scored in the Comprehensive Form's Written Expression subtest. Therefore you are allowed to tell an examinee how to spell a word if he or she asks.

noted in the Don't Forget insert, you may also tell a student how to spell a word, if they ask (spelling is not scored in this subtest). However, you should not spontaneously correct a child's spelling or offer similar assistance unless asked by the examinee.

To administer the Brief Form's Writing subtest, you need the response booklet, a pencil, and the KTEA-II Brief Easel. Students are administered an item set based on their grade. After a student has completed a set, if they have earned 4 or more scores of 0, stop testing, but if they have earned 3 or fewer scores of 0, then continue until the next stop point. In the Writing subtest, spelling items are interspersed among items that demand skills such as capitalization, punctuation, and word form. Because spelling is an important component of the Brief Form's Writing subtest, you may not help students spell words during the subtest (which is unlike the rules of administration for the Comprehensive Form's Written Expression subtest).

Spelling

Spelling is administered to children in first grade and beyond. Examinees write their responses in the Student Response Booklet using a pencil with an eraser (it is a good idea to have extras on hand, in case of broken pencil points). The first four items require examinees to write a letter to complete a word, but the remaining items require the spelling of complete words. Watch the child on each item to make sure that he or she is writing the response on the correct line. You should ask the child to clarify what he or she wrote if the child's handwriting is unclear, or if you suspect he or she has reversed a letter (e.g., writing *b* for *d* or *p* for *q*). Children will not be penalized for such reversals if they say the correct letter. Children are allowed to erase and correct a response if they want. If a child does not respond immediately after you have said a word, or if the child asks you to repeat something, you may repeat the word or sentence.

If the child you are testing has a motor disability or an inability to write for any other reason, you may permit the child to respond orally. If a child responds orally, then write the response on the record form as he or she spells it. However, this alternative procedure for responding should only be used after every attempt is made to have the student give a written response.

Listening Comprehension

Listening Comprehension is administered via a CD player. In an emergency, or if you experience technical problems with your CD player, you can read the subtest's passages aloud, as they are written in the test easel. Similar to Reading Comprehension, Listening Comprehension items are grouped into item sets, and the child's grade level determines where to begin. Prior to beginning this subtest you should check the volume on your CD player, to ensure that the examinee will be able to hear adequately, and cue the CD to the proper track. Before playing each passage, be sure that the child is ready to listen, because examinees are not allowed to hear the passage more than once. Immediately after the passage has been played, pause the CD player and ask the questions about the story. Although the passage itself may not be replayed, you may repeat a test question at the student's request. The Don't Forget insert reminds you of important points about administering Listening Comprehension.

DON'T FORGET

Reminders for Administering Listening Comprehension

Introduce the test before beginning the first passage.

Say, "You are going to hear a short story. Listen carefully, and then I will ask you some questions about the story. Ready? Listen."

Read the response choices for multiple-choice questions twice.

When administering multiple-choice questions, say the letter as well as the text of each answer choice, and then pause slightly after each choice. After completing the list of choices, say the list a second time.

Prompt examinees for a second answer on questions with two-part answers.

If a question asks for a two-part answer and the student only gives one part, then say: "Yes, and what else?"

Play the passage only one time.

You may play the passage only once and may not answer any questions that the student asks about the story.

Test questions may be repeated.

You may repeat a test question if a child asks for repetition or if you suspect that the student did not hear the question the first time.

Oral Expression

Oral Expression is administered in item sets and begins with the set determined by the child's grade (these starting points are listed in the easel). During administration, you may repeat an item if the child requests or if you believe that he or she did not hear it. Some items require examinees to start their response with a particular word. If a child does not start with the requested word, then you should give the child a second trial and give credit if he or she responds correctly upon the second administration of the item.

Word Recognition Fluency

Prior to administering Word Recognition Fluency make sure that you have the Word Recognition Fluency Card and a stopwatch in hand. Some of the words in this subtest are quite challenging, and it is recommended that you review the pronunciation of these words on the CD prior to administering the subtest. The starting point for Word Recognition Fluency is based on a child's performance on Letter and Word Recognition. Children who reached item 84 on Letter and Word Recognition start Word Recognition Fluency at item 31; all other children begin Word Recognition Fluency at item 1.

Introduce the test with the text printed in the easel (also on the record form). Once you say "Go," begin timing. After 60 seconds, say, "Stop," and draw a line in the record form after the last word attempted. Some children may complete the task before 60 seconds have elapsed—if so, record their completion time on the record form. During administration of this subtest, children may hesitate or get stuck on a word. When such a pause occurs, encourage the examinee to keep going and move on to the next word. As children read the words, record any words that they misread or skip by putting a slash through the appropriate word on the record form. However, do not penalize examinees for articulation errors or variations due to regional speech patterns.

Decoding Fluency

Administration of Decoding Fluency is very similar to administration of Word Recognition Fluency. For administration, you need the Decoding Fluency Card and a stopwatch or watch that shows seconds. Prior to administration, you should listen to the CD to hear examples of how to pronounce the nonsense words. To begin administration, you should introduce the subtest with the instructions printed in the manual and the record form. After you say, "Go," immediately begin timing the examinee, and after 60 seconds, instruct the examinee to stop. Make a slash on the record form after the last word that the examinee read. If an examinee pauses or hesitates during the task, encourage him or her to keep going or move on to the next one. As the examinee is reading the words, make a slash through any of the words that are mispronounced or skipped. If a child completes the Decoding Fluency Card before 60 seconds have elapsed, record the completion time in seconds.

Associational Fluency and Naming Facility

As mentioned earlier in this chapter, Associational Fluency and Naming Facility are administered together in task pairs (one Associational Fluency task with one Naming Facility task). Although these are the final tests listed in the easel and in the record form, they must be administered throughout the test battery, and each of the four task pairs should be separated by other subtests. In Rapid Reference 3.5 we provide a suggested order for subtests administration when these two tasks are included in the battery.

The specific directions to administer each of the task pairs are listed in the record form. Generally, on the Associational Fluency tasks (two semantic fluency tasks, such as naming foods, noisy objects, animals, and toys, and two phonemic fluency tasks), you give the child 30 seconds to say as many of the words in a category that he or she can think of. If children stop or say that they cannot think of more, you should encourage them to try to say more if they have more time left. Children under grade 1 are administered only the first two Associational Fluency tasks which include semantic fluency from Task Pair 1 and 2 but not phonemic fluency from Task Pair 3. You should attempt to record the examinee's words verbatim, but sometimes a child responds so rapidly that such recording is difficult. In those instances, you should simply make a checkmark on a line of the record form to indicate that the child gave a correct response.

For the Naming Facility tasks, you first need to determine that the examinee knows the names of the objects, colors, and letters. If the examinee uses a different name for one of the objects, tell him or her the correct name to use. However, on the color and letter-naming tasks, if the student does not name a color or letter correctly, then do not administer that task (see the accompanying Caution).

Students in PreK and kindergarten should only be administered the first two Naming Facility (RAN) tasks (not letter naming). As the examinee is responding, you should mark on the record form any stimulus that he or she names incorrectly. When the child completes naming all of the stimuli on the card, you should record the child's completion time.

> ### CAUTION
>
> Prior to administering Naming Facility (RAN), check to make sure that the student knows the names of the objects, colors, and letters. You may tell them the correct name of an object if they use a different term. However, do not administer the task if the student does not correctly name a color or letter.

HOW TO SCORE THE KTEA-II

The KTEA-II yields several types of scores: raw scores, standard scores (subtests, domain composites, and the Comprehensive Achievement Composite or Brief Achievement Composite), grade equivalents, age equivalents, and percentile ranks. Raw scores reflect the number for points earned by the student on each subtest. These scores, by themselves, are meaningless, because they are not norm-based. When they are converted to standard scores, which are norm-based, they then allow the student's performance to be compared to that of others. The KTEA-II standard scores have a mean of 100 and a SD of 15. The range of standard scores for the subtests and composites is 40 to 160. We assume that achievement-test performance is distributed on a normal curve, with the majority of students scoring within ±1 SD of the mean. Thus, about two-thirds (68 percent) of students score in the range of 85 to 115. Less than 3 percent of students score above 130 or below 70.

Types of Scores

Each type of the KTEA-II's scores is described in the following pages.

Raw Scores

Subtest raw scores are calculated in a variety of ways. Five of the KTEA-II Comprehensive Form subtests' raw scores are calculated by subtracting the number of errors from the ceiling item (i.e., Letter and Word Recognition, Math Concepts and Applications, Math Computation, Nonsense Word Decoding, and Spelling). Phonological Awareness and Associational Fluency require examiners to sum the scores from various sections to determine the raw scores. Similarly, the raw scores for the Math and Reading subtests of the Brief Form are calculated by subtracting the total number of errors from the ceiling number. Some subtests require examiners to use a table to convert the total number of points in a section to the final raw score (i.e., Reading Comprehension, Written Expression, Listening Comprehension, Oral Expression, and the Writing subtest of the Brief Form). Three tasks that are timed (Word Recognition Fluency, Decoding Fluency, and Naming Facility) require examiners to use a chart to convert an examinee's completion time to a point value, which is then part of the calculation of the raw score.

Standard Scores

To be meaningfully interpreted, the raw scores of the KTEA-II must be converted to standard scores. When converting from raw to standard scores, you must first decide whether to use age-based or grade-based norms. This decision

CAUTION

Why Differences Occur When Basing Standard Scores on Age versus Grade

QUESTION:

I recently administered the KTEA-II to a child age 8:11 who just completed third grade. I looked up her standard scores according to age norms (as is typically my practice), but then, out of curiosity, I looked up her scores according to grade norms, too. The scores were quite different in some cases (e.g., both Reading Comprehension and Math Computation were 9 points lower when calculated according to the Grade Norms). Could you tell me why Age and Grade norms may yield different scores and give me your opinion about when each type of norm is most useful?

ANSWER:

The explanation of the difference is pretty simple. Assuming that children start kindergarten when they are 5 years old, then children start grade 3 when they are 8 years old. Therefore, virtually all children aged 8:11 are in grade 3. Children turn 8:11 at a steady rate throughout the grade 3 school year—some turn 8:11 in September, others in June. Therefore, about half of the students turn 8:11 in the fall, and about half in the spring. Thus, the norm sample for age 8:11 contains students from the beginning through the end of grade 3. That sample performs lower, as a group, than the norm sample for the spring of grade 3.

Thus, for a student who turns 8:11 in the spring, the age norms will give higher standard scores than the grade norms. The reverse is true for a student who turns 8:11 in the fall. (The direction of the difference by time of year can't be generalized: it depends on what the month of age is. For a student aged 8:3 in the fall, age-based scores are higher than grade-based scores, because some students who turn 8:3 in the fall are in grade 2.)

In principle, there is no good, practical solution for taking curriculum exposure into account in age norms, and all of the achievement batteries have this problem. The ideal might be to have age-by-grade norm tables (e.g., age 8:6 in the fall of grade 3, age 8:6 in the spring of grade 3, age 8:6 in the spring of grade 2), but that is too complex. Simply subdividing age norms into fall and spring, as we used to do, is flawed because at most months of age a student could be in either of two grades, which would be an even greater distortion for some students.

The bottom line is that the situation is complicated—the deeper you look into it, the messier it becomes. In these days, when grade retention is rare, there might be a good argument to be made for using grade norms rather than age norms for clinical evaluations. The concern used to be that grade norms would make a student who had repeated a grade or two look "too good." These days, there would seem to be a better argument that age norms are problematic because they mix students with different amounts of curriculum exposure. However, examiners must follow requirements set forth by their state and school district based on IDEA Reauthorized, so for some that will mean using age norms for special-ed classification and for others that will require using grade norms. Examiners should just be aware that occasionally differences do occur between them.

Note: The "Answer" is based on a personal communication from Mark Daniel (7/13/2004), Executive Director of Assessment Development and Director of the KABC-II/KTEA-II Project at AGS.

depends on whether you want to compare the student's test performance with that of the same-age peers or same-grade peers. In most cases, the resulting standard scores will be similar. However, important differences can occur if the student has been retained or has received an accelerated grade placement, or if the student began school earlier or later in the year than is typical. In these cases, the age-based norms are probably more relevant. However, if you are planning on comparing performance on the KTEA-II with performance on an ability measure such as the KABC-II, always use age-based norms, because they are the basis for the standard scores on ability measures. The Caution box provides further information about the differences between age-based and grade-based standard scores.

When selecting grade-norms to convert raw scores to standard scores, you must select from one of two sets: Fall (indicating that a child was assessed in August–January), or Spring (indicating that a child was assessed in February–July). The front of the record form has a box that you can check to indicate whether you have used the Fall or Spring grade norms or the age-norms. In addition to separating each of the grade norms into Fall and Spring, the *KTEA-II Comprehensive Form Norms Book* also has two columns for each subtest (one for Form A and one for Form B). Carefully select the correct column and the correct page of the norms book when you are determining the standard scores. The Don't Forget box reminds examiners about which tables to use to find various standard scores.

Because scores have error associated with them, it is wise to report standard scores with a band of error or within a confidence interval. The KTEA-II allows you to choose from 85 percent, 90 percent, or 95 percent confidence levels (the

DON'T FORGET
....

Where to Find Standard Scores

	Fall Grade Norms	Spring Grade Norms	Age-Based Norms
Subtest Standard Scores	Table N.1	Table N.2	Table N.4
Domain Composites		Table N.3	Table N.5
Comprehensive Achievement Composite		Table N.3	Table N.5

Note: Tables referenced in this Don't Forget are from the *KTEA-II Comprehensive Form Norms Book*. Table N.1 is found on pages 2–53, Table N.2 is found on pages 54–105, Table N.3 is on pages 107–115, Table N.4 is on pages 116–283, and Table N.5 is on pages 284–299.

record form directs you to circle which level of confidence you are reporting). Tables N.6 and N.7 in the *KTEA-II Comprehensive Form Norms Book* provide the bands of error for age-based standard scores and grade-based standard scores.

Grade and Age Equivalents

Grade and age equivalents may be found in Tables N.9 and N.10, respectively, in the *KTEA-II Comprehensive Form Norms Book* (similar tables are also available in the Brief Form manual). However, we recommend that they be reported with caution, as they are frequently misunderstood. They are not precise, as are standard scores or percentile ranks, and they often suggest large differences in performance, when the differences are actually insignificant. For example, a raw score of 71 on Reading Comprehension yields an age equivalent of 14:8 and earning just two more points for a raw score of 73 corresponds to an age equivalent of 16:6. On the same subtest, an examinee age 15:5 would earn an age-based standard score of 99 (for a raw score of 71) and an age-based standard score of 101 (for a raw score of 73). Thus, this 2-point standard score difference appears much smaller than the nearly 2-year-difference in age-equivalents, when comparing scores based on the same raw scores.

Percentile Ranks

Percentile ranks are an excellent metric to communicate results to parents, teachers, and other nonpsychologists. They are often readily understood and interpreted. Regardless of whether age-based standard scores or grade-based standard scores are used, the percentile rank has the same meaning: it is the percentage of individuals that the student outperformed at his or her age (age norms) or grade level (grade norms). For example, a 12-year-old who scored at the 75th percentile on Nonsense Word Decoding performed better than 75 per-

CAUTION

Age-equivalents and grade-equivalents are not as precise as standard scores, and may make small differences appear larger than they actually are, as shown in the example that follows:

Reading Comprehension Raw Score	Age Equivalent	Standard Score
71	14:8	99
73	16:6	101
Difference:	Nearly 2 years	2 standard score points

cent of 12-year-olds on that subtest. A first grader who scored at the 5th percentile on Phonological Awareness scored better than only 5 percent of first graders. Each standard score can be converted to a percentile rank by using Table N.8 of the *KTEA-II Comprehensive Form Norms Book* or Table C.9 in the *KTEA-II Brief Form Manual*.

> **CAUTION**
>
> **Percentile Ranks are not Percent Correct**
>
> Clearly communicate to parents that a percentile rank is the percent of children that an examinee scored better than. A percentile rank is *not* the percentage of items answered correctly.

Descriptive Categories

Rapid Reference 3.6 presents the descriptive categories that the test authors selected for KTEA-II subtests and composites. These verbal descriptions correspond to commonly used standard score ranges. The categories shown in this table are intended to reflect in words the approximate distance of each range of scores from the group mean—a verbal translation of the normal curve. This system differs from the system used for the original K-TEA and from many other classification systems, such as Wechsler's (2002a, 2003).

The KTEA-II system depends on a standard deviation of 15 to define its categories, with the Average range of 85 to 115 corresponding to ± 1 standard deviation (SD) from the mean (100 ± 15); Below Average is defined as 1 to 2 SDs below the mean (70 to 84), and so forth. You should use these categories to describe standard scores on the global scales and scale indexes. This system avoids the narrow 10-point categories (e.g., 70 to 79, 110 to 119) that appear frequently in other

≡Rapid Reference 3.6

Descriptive Category System for the KTEA-II Comprehensive and Brief Forms

Range of Standard Scores	Name of Category	SDs from Mean
131–160	Upper Extreme	+2 to +4
116–130	Above Average	+1 to +2
85–115	Average Range	−1 to +1
70–84	Below Average	−1 to −2
40–69	Lower Extreme	−2 to −4

systems (including the one used for the original K-TEA). One problem with 10-point categories is that when confidence intervals are used to provide a reasonable band of error, it is common for the confidence interval to span three different categories. That broad span of ability levels can be confusing, for example, when explaining a child's test performance to a parent.

It is inappropriate to overwhelm readers of a case report by providing descriptive categories for each standard score. These labels serve best when they either summarize an individual's performance on all scales via a composite score or highlight significant discrepancies among the scales. Generally, the use of descriptive labels with subtests should be reserved for standard scores that are significantly above or below the child's own mean values, or for standard scores that are high or low relative to other children of the same age.

Subtest-by-Subtest Scoring Keys

Most of the items on the KTEA-II have a simple, dichotomous scoring system, requiring examiners to circle either a 1 (for correct) or a 0 (for incorrect) on the record form. However, there are differences in how raw scores are calculated across the subtests. Regardless of how the raw score is calculated, you need to score the items (at least in a preliminary fashion) as you are testing. This score-as-you-go procedure is necessary, so that you know when to discontinue a subtest or when you need to drop back to an earlier start point. We recommend that you double-check the accuracy of each item's score when you are completely done with the test administration, prior to calculating the raw score. The Caution box

CAUTION

Common Errors in Scoring

- Calculating the raw score incorrectly
- Transferring the raw score to the front page of the record form incorrectly
- Adding the subtest standard scores incorrectly when calculating the sum for the composite scores
- Using the wrong tables for standard score conversions
- Misreading the norms tables—for example, using the wrong line or wrong column
- Subtraction errors in comparing composites and subtest scores
- Errors in conducting the error analysis—for example, totaling the error columns incorrectly

DON'T FORGET

Scoring Keys for the Brief Form Subtests

Brief Form Subtest	Scoring Keys
Reading Part 1	• Each correctly pronounced word is awarded 1 point. • To be correct, the word must be said as a connected, relatively smooth whole, with accent properly placed. • Multiple pronunciations are not penalized as long as the final pronunciation is correct. • Be aware that some words have multiple correct pronunciations. • Although there is no error analysis in the Brief Form, examiners should still carefully record incorrect responses as part of their qualitative observations.
Reading Part 2	• Each correct response is awarded 1 point. • Parts of some responses may be optional and not required to earn credit (i.e., responses shown in parentheses in the manual). • Refer to the complete scoring rules on the easel when scoring. • Mispronunciations due to regional speech patterns are not penalized. • Total Reading score is based on the sum of correct scores for Parts 1 and 2 for children in 1–12th grades, but only includes Part 1 for children under first grade.
Math	• Each correct response is awarded 1 point. • Credit can be given even if a response is not reduced to the lowest terms. • Units of measurement are not required to credit a correct response. • Total score is based on the total number of correct items (any nonadministered items before the basal are also given credit).
Writing	• Items are scored 1 point for each scoring criteria correctly met (i.e., some items have more than one scoring criteria, such as "correctly spelled" and "no punctuation errors." • Specific scoring criteria are listed in the easel and in the record form. • Calculate the raw score by totaling the number of points earned in the item set and using the table on page 8 of the record form to convert that point total to the raw score.

lists some common errors in scoring. Scoring keys for each of the Comprehensive Form subtests are listed in the following pages, and scoring keys for the Brief Form subtests are listed in the Don't Forget insert.

Phonological Awareness

Children should not be penalized for articulation errors or for variations in speech due to regional speech patterns. In Sample A and items 1 through 4, children's responses should be scored as correct if they rhyme with the stimulus word, even if they are nonsense words (e.g., if a child says "*jook* rhymes with *book*"). The Phonological Awareness total raw score is the sum of scores from sections 1 through 6 (the Long form) for kindergartners, but is the sum for only sections 1, 4, and 5 (the Short form) for children in first grade and above. However, the Long form can also be administered and scored for students in first grade and above if deemed clinically necessary.

Letter and Word Recognition

Similar to proper administration of this subtest, the key to properly scoring Letter and Word Recognition is having knowledge of the proper pronunciation of all the stimulus words. You need to be proficient in recording a response phonetically (either with the phonetic key or sound-by-sound). A bright child or adolescent may rapidly read the six words listed on a stimulus page, and if you struggle with how to record what they say, you will undoubtedly run into trouble with scoring.

Note that some words have multiple correct pronunciations (e.g., items 72, 74, 85, 88, and 95 of Form A), and the various pronunciations are listed on both the record form and the easel. Sometimes examinees will sound out a word two or three times (perhaps incorrectly) before they read it smoothly as their final response. Give credit to children for their final response if it is correctly pronounced in a relatively smooth manner, with the accent properly placed. However, if a child's regional speech pattern leads to a different pronunciation, give credit for an item if it is the region's common pronunciation. For example, reading "car" with a Bostonian accent of "caw." To calculate the raw score, subtract the number of errors (0 scores) from the ceiling item. An error analysis may be conducted after the test is administered.

Math Concepts and Applications

Some Math Concepts and Applications items have multiple questions, and to give credit, examinees must answer all parts of the question correctly (e.g., items 27 and 28 on Form A). Some items have multiple ways that the child can correctly respond (e.g., 3/5 or 60% or 0.6). Note that the record form only lists one of the correct responses, but the manual lists all the possible correct ways of responding. Some items are problems requiring calculations with units of measure (e.g., inches, feet, pounds). In most instances, children are not required to include the unit of measurement in their response. For such items, the fact that the unit of measurement is optional is indicated on the record form by being printed in parentheses. To calculate the raw score, subtract the number of errors (0 scores) from the ceiling item. An error analysis may be conducted after the test is administered.

Nonsense Word Decoding

Scoring for this subtest is very similar to that of Letter and Word Recognition. Correct recording of the examinee's responses is crucial if you intend to complete a detailed error analysis. Each item is scored 1 point for a correct response and 0 points for an incorrect response. Six of the 50 items have more than one correct pronunciation, and all of these correct pronunciations are listed on both the record form and in the easel. Children should not be penalized for misplacing the accent of a word or if they have articulation errors. Correct responses are those in which the child pronounces the word in a connected, relatively smooth whole (even if they must make several attempts before being able to finally pronounce the word in that manner). To calculate the raw score, subtract the number of errors (0 scores) from the ceiling item. An error analysis may be conducted after the test is administered.

Math Computation

Binary scoring is used for Math Computation, with 1 point given for correct responses and 0 points for incorrect responses. You should score examinees' responses as they finish each problem so that you know when to discontinue the subtest. As mentioned in the section of this text on administration, it is important to watch examinees as they write their responses, to ensure that you know which number is their final response and also to ensure that you can read their handwriting. When handwriting is unclear, you should ask examinees what their final written response is. Some items allow different versions of a number as a correct response. For example, a response reduced to the lowest terms is correct (e.g., 1½), but also an equivalent improper fraction is correct (3/2), or an equivalent decimal (1.5). Acceptable versions of a response are printed in the record form. To calculate the raw score, subtract the number of errors (0 scores) from the ceiling item. An error analysis may be conducted after the test is administered.

Reading Comprehension

Reading Comprehension is one of the few KTEA-II subtests that requires a bit of judgment in scoring. The first few items, which require a pointing response or have examinees follow a specific command, are easy to score as correct or not correct. Of the remaining items, just over one quarter are multiple-choice questions, which are also straightforward to score. The passage items that have open-ended questions generally are not difficult to score, as the easel has examples of correct and incorrect answers and the general criteria that is necessary for an item to be scored correctly. In most cases, the reasons behind the decisions regarding correct and incorrect responses are implicitly clear. However, for nine Reading Comprehension items, additional information is provided in Appendix C of the *KTEA-II Comprehensive Form Manual* regarding the explanation for scoring decisions. Additional examples of correct and incorrect responses are also provided in Appendix C of the *KTEA-II Comprehensive Form Manual* for these nine items.

To calculate the total raw score for Reading Comprehension, first compute the number of points obtained on the set (or last pair of adjacent sets) that the examinee took. Then you must use the conversion table on pages 12 and 13 of the record form to convert this point total to the raw score (see figure 3.5 for an example).

Written Expression

Thorough scoring must be completed after the test is administered. Detailed, item-by-item Written Expression scoring instructions are provided in Appendix E of the *KTEA-II Comprehensive Form Manual* (pp. 159–222). The one exception to scoring at the end of the test is for first grade students in the Spring: For these children, Level 2 must be preliminarily scored after item 23 to determine whether the rest of Level 2 should be administered. Each item of this subtest has one or more scoring categories, which is scored 1 or 0. The most common categories include task, sentence structure, capitalization, punctuation, grammar, and other mechanical errors. In addition to the specific error categories, you should familiarize yourself with the general scoring guidelines for Written Expression (see the Don't Forget box for a review of these).

Once you have scored each of the categories 1 or 0, then sum the total number of points obtained within the item set administered. This total number of points is then converted to a raw score, using a conversion table. The table that converts the total points earned at a particular level of the Written Expression subtest to the raw score is provided on pages 223–224 of the *KTEA-II Comprehensive Form Manual*. Some children will end up taking more than two sets of items; in such cases, use the last two sets administered for scoring purposes. An error analysis may be conducted after the test is administered.

6. Reading Comprehension

Range: Grades 1–12+

Basal: If starting at Set B, must pass first 3 items or drop back to item 1. If Starting at Set C or above, must pass at least 2 items in the first passage administered, or drop back one start point as needed.

Discontinue: at stop point (■) for set if there are at least 4 failures and 4 passes in a set or pair of sets; or after 5 consecutive failures

Note: Mark skill categories only for items within the set or pair of sets

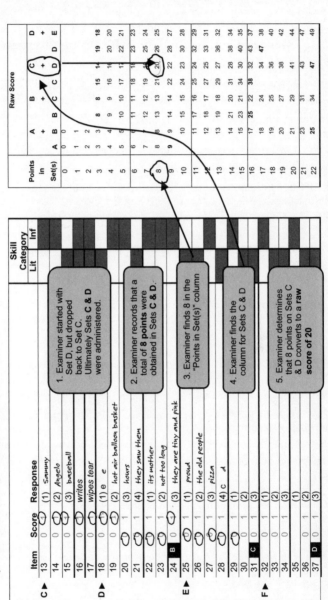

Figure 3.5 Example of how to convert the total number of points in an Item Set to the raw score on Reading Comprehension of the KTEA-II Comprehensive Form

DON'T FORGET

General Scoring Guidelines for Written Expression

Error categories are independent.

Score each error category independent of the others. Try not to let poor performance in one category influence the scores for other categories in that item.

Structure and grammar errors should be obvious.

Score 0 for sentence structure and word form (grammar) only if the error is obvious and would stand out in semiformal writing, such as a class paper.

Use judgment to choose best-fitting category.

Sometimes a response is clearly erroneous, but it is not immediately evident which category should be scored 0. In those instances, choose the category that in your judgment best fits the error. The overall subtest score will not be affected.

Most often, ignore extra writing.

If the task criterion specifies a limited product (e.g., one word or one sentence) and the student produces a response which partly satisfied this criterion, ignore any additional material the student has written when scoring the task criterion. However, if the task criterion is open-ended (e.g., "one or more sentences"), score according to the entire response. For the sentence structure criterion, scoring usually is based on the student's entire response, except when the scoring rule for an item specifies otherwise.

Give no credit for incomprehensible responses or no response.

If a student doesn't respond to an item, or if the response is incomprehensible (the meaning cannot be understood), score 0 on all categories for that item.

Give no credit for task criterion and sentence structure for misplaced sentence parts.

On later items, misplacement of a part of the sentence can cause failure on both the task criterion (because the sentence does not make sense or says something false) and the sentence structure criterion (because of the misplacement). In such cases, score 0 for both criteria.

If a word is recognizable it is phonetically readable.

"Phonetically readable," a term used in Level 2 and 3 scoring, is not a technical term; it means that the word is recognizable.

Try not to penalize for poor handwriting or poor spelling.

If a response is difficult to read due to poor spelling or poor handwriting, score as much of it as possible.

Note: From Appendix E of KTEA-II Comprehensive Form Manual (Kaufman & Kaufman, 2004a).

Spelling

Scoring for spelling is straightforward: score 1 for correctly spelled words and 0 for misspelled words. Poorly formed letters, capitalization, and mixing printing with handwriting are not penalized. The key to scoring Spelling is making sure that you know what the child intended to write during administration. Thus, as mentioned in the administration section, you must carefully watch children write their responses and ask them to name any letters that are unclear or ambiguous. To calculate the raw score, subtract the number of errors (0 scores) from the ceiling item. An error analysis may be conducted after the test is administered.

Listening Comprehension

The record form lists correct responses (that is, the most common correct responses). However, other correct responses are listed in the easel. For some items, specific criteria that a response must satisfy in order to be scored correct are listed (along with examples). Some responses have optional portions, which are shown in parentheses in the easel. When scoring, you should not penalize students for immature speech or articulation errors.

The total number of points for Listening Comprehension is based on the scores from administration of a complete item set or pair of adjacent tests. You should base the final score on the last two item sets administered. Once you have calculated the total points, use the conversion table on pages 20 and 21 of the record form to convert the point total to the raw score.

Oral Expression

Similar to Written Expression, the *KTEA-II Comprehensive Form Manual* provides detailed, item-by-item scoring instructions, which should be applied after the subtest is administered. However, you must give a preliminary score while the subtest is being administered to determine if the basal or discontinue rules have been met (preliminary scores are listed on the left side of the record form, just beside the item number). When you are unsure whether a preliminary item score should be 0 or 1, you should err on the side of caution and give the child credit. This procedure is less likely to lead you to prematurely discontinue the subtest.

The item-by-item scoring categories listed in Appendix F of the manual (pp. 225–257) are four-fold: task (pragmatics), sentence structure (syntax), word meaning (semantics), and word form (grammar). These categories are explained in depth and exemplified in the manual. General scoring guidelines are also provided and are summarized in the Don't Forget insert. Once scoring is completed, total the points in the item set (or last pair of adjacent item sets) taken by the examinee. Then use the conversion table on pages 258–259 of the *KTEA-II Com-*

DON'T FORGET

General Scoring Guidelines for Oral Expression

Error categories are independent.

Score each error category independently of the others. Try not to let poor performance in one category influence the scores for other categories in that item.

Base scoring on commonly heard speech.

Score 0 for sentence structure, word meaning, and word form (grammar) only if the error is obvious and would stand out in semiformal speech, such as speaking to the class.

Use judgment to choose best-fitting category.

Sometimes a response is clearly erroneous, but it is not immediately evident which category should be scored 0. In those instances, choose the category that in your judgment best fits the error. The overall subtest score will not be affected.

Give no credit for incomprehensible responses or no response.

If a student doesn't respond to an item, or if the response is incomprehensible (the meaning cannot be understood), score 0 on all categories for that item.

Do not penalize false starts, self-corrections, or interjections.

For example, give credit if a child says: "Before she went home—I want to go home—she went to the grocery store with her mom."

Most often, ignore extraneous words or sentences.

If the student says something that is not related to the task, but gives a correct response, ignore anything else he or she says.

Give no credit for task criterion and sentence structure for misplaced sentence parts.

On later items, misplacement of a part of the sentence can cause failure on both the task criterion (because the sentence does not make sense or says something false) and the sentence structure criterion (because of the misplacement). In such cases, score 0 for both criteria.

Do not penalize for articulation errors.

Note: From Appendix F of KTEA-II Comprehensive Form Manual (Kaufman & Kaufman, 2004a).

prehensive Form Manual to determine the raw score, based upon the total points in the set.

Word Recognition Fluency

Scoring for this subtest involves calculating the number of correct items read within the time limit. The scores are calculated in a slightly different manner for children who start with item 31, in contrast to those who start with item 1 (see the accompanying Don't Forget box). Children who reach the end of the card in less

DON'T FORGET

How to Calculate Word Recognition Fluency's Raw Score

If examinee started at item 1	If examinee started at item 31, but did not reach the end of the card in less than 60 seconds	If examinee started at item 31, reached the end of the card in less than 60 seconds, and has a total raw score of 83 or more
1. Subtract the number of errors (and skips) from the number of the last item reached to calculate the raw score.	1. Subtract the number of errors (or skips) from the last item number reached. 2. Subtract 6 from the result.	1. Subtract the number of errors (or skips) from the last item number reached. 2. Subtract 6 from the result. 3. Use the Completion Time table in the record form to determine how many extra points to add to the raw score.

than 1 minute and have a total raw score of 83 or greater will have extra points added to their total raw score at the end.

Decoding Fluency

The total raw score for Decoding Fluency is calculated by subtracting the number of errors (which includes the number of words skipped) from the number of the last item reached. However, if an examinee finishes reading all of the words in less than 60 seconds and has a total raw score of 45 or greater, add extra points to his or her score. The number of extra points to add is determined by referring to the Completion Time chart in the record form, which states how many extra points are awarded for various completion times. There are a maximum of 13 possible extra points for the fastest responses.

Associational Fluency

Scoring for the four associational fluency tasks (foods, noisy, /d/, /t/ or animals, toys, /k/, /m/) is based on the number of different responses spoken by the examinee in 30 seconds that meet the task demand. Appendix G of the *KTEA-II Comprehensive Form Manual* (pp. 261–263) lists the specific requirements for each of the Associational Fluency tasks. For all tasks, credit is not given for made-up words or words that were given as examples. Although words that are repetitions are not credited, you may give a child credit if he or she uses a homophone (words that sound the same but have different meanings, e.g., too, two, to; seem, seam). Total raw scores for children in Pre-K and kindergarten is based only on the sum of the two semantic fluency tasks, but the total raw scores for children in first grade and above are based on the sum of the two semantic fluency tasks plus the two phonemic fluency tasks.

Naming Facility

The raw score for each of the three Naming Facility tasks is based on the examinee's completion time as well as the number of errors that he or she makes. If an examinee makes more than three errors on a task, then you should not score that task. If a child makes two or fewer errors, then you should convert the examinee's completion time to a point score, using the table on the record form. The total raw score for Naming Facility for children in Pre-K and kindergarten is based only on the first two Naming Facility tasks; the total raw score for children in grades one and above is based on the sum of all three Naming Facility tasks.

Computer Scoring Procedures

The KTEA-II ASSIST computer scoring program offers an alternative to hand scoring the test. Raw scores can quickly be converted to derived scores with the

KTEA-II ASSIST. The software contains both Macintosh and Windows programs on one CD-ROM. The printout from the KTEA-II ASSIST includes a summary of student performance by composite or subtest, comparisons of skill areas or subtests for easy interpretation of results, achievement/ability comparisons, and error analysis for all standard subtests. It also offers additional information, including best practices instructional suggestions for designing Individualized Education Program (IEP) goals that match students' score information with remediation strategies, and lists of math problems or reading or spelling words similar to those that were difficult for the student. The KTEA-II ASSIST works on the same platform as the KABC-II ASSIST, so examinee information (e.g., name, date of birth, dates of testing) will be saved and can transfer from one program to the next.

HOW TO INTERPRET THE KTEA-II

Once you have completed administration and scoring you may begin a systematic system of interpreting the scores yielded from the KTEA-II. Because the KTEA-II Comprehensive Form yields so much information (14 possible subtest scores, four domain composites, four reading-related composites, and a Comprehensive Achievement Composite), examiners need to methodically employ an efficient process of interpretation to glean the most from the data. In this section of the book, we provide readers with such a systematic method.

Introduction to Interpretation

A child's or adolescent's reason for referral typically dictates the battery of tests administered during an assessment. In the case of the KTEA-II, either the full battery may be administered or a partial battery may be administered to answer a question about a particular area of academic functioning. We present an approach to interpreting the comprehensive battery of the KTEA-II as well as an alternative approach if only part of the KTEA-II Comprehensive Form is administered. The interpretive approaches advocated in this book begin at the global level, by looking at the Comprehensive Achievement Composite (CAC) and domain composites, then moving to subtests, and finally looking at specific patterns of errors. One goal of KTEA-II interpretation is to identify and promote understanding of the student's strong and weak areas of academic functioning, from both a *normative* (age-based or grade-based) and *ipsative* (person-based) perspective. Similar to interpretive approaches presented for various cognitive instruments, such as the KABC-II (Kaufman, Lichtenberger, Fletcher-Janzen, & Kaufman, 2005) and the

WISC-IV (Flanagan & Kaufman, 2004), we support the notion of backing interpretive hypotheses with multiple pieces of supportive data. Such supportive data may be in the form of multiple test scores, behavioral observations, teacher reports, school records, or parent reports. In other words, test scores are not interpreted in isolation.

Interpretation of the complete KTEA-II Comprehensive Form involves five steps:

1. Interpret the Comprehensive Achievement Composite.
2. Interpret domain composites and subtest scores.
3. Identify domain composite strengths and weaknesses.
4. Identify subtest strengths and weaknesses.
5. Determine the significance and unusualness of planned comparisons.

When you administer only portions of the KTEA-II Comprehensive Form, you may conduct an abbreviated interpretation, as the CAC and some domain composites will not be available for the interpretive analyses. In the abbreviated interpretation of a partial battery you will conduct only two of the steps listed earlier.

2. Interpret the domain composite scores and subtest scores obtained.
5. Determine the significance and unusualness of planned comparisons.

Interpretation of the KTEA-II Brief Form is analogous to what we describe for interpreting a partial KTEA-II Comprehensive Form battery. The KTEA-II Brief Form was designed to be a screening instrument that can determine when further, more comprehensive assessment is necessary; therefore, the level of interpretation is not as in-depth as it is with the Comprehensive form (i.e., no error analysis is available on the KTEA-II Brief Form). There are two steps to interpreting the Brief Form: (1) interpret the Brief Achievement Composite, and (2) compare subtest standard scores. Readers are directed to Step 1 for interpreting the Achievement Composite for both the Brief and Comprehensive forms. For information on how to conduct a comparison of subtest scores in the Brief Form, readers are directed to Step 5, following.

The data and calculations needed to conduct each of the interpretive steps outlined in this chapter are recorded on the KTEA-II record form. For the Comprehensive Form, the data for Steps 1 and 2 are recorded on pages 1 and 3 of the record form. The data for Steps 3 and 4 are recorded on page 3 of the record form, and the data for Step 5 are recorded on the back page of the record form. All data for the Brief Form are recorded on the front cover of the record form.

After either the interpretation of the complete or partial KTEA-II Comprehensive Form battery, examiners may wish to obtain more detailed information by analyzing an examinee's errors. The final section on interpretation details a process of error analysis for each KTEA-II subtest.

Step 1. Interpret the Comprehensive Achievement Composite (CAC)

The CAC is composed of four subtests for preschoolers and kindergarteners and six subtests for students in grades 1 and above. The CAC subtests for these two groups are shown earlier in this chapter in Figure 3.1. If a partial KTEA-II battery is administered, and all four or six of the subtests that comprise the CAC are not obtained, then the CAC cannot be calculated, and this interpretive step can be skipped. The function of the CAC and the Brief Achievement Composite (BAC) on the Brief Form is to provide a global overview of a student's academic achievement across four domains: reading, math, written language, and oral language. The CAC standard score is also used in later interpretive steps, as it represents a student's average academic ability or the midpoint of all their academic skills. Thus, in the later interpretive steps, the CAC is the basis of comparison for determining the student's relatively strong and weak areas of achievement.

When interpreting the CAC or BAC in written reports, you should report the CAC or BAC standard score, the confidence interval, percentile rank, and descriptive category. If the BAC's or CAC's confidence interval spans more than one descriptive category, we suggest reporting the descriptive category as a range (e.g., if the confidence interval is 111 to 119, then write in the report: "Eliza's CAC was in the Average to Above Average range of academic functioning.").

In addition to reporting the CAC standard score, the confidence interval, percentile rank, and descriptive category, you should report whether the CAC is a Normative Strength or Normative Weakness. A Normative Strength (*NStr*) is defined as a standard score that is greater than 115 and a Normative Weakness (*NWk*) is defined as a standard score that is lower than 85. Thus, Normative Strengths and Weaknesses are those scores that fall outside of the Average range of academic functioning. Page 3 of the KTEA-II Comprehensive Record Form has a place to record whether the CAC is a Normative Strength or Normative Weakness by circling the appropriate abbreviation (See Figure 3.6).

Some children's CAC (or BAC) standard scores are composed of scores that vary widely across the four academic domains. In such cases, the CAC should be interpreted with an appropriate explanation. For example:

Tomás earned Reading Comprehension and Letter Word Recognition standard scores of 74 and 75, respectively, but also earned much higher Math

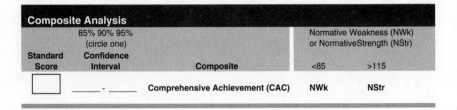

Figure 3.6 Analysis of Comprehensive Achievement Composite

Note: Excerpt from p. 3 of the *KTEA-II Comprehensive Form* Record Form that can be used to record data for interpretive Step 1.

Computation and Math Concepts and Applications standard scores of 124 and 125, respectively. His CAC standard score was 100, which represents the midpoint of very diverse abilities. Because of the variability in the scores that comprise Tomás' CAC score, a more meaningful understanding of his diverse academic abilities can be obtained by examining his performance on the separate academic domain composites.

Thus, the examiner's written report will communicate that although Tomás earned a CAC in the Average range, his academic skills are highly variable, ranging from Below Average to Above Average. The report will then go on to focus on those separate academic domains, as the Average CAC does not provide as much useful and meaningful information as does his scores on the separate academic domains.

Step 2. Interpret the Domain Composite Scores and Subtest Scores

In the second interpretive step, a procedure similar to that of Step 1 is followed for interpreting the domain composite scores and the subtest scores. Step 2 is conducted whether a complete or partial KTEA-II battery was administered. For whichever subtests were administered, report the standard score, the confidence interval, and percentile rank. We do not recommend reporting the descriptive categories for each of the subtests, as that amount of information (scores plus descriptive categories) is a bit overwhelming and unnecessary. However, we do recommend reporting the descriptive categories for the four domain composites and four reading-related composites, in addition to the standard scores, the confidence intervals, and percentile ranks.

The final part of Step 2 for each composite and subtest is to determine whether each is a Normative Strength or Normative Weakness. Like interpretation of the CAC, you can circle NWk (scores < 85) and NStr (scores > 115) on page 3 of the record form, to indicate the Normative Weaknesses and Strengths (see Figure 3.7).

Step 3. Identify Domain Composite Strengths and Weaknesses

In Steps 1 and 2 you compare the examinee's abilities to that of the normative group (i.e., determining Normative Strengths and Weaknesses), but in Step 3 you compare the examinee's abilities to his or her own average level of academic performance (i.e., determining Personal Strengths and Weaknesses). The CAC standard score is used as the value that represents a student's average level of performance, which is compared to the student's performance on the separate domain composites (Rapid Reference 3.7 gives the rationale for using the CAC to represent the student's average level of performance). Thus, for each of the four domain composites (Reading, Math, Written Language, and Oral Language) and the four reading-related composites (Sound Symbol, Oral Fluency, Decoding, and Reading Fluency), subtract the domain composite standard score from the CAC standard score. Then record this difference on page 3 of the record form in the column labeled "Diff. from CAC." A student's domain composite that is significantly higher than the CAC is labeled a Personal Strength (*PStr*) and a domain composite that is significantly lower than the CAC is labeled a Personal Weakness (*PWk*). Tables in the *KTEA-II Comprehensive Form Manual* provide the specific difference values necessary to be considered significant at the .05 level (refer to the "Significance" column of Table I.1 for grade norms or Table I.3 for age norms). If the difference between the CAC and a domain composite is equal to or greater than the value indicated in the table then that composite is deemed significantly different. A significant difference in which the domain composite is greater than the CAC is a Personal Strength and a significant difference in which the domain composite is less than the CAC is a Personal Weakness.

After determining which composites are Personal Strengths and Personal Weaknesses, you must determine how usual the difference is in the norm sample. If the value of the difference is unusually large (occurring in fewer than 10 percent of the norm sample cases), then you should check the box in the column labeled "Infrequent" on page 3 of the record form. To determine whether a discrepancy is unusually large, refer to the "Frequency" column of Table I.1 or Table I.3 of the *KTEA-II Comprehensive Form Manual*.

Personal Strengths or Weaknesses that are also "Infrequent" and a Normative Strength or Weakness are especially noteworthy and demand special attention when translating scores for diagnostic and educational considerations. Per-

Composite Analysis

Standard Score	Confidence Interval (85% 90% 95% circle one)	Composite	Normative Weakness (NWk) or Normative Strength (NStr)		Personal Weakness (PWk) or Personal Strength (PStr)			
			<85	>115	Diff. from CAC	Sig. (p<.05)		Infrequent (<10%)
☐	__ - __	Comprehensive Achievement (CAC)	NWk	NStr				
☐	__ - __	Reading	NWk	NStr	___	PWk	PStr	☐
☐	__ - __	Math	NWk	NStr	___	PWk	PStr	☐
☐	__ - __	Written Language	NWk	NStr	___	PWk	PStr	☐
☐	__ - __	Oral Language	NWk	NStr		PWk	PStr	☐
☐	__ - __	Sound Symbol	NWk	NStr	___	PWk	PStr	☐
☐	__ - __	Decoding	NWk	NStr		PWk	PStr	☐
☐	__ - __	Reading Fluency	NWk	NStr	___	PWk	PStr	☐
☐	__ - __	Oral Fluency	NWk	NStr		PWk	PStr	☐

Figure 3.7 Analysis of Domain Composites

Note: Excerpt from p. 3 of the KTEA-II Comprehensive Form Record Form that can be used to record data for interpretive Steps 3 and 4.

≋Rapid Reference 3.7

Rationale for Using CAC as Student's Average Level of Performance

Interpretive Steps 3 and 4 suggest using the CAC as the midpoint or average level of student's academic performance when conducting comparisons with specific academic skill areas. This procedure is slightly different than that suggested in the previous version of the K-TEA, which compared subtest scores to the mean score on all subtests. By using the CAC rather than the mean of the subtests administered, examiners are not burdened with having to calculate the mean composite or mean subtest scores. The CAC includes one or two subtests from each of the academic domains, and it serves as an appropriate reference point for evaluating a broad range of individual composites and subtests.

Note: This explanation is adapted from pages 30–31 of the KTEA-II Comprehensive Form Manual (Kaufman & Kaufman, 2004a). Further detail regarding the technical procedures used in the interpretive procedures can also be found on pages 30–31 of the manual.

sonal Strengths and Weaknesses, by definition, are scores that are significantly different from a student's CAC; that is, the differences are very unlikely to have occurred by chance. Some significant differences may be quite common in the population. Thus, these significant differences, in and of themselves, may not be of particular clinical interest. However, if a difference is so large that it rarely occurs in the population (i.e., it is "Infrequent"), then it is usually worth investigating further.

Step 4. Identify Subtest Strengths and Weaknesses

Step 4 is similar to Step 3 in that you are comparing a student's performance to his or her own average level of performance. However, Step 3 determined Personal Strengths and Weaknesses for domain composites—Step 4 determines them for subtest scores. To identify subtest strengths and weaknesses, follow the same procedure outlined in Step 3: Subtract each subtest standard score from the CAC standard score. Record the absolute difference between the scores on page 3 of the record form in the appropriate blank under "Diff. from CAC." Then refer to Table I.2 (grade norms) or I.4 (age norms) in Appendix I of the *KTEA-II Comprehensive Form Manual* to determine whether each difference is statistically significant at the .05 level. If a difference is large enough to be considered significant and the subtest score is higher than the CAC score, then that subtest is a Personal Strength (circle *PStr* on the record form). If a difference is large enough to be considered significant and the subtest score is lower than the CAC score, then that subtest is a Personal Weakness (circle *PWk* on the record form).

If a difference is statistically significant (deeming a subtest a Personal Strength or Personal Weakness), then determine how unusual it is in the norm sample. Refer to the columns labeled "Frequency" in Table I.2 (grade norms) or Table I.4 (age norms) in Appendix I of the *KTEA-II Comprehensive Form Manual.* If the value of the difference occurs in fewer than 10 percent of the norm sample cases, put a checkmark on page 3 of the record form in the "Infrequent" column. The subtests that are both a Personal Strength or Weakness and are labeled "Infrequent" are worthy of further investigation, as they may provide useful diagnostic information or information related to educational considerations.

Step 5. Determine the Significance and Unusualness of Planned Comparisons

Step 5 is useful for evaluating hypotheses about specific strong and weak areas of achievement or for evaluating a comparison between particular academic or reading-related skills. At times, specific planned comparisons of composites or subtests may provide useful information for diagnosis or instructional planning.

On the Comprehensive Form, there are numerous planned comparisons that can be made depending on the examiners needs. However, the test authors recommend routinely making at least two comparisons in the Comprehensive Form:

DON'T FORGET

What Can be Learned from the Expression and Comprehension Comparisons?

Oral Expression vs. Written Expression	Reading Comprehension vs. Listening Comprehension
These two expression subtests both require students to use expressive language in realistic situations. Both subtests are scored along similar dimensions: task (pragmatics), sentence structure (syntax), and word form (grammar). Thus, the comparison between these tasks may point to a particular difficulty in either written or spoken expression.	These two comprehension tasks both assess the literal and inferential comprehension of connected text (particularly the passage-reading tasks of Reading Comprehension and Listening Comprehension). Thus, the comparison between these subtests may help identify a problem specific to reading (that is distinct from a more general language problem).

(1) Oral Expression subtest with Written Expression subtest, and (2) Reading Comprehension subtest with Listening Comprehension subtest. The Don't Forget box reminds readers what can be learned from these expression and comprehension comparisons.

On the KTEA-II Brief Form, there are three subtest comparisons to make: (1) Reading versus Math, (2) Reading versus Writing, and (3) Math versus Writing. These three comparisons should be routinely made to discover if there are any relative academic strengths or weaknesses.

The methods for evaluating planned comparisons between composites or subtests is very similar to those employed in Steps 3 and 4. Once you have determined which comparisons you would like to make, follow the substeps of Step 5 as outlined in Rapid Reference 3.8. Calculate the difference between the scores, then determine the significance and frequency of that difference. The back page of the KTEA-II Comprehensive Form record form and the front page of the KTEA-II Brief Form have places to record the data for these planned comparisons.

≋ Rapid Reference 3.8

Substeps of Interpretive Step 5

A. Record the standard scores for the two composites or subtests of each comparison in the appropriate boxes of the back page of the KTEA-II Comprehensive Record Form or the front page of the KTEA-II Brief Form Record Form.

B. Record the absolute value of the difference between them in the space between the boxes.

C. Determine whether the difference is statistically significant by referring to the appropriate table (I.5 through I.8 in Appendix I of the *KTEA-II Comprehensive Form Manual*, or Tables C.14 and C.15 of the *KTEA-II Brief Form Manual*). Find the column for the smallest significance level in which the observed difference computed in Step B is equal to or greater than the value in the table, and circle the appropriate number (.05 or .01) on the record form. Then draw a circle around the name of the composite or subtest having the higher score.

D. If the difference is statistically significant, refer again to the appropriate table in the manual (Table I.5, I.6, I.7 or I.8 in Appendix I of the *KTEA-II Comprehensive Form Manual* or Table C.16 and C.17 of the *KTEA-II Brief Form Manual*) to see whether the difference is also unusually large, meaning that it occurred infrequently in the norm sample. Find the column for the smallest percentage frequency in which the observed difference (computed in Step B) is equal to or greater than the value in the table, and circle the appropriate number (15%, 10%, or 5%) on the record form.

Clinical Analysis of Errors

The KTEA-II authors believe that understanding test performance by studying students' incorrect responses is a profitable method of helping students' progress, and that efforts to objectify and substantiate the value of various error analysis methods should be intensified (Kaufman & Kaufman, 2004a). Many good teachers intuitively apply error analysis skills in their everyday teaching. In today's schools, however, where psychologists, educational diagnosticians, special educators, and classroom teachers exchange information about students, a more formal, systematic approach to error analysis, using a common language, is necessary for effective communication of information about students' academic functioning and teachers' instructional strategies (Kaufman & Kaufman, 2004a).

During development of the original K-TEA Comprehensive Form and its revision, the KTEA-II, the authors were aided by curriculum experts in reading, mathematics, spelling, writing, and oral language in defining the specific skills making up each subtest and examining the types of errors students are likely to make on subtest items. Based on the recommendations of these experts, a review of the literature on instructional theory and practice, discussions with many practicing school psychologists and educational diagnosticians, and the actual errors made by students participating in the standardization programs, the KTEA-II error analysis method was developed (Kaufman & Kaufman, 2004a). It is built on the method used with the original K-TEA, but for some subtests it has been enhanced to provide a greater amount of detail. This procedure uses information documented on the record form during KTEA-II administration to identify specific areas in which the student demonstrates strong, weak, or average skill development as defined by the performance of the standardization sample.

The error analysis procedures provide examiners with more specific information about a student's performance than can be obtained from composite or subtest standard scores or comparisons. Some uses for the error analysis data are described by Kaufman and Kaufman (2004a) as follows:

- Obtaining a more precise level of diagnostic information than subtest standard scores.
- Determining the concentration of skill problems.
- Determining the location of weak skills on a skill continuum.
- Gauging the severity of skill deficiencies.
- Identifying common sources of difficulty underlying several skill areas.
- Integrating results from multiple subtests, to help substantiate hypotheses about the sources of skill difficulties.
- Error analyses are a valuable part of the interpretive process.

Thus, the KTEA-II Comprehensive Form offers detailed information beyond the examinee's subtest and composite scores that can provide important and specific information that becomes a basis for intervention. The details about a child's skills come from a system for analyzing specific errors made on 10 of the KTEA-II's 14 subtests. The system of error analysis determines both strong and weak skill areas across global skills (such as reading and math) and more specific skills (such as Math Computation and Math Concepts and Applications).

The KTEA-II Comprehensive Form error analysis uses norm-referenced methodology to determine a child's relative mastery of specific skills, which can then lead to effective remediation of skill deficiencies. Each student's performance on certain skills is labeled "strong," "average," or "weak," compared with other students in the same grade level. The Don't Forget box explains how each of these levels of skill status are defined and what the implications are for each.

There are two basic types of error classification methods: item-level error clas-

DON'T FORGET

Skill Status Defined According to Average Number of Errors

Skill Status Category	Definition	Implications for Obtaining Each Level of Skill Status
Strong	Average number of errors made by the top 25 percent of the national grade-level reference group.	A student's skill acquisition is considerably above that of typical students at that grade level. These areas require less instructional attention and may be used to teach to the student's strengths.
Average	Average number of errors made by middle 50 percent of the national grade-level reference group (i.e., those between the 25th and 75th percentiles).	The student has demonstrated acquisition of that skill to a degree typical for pupils at that grade level. These areas require less instructional attention and may be used to teach to the student's strengths.
Weak	Average number of errors made by the bottom 25 percent of the national grade-level reference group.	The student has a possible deficiency in that skill area and further diagnostic evaluation is warranted. Appropriate remediation strategies may be needed to help the student with the deficiency.

sification and within-item classification. In the item-level error classification, each item is classified according to the process, concept, or skill that it assesses. If an item is incorrect, the error type is automatically assigned. For example, each of the Reading Comprehension and Listening Comprehension items are classified as either literal or inferential. Thus, if a student's response to Reading Comprehension item 13 is incorrect, it is automatically classified as a literal error, whereas an incorrect response to item 15 is automatically counted as an inferential error. Other item-level classifications are conducted on Written Expression items, which are classified in the following categories: task, structure, word form, capitalization, and punctuation. Oral Expression items are classified along similar categories: task, sentence structure, word meaning, and word form. In contrast to item-level classification's automatic error assignment, within-item classification requires judgment on the part of the examiner to determine the error type. That is, the specific details of the student's response will lead examiners to select which of many types of errors the examinee made. For example, on Letter and Word Decoding, examiners must examine the incorrect pronunciation of a word to determine if an

DON'T FORGET

Types of Error Analysis Methods for KTEA-II Subtests

Subtests Using Item-Level Error Classification	Subtests Using Within-Item[a] Error Classification
Reading Comprehension	Math Computation
Listening Comprehension	Letter and Word Recognition
Written Expression	Nonsense Word Decoding
Oral Expression	Spelling
Phonological Awareness	
Math Concepts and Applications	
Math Computation	

Note: Subtests with errors categorized according to item-level error classifications are automatically assigned an error category when an item is incorrect. Subtests with errors categorized according to within-item error classification are assigned an error category or categories according to the examiner's qualitative analysis of the student's incorrect response.

[a]Because within-item error analysis has a large number of error categories, the grids for classifying and counting errors on these four subtests are too large to be included in the record form. Thus, a separate Error Analysis Booklet contains the worksheets for tabulation errors on these subtests.

CAUTION

When to Conduct Error Analyses

Error analysis should be done after the *entire* assessment is complete.

error was made in categories such as: short vowel, long vowel, silent letter, prefix, suffix, and so forth. Multiple-error categories may be marked in the within-item classification. The Don't Forget insert lists the types of error analysis that are used for the KTEA-II subtests.

General Procedures for Using the Error Analysis System

The error analysis system differs according to whether the subtest is being analyzed by item-level classification or by within-item classification. However, there are some general procedures that should be followed in any of the error analysis methods. Rapid Reference 3.9 lists the general procedures for conducting error analysis. The Caution box reminds examiners about when the appropriate time is to conduct the error analysis. In the next several Rapid References (3.10–3.15), specific information about conducting error analysis for each of the subtests is outlined. These Rapid References are grouped according to subtests which have similar error analysis procedures.

Error Analysis in Reading Comprehension and Listening Comprehension

Reading comprehension can be defined as the process of deriving meaning from text by reflecting on what is read. On the KTEA-II, items from Reading Comprehension and Listening Comprehension are divided into literal and inferential comprehension. Literal comprehension requires recognizing or recalling ideas, information, or events that are explicitly stated in an oral or written text. In contrast, inferential comprehension requires the generation of new ideas from those stated in the text. Students derive inferences from relating different concepts presented in the text or by combining information with previously acquired knowledge. Sometimes inferences require students to evaluate the writer's or speaker's viewpoint. Literal questions do not require the student to go beyond the viewpoints of the writer or speaker, and are usually paraphrased portions of the text. The questions asked on the KTEA-II Reading Comprehension subtest (except for the simple command items) and the Listening Comprehension subtest either demand literal comprehension or inferential comprehension, and errors on the items are categorized accordingly.

Error Analysis in Written Expression and Oral Expression

Students are required to communicate their ideas in words for both KTEA-II's Written Expression and Oral Expression subtests. The skills needed to commu-

≡ *Rapid Reference 3.9*

General Procedures for Using the Error Analysis System

1. After test administration, place one or more check marks in the appropriate error category column for each item answered incorrectly.

   a. For *item-level error analysis*, make a mark in every column with an open (unshaded) box if an item was incorrectly answered.

   b. For *within-level error analysis*, make a mark in the open (unshaded) boxes in columns that apply to the student's incorrect responses.

2. After error categories have been checked for all failed items, sum the number of checks in each column, and record the total number for each category.

3. Transfer the error totals for the ten subtests to pages 28 and 29 of the *KTEA-II Comprehensive Record Form* under the column labeled "Student's # of Errors."

4. Refer to the error analysis norm tables in Appendix K of the *KTEA-II Comprehensive Form Manual* and record the following on the record form:

   a. The number of items that the examinee attempted. Calculate this number by counting the number of white boxes in the column between item 1 and the discontinue point, even if the examinee was not administered all of the earliest items.

   b. The "Average Number of Errors" for each error category made by students in the norm sample, who are in the same grade and who attempted the same item.[a]

   c. If the examinee made more than the "Average Number of Errors" then mark that error category as a weakness (circle *W*) on the record form.

   d. If the examinee made fewer than the "Average Number of Errors" then mark that error category as a strength (circle *S*) on the record form.

   e. If the number of errors made by the examinee was equal to or within the range of the "Average Number of Errors" then mark that error category as average (circle *A*) on the record form.

Note: The four subtests analyzed by within-level error categorizations are Letter and Word Recognition, Nonsense Word Decoding, Math Computation, and Spelling.

[a] In the norms tables, the "average" is defined as the number of errors made by the middle 50% of students.

nicate orally are similar to those needed to communicate in written form. However, oral communication is typically more spontaneous and natural, whereas writing is more deliberate and structured. Difficulty in both oral and written communication can be caused by a variety of errors, which the error analysis procedures attempt to quantify.

To quantify students' communication ability, the error analysis examines several aspects of communication.

≡Rapid Reference 3.10

Using the Error Analysis System for Reading Comprehension and Listening Comprehension

	Reading Comprehension	Listening Comprehension
Where error analysis is recorded	Record form pp. 12–13 and summarized on p. 28	Record form pp. 20–21 and summarized on p. 28
Types of errors recorded	Either literal or inferential	
Items for which errors are recorded	Error analysis is based on the set, or pair of adjacent sets, used for scoring the case	

≡Rapid Reference 3.11

Using the Error Analysis System for Written Expression and Oral Expression

	Written Expression	Oral Expression
Where error analysis is recorded	Record form pp. 14–18 and summarized on p. 29	Record form pp. 22–25 and summarized on p. 29
Types of errors recorded	Task Structure Word Form Capitalization (Written only) Punctuation (Written only) Word Meaning (Oral only)	
Items for which errors are recorded	Error analysis is based on a level (or booklet) administered	Error analysis is based on the set, or pair of adjacent sets, used for scoring the case

- How well the writing or speech adheres to the task demands, to communicate in a comprehensible and functional manner (pragmatics)
- How well-constructed the student's sentences are (syntax)
- Appropriateness of the word forms (grammar)
- Correct use of words (semantics)
- Mechanics (capitalization and punctuation for written expression)

When contrasting the errors made in Written Expression with those from Oral Expression, examiners can differentiate language structure problems from writing problems. Some children have deficits in their basic knowledge of language (which will likely be evident in errors on both tests), but some children with intact Oral language skills may have strong language structure, yet have deficits in their Written Expression.

Error Analysis in Phonological Awareness

The particular aspects of sound awareness and manipulation that a student has or has not mastered will be evident in the errors that are made on the Phonological Awareness subtest. The development of skills tapped in this subtest (rhyming, sound matching, blending, segmenting, and deleting sounds) are important precursors to reading. Teachers can use information about deficits in certain areas of phonological awareness when trying to teach early reading skills.

Phonological Awareness involves skills that allow students to manipulate phonemes heard in spoken language. Children with poor phonological awareness may be unable to identify sounds in words, manipulate sounds in words, perceive a word as a sequence of sounds, or isolate beginning, medial, or final sounds.

≡ Rapid Reference 3.12

Using the Error Analysis System for Phonological Awareness

	Phonological Awareness
Where error analysis is recorded	Record form p. 5 and summarized on p. 29
Types of errors recorded	Rhyming, sound matching, blending, segmenting, and deleting sounds
Items for which errors are recorded	Error analysis is based on the sections administered (sections 1–5 for kindergarten and sections 1, 4, and 5 for Grades 1+)

These subskills are assessed by the error analysis, which is divided into either three or five skills, depending on the child's grade. Error analysis of the kindergarten form of Phonological Awareness (the long form) contains five task categories: rhyming, sound matching, blending, segmenting, and deleting sounds. For grades 1 through 6, errors are analyzed for a short form, containing rhyming, segmenting, and deleting sounds.

Error Analysis in Math Concepts and Applications

This subtest contains two related sets of abilities: concepts and applications. Concepts are the basic ideas and relationships on which the system of mathematics is built. Acquisition of math concepts is hierarchical, which requires students to master basic concepts before more advanced concepts can be learned. Applications involve using these concepts and skills to solve actual and hypothetical problems (e.g., reading graphs, balancing a checkbook). If a child has not yet mastered a certain concept or skill, he or she will not be able to apply that concept to solve an actual or hypothetical problem.

Each Math Concepts and Applications item is associated with one primary skill. Thus, if a child responds incorrectly to an item, in the error analysis that item is marked as an error in one of 15 categories. However, the final skill category (Word Problems) will be marked as an additional error along with one other error category. That is, on the six items that are word problems, children who re-

≡Rapid Reference 3.13

Using the Error Analysis System for Math Concepts and Applications

	Math Concepts and Applications
Where error analysis is recorded	Record form pp. 8–9 and summarized on p. 29
Types of errors recorded	Number concepts, addition, subtraction, multiplication, division, tables and graphs, time and money, geometry, measurement, fractions, decimals and percents, data investigation, advanced operations, multi-step problems, word problems
Items for which errors are recorded	Error analysis is based on all administered items until the ceiling is reached

spond incorrectly will have an error in Word Problems as well as one of the other 14 skill categories (such as addition, multiplication, division, etc.).

Error Analysis in Math Computation

The error analysis system for Math Computation gives information about nine skill areas (such as addition, multiplication, fractions) and about 10 specific processes (such as regrouping, converting to common denominators, or placing decimal points) in which the student has made errors. Useful information is gleaned from understanding a student's skill deficits, but even more instructionally relevant information may be revealed from the process errors that students make. Understanding the reason that a child missed an item (e.g., because they added when they should have subtracted or because they made an error when regrouping) can help determine how and where to provide additional remedial instruction for a child.

The first two error categories of the specific processes (listed under Within-Item Errors) are *Wrong Operation and Fact* or *Computation Error.* These two error categories can be applied to all items. However, if an error is better described by another type of error category, then the *Wrong Operation* category should not be marked. For example, if the child solves a problem involving division by a frac-

≡Rapid Reference 3.14

Using the Error Analysis System for Math Computation

	Math Computation
Where error analysis is recorded	Error Analysis booklet pp. 6–7 and summarized on Record Form p. 29
Types of errors recorded	*Item-level errors:* addition, subtraction, multiplication, division, fraction, decimal, exponent or root, algebra *Within-item errors:* wrong operation, fact or computation regrouping addition, regrouping subtraction, subtract smaller from larger, add or subtract numerator and denominator, equivalent fraction/common denominator, multiply/divide fraction, mixed number, incorrect sign
Items for which errors are recorded	Error analysis is based on all administered items until the ceiling is reached

tion by dividing the numerators and denominators instead of inverting and multiplying, then you should employ the *Multiply/Divide Fraction* category instead of the *Wrong Operation* category. Pages 44–45 of the *KTEA-II Comprehensive Form Manual* define and give examples of the within-item errors.

Error Analysis in Letter and Word Recognition, Nonsense Word Decoding, and Spelling

The decoding of words requires that students connect speech sounds to letter patterns. Three subtests tap this skill in slightly different ways. Letter and Word Recognition taps a student's ability to read words with unpredictable letter patterns. Nonsense Word Decoding assesses a students' ability to apply decoding and structural analysis skills to typically occurring letter patterns. Spelling requires students to relate speech sounds that they hear to letter patterns that they write.

The error analysis system for Letter and Word Recognition, Nonsense Word Decoding, and Spelling is made up of "categories corresponding to letters and letter combinations that have a predictable relationship to their sound. Errors involving unpredictable letter-sound relationships are qualitatively different from the other error categories, because by definition those errors are not generalizable to other words" (Kaufman & Kaufman, 2004a, p. 46). A separate error category is provided for words with unpredictable patterns, which gives a clearer indication of the student's problem areas in the decoding or spelling of predictable patterns.

The error analysis system is set up in such a way that words are divided into parts based on orthographically predictable patterns. The Don't Forget insert explains how words are divided with this system. Other error categories include those such as: incorrect initial or final sound or letter, wrong vowel, omitted or incorrectly inserted syllables, or, in Spelling, a nonphonetic misspelling. In the *KTEA-II Comprehensive Form Manual,* definitions and examples of the error categories for these three subtests are outlined, in Table 4.2 (Kaufman & Kaufman, 2004a, p. 48). Although the categories are very similar for Letter and Word Recognition, Nonsense Word Decoding, and Spelling, some differences do exist, which are articulated in the Caution box.

The last category in Letter and Word Recognition, Nonsense Word Decoding, and Spelling is *Whole Word Error.* Generally, if an examinee's response is significantly different from the stimulus word, it is usually better to mark the item as a *Whole Word Error* rather than trying to identify numerous, specific errors. There are several times when it is best to mark a student's response in the *Whole Word Error* category (Kaufman & Kaufman, 2004a, p. 50).

1. If the response contains more than four incorrect parts, don't try to identify them, but write *UN* (unclassifiable) in the *Whole Word Error* box.
2. If the response is a different word or a read word that approximates the stimulus word or nonsense word, use the word-parts error analysis grid for those errors that can be easily identified, and write *WS* (word substitution) in the *Whole Word Error* box. If the response contains more than four identifiable errors, follow guideline 1 above.
3. In Letter and Word Recognition, if the mispronunciation contains a misplaced accent, write *MPA* (misplaced accent) in the *Whole Word Error* box.

≣Rapid Reference 3.15

Using the Error Analysis System for Letter and Word Recognition, Nonsense Word Decoding, and Spelling

	Letter and Word Recognition	Nonsense Word Decoding	Spelling
Where error analysis is recorded	Error Analysis booklet pp. 2–3 and summarized on Record Form p. 28	Error Analysis booklet pp. 4–5 and summarized on Record Form p. 28	Error Analysis booklet p. 8 and summarized on Record Form p. 28
Types of errors recorded[a]	Single/double consonant, initial blend, consonant blend, medial/final blend, consonant digraph, wrong vowel, short vowel, long vowel, vowel team/diphthong, r-controlled vowel, silent letter, prefix/word beginning, suffix/inflection, prefix/word beginning and suffix inflection/hard or soft C, G, S, unpredictable pattern, initial/final sound, insertion/omission, nonphonetic, misordered sounds		
Items for which errors are recorded	Error analysis is based on all administered items until the ceiling is reached		

[a] Errors for these subtests are defined and exemplified on page 48 of the *KTEA-II Comprehensive Form Manual*. Some error categories are not scored for each of these subtests. Specifically, nonphonetic errors are only scored for the Spelling subtest, errors due to an unpredictable pattern are scored only for Letter and Word Recognition and Spelling only. Errors due to a wrong vowel and initial or final sounds are only scored in Letter and Word Recognition and Nonsense Word Decoding.

DON'T FORGET

Dividing Words into Parts Based on Orthographically Predictable Patterns for Error Analysis

Number of Syllables	How Words Are Divided	Example
One-syllable words	Divided into vowel and consonant parts	*what* is divided into: *wh* (consonant digraph) *a* (short vowel) *t* (single consonant)
Multisyllabic words	Divided into words with roots and affixes, with the affixes as whole words and the roots further divided into vowel and consonant parts	*roasted* is divided into: *r* (single consonant) *oa* (vowel team) *st* (medial/final consonant blend) *ed* (suffixes and inflections)

CAUTION

Differences between Skill Categories for Letter and Word Recognition, Nonsense Word Decoding, and Spelling

- All three subtests include a category for *Consonant Blends,* but in Nonsense Word Decoding and Spelling this category is divided into *Initial* and *Medial/Final* consonant blends because these subtests include a large number of instances of each subtype.

- Because the pseudowords in Nonsense Word Decoding were created to be decodable based on predictable patterns, error analysis for this subtest does not include the *Unpredictable* Pattern category.

- Spelling error analysis does not contain the *Wrong Vowel* category. Writing a wrong vowel is categorized as a short or a long vowel error.

- All three subtests include *Prefixes and Word Beginnings* and *Suffixes and Inflections* categories. They are merged into one category in Nonsense Word Decoding because that subtest has few prefixes.

- In Spelling, if a student inserts a grapheme (smaller than a syllable) that is not in the sound of the word, count this as a *silent letter* error.

Note: This information is adapted from the *KTEA-II Comprehensive Form Manual* (Kaufman & Kaufman, 2004a, p. 47).

4. If the student doesn't know or doesn't respond, write *NR* (no response) in the *Whole Word Error* box. If a student stops before finishing a set of items on the easel page, fill in the remaining items for that set with *NR*.

As we stressed in the administration and scoring sections, recording a student's exact responses is crucial for these subtests. In addition to being familiar with how to record student's responses phonetically, you should be familiar with the error categories before testing, as this will aid you during the error analysis.

USING THE KTEA-II COMPREHENSIVE FORM WITH THE KABC-II

Earlier in this chapter we described the relationship between the KTEA-II Comprehensive Form and the KABC-II that was revealed by the psychometric data. These data (see Table 3.5 in the section on validity) showed that moderate relationships between the two measures (KTEA-II CAC correlations of .74 to .80 with the KABC-II's global scores–the Fluid-Crystallized Index [FCI] and Mental Processing Index [MPI]), which are indicative of the concurrent validity of the tests. In practical terms, these data mean that you can interpret the two test batteries together and be confident that they relate to each other very well. In addition to examining correlational data, another quantitative method of understanding the relationship between the KABC-II and the KTEA-II can be gained by examining significant differences between standard scores on both batteries. One of the benefits of conorming an achievement battery with a measure of cognitive abilities is that it provides a basis for more accurate comparisons between achievement and ability.

Currently, many states and school districts require that a discrepancy between achievement and ability be documented in order to qualify for the diagnosis of a specific learning disability under the Education for All Handicapped Children Act of 1975 (P.L. 94-142) and the Individuals with Disabilities Education Act (IDEA) Amendments of 1997. However, changes are on the horizon for how learning disabilities are identified. On December 3, 2004, President Bush signed into law new IDEA reforms under the Individuals with Disabilities Education Improvement Act, making it officially known as P.L. 108-446. The signing marked the end of a 3-year IDEA reauthorization process and represented the first update to the nation's special education law in 7 years. The ramifications for P.L. 108-446 on learning disability identification, including the elimination of the IQ-achievement discrepancy requirement, are discussed in the Clinical Applications chapter of this book. Although the new law does not require the IQ-achievement discrepancy, it does not prohibit its use as a mechanism to identify children for services. States, in collaboration with local education agencies, will determine the criteria for determining a specific learning disability. Bearing these forthcoming changes in mind, in the following section we present the procedures for determining whether significant discrepancies exist between global cognitive ability and achievement for examiners who desire to use them.[1]

Calculating Significant Differences between KTEA-II and KABC-II Scores

The two primary methods of comparing ability with achievement are the simple-difference method and the regression (or predicted-score) method. In the former, a standard score from an ability test is compared with achievement standard scores, and the differences may be evaluated for statistical significance or unusualness. In the regression method, the correlation in the population between ability and achievement scores is used to calculate the expected (average) achievement standard score for students having a given ability score, and the individual student's actual achievement score is compared with this predicted value (Rapid Reference 3.16 outlines the steps for using the regression method). Both the simple-difference method and the regression method require that the achievement test be scored using age norms, because ability tests typically do not provide grade norms. Interpretive tables for both methods are provided in the *KTEA-II Comprehensive Form Manual* (Appendix I, Kaufman & Kaufman, 2004a), although we prefer the regression approach to the simple difference method because it has a stronger psychometric rationale.

STRENGTHS AND WEAKNESSES OF THE KTEA-II

The KTEA-II has several major strengths: it has an extended age range, from 4:6 to age 25; it has two parallel, independent forms; it measures achievement in the seven specific learning disability areas identified in IDEA (IDEA, 1997) and P.L. 108-446; and its content was developed with the help of curriculum experts, so that the errors on the test reveal direction for instructional intervention. The emphasis on reading, with four new reading-related composites, allows examiners to adequately assess one of the top referral concerns for students, and the extensive, norm-based error analysis system provides insight into numerous, specific skill

---

[1] Typically, achievement-ability discrepancy analyses are not conducted when administering a screening measure like the KTEA-II Brief Form. Such analyses are more appropriate when conducting a comprehensive assessment with the KTEA-II Comprehensive Form. However, examiners may administer a brief test of cognitive ability along with the KTEA-II, such as the conormed Kaufman Brief Intelligence Test–Second Edition (KBIT2; Kaufman & Kaufman, 2004c) in order to have an understanding of a person's general level of cognitive functioning.

≡Rapid Reference 3.16

Steps for Using the Regression Model in Ability-Achievement Discrepancy Analysis

1. Record the student's KABC-II standard score (either FCI, MPI, or NVI) and the KTEA-II standard score in the designated boxes on the back page of the KTEA-II Comprehensive Record Form.

2. Refer to Table I.9 in Appendix I of the *KTEA-II Comprehensive Form Manual* to find the correlation between the KABC-II ability scale and the achievement composite or subtest.

3. Using that correlation value, refer to Table I.10 in Appendix I of the *KTEA-II Comprehensive Form Manual* to obtain the predicted achievement score corresponding to the ability score, and write the predicted achievement score in the designated box on the KTEA-II Comprehensive Record Form.

4. If the actual achievement score is lower than the predicted score, compute the difference between the predicted and actual achievement scores, and write it on the designated line of the KTEA-II Comprehensive Record Form.

5. Refer to Table I.11 in Appendix I of the *KTEA-II Comprehensive Form Manual* to find the values of the difference required for statistical significance. Find the column for the smallest significance level in which the observed difference (computed in step 4) is equal to or greater than the values in the table, and circle the appropriate number (.05 or .01) on the KTEA-II Comprehensive Record Form.

6. If the difference between the predicted and actual achievement scores is statistically significant, refer again to Table I.11 to determine whether the difference is unusual. Find the column for the smallest percentage frequency in which the observed difference (computed in step 4) is equal to or greater than the value in the table, and circle the appropriate number (10%, 5%, 2%, or 1%) on the record form. The frequencies in Table I.11 are one-tailed, meaning that they represent the percentage of the population having an actual achievement score that is lower than the predicted achievement score by the specified amount or more.

Note: Steps are adapted from p. 32 of the *KTEA-II Comprehensive Form Manual* (Kaufman & Kaufman, 2004a).

deficits and strengths for each student. Additionally, the KTEA-II was conormed with an individually administered test of cognitive ability, the KABC-II, allowing rich information to be gleaned about how academic strengths and weaknesses may reflect strengths and weaknesses in processing and reasoning.

We feel that the KTEA-II has no major weaknesses. However, there are a few minor weaknesses, which we list in Rapid Reference 3.17 alongside the many strengths of the test. We separate strengths and weaknesses of the test into the following areas: test development, administration and scoring, reliability and validity, standardization, and interpretation.

≡ Rapid Reference 3.17

....

Strengths and Weaknesses of the KTEA-II

Test Development	
Strengths	**Weaknesses**
• The rationale for item selection, using curriculum consultants, and basing item selection on content of widely used textbooks	• Limited ceiling for some subtests for the oldest students in the Above Average range. (See Table 3.7 for specific data on highest possible subtest and composite scores for ages 21–25 and grade 12.) Although most subtests have a ceiling that is at least 2 SD above the mean, the ceilings for Spelling, Associational Fluency, and Naming Facility range from 122–129. At the highest age range, 12 of the 14 subtests have ceilings ≤ 144
• Includes subtests that measure achievement in all seven specific learning disability areas identified in the Individuals with Disabilities Education Act Amendments of 1997 (IDEA, 1997)	
• Extensive tryout data using samples with approximate proportional representation by sex and ethnicity	
• Easel format for presenting subtest items	• Limited floor for some subtests for the youngest students with the lowest ability levels. For students younger than age 6, raw scores of 0 correspond to standard scores ranging from 67–82 for Letter and Word Recognition, from 72–81 for Math Computation, from 67–77 for Listening Comprehension, from 69–77 for Phonological Awareness, from 64–72 for Associational Fluency, and from 71–83 for Naming Facility. (See Table 3.8 for specific data.)
• More reading-related subtests were added, yielding four reading-related composites	
• Innovative item types, especially in Reading Comprehension, Written Expression, and Phonemic Awareness	
• Use of extensive item analysis procedures to eliminate biased items (gender or race) and items with poor psychometric properties	• Error-analysis procedures may be difficult for examiners lacking a background in curriculum
• Error analysis procedures were expanded	
• It is conormed with the KABC-II to allow for understanding of the student's academic strengths and weaknesses within the context of the student's cognitive abilities	
• Novel and stimulating artwork is used throughout the test	

(continued)

Standardization	
Strengths	**Weaknesses**
• The standardization sample is well stratified to match the U.S. population • Two separate representative nationwide standardizations were conducted, one in the fall and one in the spring, yielding a large normative group ($N = 3,000$ for the age-norm sample and $N = 2,400$ for the grade-norm sample) for the KTEA-II Comprehensive Form • The standardization sample included students receiving special education services • Very detailed information on standardization procedures and sample are included in the manual • Expanded age range down to 4:6 years for both the Comprehensive and Brief Forms and up to 25 years for the Comprehensive form and up to 90 years for the Brief Form	• The age-norm sample has smaller adult norm samples than for the younger age samples. From ages 5–14 the samples range in size from 200–225; for 15–17 the samples are 140–145. The 18-year-old sample is $N = 100$, age 19 sample is $N = 80$, and for the sample age 20–22, $N = 125$, as well as for the age 23–25 sample

Reliability and Validity

Strengths	Weaknesses
• High mean split-half reliabilities of subtests and composites (CAC = .97; other composites range from .93 to .97, with the exception of Oral Language and Oral Fluency, which range from .85 to .87)	• The Oral Language Composite has variable correlations with similar measures on other achievement instruments. However, this may be due to the very different approaches taken by different test batteries in measuring and defining oral expression and listening comprehension
• Two alternate forms are available for the KTEA-II Comprehensive, resulting in reduced practice effects for children who are assessed more than once	• Standard Errors of Measurement (SEM) are high for the age-norm sample for Oral Language (ranging from 4.45–6.96) and Oral Fluency (ranging from 4.25–10.28)
• Alternate form reliability coefficients (adjusted for the variability of the norm group) are very strong, ranging from .92 to .95 for the CAC. Most composite's alternate form reliability coefficients range from .85–.94. Oral Fluency and Oral Language are the weakest, ranging from .59–.81	
• KTEA-II Comprehensive Form Manual offers correlational data with four other tests of academic achievement and the original K-TEA	
• Moderate to strong correlations between KTEA-II and other measures of achievement for concurrent validity (.86–.90)	
• KTEA-II CAC correlates approximately .80 with the global scores of cognitive ability batteries (e.g., KABC-II and WISC-III)	
• Strong face validity based on use of textbook content and skill development in reading and mathematics	
• Construct validity indicated by increasing scores across grades and ages	

(continued)

Administration and Scoring

Strengths	Weaknesses
• The test protocol has a user-friendly layout	• Need to write oral responses phonetically to use error analysis for Letter and Word Recognition and Nonsense Word Decoding, which can be especially challenging when testing students who respond very quickly
• Easel format simplifies administration	
• Starting points and discontinue rules are clearly labeled on the record form and easels for all subtests	
• Children find Pepper the puppet very engaging in Phonemic Awareness	• Need to remember to use conversion table to convert points earned in a set to the raw score for Reading Comprehension, Written Expression, Listening Comprehension, and Oral Expression
• Students find the storybook format of Written Expression much less tedious than a more traditionally formatted test of written expression	
• Most test items are scored in a dichotomous manner	• When Associational Fluency and Naming Facility are administered, they must be given out of easel order, which may be confusing for some examiners
• A large number of Written Expression scoring examples are provided in the manual	
• A large number of Oral Expression scoring examples are provided in the manual	• The new descriptive categories are different from those from the original K-TEA as well as many other achievement and ability measures, which may be confusing to those familiar with the old categories
• Both age and grade norms are available	
• New descriptive categories reflect a simpler system of categorizing ability level, based on the test's SD of 15	
• A separate error analysis booklet is provided for the subtests that have large numbers of skill categories, thereby making the main record form less cumbersome	

(continued)

Interpretation

Strengths	Weaknesses
• Both composites and subtests can be interpreted due to high reliability data • Error analysis procedures pinpoint specific skill deficits • The composites and error analysis yield much diagnostic information directly relevant to instructional remediation • Subtest and battery composite intercorrelations are presented by age and grade in the *KTEA-II Comprehensive Form Manual* • Interpretive procedures were simplified by comparing composites and subtests to CAC rather than to the mean of all composites • Integrated normative and ipsative comparisons are included in the interpretive process • Pairs of KTEA-II Comprehensive subtests (i.e., Reading Comprehension and Listening Comprehension, and Written Expression and Oral Expression) were developed to have similar formats, to enable useful comparisons that can help the examiner distinguish specific problems in reading or writing from more general language problems • Growth Scale Values (GSV) are provided to provide a mechanism by which a student's absolute (rather than relative) level of performance can be measured • The manual encourages examiners to verify hypotheses with other data • The KTEA-II Record Form provides a place to record the basic analysis of the scale composites, including strengths and weaknesses, composite comparisons, subtest comparisons, and ability-achievement discrepancies • Because it is conormed with the KABC-II, the KTEA-II is easily interpreted within the CHC theoretical framework	• Caution needs to be taken when interpreting the scores with a nonoptimal ceiling for ages 21–25 (see Table 3.7) or a nonoptimal floor for children under age 6 (see Table 3.8). • If all of the CAC subtests are not administered, then the Composite Analysis and Subtest Analysis cannot be completed because the CAC is used in all of these comparisons. However, pairwise composite comparisons or pairwise subtest comparisons are still possible • Little information is provided in the *KTEA-II Comprehensive Form Manual* on how to utilize the growth scale values (GSV)

Table 3.7 Ceiling for Students Age 21:0–25:11 and Grade 12: Highest Possible Subtest and Composite Scores

KTEA-II Subtest/Composite	Age 21:0–25:11		Grade 12[a]	
	Form A	Form B	Form A	Form B
Letter and Word Recognition	139	136	140	135
Reading Comprehension	135	131	144	139
Reading Composite	**160**	**160**	**160**	**160**
Math Concepts & Applications	138	138	160	160
Math Computation	136	136	148	148
Mathematics Composite	**153**	**153**	**147**	**147**
Written Expression	160	160	160	160
Spelling	129	122	143	133
Written Language Composite	**160**	**160**	**160**	**160**
Listening Comprehension	134	134	131	131
Oral Expression	140	131	136	130
Oral Language Composite	**160**	**160**	**160**	**160**
Phonological Awareness				
Nonsense Word Decoding	134	134	136	136
Sound-Symbol Composite				
Word Recognition Fluency	144	144	160	160
Decoding Fluency	137	137	140	140
Reading Fluency	**160**	**160**	**160**	**160**
Decoding Composite	**160**	**160**	**160**	**160**
Associational Fluency	123	123	135	135
Naming Facility (RAN)	122	122	127	127
Oral Fluency Composite	**160**	**160**	**160**	**160**
Comprehensive Achievement	**160**	**160**	**160**	**160**

Note: From Tables N.2, N.3, N.4, and N.5 of the *KTEA-II Comprehensive Form Norms Book* (Kaufman & Kaufman, 2004b). The maximum standard score on all subtests is 160. Scores ≥ 130 (+2 SD) are in the Upper Extreme and scores ranging from 116 to 130 (+1 to +2 SD) are in the Above Average range.

[a] Spring grade norms are reported here. The values for the Fall grade norms (available in Table N.1 of the *KTEA-II Comprehensive Form Norms Book*) for 12th grade students are very similar to those reported here.

Table 3.8 Floor for Students Age 4:6–4:8 and Grade K: Lowest Possible Subtest and Composite Scores

KTEA-II Subtest/Composite	Age						Grade[a]	
	4:6–4:8	4:9–4:11	5:0–5:2	5:3–5:5	5:6–5:8	5:9–5:11	K	1
Letter and Word Recognition	82	79	76	73	70	67	59	44
Reading Comprehension								63
Reading Composite								**44**
Math Concepts & Applications	60	59	58	57	54	50	50	43
Math Computation			81	78	75	72	66	52
Mathematics Composite	**42**	**42**	**42**	**42**	**42**	**42**	**46**	**46**
Written Expression	48	40	40	40	40	40	40	40
Spelling								62
Written Language Composite								**46**
Listening Comprehension	77	74	71	69	68	67	67	61
Oral Expression	68	65	63	63	62	61	55	50
Oral Language Composite	**42**	**42**	**42**	**42**	**42**	**42**	**46**	**46**
Phonological Awareness			77	73	69	67	63	53
Nonsense Word Decoding								76
Sound-Symbol Composite								**40**
Word Recognition Fluency								
Decoding Fluency								
Decoding Composite								**40**

Table 3.8 (Continued)

KTEA-II Subtest/Composite	Age							Grade[a]	
	4:6–4:8	4:9–4:11	5:0–5:2	5:3–5:5	5:6–5:8	5:9–5:11		K	1
Associational Fluency	72	70	69	67	65	64		53	46
Naming Facility (RAN)	83	81	79	76	73	71		68	45
Oral Fluency Composite	**40**	**40**	**40**	**40**	**40**	**40**		**40**	**40**
Comprehensive Achievement	**40**	**40**	**40**	**40**	**40**	**40**		**40**	**43**

Note: From Tables N.2, N.3, N.4, and N.5 of the *KTEA-II Comprehensive Form Norms Book* (Kaufman & Kaufman, 2004b). The minimum standard score on all subtests is 40. Scores ≤ 69 (−2 SD) are in the Lower Extreme and scores ranging from 70 to 84 (−1 to −2 SD) are in the Below Average range. Data are reported for Form A only. However, in most cases the data for Form B are equivalent to Form A or only 1–2 points different. Values shown here are standard scores corresponding to raw scores of zero.

[a] Spring grade norms are reported here. The values for the Fall grade norms (available in Table N.1 of the *KTEA-II Comprehensive Form Norms Book*) for kindergarten and first grade students are very similar to those reported here.

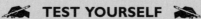

TEST YOURSELF

1. In addition to Reading, Mathematics, Written Language, and Oral Language composite standard scores, the KTEA-II offers four Reading-Related composites. True or False?

2. Which two domain composites does the KTEA-II yield for children who have not yet begun kindergarten?

   (a) Reading and Mathematics

   (b) Mathematics and Written Language

   (c) Oral Language and Reading

   (d) Written Language and Oral Language

3. Knowledge of proper pronunciation of all the stimulus words is key to administering which KTEA-II subtests?

4. Students are not penalized for misspelled words on the Written Expression subtest. True or False?

5. All KTEA-II subtests offer an error analysis. True or False?

6. What value is used to represent a student's overall average level of performance on the KTEA-II during the interpretive process?

   (a) The mean of all domain composites

   (b) The Comprehensive Achievement Composite (CAC)

   (c) The mean of only Reading and Math Composites

   (d) The mean of Reading, Math, and Writing Composites

7. The suggested KTEA-II interpretive steps base academic strengths on normative comparisons as well as ipsative (person-based) comparisons. True or False?

8. Of the two primary methods of comparing ability with achievement, the simple-difference method and the regression method, which has a stronger psychometric rationale (and is therefore the preferred approach)?

   (a) Regression method

   (b) Simple-difference method

9. Pairs of KTEA-II Comprehensive subtests (i.e., Reading Comprehension and Listening Comprehension, and Written Expression and Oral Expression) were developed specifically to have similar formats to enable useful comparisons that can help the examiner distinguish specific problems in reading or writing from more general language problems. True or False?

(continued)

10. Which one of the four academic domains measured in the KTEA-II Comprehensive Form is *not* measured by the KTEA-II Brief Form?

(a) Reading

(b) Mathematics

(c) Written Language

(d) Oral Language

Answers: 1. True; 2. d; 3. Letter and Word Recognition, Nonsense Word Decoding, Word Recognition Fluency, and Decoding Fluency; 4. True; 5. False; 6. b; 7. True; 8. a; 9. True; 10. d

Four

CLINICAL APPLICATIONS

n this chapter we focus on some key clinical applications of the WIAT-II and KTEA-II. In the first half of this chapter we discuss topics related to utilizing the relationship between measures of achievement and intelligence. Both the WIAT-II and KTEA-II were conormed with tests of cognitive ability and were designed to work in tandem with these cognitive instruments to identify skill deficits as well as potential process deficits. When the KTEA-II is used with the KABC-II, or the WIAT-II is used together with other Wechsler instruments (e.g., WPPSI-III, WISC-IV) and specialized instruments such as the Process Assessment of the Learner: Test Battery for Reading and Writing (Berninger, 2001) examiners can develop a more comprehensive understanding of the reasons for underachievement. (At the same time, WIAT-II and KTEA-II are widely used in the assessment of children for placement in accelerated or gifted programs, and use of these instruments with individuals of varying levels of achievement is discussed later in this chapter.)

The linking of these achievement measures with other assessment measures provides for efficient collection of in-depth data that can help the examiner to test hypotheses, to formulate a diagnosis, to make decisions related to eligibility, and most importantly, to bridge the gap between assessment and intervention. Although an ability-achievement discrepancy is no longer required to identify learning disabilities, it still can serve an important role in understanding all of the issues that place a student at risk for academic failure. In chapters 2 and 3 we discussed the procedures for determining achievement-ability discrepancies. However, here we provide information on the conceptual and theoretical relationships between achievement and ability as measured by the WIAT-II and WISC-IV and the KTEA-II and KABC-II.

In the second half of this chapter we review some of the data on the clinical application of the WIAT-II and KTEA-II in special populations, including reading, math, and writing disabilities, as well as Attention-Deficit/Hyperactivity Disorder. Based on these special population studies, we attempt to draw inferences about the relationships between WIAT-II–WISC-IV and KTEA-II–KABC-II, to provide useful information for clinicians who assess such children and strive to develop the best possible interventions for them.

WIAT-II AND THE WECHSLER INTELLIGENCE SCALES

David Wechsler based his original Wechsler–Bellevue on the premise that intelligence is a *global* entity because it characterizes the individual's behavior as a whole, and it is also *specific* because it is composed of elements or abilities that are distinct from each other. Wechsler developed subtests that highlighted the cognitive aspects of intelligence: verbal comprehension, abstract reasoning, perceptual organization, quantitative reasoning, memory, and processing speed. All of these areas have been confirmed as important in more contemporary theories and measures of intelligence (Carroll, 1993, 1997; Horn, 1991). A significant change in the Wechsler scales occurred with the publication of the WISC-IV, in that instead of reporting scores within two domains, Verbal and Performance, emphasis was placed on the measure of more discrete domains of cognitive functioning (e.g., verbal comprehension, perceptual reasoning, processing speed, working memory), while continuing to provide a measure of global intelligence (FSIQ). The new four-factor structure of the cognitive measure is appropriate for several reasons. First of all, cognitive functions are interrelated, functionally and neurologically, making it difficult to measure a pure domain. Various aspects of cognition are required to perform the tasks used to measure a domain. For example, a measure of processing speed, such as the WISC-IV's Coding subtest, requires visual scanning and discrimination of information, short-term memory, paired-associative learning, and a grapho-motor response. Second, including subtests that require the use of multiple cognitive abilities is ecologically valid in that cognitive tasks are rarely performed in isolation. As Wechsler (1975) observed:

> . . . the attributes and factors of intelligence, like the elementary particles in physics, have at once collective and individual properties, that is, they appear to behave differently when alone from what they do when operating in concert. (p. 138)

The measurement of general intelligence (g) is supported by its strong ecological validity in predicting such things as academic achievement, job performance, and overall psychological well-being. Measures of more discrete domains do not show the same degree of predictive ability (Gottfredson, 1998). Measuring psychometrically pure factors of discrete domains may be useful to research, but it does not necessarily result in information that is useful for real-world application

(Zachary, 1990). Because it is unreasonable to expect any single measure of intelligence to adequately test all domains of cognitive functioning in a meaningful and practical way (Carroll, 1997), Wechsler selected measures that sampled a wide variety of domains (e.g., verbal comprehension, perceptual organization, memory), which have since proven to be important aspects of cognitive functioning. He also acknowledged the possibility of obtaining invalid results when examiners or examinees become fatigued. As a result, he selected a sufficient number of subtests to provide clinically meaningful information about an individual's cognitive functioning in a reasonable time period. Wechsler believed that other related factors, such as achievement, executive functioning, and motor skills, which could impact performance on an intelligence test, should be assessed by tests specifically designed to measure those abilities. Finally, Wechsler recognized that performance on measures of cognitive ability reflects only a portion of what comprises intelligence. He defined intelligence as the "capacity of the individual to act purposefully, to think rationally, and to deal effectively with his environment" (p. 3, 1975). He avoided defining intelligence in purely cognitive terms because he believed that these factors only comprised a portion of intelligence. He proposed that attributes such as planning and goal awareness, enthusiasm, field dependence and independence, impulsiveness, anxiety, and persistence, which are not directly tapped by standard measures of intelligence, influence a person's performance on these measures, as well as his or her functioning in the real world (Wechsler, 1975). Assessing an individual's intelligence involves more than simply obtaining a score on an intelligence test. As Wechsler (1975) noted:

> What we measure with tests is not what tests measure—not information, not spatial perception, not reasoning ability. These are only a means to an end. What intelligence tests measure is something much more important; the capacity of the individual to understand the world about him and his resourcefulness to cope with its challenges. (p. 139)

The WIAT-II was designed to be used with the three age-specific Wechsler scales as the foundation of the psychoeducational assessment. Consequently, subsets of the WIAT-II standardization sample were administered the appropriate cognitive measure according to age. The data related to the linking sample of WIAT-II and WAIS-III were published with the achievement test in 2002. New linking studies were conducted as part of the standardizations of the WPPSI-III (2002) and the WISC-IV (2003). As a result, WIAT-II can be used with any of the Wechsler scales to identify ability-achievement discrepancies and to explore the relationship between higher-order cognitive ability domains and acquired achievement skills. Special attention will be placed on using WIAT-II with WISC-IV in this section, as this is the predominant pairing of the tests for school-age children.

Description of the WISC-IV

Because the WISC-IV and WIAT-II were designed to be used together, it is important to understand the structure of the WISC-IV and the WISC-IV Integrated (2004), and to identify the cognitive abilities measured by each index. Correlational studies between the WISC-IV and the WIAT-II and the WISC-IV Integrated and the WIAT-II are discussed. Clinical studies, which are addressed later in this chapter, reveal unique patterns of performance between the WIAT-II and the WISC-IV and the WISC-IV Integrated.

Rapid Reference 4.1 presents the four-factor structure of the WISC-IV. Its subtests were designed to measure a broad range of cognitive abilities. The new framework of the WISC-IV is based on theory and is supported by clinical research and factor-analytic results (see a discussion in Chapter 5 of the *WISC-IV Technical and Interpretive Manual* [2004]). The framework is similar to that of the WAIS-III, which was published in 1997. Subtests are either *core* (required for calculation of the index scores and FSIQ) or *supplemental* (intended to substitute for

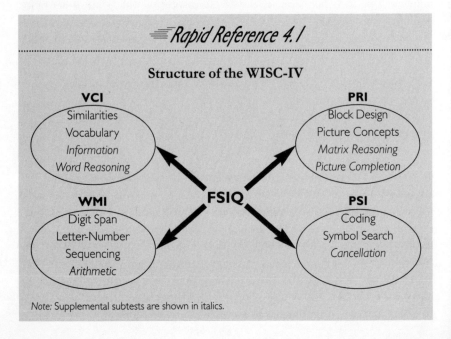

Rapid Reference 4.1

Structure of the WISC-IV

VCI
Similarities
Vocabulary
Information
Word Reasoning

PRI
Block Design
Picture Concepts
Matrix Reasoning
Picture Completion

FSIQ

WMI
Digit Span
Letter-Number
Sequencing
Arithmetic

PSI
Coding
Symbol Search
Cancellation

Note: Supplemental subtests are shown in italics.

a core under certain conditions, or to extend the range of cognitive skills measured by the core), and an individual's performance can be evaluated using the index scores—Verbal Comprehension Index (VCI), Perceptual Reasoning Index (PRI), Working Memory Index (WMI), Processing Speed Index (PSI), the composite Full Scale IQ (FSIQ), and an alternate General Ability Index (GAI, which is a composite of VCI and PRI). Each subtest yields a scaled score (mean [M] = 10; SD = 3) and each index produces a derived standard score (M = 100; SD = 15). In addition to the WISC-IV subtest and composite scores, seven *process* scores (Block Design No Time Bonus, Digit Span Forward, Digit Span Backward, Longest Digit Span Forward, Longest Digit Span Backward, Cancellation Random, and Cancellation Structured) can be obtained for the purpose of providing more in-depth information about an examinee's performance.

The WISC-IV introduced new subtests to improve the measurement of fluid reasoning, working memory, and processing speed. The importance of fluid reasoning is emphasized in many theories of cognitive functioning (Carroll, 1997; Cattell, 1943, 1963; Cattell & Horn, 1978; Sternberg, 1995). Tasks that require *fluid reasoning* involve the process of "manipulating abstractions, rules, generalizations, and logical relationships" (Carroll, 1993, p. 583). The measurement of fluid reasoning is incorporated in the new subtests: Matrix Reasoning, Picture Concepts, and Word Reasoning. The first two appear on the PRI index, whereas the latter is a VCI supplemental subtest. *Working memory* is the ability to actively maintain information in conscious awareness, perform some operation or manipulation with it, and produce a result. Working memory is an essential component of fluid reasoning and other higher-order cognitive processes, and is closely related to achievement (Fry & Hale, 1996; Perlow, Jattuso, & Moore, 1997; Swanson, 1996). Working memory is assessed with Digit Span the new Letter-Number Sequencing subtest and by the reworking of the former Arithmetic subtest to increase working memory demands. Because research indicates that greater demands on working memory occur for Digit Span Backward than Digit Span Forward, separate process scores were developed for this subtest. Speed of processing is dynamically related to mental capacity (Kail & Salthouse, 1994), reading performance (Berninger, 2001), reasoning, and the efficient use of working memory for higher-order fluid reasoning tasks (Fry & Hale, 1996). Processing speed is also sensitive to such neurological conditions as epilepsy, ADHD, and traumatic brain injury (Donders, 1997). In children, more rapid processing of information may reduce demands on working memory and facilitate reasoning. The new Cancellation subtest was developed for the WISC-IV as a supplemental measure of processing speed. By comparing performance on Cancellation when stimulus materials are structured (Cancellation Structured [CAS]) as opposed to when they are random (Cancellation Random [CAR]), additional information related to visual selective attention, visual neglect, response inhibition, and motor perseveration is acquired.

Description of the WISC-IV Integrated

Rapid Reference 4.2 shows the structure of the WISC-IV Integrated (2004) which adds 16 process subtests to the WISC-IV battery. Seven of the process subtests are *adaptations* of the core and supplemental subtests of the WISC-IV (Similarities Multiple Choice, Vocabulary Multiple Choice, Picture Vocabulary Multiple Choice, Comprehension Multiple Choice, Information Multiple Choice, Arithmetic Process Approach, and Written Arithmetic). These subtests include the same item content as their corresponding core or supplemental subtests, but also contain modifications to the mode of presentation or response format. Six of the process subtests are *variations* of the core and supplemental subtests (Block Design Multiple Choice, Block Design Process Approach, Visual Digit Span, Spatial Span, Letter Span, and Letter-Number Sequencing Process Approach). The variations include new item content and modifications to the mode of presentation or response format. Three process subtests are designed to expand the scope of construct coverage (i.e., Elithorn Mazes) or to provide information that can be used to better understand a child's performance on other subtests (i.e., Coding Recall and Coding Copy). The process subtests provide additional measures of cognitive abilities and may be used to test specific hypotheses regarding underlying cognitive processes and test-taking behaviors that contribute to performance on the core and supplemental subtests. On occasion, a process subtest may not measure the same construct as the core and supplemental subtest within a cognitive domain. For example, if a child performs poorly on Coding B (a measure of processing speed), the examiner may elect to administer Coding Recall (a measure of incidental learning) to see if the child remembers the pairings of numbers and symbols on Coding B. Although it is not a measure of processing speed, Coding Recall is included in the Processing Speed domain because it provides additional information about the cognitive processes contributing to performance on Coding B.

One of the primary benefits of adding select subtests from the WISC-IV Integrated to a psychoeducational battery that includes WIAT-II is to delve more deeply into the role played by executive functions, working memory, and processing speed in learning. For example, empirical data gathered from clinical populations suggests that working memory may be affected differentially by neurodevelopmental problems or brain injury. Studies have identified distinct neu-

≡Rapid Reference 4.2

Structure of the WISC-IV Integrated

Perceptual Domain

Core Subtests
- Block Design
- Picture Concepts
- Matrix Reasoning

Supplemental Subtests
- Picture Completion

Process Subtests
- Block Design Multiple Choice
- Block Design Process Approach
- Elithorn Mazes

Verbal Domain

Core Subtests
- Similarities
- Vocabulary
- Comprehension

Supplemental Subtests
- Information
- Word Reasoning

Process Subtests
- Similarities Multiple Choice
- Vocabulary Multiple Choice
- Picture Vocabulary Multiple Choice
- Comprehension Multiple Choice
- Information Multiple Choice

Working Memory Domain

Core Subtests
- Digit Span
- Letter-Number Sequencing

Supplemental Subtests
- Arithmetic

Process Subtests
- Visual Digit Span
- Spatial Span
- Letter Span
- Letter-Number Sequencing Process Approach
- Arithmetic Process Approach
- Written Arithmetic

Processing Speed Domain

Core Subtests
- Coding
- Symbol Search

Supplemental Subtests
- Cancellation

Process Subtests
- Coding Recall
- Coding Copy

roanatomical locations for verbal, visuospatial, and executive working memory functions (Gathercole, Pickering, Armbridge, & Wearing, 2004). The WISC-IV Integrated measures both the auditory-verbal (i.e., Digit-Span and Letter-Number Sequencing Process Approach) and the visuo-spatial (i.e., Visual Digit Span and Spatial Span) components. Further, several of the subtests (e.g., Block Design and Block Design No Time Bonus, Arithmetic and Arithmetic With Time Bonus) provide scaled scores that are derived from total raw scores with and without time-bonus points. This type of information is especially helpful when making recommendations for instruction and accommodations in the classroom.

Integrating the WIAT-II and WISC-IV—Quantitative Analyses

When comparing ability, as measured by the WISC-IV, to achievement measured by WIAT-II, FSIQ or GAI and individual achievement subtest standard scores or composites are typically used. With some achievement tests it is necessary to use the composite scores to identify ability-achievement discrepancies, because of the lower reliability scores on the individual achievement subtests. This is not the case with the WIAT-II because subtest reliabilities across ages fall in the same range as the composite reliabilities. In fact, there are times when a discrepancy among subtests contributing to a composite exists; individual subtest scores should then be used, because the composite score could mask important deficits and be misleading.

Coefficients of correlation between WIAT-II scores and WISC-IV scores demonstrate the strong relationship between the Wechsler tests of cognitive ability and achievement. The WISC-IV and the WIAT-II were administered to 550 children aged 6 to 16 with a testing interval of 0 to 39 days (M = 12 days). The correlations between the two tests are highest at the composite level, ranging from .49 (for PSI and Oral Language) to .87 (for FSIQ and Total Achievement). The VCI was moderately to highly correlated with all of the WIAT-II composites (range of .67 for Written Language to .75 for Oral Language). VCI correlated highest (.80) with Total Achievement. The moderate correlations between PRI and the WIAT-II composites range from a low of .61 with Written Language to a high of .67 with Mathematics, with a .71 correlation between PRI and Total Achievement. WMI correlates highest with the Reading composite (.66) and lowest with the Oral Language composite (.57). The correlation between Total Achievement and WMI is .71. The PSI correlates highest with Written Language (.55) and lowest with Oral Language (.49). The correlation between PSI and Total Achievement is .58. At the subtest level, the strongest relationships are found between WISC-IV Arithmetic and Math Reasoning (.77), Vocabulary and Listening Comprehension (.75), Information and Listening Comprehension (.74), Vocabulary and Reading Comprehension (.70), and Similarities and Listening Comprehension (.70). The Cancellation subtest correlated minimally with any of the WIAT-II subtests (range of .10 to .18). See Table 5.15 in the *WISC-IV Technical and Interpretive Manual* (2003) for the complete correlation data.

Conceptually and psychometrically, the WISC-IV and WISC-IV Integrated paired with the WIAT-II have enhanced clinical utility, especially in the assessment of children with various types of learning disabilities, children with ADHD, children with language disorders, children with open or closed head injury, children with Autistic Disorder, and children with Asperger's Disorder. Later in this chapter, information related to some of these clinical groups will be presented.

WIAT-II AND PROCESS ASSESSMENT OF THE LEARNER (PAL)

The Process Assessment of the Learner: Test Battery for Reading and Writing (PAL-RW) was designed as a companion to the WIAT-II, and provides in-depth assessment of the processing skills that are necessary for the development of the academic skills measured by the WIAT-II reading and writing subtests (i.e., Word Reading, Pseudoword Decoding, Reading Comprehension, Spelling, and Written Expression). The PAL-RW is a norm-referenced tool, designed for assessing the development of reading and writing processes in children in kindergarten through grade 6. One of its primary functions is to be used in diagnosing the *nature* of reading- or writing-related processing problems in students who have exhibited a discrepancy between ability and achievement or have other indicators of a possible learning disability. Preliminary research has also indicated that the PAL-RW process measures can be used to identify processing problems in older students with average or better intelligence who are functioning at developmental levels below grade placement. The PAL-RW does not target all reading- or writing-related processes; rather, it provides measures of many of the processes that have been shown to be the best predictors of reading and writing achievement. A description of the PAL-RW subtests is found in Rapid Reference 4.3. Rapid Reference 4.4 presents a model of how the PAL-RW subtests can be used to better understand performance on the WIAT-II subtests by focusing on the processing skills required to perform the reading or writing tasks. The PAL-RW is designed to be used as a follow-up assessment when deficits in reading and/or writing are identified using WIAT-II. The purpose of the follow-up testing is to identify those processing deficits that require remediation, as part of an intervention plan. Once a process deficit is identified, the PAL-RW is directly linked to research-based interventions (i.e., *PAL Guides for Intervention,* Berninger, 1998;

≡ Rapid Reference 4.3

Process Assessment of the Learner: Test Battery for Reading and Writing Subtests

Subtest	Description	Measures
Receptive Coding	The child is asked to compare whole words, single letters, and letter groups to the target words presented visually in the stimulus booklet.	Measures the child's ability to quickly code written words into short-term memory and then to segment each word into units of different size.
Expressive Coding	The child is presented the word in the stimulus booklet and then asked to write the whole word or targeting single letter or letter group from the word by memory.	Measures the child's ability to quickly code whole written words into short-term memory and then reproduce the words or parts of words in writing.
RAN Letters	The child is asked to name aloud familiar letters and letter groups quickly and accurately.	Measures automaticity of integrating visual symbols processed by the language-by-eye system with phonologically referenced name codes processed by the language-by-mouth system.
RAN Words	The child is asked to read familiar words aloud, quickly and accurately.	Measures automaticity of word-specific mechanism by naming highly frequent words that cannot be completely decoded on the basis of the alphabet principle.
RAN Digits	The child is asked to read digits aloud, quickly and accurately.	Measures automaticity of naming known digits.
RAN Words & Digits	The child is asked to alternately name aloud familiar words and double-digit numbers, quickly and accurately.	Measures the executive functions required to coordinate cross-category naming processes.

Alphabet-Writing	The child is asked to write the lowercase letters of the alphabet in order, quickly and accurately.	Measures the child's automaticity in writing (including the ability to retrieve from long-term memory).
Note-Taking, Task A	The child is asked to listen to a simulated classroom lecture and to take notes on the information presented.	Measures the child's listening and note-taking skills.
Note-Taking, Task B	After administration of other subtests, the child is asked to write a paragraph using the notes.	Measures the child's ability to use his or her notes to accurately reconstruct with detail what was heard. Task requires integration of listening and written retelling.
Rhyming	The child is asked to listen to three words and to select the word that does not rhyme with the other two. Then the child is asked to generate a list of words that rhyme with a spoken target word.	Measures phonological awareness (the child's ability to discriminate between words that have the same ending sounds and to generate real words that have the same ending sounds).
Syllables	The child is asked to repeat a polysyllabic word presented by the examiner and then to say the syllable(s) remaining when a targeted syllable is omitted.	Measures the child's ability to segment spoken words into syllables.
Phonemes	The child is asked to repeat a monosyllabic or polysyllabic word presented by the examiner; to provide the phonemes remaining when a targeted phoneme is omitted.	Measures the child's ability to segment spoken words into phonemes.
Rimes	The child is asked to say the portions of a monosyllabic or polysyllabic word remaining when the targeted rime is omitted.	Measures the child's understanding of rimes. A rime is the portion of the syllable that is left when the initial phoneme or phonemes of the syllable are omitted.

(continued)

Subtest	Description	Measures
Word Choice	The child is presented with a response booklet and asked to circle from a choice of three the word that is spelled correctly.	Measures the child's ability to identify the correct spelling of a word presented with two misspelled distractors that have the same or nearly the same pronunciation as the correctly spelled word.
Pseudoword Decoding[a]	The child is asked to read aloud from a list of printed nonsense words. The pseudowords are designed to mimic the phonological structure of words in the English language.	Measures the child's ability to apply phonological decoding skills.
Story Recall	The child is asked to listen to a short story, answer questions about the story, and then retell the story in his or her own words.	Measures the child's ability to abstract information from text, to relate that information to prior knowledge, to organize the resulting representations in working memory, and to plan and produce a response.
Finger Sense	Five tasks are included, to elicit repetition, succession, localization, recognition, and fingertip writing for both hands.	Measures the child's finger function related to written output.

Sentence Sense	Each item requires the child to identify the meaningful (correct) sentence from among three very similar sentences, which contain only read words and which differ by only one word. Each of the two distractor sentences has one erroneous word (e.g., homonym) that does not make sense in the sentence context.	Measures the child's ability to coordinate word-recognition and sentence-comprehension processes when reading for meaning under timed conditions.
Copy Task A	The child is asked to copy, quickly and accurately, a sentence that contains all of the letters of the alphabet.	Measures the child's handwriting and ability to copy accurately without memory requirements.
Copy Task B	The child is asked to copy, quickly and accurately, a paragraph.	Measures the child's handwriting and ability to copy longer text accurately without memory requirements.

[a]Pseudoword Decoding is the same subtest for both PAL-RW and WIAT-II.

≡ Rapid Reference 4.4

Process Assessment of the Learner: Test Battery for Reading and Writing Subtests and Processes

Component Reading or Writing Skill (WIAT-II Subtest)	Process	PAL-RW Subtest(s)
Word Recognition (Word Reading and Pseudoword Decoding)	1. Orthographic coding in short-term memory 2. Orthographic representation in long-term memory 3. Phonological coding in short-term memory 4. Rapid Automatic Naming (RAN)	1. Receptive Coding 2. Word Choice 3. Phonemes, Rimes 4. RAN-Letters, RAN-Words
Comprehension (Reading Comprehension)	Verbal Reasoning	VCI from WISC-IV
Reading Rate (Word Reading and Reading Comprehension)	1. Automaticity of letter coding 2. Word automaticity 3. Automaticity of word-specific mechanism	1. RAN-Letters, Receptive Coding (Tasks B, C, D, E) 2. RAN-Words 3. RAN-Words
Handwriting (Written Expression)	1. Handwriting automaticity 2. Finger function 3. Storing or retrieving letter forms in memory	1. Alphabet Writing, Copying 2. Finger Sense 3. Receptive Coding, Expressive Coding

Spelling (Spelling and Written Expression)	1. Vocabulary knowledge and verbal skills 2. Phonological coding in short-term memory 3. Orthographic coding in short-term memory 4. Integrating receptive coding with written output 5. Representation in long-term memory	1. VCI from WISC-IV 2. Phonemes, Rimes 3. Receptive Coding 4. Expressive Coding 5. Word Choice
Composition Fluency (Written Expression)	1. Handwriting automaticity 2. Orthographic coding in short-term memory 3. Finger function 4. Integrating receptive coding with written output 5. Representation in long-term memory	1. Alphabet Writing 2. Receptive Coding 3. Finger Sense 4. Expressive Coding 5. Word Choice
Composition Quality (Written Expression)	1. Verbal reasoning 2. Handwriting automaticity 3. Orthographic coding in short-term memory 4. Finger function 5. Integrating receptive coding with written output 6. Representation in long-term memory	1. VCI from WISC-IV 2. Alphabet Writing 3. Receptive Coding 4. Finger Sense 5. Expressive Coding 6. Word Choice

Source: Adapted from Table 4.4 of *PAL Test Battery for Reading and Writing Administration and Scoring Manual* (The Psychological Corporation, 2001).

PAL Research-Based Reading and Writing Lessons, Berninger & Abbott, 2003) that target instruction at the processes specific to reading and writing.

To further explore the relationship between the two instruments, the WIAT-II and the PAL-Test Battery for Reading and Writing (PAL-RW) were administered to a sample of 101 children aged 5 to 12 (Mean = 8 years) in grades K to 6. The correlation coefficients by grade groupings are reported in Rapid Reference 4.5. The WIAT-II subtests that evaluate reading skills are moderately correlated with PAL-RW subtests that measure the processing skills of orthographic and phonological coding (e.g., Receptive Coding, Expressive Coding, Rhyming, Syllables, Phonemes, and Rimes). The PAL-RW tasks that require orthographic awareness—Receptive Coding, Expressive Coding, Word Choice, and RAN-Letters—correlate most highly with the WIAT-II Spelling subtest. Low to moderate correlations are reported for all PAL-RW subtests and the WIAT-II math subtests; moderate correlations may be the result of the language component, particularly present in the Math Reasoning subtest.

Additional testing using the PAL-RW is not warranted for every examinee; however, for those students referred for possible reading and/or writing disabilities, the use of PAL-RW with WIAT-II can provide both diagnostic data and instructional guidance for improving learning outcomes.

INTEGRATION OF THE KTEA-II AND THE KABC-II WITH CHC THEORY

The KTEA-II and the KABC-II are designed to fit hand-in-glove.[1] The advantages of conorming the two batteries are numerous: the theoretical basis for the ability test and the achievement tests are similar and cohesive; administration and interpretive systems are similar in design; more accurate comparisons can be made between achievement and ability; each test can enhance the diagnostic reach of the other; and the combination of tests conveniently provides a cohesive and substantial portion of a comprehensive assessment.

This section introduces the reader to the design and make-up of the KABC-II and to the Cattell-Horn-Carroll (CHC) broad and narrow abilities, which both the KTEA-II and KABC-II were designed to assess. Different aspects of the integration of the KTEA-II and the KABC-II are explored by examining

[1] The section titled "Integration of the KTEA-II and KABC-II with CHC Theory" is adapted with permission from Chapter 6 of *Essentials of KABC-II Assessment* (Kaufman, Lichtenberger, Fletcher-Janzen, & Kaufman, 2005).

Correlations between the WIAT-II and Selected PAL-RW Subtests

WIAT-II Subtests and Supplemental Scores	Receptive Coding	Expressive Coding	RAN-Letters	RAN-Words	RAN-Digits	RAN-Words & Digits	Note-Taking Task A	Note-Taking Task B	Rhyming	Syllables	Phonemes	Rimes	Word Choice	Story Retell	Sentence Sense	Copying Task A (20" Score)	Copying Task B (90" Score)
Word Reading	.77	.80	−.78	−.54	−.73	−.72	.64	.65	.45	.47	.61	.48	.82	.07	.30	.60	.46
Numerical Operations	.66	.46	−.66	−.48	−.63	−.47	.48	.48	.46	.21	.52	.35	.82	.12	.35	.54	.42
Reading Comprehension	.63	.48	−.74	−.50	−.73	−.54	.46	.49		.48	.42	.50	.70		.20	.47	.53
Spelling	.77	.81	−.78	−.48	−.74	−.62	.58	.65	.50	.43	.59	.42	.79	.28	.26	.68	.56
Pseudoword Decoding	.69	.83	−.72	−.54	−.72	−.56	.54	.59		.49	.56	.52	.80		.28	.57	.32
Math Reasoning	.73	.77	−.75	−.57	−.69	−.57	.60	.60	.34	.42	.61	.42	.81	.20	.31	.60	.48
Written Expression	.69	.70	−.78	−.39	−.73	−.69	.46	.48	.49	.30	.50	.32	.75	.17	.31	.66	.61
Listening Comprehension	.51	.41	−.64	−.38	−.58	−.39	.57	.59	−.12	.30	.53	.19	.48	.13	.23	.59	.43
Oral Expression	.49	.56	−.35	−.32	−.32	−.21	.57	.60	.24	.20	.48	.21	.08	.67	−.02	.41	.26

PAL-RW Subtests

Note: $N = 101$. For Receptive Coding, Phonemes, and Rimes, correlations were calculated separately for grades K–3 and 4–6, and then averaged using Fisher's z transformation. For Syllables, correlations were calculated separately for grades 1–3 and 4–6, and then averaged using Fisher's z transformation. For all other subtests, correlations were calculated separately by test order, and averaged using Fisher's z transformation.

theoretical, quantitative, clinical, qualitative, and procedural points of view. It should be noted that the formal integration of the KTEA-II and the KABC-II is in its infancy, because the batteries have just been published. There are limits to the amount of prepublication research that can be performed. We look forward to the future field research that will explore and define the boundaries of KTEA-II/KABC-II integration.

Description of the KABC-II

The KABC-II is a measure of the processing and cognitive abilities of children and adolescents between the ages of 3:0 and 18:11. The KABC-II is founded on two theoretical models: Luria's (1966, 1970, 1973) neuropsychological model, featuring three Blocks, and the Cattell-Horn-Carroll (CHC) approach to categorizing specific cognitive abilities (Carroll, 1997; Flanagan, McGrew, & Ortiz, 2000). The KABC-II yields a separate global score for each of these two theoretical models: the global score measuring general mental processing ability from the Luria perspective is the Mental Processing Index (MPI), and the global score measuring general cognitive ability from the Cattell-Horn-Carroll perspective is the Fluid-Crystallized Index (FCI). The key difference between these two global scores is that the MPI (Luria's theory) *excludes* measures of acquired knowledge, whereas the FCI (CHC theory) *includes* measures of acquired knowledge. Only one of these two global scores is computed for any examinee. Prior to testing a client, examiners choose the interpretive system (i.e., Luria or CHC) that best fits with both their personal orientation and the reason for referral.

In addition to the MPI and FCI, the KABC-II offers from one to five scales, depending on the age level of the child and the interpretive approach that the clinician chooses to take. At age 3, there is only one scale, a global measure of ability, composed of either five subtests (Mental Processing Index—MPI) or seven subtests (Fluid-Crystallized Index—FCI). For ages 4 to 6, subtests are organized into either three scales (Luria model) or four scales (CHC model): Sequential/*Gsm,* Simultaneous/*Gv,* and Learning/*Glr* are in both models, and Verbal/*Gc* is only in the CHC model. For ages 7 to 18, four scales (Luria) or five scales (CHC) are available, with the Planning/*Gf* scale joining the aforementioned KABC-II scales. The KABC-II scales for each age level are shown in Rapid Reference 4.6.

From the Luria perspective, the KABC-II scales correspond to learning ability, sequential processing, simultaneous processing, and planning ability. From the vantage point of the CHC model, as applied to the KABC-II, the scales mea-

≡Rapid Reference 4.6

Number of KABC-II Scales at Each Age Level

Age 3	Age 4–6	Age 7–18
MPI, FCI, or NVI	MPI, FCI, or NVI	MPI, FCI, or NVI
(no additional	Learning/*Glr*	Learning/*Glr*
scales are obtained	Sequential/*Gsm*	Sequential/*Gsm*
at age 3)	Simultaneous/*Gv*	Simultaneous/*Gv*
	Knowledge/*Gc*	Planning/*Gf*
		Knowledge/*Gc*

Note: MPI from the Luria system *excludes* Knowledge/*Gc* subtests (age 3) and scale (ages 4–18). The FCI of the CHC system *includes* the Knowledge/*Gc* subtests (age 3) and scale (ages 4–18).

sure the following Broad Abilities: Short-term memory, visualization, long-term memory, fluid reasoning, and crystallized ability (Rapid Reference 4.7 describes how the scales are conceptualized by each theoretical perspective). The names of the KABC-II scales reflect both the Luria process it is believed to measure and its CHC Broad Ability, as indicated in Rapid Reference 4.7: Learning/*Glr,* Sequential/*Gsm,* Simultaneous/*Gv,* and Planning/*Gf.* However, the Verbal/*Gc* scale that measures crystallized ability reflects only CHC theory, as it is specifically excluded from the Luria system.

In addition to the MPI and FCI and the five scales, the KABC-II has a Non-verbal Scale, composed of subtests that may be administered in pantomime and responded to motorically. The Nonverbal Scale permits valid assessment of children who are hearing impaired, have Limited English Proficiency, or have moderate to severe speech or language impairments or other disabilities that make the Core Battery unsuitable. This special scale comprises a mixture of Core and supplementary subtests for all age groups. The interested reader can find more information about this scale in *Essentials of KABC-II Assessment* (Kaufman, Lichtenberger, Fletcher-Janzen, and Kaufman, 2005).

The KABC-II includes 18 subtests (described in Rapid Reference 4.8), which comprise a Core battery and an Expanded battery. The Expanded battery offers supplementary subtests to increase the breadth of the constructs that are measured by the Core battery, to follow up hypotheses, and to provide a comparison of the child's initial learning and delayed recall of new learning. The scale struc-

≡ Rapid Reference 4.7

Definitions of Luria and CHC Terms

Luria Term	CHC Term
Learning Ability	**Long-Term Storage & Retrieval (Glr)**
Reflects an integration of the processes associated with all three Blocks, placing a premium on the attention-concentration processes that are in the domain of Block I, but also requiring Block 2 coding processes and Block 3 strategy generation to learn and retain the new information with efficiency. Sequential and simultaneous processing are associated primarily with Luria's Block 2, and pertain to either a step-by-step (sequential) or holistic (simultaneous) processing of information.	Storing and efficiently retrieving newly learned or previously learned information
Sequential Processing	**Short-Term Memory (Gsm)**
Measures the kind of coding function that Luria labeled "successive," and involves arranging input in sequential or serial order to solve a problem, where each idea is linearly and temporally related to the preceding one.	Taking in and holding information, and then using it within a few seconds
Simultaneous Processing	**Visual Processing (Gv)**
Measures the second type, or simultaneous, coding function associated with Block 2. For its tasks, the input has to be integrated and synthesized simultaneously (holistically), usually spatially, to produce the appropriate solution. As mentioned earlier, the KABC-II measure of simultaneous processing deliberately blends Luria's Block 2 and Block 3 to enhance the complexity of the simultaneous syntheses that are required.	Perceiving, storing, manipulating, and thinking with visual patterns

Planning Ability

Measures the high-level, decision-making, executive processes associated with Block 3. However, as Reitan (1988) states, "Block 3 is involved in no sensory, motor, perceptual, or speech functions and is devoted exclusively to analysis, planning, and organization of programs for behavior" (p. 335). Because any cognitive task involves perception of sensory input and either a motor or verbal response, the KABC-II measure of planning ability necessarily requires functions associated with the other two Blocks as well.

Fluid Reasoning (Gf)

Solving novel problems by using reasoning abilities such as induction and deduction

(Crystallized ability does not have an analogous ability that is included in the Luria model)

Crystallized Ability (Gc)

Demonstrating the breadth and depth of knowledge acquired from one's culture

Note: The names of the KABC-II scales were chosen to reflect both their Luria and CHC underpinnings. Verbal/Gc is included in the CHC system for the computation of the FCI, but it is excluded from the Luria system for the computation of the Mental Processing Index (MPI). The Planning/Gf scale is for ages 7–18 only. All other scales are for ages 4–18. Only the MPI and FCI are offered for 3-year-olds.

Description of KABC-II Subtests

Sequential/Gsm Subtests

	Description
Word Order	The child touches a series of silhouettes of common objects in the same order as the examiner said the names of the objects; more difficult items include an interference task (color naming) between the stimulus and response.
Number Recall	The child repeats a series of numbers in the same sequence as the examiner said them, with series ranging in length from 2 to 9 numbers; the numbers are single digits, except that 10 is used instead of 7 to ensure that all numbers are one syllable.
Hand Movements	The child copies the examiner's precise sequence of taps on the table with the fist, palm, or side of the hand.

Simultaneous/Gv Subtests

Rover	The child moves a toy dog to a bone on a checkerboard-like grid that contains obstacles (rocks and weeds), and tries to find the "quickest" path—the one that takes the fewest moves.
Triangles	For most items, the child assembles several identical rubber triangles (blue on one side, yellow on the other) to match a picture of an abstract design; for easier items, the child assembles a different set of colorful rubber shapes to match a model constructed by the examiner.
Conceptual Thinking	The child views a set of four or five pictures and the child identifies the one picture that does not belong with the others; some items present meaningful stimuli and others use abstract stimuli.

Face Recognition	The child attends closely to photographs of one or two faces that are exposed briefly, and then selects the correct face or faces, shown in a different pose, from a group photograph.
Gestalt Closure	The child mentally "fills in the gaps" in a partially completed "inkblot" drawing and names (or describes) the object or action depicted in the drawing.
Block Counting	The child counts the exact number of blocks in various pictures of stacks of blocks; the stacks are configured such that one or more blocks is hidden or partially hidden from view.

Planning/Gf Subtests

| Pattern Reasoning[a] | The child is shown a series of stimuli that form a logical, linear pattern, but one stimulus is missing; the child completes the pattern by selecting the correct stimulus from an array of four to six options at the bottom of the page (most stimuli are abstract, geometric shapes, but some easy items use meaningful stimuli). |
| Story Completion[a] | The child is shown a row of pictures that tell a story, but some of the pictures are missing. The child is given a set of pictures, selects only the ones that are needed to complete the story, and places the missing pictures in their correct locations. |

Learning/Glr Subtests

| Atlantis | The examiner teaches the child the nonsense names for fanciful pictures of fish, plants, and shells; the child demonstrates learning by pointing to each picture (out of an array of pictures) when it is named. |
| Atlantis—Delayed | The child demonstrates delayed recall of paired associations learned about 15–25 minutes earlier during Atlantis by pointing to the picture of the fish, plant, or shell that is named by the examiner. |

(continued)

Learning/Glr Subtests (continued)

Rebus Learning	The examiner teaches the child the word or concept associated with each particular rebus (drawing) and the child then "reads" aloud phrases and sentences composed of these rebuses.
Rebus Learning—Delayed	The child demonstrates delayed recall of paired associations learned about 15–25 minutes earlier during Rebus by "reading" phrases and sentences composed of those same rebuses.

Knowledge/Gc Subtests

Riddles	The examiner provides several characteristics of a concrete or abstract verbal concept and the child has to point to it (early items) or name it (later items).
Expressive Vocabulary	The child provides the name of a pictured object.
Verbal Knowledge	The child selects from an array of six pictures the one that corresponds to a vocabulary word or answers a general information question.

Note: Descriptions are adapted from KABC-II Technical Manual (Kaufman & Kaufman, 2004b).

[a]At ages 5–6 Pattern Reasoning and Story Completion are categorized as Simultaneous/Gv subtests.

ture for each age group varies slightly, and is described in detail in the *KABC-II Manual* (Kaufman & Kaufman, 2004b).

Integrating the KTEA-II and KABC-II—Quantitative Analyses

Coefficients of correlation between KTEA-II global scores and scores on cognitive tests were presented and discussed in the validity section of Chapter 3 in this book. Overall, the KABC-II FCI and MPI correlated substantially (mean $r = .74–.79$) with the KTEA-II CAC. The KTEA-II Comprehensive Form Reading and Math Composites also strongly correlated with the KABC-II FCI and MPI (ranging from .68 to .74). KTEA-II Written Language and Oral Language had slightly lower correlations with the KABC-II (i.e., ranging from .60 to .67).

To further examine the cognitive-achievement relationships we can study how each KABC-II scale index correlates with major KTEA-II composites. Rapid Reference 4.9 and 4.10 show these correlations; asterisks are used to indicate the KABC-II index that correlates highest (**) and second-highest (*) with each KTEA-II composite.

≡ *Rapid Reference 4.9*

KABC-II Scale Index Correlations with KTEA-II Composites (Ages 7–18 Years)

KTEA-II Composite

KABC-II Scale	Total	Reading	Math	Written Language	Oral Language
Learning/*Glr*	.58	.55	.49	.53*	.48
Sequential/*Gsm*	.50	.48	.44	.44	.44
Simultaneous/*Gv*	.54	.47	.53	.40	.43
Planning/*Gf*	.63*	.56*	.59*	.51	.51*
Knowledge/*Gc*	.75**	.71**	.62**	.59**	.68**

**Highest correlate of each KTEA-II Achievement Composite.

*Second-highest correlate of each KTEA-II Achievement Composite.

Note: Total = Comprehensive Achievement Composite. $N = 2,025$. All correlations were corrected for the variability of the norm group, based on the standard deviation obtained on the KTEA-II, using the variability correction of Cohen et al. (2003, p. 58). Data are adapted from Kaufman and Kaufman (2004b).

≡Rapid Reference 4.10

KABC-II Scale Index Correlations with KTEA-II Composites (Ages 4:6–6 Years)

KTEA-II Composite

KABC-II Scale	Total	Reading	Math	Written Language	Oral Language
Learning/Glr	.54	.58**	.52	.62**	.42
Sequential/Gsm	.59	.57*	.57*	.58	.49
Simultaneous/Gv	.65**	.57*	.65**	.59*	.50*
Knowledge/Gc	.60*	.49	.49	.47	.62**

**Highest* correlate of each KTEA-II Achievement Composite.

Second-highest correlate of each KTEA-II Achievement Composite.

Note: Total = Comprehensive Achievement Composite. N = 491 for Total and Oral Language; N = 301 for Math; N = 122–124 for Written Language. All correlations were corrected for the variability of the norm group, based on the standard deviation obtained on the KTEA-II, using the variability correction of Cohen et al. (2003, p. 58). Data are adapted from Kaufman and Kaufman (2004b).

For the older children, ages 7 to 18, the Knowledge/Gc scale was the strongest correlate of all areas of achievement (Rapid Reference 4.9). For this age group, the Knowledge/Gc Index correlated .75 with KTEA-II Comprehensive Achievement, about .70 with Reading and Oral Language, and about .60 with Math and Written Language. The second-best correlate for ages 7 to 18 was typically Planning/Gf (r's of .51 to .63), although Learning/Glr was the second-best correlate of Written Language (.53). The poorest relationships with all areas of academic achievement for ages 7 to 18 tended to be analogs of the original KABC-II processing scales—Sequential/Gsm and Simultaneous/Gv (r's of .40 to .54).

Given that the KABC-II's Knowledge/Gc Index is designed to measure the depth and breadth of knowledge acquired from one's culture (including schooling), the strong relationship between it and all areas of achievement for school-age children and adolescents was not surprising. The good correlations with achievement for the new KABC-II scales—Planning/Gf and Learning/Glr—attest to the importance in the classroom of the ability to solve problems and learn new material during a clinical evaluation of general cognitive ability.

Intriguingly, the patterns of relationship between ability and achievement observed for school-age children and adolescents differed quite a bit from the patterns seen at ages 4:6 to 6 years (Rapid Reference 4.10), when academic abilities are first emerging. Despite its obvious link to vocabulary and acquisition of facts, the Knowledge/*Gc* Index was *not* the highest correlate of achievement for young children. That distinction went to the Simultaneous/*Gv* Index (*r* = .65 with KTEA-II Comprehensive Achievement) with Knowledge/*Gc* (.60) and Sequential/*Gsm* (.59) in a virtual deadlock for second best. So, contrary to ages 7 to 18, the KABC-II Sequential/*Gsm* and Simultaneous/*Gv* Indexes were among the best correlates of achievement for ages 4:6 to 6 years. In addition, rather than the Knowledge/*Gc* scale emerging as the automatic best predictor of each area of achievement, the highest correlates for young children varied by area. Simultaneous/*Gv* was the highest correlate of Math (.65), Learning/*Glr* was best for Written Language (.62), and Knowledge/*Gc* was best for Oral Language (.62). Three of the four Indexes (all *except* Knowledge/*Gc*) were about equal as predictors of Reading (.57 to .58).

Thus, for ages 7 to 18, mental processes such as reasoning and planning were important for academic achievement, but not as important as a child's previously acquired knowledge. For ages 4:6 to 6, the roles were reversed. During the stage when school skills are emerging, the amount of knowledge a child has already acquired is secondary to the cognitive processes that are needed to learn to read, write, compute, and speak. Indeed, the one aspect of achievement for which Knowledge/*Gc* was easily the best predictor was Oral Language—undoubtedly relating to the fact that both subtests for this age group (Riddles and Expressive Vocabulary) emphasize children's oral language skills.

The increase in the Knowledge/*Gc* scale's importance from ages 4:6 to 6 to 7 to 18 probably reflects the increased experience with language and academic information as age increases. Also, the strong correlations at ages 4:6 to 6 between Simultaneous/*Gv* and achievement most likely relates to the fact that this scale measures *both* Visual Processing (*Gv*) and Fluid Reasoning (*Gf*) for young children, because a separate Planning/*Gf* scale does not emerge until age 7.

Further examination of Rapid References 4.9 and 4.10 indicates that coefficients between KABC-II scale indexes and the five major KTEA-II composites ranged from .40 to .75, with median values of .53 (ages 7 to 18) and .57 (4:6 to 6). Most values (about 70%) were in the .50 to .75 range, indicating an acceptable level of relationship between the individual scales of the KABC-II and the major KTEA-II composites. If the majority of values were below this moderate range then there would be a concern that there would not be a reasonable level of association between the two tests. On the other hand, individual scales indicating much higher levels would raise the issue of redundancy and the possibility that the tests measure the same constructs. Even the highest correlation—.75 between Knowledge/Gc and total KTEA-II achievement for ages 7 to 18—denotes an overlap of 56 percent, indicating that each test has its own uniqueness. Therefore, the fact that the majority of coefficients fall in this moderate to strong area indicates an acceptable level of relationship between the two tests.

The KABC-II scales that correlate most highly with the Comprehensive Achievement scale of the KTEA-II differ, again, by age level. The Knowledge scale, as expected, has the highest correlation coefficients with the Comprehensive Achievement scale across all age levels except ages 4:6 and grade 1. The latter groups have highest coefficients on the Simultaneous and Sequential scales, respectively, rather than the Knowledge scale. This is another way of reflecting the makeup of the FCI, MCI, and Comprehensive Achievement relationship. The increase in Knowledge scale importance probably reflects the increased experience with language and academic information as age increases.

Integrating the KTEA-II and KABC-II—Theory

The integration of the KTEA-II and KABC-II was designed to sample the spectrum of broad and narrow abilities defined by the Cattell-Horn-Carroll (CHC) model. The CHC model includes 10 broad abilities and about 70 narrow abilities (Flanagan & Ortiz, 2001). The KABC-II addresses five of the CHC broad abilities: Short-Term Memory (Gsm), Visual Processing (Gv), Long-Term Storage and Retrieval (Glr); Fluid Reasoning (Gf); and Crystallized Ability (Gc). The KTEA-II Comprehensive Form measures three additional broad abilities: Auditory Processing (Ga), Reading and Writing (Grw), and Quantitative Knowledge/Gq ability. It also measures Glr narrow abilities, which increase the breadth of the Glr narrow abilities measured by the KABC-II when the two batteries are administered together. The KABC-II also indirectly measures one of the Gq narrow abilities (i.e., Mathematics Achievement, by virtue of the fact that Rover and Block Counting each require the child to count).

There are two broad abilities of the CHC model that are not measured by either the KABC-II or the KTEA-II: Processing Speed (Gs), and Decision Speed/Reaction Time (Gt). These two broad abilities are not measured by either battery because they are only concerned with speed, not quality, of processing; they lack the requisite complexity for inclusion; and they are weak measures of g in Carroll's (1993) factor-analytic survey (Kaufman & Kaufman, 2004b). Measures of gs are readily available in other tests, most notably the WJ III and WISC-IV, but Gt is not measured by any major test battery.

Figure 4.1 displays the alignment of narrow abilities measured by the KABC-

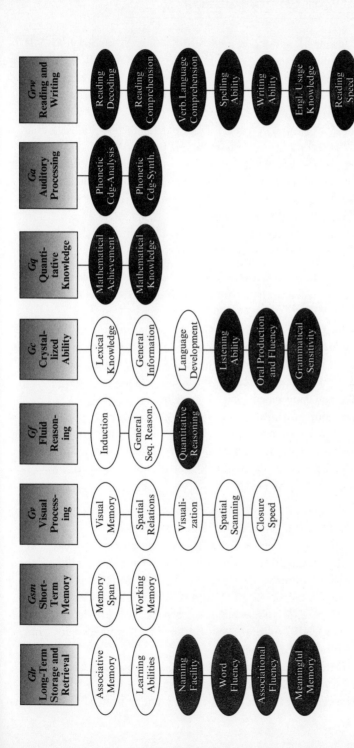

Figure 4.1 CHC broad and narrow abilities measured by the KABC-II and the KTEA-II

Note: The CHC broad abilities are shown in gray squares. CHC narrow abilities that are measured by only KABC-II subtests are represented by white ovals; narrow abilities that are measured only by KTEA-II subtests are represented by black ovals. Two KABC-II subtests also measure math achievement, but are primarily measures of other narrow abilities.

Source: Kaufman, Lichtenberger, Fletcher-Janzen, & Kaufman (2005).

II and KTEA-II, grouped by the pertinent broad ability. Alone, the KTEA-II measures 19 narrow abilities and six broad abilities. For the KABC-II, the 14 narrow abilities are measured, including two or more associated with each of five broad abilities. The total of 33 is just under half of the 70 or so narrow abilities hypothesized, and often documented empirically, by Carroll (1993).

Rapid References 4.11 through 4.18 provide specific information regarding the precise KABC-II and KTEA-II subtests that are believed to measure each of the 34 narrow abilities. The Rapid References are organized by broad ability (e.g., Rapid Reference 4.11 covers the subtests that measure *Glr* narrow abilities, Rapid Reference 4.12 is confined to *Gsm* narrow abilities, and so forth). The broad abilities measured by the KABC-II were defined earlier in Rapid Reference 4.7. The remaining three broad abilities, which are measured only by the KTEA-II, are defined as follows (Flanagan, McGrew, & Ortiz, 2000).

> **Quantitative Knowledge (*Gq*):** The *Gq* store of acquired knowledge represents the ability to use quantitative information and manipulate numeric symbols.
>
> **Reading/Writing Ability (*Grw*):** The *Grw* ability is an acquired store of knowledge that includes basic reading and writing skills required for the comprehension of written language and the expression of thought via writing. It includes both basic (e.g., reading decoding, spelling) and complex abilities (e.g., reading comprehension and the ability to write a story).
>
> **Auditory Processing (*Ga*):** Auditory processing is the ability to perceive, analyze, and synthesize patterns among auditory stimuli, and to discriminate subtle nuances in patterns of sound and speech when presented under distorted conditions. *Ga* subsumes most of those abilities referred to as phonological awareness/processing.

One of the most important expectations that you may have about using the KABC-II and the KTEA-II together is that there is a cohesive theoretical design that acts like an umbrella over the two tests. This expectation is met in that there are no redundancies between the tests, which would result in a waste of time. (No examiner has time to waste duplicating subtests!) The definition of cognitive processing and achievement on the KABC-II and KTEA-II is theoretically based and evidence-based; the results of combining the two tests will give the examiner a comprehensive and fruitful examination of the child's cognitive abilities and how they translate into academic skills.

That is not to say that the two batteries do not overlap in broad or narrow abilities; as is evident from Figure 4.1 and Rapid References 4.11 to 4.18, there is some overlap. However, there is no redundancy. For example, both batteries measure *Glr* and *Gc* narrow abilities, but each measures a separate set. When they do measure the same narrow ability, they do it in quite different ways: Mathematical Achievement is a minor aspect of two KABC-II subtests, but this *Gq* ability is the major thrust of Mathematics Computation; in contrast, the *Gf* narrow ability of Induction is a key component of the KABC-II Planning/*Gf* subtests.

Flanagan and Ortiz (2001) suggest that you need at least two different, primary narrow ability measures to adequately measure a broad ability from a cross-battery perspective. Examiners who integrate the KABC-II with the KTEA-II should easily be able to achieve adequate measurement of seven broad abilities: *Gv, Gf, Gc, Glr, Gsm, Grw,* and *Gq*. However, assessment of *Ga* depends on a single KTEA-II subtest (Phonological Awareness) that is only normed from age 4:6 to grade 6.

Of course, no one battery can cover the CHC model in its entirety, but the KABC-II and the KTEA-II—like the WJ III Cognitive and Achievement Batteries—provide a substantially positive start for the clinician to examine a child's performance from a CHC perspective. The KTEA-II can be supplemented via cross-battery assessment, using CHC theory as its foundation. For more in-depth study of the theory and assessment approach as it pertains to other instruments (such as the original K-ABC and Wechsler scales), consult publications by Flanagan and her colleagues (Flanagan & Kaufman, 2004; Flanagan, McGrew, & Ortiz, 2000; Flanagan & Ortiz, 2001; Flanagan, Ortiz, Alfonso, & Mascolo, 2002; McGrew & Flanagan, 1998).

Long-Term Storage & Retrieval (Glr)

Examiners can obtain a rich measurement of *Glr* by administering a variety of KTEA-II subtests. Listening Comprehension, Associational Fluency, and Naming Facility/RAN all relate to the CHC requirement of the child engaging in activities that measure the efficiency of how well information is stored and retrieved. The KABC-II Core Battery measures a single *Glr* narrow ability (Associative Memory); an additional narrow ability is assessed when examiners administer the supplementary Delayed Recall scale (Atlantis Delayed and Rebus Delayed each measure *both* Associative Memory and Learning Abilities).

KTEA-II Listening Comprehension demands that the child listen to and encode a story and then manipulate the information to answer questions about the story. Although "long-term storage and retrieval" implies that there is a long time between encoding and retrieval, this is not necessarily the case, because the information has to be retrieved by association for whatever time interval has lapsed. The CHC model calls the narrow ability measured by Listening Comprehension "Meaningful Memory."

≡Rapid Reference 4.11

CHC Analysis: Long-Term Storage and Retrieval (*Glr*) Narrow Abilities Measured by KTEA-II and KABC-II Subtests

Glr Narrow Ability

Associative Memory
KABC-II Atlantis
KABC-II Rebus
KABC-II Atlantis Delayed
KABC-II Rebus Delayed

Learning Abilities
KABC-II Atlantis Delayed
KABC-II Rebus Delayed

Naming Facility
KTEA-II Naming Facility/RAN

Associational Fluency
KTEA-II Associational Fluency (category items, e.g., foods, animals)

Word Fluency
KTEA-II Associational Fluency (category items, e.g., words that start with the /d/ sound)

Meaningful Memory
KTEA-II Listening Comprehension

The Naming Facility/RAN subtest was given its label based both on the CHC narrow ability that it measures (Naming Facility) and on the popular neuropsychological subtest that inspired it (Rapid Automatized Naming, or RAN). The Associational Fluency subtest is also named after a CHC narrow ability, but in actuality this subtest measures two different narrow abilities. The category items (e.g., name as many kinds of toys as you can) measure Associational Fluency, whereas the items that focus on naming as many words as possible that start with a specific sound (such as /k/) measure Word Fluency. For purposes of reliability, these two narrow abilities are subsumed by a single standard score. Inferences about the separate narrow abilities are only possible if the child performs at notably different levels on the two kinds of items (e.g., a child who can reel off a string of words that begin with particular sounds, but is stymied and hesitant when retrieving categorical words). See Rapid Reference 4.11 for an outline of the Long-Term Storage & Retrieval (*Glr*) narrow abilities.

Short-Term Memory (Gsm)

The primary subtest that measures auditory short-term memory on the KABC-II is Number Recall. The CHC model mostly mentions auditory short-term memory tests for *Gsm*, but visual and haptic activities such as Hand Movements also measure *Gsm*. The three subtests together measure different modalities of short-term memory, and also how short-term memory can evolve into working memory.

All three KABC-II *Gsm* subtests (Number Recall, Word Order, and Hand Movements) measure Memory Span. In addition, Word Order has a color inter-

≡Rapid Reference 4.12

CHC Analysis: Short-Term Memory (*Gsm*) Narrow Abilities Measured by KABC-II
(KTEA-II Subtests Do Not Measure Any *Gsm* Narrow Abilities)

Gsm Narrow Ability

Memory Span
    KABC-II Word Order (without color interference)
    KABC-II Number Recall
    KABC-II Hand Movements

Working Memory
    KABC-II Word Order (with color interference)

Note: Success on KTEA-II Phonological Awareness and Listening Comprehension is also dependent, to some extent, on *Gsm*.

---

ference task that definitely requires the narrow ability of Working Memory. Consequently, for young children (ages 3 to 5 or 6), who are not likely to reach the color interference items in Word Order, the KABC-II measures only a single CHC narrow ability—Memory Span. However, for children 6 to 7 or older, the KABC-II measures both Memory Span and Working Memory. See Rapid Reference 4.12 for an outline of the Short-Term Memory (*Gsm*) narrow abilities.

Visual Processing (Gv)

The KABC-II provides rich measurement of five *Gv* narrow abilities, although examiners need to administer supplementary subtests such as Gestalt Closure (Closure Speed) and Hand Movements (Visual Memory) to measure all five. See Rapid Reference 4.13 for an outline of the Visual Processing (*Gv*) narrow abilities.

Fluid Reasoning (Gf)

Fluid reasoning is specifically measured by the subtests that constitute the KABC-II Planning/*Gf* scale (Pattern Reasoning, Story Completion), and also by subtests on the Simultaneous/*Gv* scale (Rover, Conceptual Thinking) and the Knowledge/*Gc* scale (Riddles). KTEA-II Mathematics Concepts and Applications is primarily a *Gq* task, but it also requires considerable *Gf* for success, specifically the narrow ability Quantitative Reasoning. On the Planning/*Gf* scale, Pattern Reasoning primarily measures the narrow ability of Induction, whereas Story Completion measures *both* Induction (figuring out what the story is about) and General Sequential Reasoning, or deduction (selecting and sequencing the correct pictures). See Rapid Reference 4.14 for an outline of the Fluid Reasoning (*Gf*) narrow abilities.

≡ *Rapid Reference 4.13*

CHC Analysis: Visual Processing (*Gv*) Narrow Abilities Measured by KABC-II (KTEA-II Subtests Do Not Measure Any *Gv* Narrow Abilities)

Gv Narrow Ability

Visual Memory
  KABC-II Face Recognition
  KABC-II Hand Movements

Spatial Relations
  KABC-II Triangles

Visualization
  KABC-II Triangles
  KABC-II Conceptual Thinking
  KABC-II Block Counting
  KABC-II Pattern Reasoning
  KABC-II Story Completion

Spatial Scanning
  KABC-II Rover

Closure Speed
  KABC-II Gestalt Closure

Note: Success on KTEA-II Written Expression is also dependent, to some extent, on Visual Processing.

Crystallized Ability (Gc)

The narrow ability of Lexical Knowledge is measured by all three KABC-II Knowledge/*Gc* subtests, with Riddles (Language Development) and Verbal Knowledge (General Information) each measuring an additional *Gc* narrow ability as well. When the KABC-II and KTEA-II are administered together, the measurement of *Gc* narrow abilities expands to six, indicating breadth of coverage of this broad ability. See Rapid Reference 4.15 for an outline of Crystallized Ability (*Gc*) narrow abilities.

Auditory Processing (Ga)

Ga "requires the perception, analysis, and synthesis of patterns among auditory stimuli as well as the discrimination of subtle differences in patterns of sound" (Flanagan & Ortiz, 2001, p. 18). It is assessed on the KTEA-II by the supplementary Phonological Awareness, and measures both the analytic and synthetic narrow abilities associated with the *Ga* broad ability. However, the KTEA-II subtest is of appropriate difficulty primarily for young children (PreK to grade 2), and is only standardized through grade 6. In addition, it yields an overall score rather than separate scores for its two narrow abilities. Nonetheless, the KTEA-II Error Analysis procedure for Phonological Awareness permits examiners to determine whether the child performed at a "Strong," "Average," or "Weak" level

≡Rapid Reference 4.14

CHC Analysis: Fluid Reasoning (*Gf*) Narrow Abilities Measured by KTEA-II and KABC-II Subtests

Gf Narrow Ability

Induction
KABC-II Conceptual Thinking
KABC-II Pattern Reasoning
KABC-II Story Completion

General Sequential Reasoning
KABC-II Story Completion
KABC-II Rover
KABC-II Riddles

Quantitative Reasoning
KTEA-II Mathematics Concepts and
Applications

Note: Success on KABC-II Rebus and four KTEA-II subtests (Reading Comprehension, Listening Comprehension, Oral Expression, and Written Expression) is also dependent, to some extent, on Fluid Reasoning.

≡Rapid Reference 4.15

CHC Analysis: Crystallized Ability (*Gc*) Narrow Abilities Measured by KTEA-II and KABC-II Subtests

Gc Narrow Ability

General Information
KABC-II Verbal Knowledge (items that
measure general information)
KABC-II Story Completion

Language Development
KABC-II Riddles

Lexical Knowledge
KABC-II Riddles
KABC-II Verbal Knowledge (items that
measure vocabulary)
KABC-II Expressive Vocabulary

Listening Ability
KTEA-II Listening Comprehension

Oral Production and Fluency
KTEA-II Oral Expression

Grammatical Sensitivity
KTEA-II Oral Expression
KTEA-II Written Expression

Note: Success on KABC-II Rebus is also dependent, to some extent, on Grammatical Sensitivity.

≡Rapid Reference 4.16

CHC Analysis: Auditory Processing (*Ga*) Narrow Abilities Measured by KTEA-II
(KABC-II Subtests Do Not Measure Any *Ga* Narrow Abilities)

Ga Narrow Ability

Phonetic Coding—Analysis
KTEA-II Phonological Awareness
(Section 1—Rhyming; Section 2—
Sound Matching; Section 4—Seg-
menting; Section 5—Deleting Sounds)

Phonetic Coding—Synthesis
KTEA-II Phonological Awareness
(Section 3—Blending)

Note: Deficits in certain *Ga* narrow abilities, such as Speech Sound Discrimination (US), may impact performance negatively on such tests as KABC-II Riddles, Word Order, and Number Recall,
and KTEA-II Listening Comprehension.

on the separate sections of the subtest (Kaufman & Kaufman, 2004a). Hence, the error analysis allows examiners to compare the child's ability on the two *Ga* narrow abilities that it measures. See Rapid Reference 4.16 for an outline of Auditory Processing (*Ga*) narrow abilities.

*Quantitative Knowledge (*Gq*)*

Gq measures the individual's store of accumulated mathematical knowledge (Flanagan & Ortiz, 2001). It is different from the *Gf* narrow ability of Quantitative Reasoning because *Gq* is more about what the child knows than how the child reasons with quantitative information. Math Concepts and Applications measures quantitative Reasoning to some extent, but that subtest is primarily a measure of *Gq,* as is Mathematics Computation. Taken together, both KTEA-II subtests that make up the Math Composite measure the two *Gq* narrow abilities, providing thorough measurement of the *Gq* broad ability. See Rapid Reference 4.17 for an outline of Quantitative Knowledge (*Gq*) narrow abilities.

≡Rapid Reference 4.17

CHC Analysis: Quantitative Knowledge (*Gq*) Narrow Abilities Measured by KTEA-II and KABC-II Subtests

Gq Narrow Ability

Mathematical Knowledge
KTEA-II Mathematics Concepts and
Applications

Mathematical Achievement
KTEA-II Mathematics Computation
KABC-II Rover
KABC-II Block Counting

≡Rapid Reference 4.18

CHC Analysis: Reading and Writing (*Grw*) Narrow Abilities Measured by KTEA-II
(KABC-II Subtests Do Not Measure Any *Grw* Narrow Abilities)

Grw Narrow Ability

Reading Decoding
   KTEA-II Letter and Word Reading
   KTEA-II Nonsense Word Decoding

Reading Comprehension
   KTEA-II Reading Comprehension
   (paragraph items)

Verbal (Printed) Language Comprehension
   KTEA-II Reading Comprehension
   (items requiring student to do what a
   sentence tells them to do)

Spelling Ability
   KTEA-II Spelling

Writing Ability
   KTEA-II Written Expression

English Usage Knowledge
   KTEA-II Written Expression

Reading Speed
   KTEA-II Word Recognition Fluency
   KTEA-II Decoding Fluency

*Reading and Writing (*Grw*)*

Grw is measured by achievement tests (Flanagan & Ortiz, 2001). The KTEA-II provides thorough measurement of five key *Grw* narrow abilities: Reading Decoding, Reading Comprehension, Spelling Ability, Writing Ability, and Reading Speed. It also measures two additional *Gc* abilities to some extent—Verbal (Printed) Language Comprehension and English Usage Knowledge. Several of the new subtests added to the KTEA-II Comprehensive Form (Nonsense Word Decoding, Written Expression, Word Recognition Fluency, and Decoding Fluency) greatly enriched the measurement of *Grw* narrow abilities relative to the original K-TEA. See Rapid Reference 4.18 for an outline of Reading and Writing (*Grw*) narrow abilities.

Clinical Analysis of the Integration of the KABC-II and KTEA-II

CHC theory and quantitative analyses (especially correlational) provide valuable ways of integrating the KABC-II and KTEA-II, but it is important to remember that (1) the KABC-II is built on a dual theoretical foundation (Luria's neuropsychological approach as well as CHC psychometric theory), and (2) both the KABC-II and KTEA-II are individually administered, clinical instruments that afford examiners rich opportunities for qualitative observations. We cannot envision the examiner obtaining the full benefit of an analysis of the KABC-II and

KTEA-II without including the important process and qualitative information. This information comes from observing a child in a standardized setting that minimizes unnecessary interactions (e.g., wording in instructions) and maximizes opportunities to actively engage learning processes (e.g., dynamic subtests like Atlantis and Rebus) with the child.

This section on clinical analysis fully takes into account the neuropsychological processing model developed by Luria, and addresses brain functions/processes involved in cognitive *and* achievement tests. For example, the Phonological Awareness test on the KTEA-II is a subtest that requires the child to remember and manipulate sounds and words. This subtest is not only a wonderful measure of auditory skills (*Ga*), but also of working memory and cognitive sequencing. These latter skills are specifically measured by the Sequential/*Gsm* scale, indicating that a complete understanding of the young child's performance on KTEA-II Phonological Awareness requires examiners to compare that performance to the child's success (or lack of it) on KABC-II Sequential/*Gsm* subtests.

It is not a coincidence that these kinds of tasks reflect years of research on auditory/sequential skills and the phonemic awareness skills needed for reading (e.g., Hooper & Hynd, 1985; Kamphaus & Reynolds, 1987; Lichtenberger, Broadbooks, & Kaufman, 2000; Lichtenberger, 2001) and associated with left-hemispheric processing (James & Selz, 1997; Lyon, Fletcher, & Barnes, 2003; Reynolds, Kamphaus, Rosenthal & Hiemenz, 1997).

For each section that follows, discussion emphasizes functional processing abilities that will hopefully help examiners with construct and skill analyses. Both the CHC and Luria theoretical approaches reflect an aspect of comprehensive assessment that needs to be buttressed by qualitative/process information. Furthermore, all cognitive test and achievement test data must be interpreted in the context of other important information such as history, medical status, medications, family involvement, quality of teaching, developmental stage, social and emotional functioning, visual-motor functioning, and responses to prior interventions.

Phonological Awareness, Sequential Processing, Short-Term Memory, and Listening Comprehension

As indicated in Rapid Reference 4.12, we believe that the KTEA-II Phonological Awareness and Listening Comprehension are each dependent, to some extent, on the CHC *Gsm* broad ability. The process rationale for each subtest follows.

Process rationale for Phonological Awareness: It is important to understand both the Lurian and CHC ways of interpreting the Sequential/*Gsm* scale because there is a great deal of research literature that combines sequential processing and auditory short-term memory with the type of phonological processing skills that are measured by the KTEA-II Phonological Awareness subtest (Siegal, 1997; Teeter, 1997). The combination of this KTEA-II subtest and the KABC-II Sequential/*Gsm* subtests provides a large window of opportunity for evaluating reading problems and the more phonologically based subtypes of learning disabilities (see the section of this chapter on "Identifying Learning Disabilities").

As a primary measure of auditory short-term memory, the Sequential/*Gsm* Core subtests help the examiner evaluate the critical listening skills that children need in the classroom. The Phonological Awareness subtest measures sound-symbol connections, but because of the way it is set up, it also measures auditory short-term memory and sequencing skills. This is an interactive subtest where the child has to listen very closely to the examiner and then reproduce sounds and manipulate word syllables and sounds. In the last part of Phonemic Awareness, the child also has to hold a multisyllable word in working memory and then remove a syllable to form a new word.

A skilled examiner can retrieve a lot of information by assessing behavioral clues about how well the child can remember sounds and use working memory. Does the child attempt to reproduce the sound? Does the child miss the examiner's cues and ask for repetitions? Is the child shy and too embarrassed to verbalize? Does the child get the sounds right but in the wrong order? When you move to the part of Phonological Awareness that needs working memory, does the child's behavior shift dramatically? Does the child pay attention or do you have to cue each item?

The reading research literature indicates that many early reading problems stem from a learning disability subtype called "auditory-linguistic or phonological form of dyslexia" (Spreen, 2001; Teeter, 1997). This is not to say that visual and other processing deficits are not important subtypes of reading problems, but for the moment, let us explore the relationship between the processing and production of phonology in young readers.

Phonological processing is basically the ability to understand and use the sound components of language. The KTEA-II Phonological Awareness subtest comprises five different activities that correspond to Adams' (1990) five levels of phonemic awareness tasks, in ascending order of difficulty: rhyming, sound matching, blending, segmenting, and manipulating phonemes.

Phonological processing is closely related to problems in speech perception, naming and vocabulary ability, and auditory short-term memory with sounds. When phonological awareness deficits are present reading comprehension suffers, because the cognitive processes that are required for comprehension are tied up in decoding and word recognition (Stanovich, 1992). This leaves the child with a myopic focus on the elements of the text and little resources for fluid reading and comprehension.

Young children who have reading problems can be helped by evaluating their ability to understand the phonetic/linguistic parts of reading. If we know which parts are problematic, then we will be able to better describe interventions that are targeted to the child's specific deficit. There is evidence to support interventions in phonemic awareness with young elementary-aged children, not only from an academic outcome perspective, but also from neuropsychological growth perspective in that neural networks that support reading can be enhanced with the appropriate instruction (Lyon et al., 2003).

As indicated, the KABC-II scale that has an important part in the assessment of phonological awareness skills, especially in younger readers, is the Sequential/ *Gsm* scale. The primary task of the Sequential/*Gsm* scale is to measure how the child processes information in a linear, step-by-step fashion. How a child performs on the Sequential/*Gsm* scale can illuminate whether the child has the prerequisite auditory sequencing and short-term memory skills to be able to put sounds together with symbols while he or she is decoding a word (Das, Naglieri, & Kirby, 1994; Kirby & Williams, 1991; Naglieri, 2001).

Process Rationale for Listening Comprehension: The Listening Comprehension subtest on the KTEA-II also supports the Sequential/*Gsm* scale because it straddles auditory short-term memory, auditory working memory, and auditory long-term encoding. The tasks are presented in a purely auditory form and therefore should be compared with Phonological Awareness and the Sequential/*Gsm* Core subtests. Does the child remember well on Phonological Awareness with small, short-term auditory segments and then do very poorly on Listening Comprehension, which requires a much higher auditory memory load? Or, the opposite; the child does not do well with small, purely auditory segments, but when the task is put in story form on Listening Comprehension he or she performs quite well? Answers to these types of processing questions will help with differential diagnosis later on.

The Simultaneous/Gv Scale and Written Expression

You may wish to compare performance on the Simultaneous/*Gv* scale with Written Expression, to examine the visual-motor aspects of written expression activities and how they relate to some of the visual-motor activities on the KABC-II subtests such as Rover or Triangles. These comparisons may help you figure out why a child has poor handwriting, or poor visual organization on writing tasks. Remember when you were administering the Written Expression test to the child.

Did you observe the child having trouble holding the pencil? Did the child lose his or her place a lot? Did the child write a lot of words or letters in a reversed way? Were there multiple erasures? Did the child have trouble figuring out where he or she should write the responses, even though you were pointing to the correct starting point?

If you do suspect that poor achievement in writing is partly due to visual-motor issues then it would be appropriate to pursue this hypothesis further, by administering tests designed specifically for assessing visual-motor problems. We believe that KTEA-II Written Expression is dependent, to some extent, on the CHC *Gv* broad ability (see Rapid Reference 4.13).

Planning, Reasoning, and Executive Functions: How They Apply to Rover and Rebus and to Several KTEA-II Subtests

Rapid Reference 4.13 indicates that KABC-II's Rover measures the *Gf* narrow ability of General Sequential Reasoning (deduction). Other subtests (Rebus and four KTEA-II tasks) are mentioned in the Note to that Rapid Reference as being dependent, to some extent, on the *Gf* broad ability. The process rationale for each of these subtests follows.

Process Rationale for Rover. Rover was designed to explore the child's ability to create numerous ways to solve a problem and then to choose the best plan. Like the game of chess, however, Rover also has a visual-spatial component that is just as essential as planning ability in order to efficiently navigate the game board. When Rover was initially developed, it was intended as a measure of Planning/ *Gf*. However, confirmatory factor analyses of National Tryout clearly pinpointed Rover as a measure of simultaneous and visual processing. Because the child has to look for different ways a dog can get to a bone on a map-like game board containing rocks, weeds, and grass, it is ultimately the child's visual mapping ability that plays the most important part in solving the problems.

Nonetheless, Rover was included in the KABC-II because, regardless of its scale membership, the task presented an interesting challenge to children and adolescents, measures both *Gf* and *Gv* narrow abilities, and demands intact executive functions for success. If a child has poor planning or executive functions, performance on this subtest is severely impacted. Even though the child's visual-spatial mapping abilities lead the way, he or she still has to figure out several plans, hold them in working memory, and then determine the value of the best plan. The latter is, most definitely, an executive functioning task.

Indeed, in a KABC-II study of 56 children with Attention Deficit/Hyperactivity Disorder (ADHD), a group that is noteworthy for having deficits in executive functions (Barkley, 2003), the children had significantly lower scores ($p <$

.001) on Rover than their non-ADHD peers (Kaufman & Kaufman, 2004a). They also had significantly lower scores on more pure measures of executive functions, such as the Planning/Gf Pattern Reasoning and Story Completion subtests ($p < .01$).

When you are evaluating the Planning/Gf scale, therefore, consider the child's performance on Rover. Was the child organized? Did he or she take the time to look for all of the possible solutions, or did he or she just blurt out the first answer? Also look at the style of processing. Did the child take time and think about the routes, and then count out the final plan (reflective style), or did he or she charge right in and then have to self-correct later (impulsive style)? Rover can supplement the Planning/Gf scale by helping you look at the differences in subtest scores, including the processing and qualitative aspects of how the child obtained the scores. If you note executive function-type deficits during Rover, see if these deficits were also evident on Pattern Reasoning and Story Completion. Also, examine your qualitative observations of the child's strategy generation and then administer other tests of executive functions to test your hypotheses.

Process Rationale for Rebus. The CHC model places Rebus safely in the narrow ability category of Associative Memory (MA); the examinee is required to learn the word associated with a particular rebus drawing and then read phrases and sentences composed of these drawings. Although Rebus primarily measures a *Glr* narrow ability it still requires a great deal of organization, not just retrieval.

Rebus also measures the process of how a child responds to the teaching/learning situation. Unlike other subtests (except Atlantis), the child has to learn more and more information and then apply the information. It is similar to a classroom situation except that it is strictly controlled and measurable, because the examiner gives standardized teaching prompts. This is a subtest where the examiner feeds information and rehearsal to the child step-by-step. The examiner is constrained by only being able to teach in a standardized fashion; however, this constraint also frees the examiner to look at how the child responds to teaching. This is a dynamic and controlled process and provides key qualitative data to the KABC-II examiner.

The reason that Rebus is considered to depend on Gf to some extent is because during administration the test demands executive functions to be at maximum alert. Many researchers (e.g., Goldberg & Bougakov, 2000) liken the executive functions to an orchestra conductor. The first and second functional areas of the brain, if you will, are the actual musicians in the orchestra—all designed to play certain instruments at certain times. The orchestra conductor is the third functional area of the brain (frontal lobe area), which has to direct complex cognitive functions that require input, processing, prioritizing, organizing, planning, and output.

Rebus taxes the orchestra conductor, because there are many first and second functional unit tasks, such as paying attention to each tiny word/picture, processing the visual information, processing the auditory information, melding the symbol and sound, only learning exactly what the examiner is teaching at paced intervals, organizing the reading of symbols and their sounds into coherent and meaningful sentences, and checking for mistakes and comprehension. It takes quite a conductor to direct the Rebus symphony!

There are many qualitative or behavioral indicators present during the application of Rebus that can give the examiner clues as to problems with attention or executive functions. Many young children performing Rebus will try very hard to learn the words and their matching symbols and then be completely oblivious to the fact that they are reading meaningful sentences. Therefore, if they make a mistake on a word and the meaning of the sentence disappears they do not mentally register the lack of meaning—they simply just continue to read isolated symbols. On the other hand, children who do have developing executive or metacognitive functions will notice the break in comprehension, skip back to where they think they went wrong, and try to figure out the mistaken symbol. This behavior is correlative of the orchestra conductor checking where lower functions went wrong, and it also makes for a difference in scores, because the child self-corrects.

An alert examiner will know by the presence or absence of self-corrective behaviors if the child has problems with organization. A low score on Rebus could mean that there is a problem with transferring information from short/recent memory to long-term memory (as the *Glr* classification implies), but a low score could also mean that there is trouble with planning/executive functions. Hence, a comparison with the strong planning subtests like Pattern Reasoning and Story Completion is appropriate. Therefore, while Rebus factorially belongs on the *Glr*/Learning Scale of the KABC-II, it can also assist in the exploration of the child's fluid reasoning ability, measured on the Planning/*Gf* scale.

Process Rationale for KTEA-II Written Expression, Reading Comprehension, Math Applications, Oral Expression, and Listening Comprehension. There are four subtests on the KTEA-II that require not only academic knowledge, but also organizational, deductive, inductive, and planning skills. Written Expression, Reading Comprehension, Oral Expression, and Listening Comprehension all require higher levels of cognition (Sattler, 2001), cognitive load (Raney, 1993), or higher-complex abilities (Mather, Wendling, & Woodcock, 2001). Sattler, and Mather et al. describe primary academic tasks in a hierarchy, ranging from ones requiring low levels of cognition, such as letter identification, to those that require higher levels, such as reading comprehension and the construction of written text. Figure 4.2 illustrates the hierarchical relationship among achievement areas and subtests on the

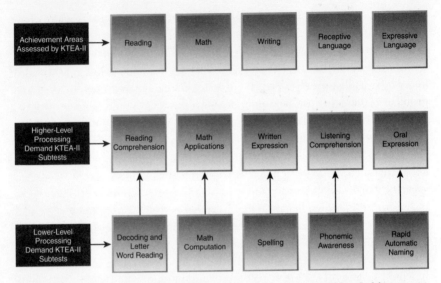

Figure 4.2 KTEA-II Hierarchy of Cognitive Processing Load by Achievement Area, Higher Level Processing Subtests, and Lower Level Processing Subtests

KTEA-II Comprehensive Form with respect to their level of cognitive processing.

Informally interpreting these subtest scores alongside the subtests that truly measure *Gf* narrow abilities acknowledges that the more sophisticated skills needed for these upper-level academic tasks should be assessed in a cognitive-processing manner. Again, the skilled and observant examiner watches how the child takes these achievement tests and looks for behavioral clues to see if the child has the organization and planning skills to do a good job.

During Reading Comprehension, for example, the child has to pick the best of several responses to answer the question about comprehension correctly. Watch for processing style here. Does the child read the passage quickly and impulsively pick an answer (impulsive, inattentive style), or does the child read the passage and then spend quite a bit of time reading the possible answers and deliberating on the correctness of a response (reflective style)? Does the child have so many problems decoding the reading passage that he or she misses the overall story? Observe the child's eye movements. Does the child read from left to right, with occasional loops back to check for comprehension (fluid movements), or does the child's eyes flicker back and forth, lose place, skip lines, or other nonfluid movements (poor eye tracking/nonfluid movements)? These types of observations can give valuable clues as to what factors bring about a low score on reading comprehension.

Comparing these kinds of observations with other subtests that require organization, executive functions, and fluid reasoning may give the examiner some keys as to why reading comprehension performance is problematic for a child. Perhaps the problem is not that the child does not know math facts; perhaps it is because he or she cannot organize the math facts to be able to apply them to a problem. If the child does have problems with organization and other *Gf* subtests, then the remediation plan calls for including prescriptions about organization (not necessarily drilling of math facts).

Similar observations about Written Expression, Oral Expression, and Listening Comprehension need to be made by the examiner, because all of these subtests require the child to have good *Gf* skills. The beauty of comparing these scores with subtests on the Planning/*Gf* scale is that the process of how a child utilizes upper-level cognitive skills to perform academic tasks is being compared, not just the concrete details that the teacher probably already knows about (e.g., reading and math levels).

There is also a quantitative method for examining the child's reasoning ability on the KTEA-II, via its Error Analysis procedure. Reading Comprehension and Listening Comprehension deliberately include items that measure inferential thinking (*Gf*) as well as literal recall of facts. The items on each subtest have been preclassified as either "Literal" or "Inferential" and the KTEA-II Error Analysis determines whether the child performed at a "Strong," "Average," or "Weak" level on each type of item (Kaufman & Kaufman, 2004b). Hence, if the child's category on the Inferential items of Reading Comprehension, Listening Comprehension (or both) is classified as "Weak" or "Strong," that classification can be used to corroborate other quantitative and qualitative data about the child's reasoning ability.

From a process point of view, information and data gleaned from the KTEA-II high-level subtests can help the examiner look at how well the "orchestra conductor" organizes complex tasks and large bodies of information. If you do suspect that the child might have executive function deficits then it is appropriate to test further, with tests that are specifically designed to measure this area. If you do not feel comfortable incorporating measures of executive functions into the Comprehensive Assessment then a referral to a colleague who is familiar with these measures is an appropriate course of action.

Auditory Processing (Ga) and Several Auditory Tasks on the KABC-II and KTEA-II

KTEA-II Listening Comprehension and three KABC-II subtests (Riddles, Number Recall, Word Order) are dependent, to some extent, on the CHC *Ga* broad ability (see Rapid Reference 4.15). The process rationale for these subtests follows.

Process Rationale for Listening Comprehension, Riddles, Number Recall, and Word Order. These subtests do not measure the CHC-defined auditory processing/*Ga* because they are more concerned with auditory memory and maintaining auditory input long enough to come up with an answer. The primary subtests that measure *Ga*—for example, KTEA-II Phonological Awareness—are more concerned with the discrimination of sounds and with phonemic analysis and synthesis. Nonetheless, Listening Comprehension and the three KABC-II subtests still all use auditory input as the main processing vehicle, and that, by nature, is serial and sequential. Because most of these auditory processes take place in similar places in the brain, and have resultant brain-behavior similarities (e.g., language problems, reading problems) the examiner should make an effort to distinguish auditory memory from auditory discrimination. Both processes require different intervention strategies and have different influences on academic performance.

Listening Comprehension, in particular, is a supportive subtest for *Ga* because it measures the kind of listening comprehension that students must do in school—that is, comprehension of relatively formal speech, rather than casual or naturalistic speech. This would serve the purpose of enhancing the relevance of the test score to a school-based evaluation. The Listening Comprehension subtest also has a second, important design objective; to parallel the passage items of the Reading Comprehension subtest. The primary difference between the two subtests is that Listening Comprehension requires the student to listen to the passages on a CD, and then answer questions spoken by the examiner. Because students perform similar tasks in Listening Comprehension and Reading Comprehension, a significantly lower score on the latter subtest may suggest the presence of a reading problem rather than a more general deficit in language development (Stanovich, 1992).

Integrating the KABC-II and KTEA-II—Qualitative/Behavioral Analyses

By comparing Qualitative Indicators (QIs) on the KTEA-II and the KABC-II, you can see how a child behaviorally responds to different types of tests. (For more detailed information about QIs, the reader is directed to the KABC-II and the KTEA-II manuals.) Examine the following scenarios to determine if there are any differences on performance for each battery.

Look for Differences with Affect and Motivation
Does the child enjoy the novel, game-like activities on the KABC-II, but then becomes quiet, sullen, or bored on the KTEA-II? Or vice versa? Does he or she act nervous and unsure on the KABC-II, but cheers up with familiar tasks on the

KTEA-II? Look for changes in behavior going from novel process tasks to familiar academic tasks.

Look for Differences with Self-Confidence

Does the child try hard on the KABC-II subtests, and knows when she or he performed well? Does the child verbalize self confidence with statements like: "I'm good at this!" "This is easy!" Do these self-confident statements reach over into the KTEA-II test performance? Or does she or he falter, make self-deprecating statements, or act unsure? Look for changes in behavior (verbalization about the self) when tasks change from process oriented to academic.

Look for Differences between Modalities

Some children have specific and significant processing styles. Many times their behavior will reflect these visual, auditory, haptic, or verbal strengths and weaknesses. Look for changes in behavior when the modality of the task changes. Does the child pay attention better when he or she has tasks that are visual, and gets fidgety when the tasks are auditory, with no visual stimulus? Does he or she chatter on verbal subtests and act unsure on visual-spatial tasks?

Look for Differences in Behavior with Cognitive Load

The KABC-II changes cognitive load from subtest to subtest and especially from basal to ceiling items on each subtest. The KTEA-II has four specific subtests that have a higher cognitive load, because they require complex skills (see Figure 4.2). Look for changes in behavior when the load level changes or items go from easy to difficult. Does the child do well on simple tasks and then get confused on ones where she or he has to organize? What strategies does the child employ on both batteries when she or he starts to approach ceiling items? Gives up? Gets impulsive? Acts like it is an enjoyable challenge? Gets frustrated, angry, or oppositional?

Look for How the Child Responds When You Teach on the Learning Scale of the KABC-II and Interactive Subtests on the KTEA-II

Note any changes in behavior when you administer the Atlantis and Rebus subtests on the KABC-II. These subtests are different from the other subtests because they are interactive; the examiner basically teaches the child each item and then requests retrieval of the information. It is important to note how a child responds to the interactive and regimented pace. Atlantis and Rebus are dynamic subtests, where there is a more intense social dependency between the examiner and the examinee; the behaviors and social strategies that the child uses in this type of teaching/learning arrangement are valuable information.

You may also want to compare the QIs from Atlantis and Rebus with the Written Expression, Phonological Awareness, Listening Comprehension, and Oral Expression subtests from the KTEA-II. They also are interactive subtests wherein the examiner engages the child throughout the test. Does the child enjoy engaging with you? Is the child nervous about being so interactive with you? Does the child act dependent and need you to lead them? Or, is the child defiant, impatient, or oppositional? It would be interesting to mention these types of behaviors to the child's teacher and see if the child's responses are similar in the classroom.

Qualitative observations need to be supported by other data. If you observe behaviors that you believe are disruptive and that hurt the child's performance on the KABC-II or the KTEA-II, check your observations out with staff and teachers to see if these QIs are present in other settings and not just the testing situation. Also, look at the scores for these subtests. If you believe that the QIs lowered the child's scores, then interventions for those behaviors may well help the child perform better in the classroom. Remember, QIs are not just about negative behaviors. QIs can provide us with valuable information about how a child gets around a disability or weakness. Watching how a child naturally compensates for learning or behavioral deficits is very valuable information, and should be included in any prescriptive recommendations.

Integrating the KABC-II and KTEA-II—Procedural Options

There are many ways to integrate the results of the KABC-II and the KTEA-II. At this point in time there is no definitive method of integrating the results of the two batteries, because it may take years of research to determine the best approach. Even then, no single approach will match the needs of all examiners. Each examiner brings a wealth of experience, "internal norms," and beliefs to the use of these tests. Additionally, every examiner has areas of diagnostic specialties and special populations with whom he or she works, with different needs and wants.

The approaches described for integrating the results of the KABC-II and the KTEA-II in this chapter are varied in their theoretical foundations, procedural complexity, and utility. It is a good idea for you to look over the different methods that have been offered and decide which work best for you. It is important, and best practice, to incorporate different interpretative systems for different circumstances.

SPECIFIC LEARNING DISABILITIES

To introduce this section on specific learning disabilities, we give a brief summary of the controversy that has surrounded the use of achievement-ability discrepancies in the diagnosis of learning disabilities, and discuss how that controversy has lead to recent legislation changing the requirements for diagnosis (i.e., P.L. 108-446). This section also reviews the available research on the WIAT-II and KTEA-II in samples of children with specific learning disabilities (SLD). We specifically examine three types of disability: Reading, Math, and Written Expression.

Controversy Surrounding Cognitive-Achievement Differences in the Diagnosis of Specific Learning Disabilities

The WIAT-II and KTEA-II are frequently used in the process of diagnosing learning disabilities—to examine individual achievement, and to compare achievement with cognitive ability. The requirements for diagnosing SLD have been hotly debated in recent years (Kaufman & Kaufman, 2001). Many researchers and clinicians have put forth strong arguments against the use of achievement-ability discrepancies as criteria for determining SLD (Berninger, Dunn, & Alper, 2005; Flanagan, et al., 2002; Siegel, 1999; Stanovich, 1999; Vellutino, Scanlon, & Lyon, 2000). Now, (as has been mentioned throughout this book), 2004 changes to the Individuals with Disabilities Education Act (i.e., P.L. 108-446) have formerly eliminated an achievement-ability discrepancy as a necessary part of determining SLD (Rapid Reference 4.19 lists where more information can be found on P.L. 108-446). Thus, assessment professionals (depending on how state and local educational authorities decide to implement P.L. 108-446) will no longer need to utilize a rigid discrepancy formula, including scores from tests such as the WIAT-II and KTEA-II in conjunction with IQ scores. Rather, WIAT-II and KTEA-II scores may be used as a mechanism to determine interindividual academic abilities, and to evaluate how academic deficits are related to or caused by deficits in basic cognitive processes. Procedures for diagnosing SLD without using an achievement-ability discrepancy have been articulated by Berninger and colleagues (Berninger, Dunn, & Alper, 2005; Berninger & O'Donnell, 2005) and Flanagan and colleagues (Flanagan, Ortiz, Alfonso, & Mascolo, 2002).

In the following sections, we describe research on specific learning disabilities in the areas of reading, mathematics, and written expression that utilizes the WIAT-II and the KTEA-II and their conormed tests. For the research described in the following, the subjects were diagnosed with learning disabilities based on a severe discrepancy between performance on an achievement measure and a measure of intellectual ability (the most prevalent definition of a learning disability at the time that the research took place).

≡Rapid Reference 4.19

Resources for the Individuals with Disabilities Education Improvement Act of 2004 (P.L. 108-446)

National Association of School Psychologists
http://www.nasponline.org/advocacy/IDEAinformation.html

National Center for Learning Disabilities
http://www.ld.org/advocacy/IDEAwatch.cfm

Council for Exceptional Children (CEC): Public Policy and Legislative Information
http://www.cec.sped.org/pp/

Learning Disabilities Association of America
http://www.ldanatl.org/

Council for Exceptional Children (CEC): Summary of Significant Issues in the New IDEA
http://www.cec.sped.org/pp/IDEA_120204.pdf

National Association of State Directors of Special Education (NASDSE) IDEA Side-by-Side: A comparison of current law to the Individuals with Disabilities Education Improvement Act of 2004. Available for purchase.
http://www.nasdse.org/

Wrights Law: IDEA 2004 Changes in Key Statutes
http://www.wrightslaw.com/law/idea/index.htm

Read the final IDEA bill posted on the website of the Committee for Education and the Workforce:
http://edworkforce.house.gov/issues/108th/education/idea/conferencereport/confrept.htm

Reading Disability

KTEA-II Study

A sample of 134 students (ages 6 to 18) with learning disabilities in reading were administered the KTEA-II Comprehensive Form (mean age 13:1) (Kaufman & Kaufman, 2004a). The scores of these students were compared to those of a non-clinical reference group that was matched on gender, ethnicity, and parent education. Compared to the nonclinical reference group, scores on all KTEA-II subtests and composites were significantly lower ($p < .001$) for the sample with Reading Disabilities. The KTEA-II domain composite scores ranged from highs of 87.1 and 85.0 on the Oral Fluency Composite and Oral Language Composite, respectively, to lows of 76.7 and 76.9 on the Decoding Composite and the Reading Composite, respectively. The mean scores for Written Language, Sound-

Symbol, and Reading Fluency Composite were at a level comparable (i.e., about one point different) to the low scores on the Reading Composite and Decoding Composite. Thus, predictably, those scores directly measuring reading skill and those related to the fluency of reading as well as phonological awareness (e.g., Sound-Symbol) show the most impairment in the Reading Disability sample. In contrast, scores in the Average range of academic ability on the Oral Language and Oral Fluency Composite (albeit in the lower end of Average), indicate that oral language skills were an area of relative integrity for the Reading Disability sample. Rapid Reference 4.20 shows the scores for this sample on all KTEA-II subtests and composites (as well as other SLD samples).

KABC-II Study

How does the pattern of scores on the KTEA-II compare with those from the conormed KABC-II for children with Reading Disabilities? A sample of 141 students ages 6 to 18 ($M = 13{:}2$ years) with documented Reading Disabilities were administered the KABC-II, and the data were compared to a matched, nonclinical reference group (Kaufman & Kaufman, 2004b). Similar to the results on the KTEA-II, scores on all KABC-II subtests and composites were significantly lower for children with Reading Disabilities than for the nonclinical reference group (all differences were $p < .001$). The Reading Disability sample's mean scores on the Sequential/*Gsm,* Learning/*Glr,* and Knowledge/*Gc* scales bordered between the Below Average and Average classifications (see Rapid Reference 4.21). The largest difference between the nonclinical group and the reading disability group was found on the Learning/*Glr* scale (with a 1 SD difference between the mean scores). Kaufman, Lichtenberger, Fletcher-Janzen, and Kaufman (2005) provide an explanation for this low score in SLD samples:

> The Learning/*Glr* scale is a demanding scale because it requires that all of the cognitive processes work together. Children must use sequential abilities to listen and organize information in a serial manner and learn in a step-by-step fashion; they must use simultaneous processing to look, organize, and remember visual information; and they must use planning abilities to prioritize information processing. The whole process utilized for the Learning/*Glr* scale is very much like a functional symphony where the first and second functional units of the brain (measured by the Sequential/*Gsm* and Simultaneous/*Gv* scales) must interact and take direction and sustain interest from the third functional unit (measured by the Planning/*Gf* scale). A disability in any of these areas can affect scores on the respective scales, but may also affect the performance on the Learning/*Glr* scale where it all has to come together. (pp. 213–214)

≋Rapid Reference 4.20

KTEA-II Scores for Students with Specific Learning Disabilities

KTEA-II Subtest or Composite	Reading Disability Mean (N = 134)	Math Disability Mean (N = 93)	Writing Disability Mean (N = 119)
Letter & Word Recognition	76.8	76.8	77.2
Reading Comprehension	80.4	79.7	80.8
Reading Composite	**76.9**	**76.8**	**77.4**
Math Concepts and Applications	82.3	78.1	82.5
Math Computation	82.9	79.1	82.3
Mathematics Composite	**81.2**	**77.2**	**81.1**
Written Expression	80.2	78.8	80.0
Spelling	76.9	77.4	76.9
Written Language Composite	**77.5**	**77.2**	**77.5**
Listening Comprehension	89.1	86.4	88.7
Oral Expression	85.2	83.5	85.0
Oral Language Composite	**85.0**	**82.6**	**84.7**
Phonological Awareness	82.8	81.7	82.4
Nonsense Word Decoding	78.9	78.8	79.3
Sound-Symbol Composite	**77.9**	**77.9**	**78.5**
Word Recognition Fluency	77.1	77.1	77.2
Decoding Fluency	78.0	78.5	78.1
Reading Fluency Composite	**77.4**	**77.7**	**77.5**
Decoding Composite	**76.7**	**76.8**	**77.3**
Associational Fluency	90.3	88.0	91.0
Naming Facility (RAN)	88.3	87.8	89.4
Oral Fluency Composite	**87.1**	**85.7**	**88.2**
Comprehensive Achievement	**78.4**	**76.1**	**78.3**

Note: All KTEA-II data on Specific Learning Disabilities (SLD) are from the *KTEA-II Comprehensive Form Manual* (Kaufman & Kaufman, 2004a): Reading Disability data are from Table 7.29, Math Disability data are from Table 7.30, and Writing Disability data are from Table 7.31. All scores from the groups with SLD are significantly lower (*p* < .001) than those of the nonclinical reference comparison groups.

WIAT-II *Study*

A sample of 162 individuals, aged 7 to 18 (M = 12 years), diagnosed with learning disability in reading (LD-R) were administered the WIAT-II (The Psychological Corporation, 2002). Their performance was compared to a non-LD control group matched on age and grade, gender, race/ethnicity, and parent education level. Rapid Reference 4.22 reports the mean performance of the two groups. The LD-R group scored significantly lower than the control group ($p < .01$) on every subtest and composite. The lowest mean scores for the LD-R group were on the reading subtests (i.e., $M = 73.49$ on Word Reading; $M = 78.55$ on Reading Comprehension; and $M = 75.87$ on Pseudoword De-coding). The highest scores for the

≡Rapid Reference 4.21

Mean KABC-II Index Scores for Children with Reading Disabilities

KABC-II Scale	Reading Disability Mean (N = 141)
Sequential/Gsm	85.4
Simultaneous/Gv	88.1
Learning/Glr	84.3
Planning/Gf	86.8
Knowledge/Gc	84.8
MPI	82.6
FCI	82.2

Note: Adapted from Kaufman and Kaufman (2004a).

LD-R group were on Oral Expression ($M = 91.79$) and Listening Comprehension ($M = 88.17$). At the composite level, the low score for the LD-R group was in reading—($M = 72.10$), compared to the non-LD sample ($M = 99.61$). The next-lowest composite score for the LD-R group was Written Language ($M = 75.01$) in comparison to the control sample ($M = 97.81$). This is not surprising, given the age of the LD-R group and the fact that many reading-disabled students have undiagnosed writing disorders that may not be identified until the intermediate or middle school grades. Both groups were studied to determine the percentage of students with a standard score that is two or more standard deviations below the mean (≤ 70) on the WIAT-II subtests and composites. For the LD-R group, 31 percent of the sample had a standard score of ≤ 70 on Word Reading (in comparison to 2 percent of the control group); 22 percent had a score of ≤ 70 on Reading Comprehension (none of the control group had a score that low); and 27 percent had a score of ≤ 70 on Pseudoword Decoding (in comparison to 1 percent of the control group). At the composite level, 19 percent of the LD-R group had a Reading score ≤ 70, whereas none of the control group scored that low. At the same time, only 5 percent of the LD-R group had Oral Expression scores ≤ 70 (in comparison to 1 percent of the control group), and only 10 percent of the

═Rapid Reference 4.22

WIAT-II Mean Performance of Children Aged 7–18 with Learning Disabilities in Reading and the Matched Control Group

	Learning Disabilities in Reading			Matched Control Group		
	Mean	SD	% With Score ≤ 70	Mean	SD	% With Score ≤ 70
Subtests						
Word Reading	73.49	10.69	31	99.21	14.06	2
Numerical Operations	82.27	14.34	17	101.43	13.86	3
Reading Comprehension	78.55	13.32	22	100.69	12.40	0
Spelling	77.28	9.35	20	99.38	13.42	1
Pseudoword Decoding	75.87	10.06	27	101.17	13.16	1
Math Reasoning	82.97	13.56	15	100.17	14.30	2
Written Expression	77.76	11.70	23	97.02	15.27	7
Listening Comprehension	88.17	14.76	10	99.77	14.81	3
Oral Expression	91.79	13.68	5	98.43	13.56	1
Composites						
Reading	73.10	10.65	19	99.61	12.46	0
Mathematics	80.72	13.86	19	100.61	14.55	2
Written Language	75.01	10.54	23	97.81	14.67	4
Oral Language	87.56	14.59	9	98.09	14.25	3
Total	77.19	9.09	11	99.06	12.70	1

Note: N = 162.
Source: Adapted from Table 6.21 of WIAT-II Manual (Wechsler, 2001).

clinical group had a Listening Comprehension score ≤ 70 (in comparison to 3 percent of the non-LD group). Individuals with reading disorders presented a distinct pattern of scores and overall performance on WIAT-II. Qualitatively, the LD-R group demonstrated more problems with automaticity, more self-corrections when reading real words, and slower silent reading speed.

WIAT-II was also administered to a sample of 41 adults in college (M = grade 14) diagnosed with a specific learning disability in reading. Rapid Reference 4.23

≡Rapid Reference 4.23

WIAT-II Mean Performance of Adults in College with Learning Disabilities in Reading and the Matched Control Group

	Learning Disabilities in Reading		Matched Control Group	
	Mean	**SD**	**Mean**	**SD**
Subtests				
Word Reading	77.62	19.81	105.44	9.05
Numerical Operations	103.58	9.69	107.10	11.41
Reading Comprehension	89.60	16.84	100.13	14.25
Spelling	82.14	14.78	101.59	10.60
Pseudoword Decoding	73.57	7.77	103.36	12.18
Math Reasoning	97.68	11.45	103.95	12.47
Written Expression	90.51	12.39	100.76	14.54
Listening Comprehension	92.02	15.40	100.95	9.77
Oral Expression	96.71	14.14	99.20	12.32
Composites				
Reading	74.14	11.77	103.19	10.79
Mathematics	99.84	9.89	105.53	11.83
Written Language	85.97	12.41	100.05	11.95
Oral Language	93.85	13.15	99.30	10.48
Total	82.79	9.83	102.94	10.28

Note: N = 41.

presents the means and standard deviations for the subtest and composite standard scores for the adult clinical group and the matched control group. Significant differences (at < .01 level) are noted between means for the two groups for Word Reading (77.62 for LD-R group; 105.44 for control group); and for Pseudoword Decoding (73.57 for LD-R group; 103.36 for control group). For the Reading Comprehension subtest differences were noted at the < .05 level between a mean of 89.60 for the LD-R group and a mean of 100.13 for the matched controls. The Reading Composite mean score was 74.14 for the LD-R sample and 103.19 for the control group ($p = < .01$). It is likely that the smaller difference between the two groups in Reading Comprehension occurs because at the college level the LD-R students have developed compensatory strategies that assist them in comprehension in spite of decoding deficits. One observation of interest in this study was the typically slow reading speed for many of the reading disabled sample. This may be where decoding deficits affect reading text. Additional time for comprehending reading materials (i.e., on exams) can be an essential accommodation for students who present this profile.

WISC-IV Study

The WISC-IV was administered to 56 children ages 7 to 13 who were identified as LD-R according to *DSM-IV-TR* criteria. Rapid Reference 4.24 (from Table 5.25 of the *WISC-IV Integrated Technical and Interpretive Manual* [2004]) reports the means and standard deviations of the WISC-IV subtest, process, and composite scores for the LD-R and a matched control group. When compared to the control group, children with LD-R obtained significantly lower mean scores for all composites, with large effect sizes for the VCI, WMI, and FSIQ. The largest effect size was for WMI. This finding is consistent with research that indicates a relationship between reading achievement and working memory (Swanson & Howell, 2001).

In the WIAT-II LD-R and the WISC-IV LD-R studies, students identified with learning disabilities in reading showed a pattern of lower Working Memory Index and FSIQ scores on the cognitive measure, and lower Word Reading, Pseudoword Decoding, and Reading Comprehension scores on the WIAT-II when compared to their matching control groups. Further, the WISC-IV study reports significantly lower scores (with large effect sizes) on the Vocabulary, Information, Arithmetic, and Letter-Number Sequencing subtests for the LD-R sample. The lower scores on Vocabulary and Information may reflect, in part, a deficiency in the general fund of information that is usually acquired through reading. The lower scores on Arithmetic and Letter-Number Sequencing suggest the role working memory may play in reading disorders.

The WISC-IV Integrated and the WIAT-II were administered to 102 children aged 7 to 13 who were diagnosed with Reading Disorder according to *DSM-IV-TR* criteria. Students with concurrent diagnosis of other learning disorders (i.e., Math LD or Writing LD) were not excluded from the study. Mean scores on the WISC-IV for students with Reading Disorder ranged from 94.7 on the Perceptual Reasoning Index to 88.1 on the Working Memory Index. This Reading Disorder sample's pattern of WIAT-II scores was similar to that reported in the *WIAT-II Manual* (discussed previously). The four lowest mean scores for the WIAT-II were Word Reading (79.5), Spelling (81.7), Pseudoword Decoding

Rapid Reference 4.24

Mean WISC-IV Performance of Reading Disorder and Matched Control Groups

Subtest/Process Score/Composite	Reading Disorder		Matched Control Group			Group Mean Comparison			Standard Difference[a]
	Mean	SD	Mean	SD	N	Difference	t value	p value	
Block Design	9.0	2.4	9.6	2.2	56	.54	1.32	.19	.24
Similarities	8.8	2.4	10.1	2.4	56	1.34	3.03	<.01	.57
Digit Span	8.0	2.6	9.8	2.5	55	1.80	3.64	<.01	.70
Picture Concepts	9.3	2.8	10.1	2.2	56	.73	1.68	.10	.29
Coding	8.2	2.5	9.4	2.5	56	1.23	2.47	.02	.49
Vocabulary	8.2	2.0	10.4	2.1	56	2.21	6.18	<.01	1.08
Letter-Number Sequencing	7.7	3.3	10.4	2.4	55	2.67	4.64	<.01	.93
Matrix Reasoning	8.9	2.2	10.0	2.1	56	1.16	2.71	.01	.54
Comprehension	8.9	2.0	10.2	2.5	55	1.36	3.09	<.01	.61
Symbol Search	9.2	2.6	10.1	2.2	56	.91	2.01	.05	.38
Picture Completion	8.9	2.7	10.4	2.5	56	1.52	3.41	<.01	.59
Cancellation	10.1	3.3	9.7	2.8	56	-.43	-.78	.44	-.14
Information	8.2	2.2	10.5	2.2	56	2.25	5.32	<.01	1.01

(continued)

Subtest/Process Score/Composite	Reading Disorder		Matched Control Group			Group Mean Comparison			
	Mean	SD	Mean	SD	N	Difference	t value	p value	Standard Difference[a]
Arithmetic	7.7	1.9	9.9	2.9	35	2.26	4.10	<.01	.92
Word Reasoning	8.9	2.1	10.1	2.7	56	1.25	2.75	.01	.52
Block Design No Time Bonus	9.1	2.6	9.6	2.4	56	.50	1.08	.29	.20
Digit Span Forward	8.4	2.9	9.8	2.7	55	1.40	2.67	.01	.51
Digit Span Backward	8.5	2.6	9.8	2.5	56	1.38	2.84	.01	.54
Cancellation Random	10.3	3.0	9.7	2.7	56	−.68	−1.26	.21	−.24
Cancellation Structured	9.6	3.3	9.5	2.8	56	−.14	−.29	.77	−.05
VCI	91.9	9.7	100.9	10.6	55	9.00	4.84	<.01	.89
PRI	94.4	11.2	99.3	9.2	56	4.91	2.96	<.01	.48
WMI	87.0	12.9	99.8	10.3	54	12.81	5.62	<.01	1.10
PSI	92.5	11.7	98.6	11.7	56	6.16	2.69	.01	.53
FSIQ	89.1	10.3	99.9	9.7	53	10.79	6.01	<.01	1.08

[a]The Standard Difference is the difference of the two test means divided by the square root of the pooled variance, computed using Cohen's (1996) Formula 10.4.

Note: VCI = Verbal Comprehension Index; PRI = Perceptual Reasoning Index; PSI = Processing Speed Index; FSIQ = Full Scale IQ.

(82.8), and Reading Comprehension (83.4). The highest subtest score was a 95.2 on Listening Comprehension. Rapid Reference 4.25 and 4.26 highlight important correlation coefficients for this study. Relative to other index scores, the VCI showed higher correlations with the WIAT-II reading scores (Reading Comprehension .43; Word Reading .41; and Pseudoword Decoding .34). The WMI correlated at the same magnitude as VCI, with Reading Comprehension (.43), while there was minimal correlation between WMI and Word Reading (.16) and WMI and Pseudoword Decoding (.13). The PSI showed almost no correlation with WIAT-II reading subtests. One factor that should be considered in light of the low correlation between PSI and the reading subtests is that reading speed and automaticity are not reflected in the subtest scores of the WIAT-II. Instead they are reported in the qualitative observations that should be referenced when a low PSI score is reported. Correlations between the scaled process scores and the WIAT-II composites are higher in the Verbal domain than in the Perceptual and Processing Speed domains. Several of the scaled process scores in the Working Memory domain correlated with Reading Comprehension, including Digit Span Backward, Spatial Span Backward, and the process scores for the arithmetic subtests. These results are consistent with research that suggests children with Reading Disorder have difficulty on verbally-mediated tasks and measures of working memory (Stanovich & Siegel, 1994; Wolf & Bowers, 1999).

≡Rapid Reference 4.25

Correlations between WIAT-II and WISC-IV Integrated Composite Scores for a Reading Disorder Group

WIAT-II Composite

WISC-IV Composite	Reading	Mathematics	Written Language	Oral Language	Total Achievement
VCI	.47	.51	.37	.44	.51
PRI	.29	.40	.27	.26	.38
WMI	.30	.35	.15	.23	.31
PSI	.22	.35	.16	.24	.29
FSIQ	.48	.61	.37	.41	.56

Note: Adapted from Table G.1 of the WISC-IV Integrated Technical and Interpretive Manual (Wechsler, 2004). VCI = Verbal Comprehension Index; PRI = Perceptual Reasoning Index; WMI = Working Memory Index; FSIQ = Full Scale IQ. N = 102.

≡Rapid Reference 4.26

Correlations between WIAT-II Subtests and WISC-IV Integrated Composite Scores for a Reading Disorder Group

WIAT-II Subtest	WISC-IV Integrated Composite				
	VCI	PRI	WMI	PSI	FSIQ
Word Reading	.41	.16	.16	.12	.34
Reading Comprehension	.43	.32	.43	.25	.51
Pseudoword Decoding	.34	.22	.13	.14	.33
Math Reasoning	.57	.40	.36	.28	.62
Numerical Operations	.38	.34	.29	.38	.52
Spelling	.26	.17	.06	.08	.25
Written Expression	.39	.28	.21	.21	.40
Listening Comprehension	.49	.42	.19	.23	.48
Oral Expression	.27	.08	.20	.19	.26

Note: Adapted from Table G.1 of the *WISC-IV Integrated Technical and Interpretive Manual* (Wechsler, 2004). VCI = Verbal Comprehension Index; PRI = Perceptual Reasoning Index; WMI = Working Memory Index; FSIQ = Full Scale IQ. $N = 102$ except Written Expression where $N = 96$.

PAL Study

WIAT-II was found to be an effective diagnostic tool when paired with the Process Assessment of the Learner Test Battery for Reading and Writing (PAL-RW; Berninger, 2001) for the identification of students at risk for a reading disorder, for instructional diagnosis, and for evaluating which students were treatment responders (Berninger, Dunn, & Alper, 2005). A group of 101 children aged 5 to 12 ($M = 8$ years) in grades K–6 was administered WIAT-II and the PAL-RW, an in-depth assessment of the processing skills related to reading and writing. The WIAT-II reading subtests were found to be moderately correlated with the PAL-RW subtests that measure the processing skills of orthographic and phonological coding (e.g., Receptive Coding, Expressive Coding, Rhyming, Syllables, Phonemes, and Rimes). To learn more about how WIAT-II and PAL-RW are being used to screen children, make instructional diagnosis, and monitor effectiveness of intervention in low-achieving schools with many at-risk students, including a number of English-learning students from low-income families, see the article "Partnership and problem solving to promote early intervention in literacy: Using the PAL" (Dunn, 2002), and the followup article "Los Angeles Unified School District (LAUSD) school psychology project bridging special and general education" (Dunn, in press).

Math Disability

KTEA-II Study

A sample of 93 students ages 6 to 18 with learning disabilities in math were administered the KTEA-II Comprehensive Form (mean age 13:6; Kaufman & Kaufman, 2004a). Similar to the KTEA-II studies on other SLD, the scores of these students were compared to those of a nonclinical reference group that was controlled for gender, ethnicity, and parent education. Compared to the nonclinical reference group, scores on all KTEA-II subtests and composites were significantly lower ($p < .001$) for the sample with Math Disabilities. An important characteristic to note about this Math Disability sample was that 81 percent had comorbid Reading Disabilities, which contributed to deficits in achievement domains such as reading and writing. Thus, the overall pattern of KTEA-II scores for the Math Disability sample was similar to that of the Reading Disability Sample, with a notably lower score on the Mathematics Composite for the Math Disability sample (see Rapid Reference 4.20). The lowest average KTEA-II domain composite scores for the Math Disability sample were on the Decoding and Reading Composites (both 76.8), and the Mathematics and Written Language Composites (both 77.2). These low scores were closely followed by standard scores for the Reading Fluency (77.7) and Sound-Symbol (77.9) Composites. In the Average range of academic ability was the Oral Fluency Composite (85.7). Rapid Reference 4.20 lists the Math Disability sample's average KTEA-II scores.

KABC-II Study

How do scores on the KTEA-II of children with mathematics disabilities compare with conormed measures of cognitive ability? A sample of 96 students ages 6 to 18 ($M = 13:7$ years) with learning disabilities in mathematics were administered the KABC-II. Similar to the Reading Disability sample, all scales were significantly lower for the group with mathematics disabilities than in the matched control group. The nonclinical reference group's average standard score for all scales was about 1 SD higher than that of the Mathematics Disability group. The greatest standard score difference between the Mathematics Disability group and the clinical reference group (about 16 points) was on the Planning/Gf scale (see Rapid Reference 4.27). Other studies have found that children with mathematics disabilities can be helped by implementing remediation strategies related to planning and fluid reasoning. Examples of such interventions include using metacog-

≡ Rapid Reference 4.27

Mean KABC-II Index Scores for Children with Mathematics Disorders

KABC-II Scale	Math Disability Mean (N = 96)
Sequential/Gsm	83.7
Simultaneous/Gv	84.6
Learning/Glr	83.7
Planning/Gf	82.7
Knowledge/Gc	82.0
MPI	79.8
FCI	79.3

Note: Adapted from Kaufman and Kaufman (2004a).

nitive approaches, teaching problem-solving rules, and planning solutions to mathematical problems with step-by-step problem solving (Rourke, 1989; Teeter & Semrud-Clikeman, 1998).

WIAT-II Study

WIAT-II was administered to a sample of 81 individuals aged 7 to 18 (M = 12 years) diagnosed with learning disabilities not specific to reading. Many of these students had been diagnosed with a learning disability specifically in math. Performance was compared to a matched control group (based on gender, age and grade, ethnicity/race, and parent education level). On the WIAT-II math subtests, the LD group showed significantly (< .01) lower scores for Numerical Operations (M = 75.76 for LD group, and M = 98.41 for non-LD group) and for Math Reasoning (M = 74.86 for LD group, and M = 97.05 for non-LD group). About a third (30 percent) of the LD group had a standard score ≤ 70 on Numerical Operations, in comparison to 6 percent of the control group, and 33 percent of the LD group had a standard score ≤ 70 on Math Reasoning in comparison to 2 percent of the control group.

A similar study was conducted with a sample of 22 college students (M = grade 14) diagnosed with learning disabilities not specific to reading, and matched controls. Several students with Math Disorder were included in the study. Although the sample is small and this is not a homogeneous group, mean scores on Numerical Operation, Math Reasoning, and Written Expression were significantly different (p = < .01) for the two groups. At the composite level, the LD-M group mean was 87.77, in comparison to the control group mean of 107.52 (p = < .01). Results of these two studies suggest that the WIAT-II may be useful in identifying achievement deficits among individuals with more generalized learning disabilities.

WISC-IV Study

WISC-IV Integrated and WIAT-II were administered to 28 children aged 8 to 13, who were diagnosed with Mathematics Disorder according to *DSM-IV-TR* criteria. Means, standard deviations, and correlation coefficients are reported in Table

G.2 of the *WISC-IV Integrated Technical and Interpretive Manual* (Wechsler et al., 2004). Among the WISC-IV Integrated index scores, the VCI and PSI exhibited the highest correlations with the WIAT-II Mathematics composite (.50 and .56, respectively), as expected. A number of moderate to high correlations are found between WIAT-II math subtest scores and the Arithmetic process scores of the WISC-IV Integrated. The highest correlations are reported between Written Arithmetic and Numerical Operations (.60) and between Written Arithmetic and Mathematics composite (.60). Given the small sample size of this study, additional research with children diagnosed with learning disability in math is warranted.

Writing Disability

KTEA-II Study

A sample of 119 students ages 6 to 18 (M = 13:3) with Written Expression Disabilities were administered the KTEA-II, along with a matched sample of students with no noted disability. All KTEA-II scores for the sample with Written Expression Disabilities were significantly lower (p < .001) than the nonclinical reference group. Most scores were in the Below Average range, with the lowest scores for the Written Expression Disability sample on the Written Language, Decoding, Reading, Reading Fluency, and Sound-Symbol Composites (all standard scores between 77 and 78). Though slightly higher, the Mathematics Composite was also in the Below Average range (81.1). Similar to the Reading Disability and Math Disability samples, the oral language skills of this sample with Written Expression Disabilities appeared to be the least affected of all the domains, with average standard scores ranging from 84.7 on the Oral Language Composite to 88.2 on the Oral Fluency Composite.

KABC-II Study

How do scores on the KTEA-II of children with writing disabilities compare with conormed measures of cognitive ability? A sample of 122 students ages 6 to 18 (M = 13:3 years) with disorders in the area of written expression were administered the KABC-II. The results of this study were very similar to the results of the sample with Reading Disabilities, which is not surprising, given that about one third of the students with Written Expression Disabilities also had Reading Disabilities. On all KABC-II scales, the group with writing disabilities scored significantly worse than the nonclinical reference group (which was a sample matched on gender, race, and parent education). The range of mean scores across the KABC-II scales was small (only about 4 points). The lowest index for the writing disability sample was on the Learning/*Glr* scale (see Rapid Reference 4.28). Kaufman, Lichtenberger, Fletcher-Janzen, and Kaufman (2005) provide some insight on why this score may be depressed in children with writing disabilities:

> Written expression does place a large [cognitive] demand on examinees, not only in terms of integrating all levels of information, but also in terms of rapidly changing thoughts and ideas as the material develops. This type of activity stretches every cognitive functional system, and perhaps the Learning/*Glr* scale suffers the most when a child has problems with overall sequential, simultaneous, and planning activities. Indeed, it follows that the evidence-based intervention techniques that work best for children with written expression deficits are those that are based on cognitive and metacognitive strategies (Kaufman et al., 1997). (p. 219)

WIAT-II Study

Included in the WIAT-II study of children diagnosed with learning disabilities not specific to reading ($N = 81$, aged 7 to 18, $M = 12$ years) were several students identified with writing disorders. Performance was compared to a matched control group (based on gender, age and grade, ethnicity/race, and parent education level). Performance of the LD group was significantly different ($< .01$) from the matched control group on the Spelling and Written Expression subtests as well as on the Written Language Composite. Specifically, the mean score on Spelling for the LD group was 79.08, compared to a mean of 101.05 in the control group. For the Written Expression subtest, the mean of the LD group was 79.85, compared to a mean of 96.24 in the control group. Whereas 21 percent of the LD group had standard scores ≤ 70 on Spelling, no one in the control group scored that low. Similarly, 21 percent of the LD group had standard scores ≤ 70 on Written Expression, but 6 percent of the control group had scores in that range. The

≡Rapid Reference 4.28

Mean KABC-II Index Scores for Children with Writing Disabilities

KABC-II Scale	Writing Disability Mean ($N = 122$)
Sequential/*Gsm*	84.6
Simultaneous/*Gv*	87.7
Learning/*Glr*	83.9
Planning/*Gf*	86.8
Knowledge/*Gc*	85.2
MPI	82.1
FCI	82.0

Note: Adapted from Kaufman and Kaufman (2004a).

Written Language Composite score for the LD group ($M = 76.77$) was significantly lower than for the non-LD group ($M = 99.13$).

Conclusions from WIAT-II and KTEA-II SLD Studies

The profile WIAT-II and KTEA-II scores for the three types of SLD reviewed here are similar to what would be expected, based on the skill deficits commonly present in students with SLD. In all of these SLD samples, deficits were seen across the board in the domains of reading, decoding, reading fluency, and written language. In contrast, oral language was an area of relative integrity for all samples with SLD. There were no discrete patterns of performance on the WIAT-II or KTEA-II that appeared to distinguish the groups of Reading, Mathematics, and Writing Disorders from one another. However, readers must be cautious for several reasons in generalizing from the data that we have summarized from the test manuals. Most of these SLD samples were not homogenous groups; they included students that had disabilities in more than one area (e.g., the KTEA-II sample with Mathematics Disabilities also had many students with comorbid Reading Disorders, and the WIAT-II samples with Mathematics and Writing Disorders also had other comorbid disorders). The students were not randomly selected for the studies and typically, independent clinicians were responsible for determining whether students fit SLD criteria. Finally, these data are group data, and may not be representative of all individuals in a diagnostic class. Therefore, the data, summarized from the manuals of the tests, should be considered a preliminary estimate of how SLD samples perform on the measures. More research would be a welcome edition to the literature on the new editions of these achievement instruments, using well-defined populations with SLD who are assessed using multiple measures.

Achievement Testing in Children with Attention-Deficit/Hyperactivity Disorder

Children with Attention-Deficit/Hyperactivity Disorder (ADHD) have tremendous difficulty in their academic performance and achievement. These difficulties include both their work productivity in the classroom and the level of difficulty they have in mastering the expected academic material (Barkley, 1998). Given these difficulties, it is not surprising that ADHD is one of the most common referrals to school psychologists and mental health providers (Demaray, Schaefer, & Delong, 2003). Typically, children who are referred to a clinic for

ADHD are doing poorly at school and are underperforming relative to their known levels of ability as determined by intelligence and academic tests. Their poor performance is likely related to their inattentive, impulsive, and restless behavior in the classroom. On standardized tests of academic achievement, children with ADHD typically score 10 to 30 standard score points lower than their peers in reading, spelling, math, and reading comprehension (Barkley, Dupaul, & McMurry, 1990; Brock & Knapp, 1996; Casey, Rourke, & Del Dotto, 1996). "Consequently, it is not surprising to find that as many as 56% of ADHD children may require academic tutoring, approximately 30% may repeat a grade in school, and 30–40% may be placed in one or more special education programs . . . [and] 10–35% may drop out [of school] entirely" (Barkley, 1998, p. 99).

Specific learning disabilities are often comorbid with ADHD. Estimates of the rates of learning disabilities coexisting with ADHD reveal that 8 to 39 percent of children with ADHD have a reading disability, 12 to 30 percent have a math disability, and 12 to 27 percent have a spelling disorder (Frick et al., 1991; Faraone, Biederman, Lehman, & Spencer, 1993; Barkley, 1990). Standardized achievement tests administered along with a comprehensive battery (including tests of cognitive ability, behavioral and emotional functioning) can help differentially diagnose ADHD from other learning and psychiatric disorders, and help determine the existence of comorbid disorders.

While achievement tests such as the WIAT-II and KTEA-II and intelligence tests such as the WISC-IV and KABC-II do not, and never were intended to, diagnose ADHD, they are of significant importance in the assessment of children with ADHD. Having knowledge of their specific areas of academic skill deficits, coupled with awareness of a child with ADHD's cognitive processing abilities, is a great benefit in planning behavioral and educational programming.

WIAT-II Study

Given what previous research on children with ADHD has shown, we would predict that children with ADHD who are tested on the WIAT-II would have significant areas of academic deficit compared to those without ADHD. To test this assumption, the WIAT-II was administered to a group of 178 individuals, ages 5 to 18 ($M = 13$ years), diagnosed with ADHD as defined in the *DSM-IV,* and a control group matched on age and grade, gender, ethnicity/race, and parent education level. Significant differences ($p < .01$) occurred between the two groups across all subtests except Oral Expression, with actual differences in mean scores ranging from 2.05 (Oral Expression) to 8.17 (Numerical Operations). Despite these significant differences, additional evidence indicates that the clinical group does not differ appreciably from the matched controls; 82 percent of the ADHD group had all subtest scores above 70, whereas 91.6 percent of the matched controls had similar results. In a second study that included 51 children, aged 7 to 18 (M = 12 years), diagnosed with both ADHD and learning disabilities, a very different profile emerged. The differences between mean scores for the ADHD-LD and the control groups are significantly large (ranging from 8.78 for Oral Expression to 25.67 on Spelling). Further, 22 percent of the ADHD-LD group had scores $\leq$ 70 on Pseudoword Decoding, 16 percent had scores $\leq$ 70 on Word Reading, and 16 percent had Numerical Operations scores $\leq$ 70. The lowest composite for the ADHD-LD group was on Written Language, where sustained attention and effort, planning, organizing, and self-monitoring are required. For the clinical group, the highest scores were on Listening Comprehension and Oral Expression. This pattern of stronger Oral Language skills was consistent across all of the clinical groups except the group with Speech and/or Language Impairment, where it was lower than every composite except Reading.

KTEA-II Study

A sample of 51 students, ages 5 to 18 (mean age 12:11), with ADHD were administered the KTEA-II, along with a matched sample of students with no noted disability. All KTEA-II composite scores for the ADHD sample were significantly lower at the $p < .001$ level than the nonclinical reference group, except for the Oral Fluency Composite ($p < .05$). Unlike the SLD samples, whose composite scores were frequently more than 1 SD below the normative mean, the ADHD sample's KTEA-II composite scores ranged from 3 to 12 points below the normative mean of 100. The mean composite scores for Reading (89.5), Mathematics (88.1), and Written Language (87.7) were not highly variable, as they differed only by about 2 points. The mean Oral Language Composite was higher at 94.5, and is clearly an area of integrity within the academic profile. The strongest performance for the ADHD group was on the Oral Fluency Composite (97.0), lending further support to the strength of this sample's oral communication skills. Thus, the overall findings from the ADHD sample tested on the KTEA-II do support previous research that found depressed academic functioning for such children. However, this sample was not as impaired as samples of children with SLD, with most of the ADHD sample's mean scores being classified within the Average range of ability. Future research administering the KTEA-II together with the KABC-II (and the WIAT-II together with the WISC-IV) to samples of children with ADHD and samples of children with comorbid ADHD and SLD will provide useful information to clinicians who work with such children.

TEST YOURSELF

1. More accurate comparisons can be made between achievement and ability when utilizing conormed tests such as the KABC-II and KTEA-II or the WIAT-II and WISC-IV. True or False?

2. Of the 4 index scores of the WISC-IV, which has the highest correlation with Total Achievement on WIAT-II?

   (a) Verbal Comprehension   *oral expression*
   (b) Perceptual Reasoning   *stable*
   (c) Working Memory
   (d) Processing Speed

3. In the WIAT-II LD-Reading and the WISC-IV LD-Reading studies discussed in this chapter, students identified with learning disabilities in reading showed which pattern of scores?

   (a) VCI was the lowest index scores on the WISC-IV, and Reading Comprehension was the lowest subtest score on the WIAT-II.
   (b) WMI and PSI were the highest index scores on the WISC-IV, and Word Reading and Pseudoword Decoding were the lowest subtest scores on the WIAT-II.
   (c) WMI was the lowest index score on the WISC-IV and Word Reading, and Pseudoword Decoding and Reading Comprehension were the lowest subtest scores on the WIAT-II.
   (d) The lowest WISC-IV index score was PRI, and Word Reading and Pseudoword Decoding were the lowest WIAT-II subtest scores.

   r = low WMI and reading

4. Why might a student with a learning disability in reading have a lower score on the Arithmetic subtest of the WISC-IV?   *b/c of memory*

5. For students ages 7 to 18, the KTEA-II Comprehensive Achievement Composite correlated most strongly with the Knowledge/Gc Index, which is not surprising given this index's link to vocabulary and acquisition of facts. Contrary to this finding for 7- to 18-year-olds, which two of the KABC-II scales were among the best correlates of achievement for ages 4:6 to 6 years?

   (a) Sequential/Gsm
   (b) Simultaneous/Gv
   (c) Learning/Glr
   (d) a & b
   (e) a & c

6. **Administration of which of the following process subtests from the WISC-IV Integrated can be especially important when evaluating a student with a possible language-based learning disorder?**

   (a) Written Arithmetic, Vocabulary, Visual Digit Span

   (b) Block Design No Time Bonus, Digit Span Forward, Digit Span Backward

   (c) Longest Digit Span Forward, Longest Digit Span Backward, Cancellation

   (d) Vocabulary Multiple Choice, Similarities Multiple Choice, and Comprehension Multiple Choice

7. **In addition to five CHC broad abilities measured by the KABC-II, the KTEA-II Comprehensive Form measures which three additional broad abilities:**

   (a) Auditory Processing (*Ga*)

   (b) Processing Speed (*Gs*)

   (c) Reading and Writing (*Grw*)

   (d) Quantitative Knowledge (*Gq*)

   (e) Speed/Reaction Time (*Gt*)

8. **The 2004 changes to the Individuals with Disabilities Education Act (P.L. 108-446) have formally eliminated an achievement-ability discrepancy as a necessary part of determining SLD. However, examining WIAT-II and KTEA-II scores alongside their conormed tests of cognitive ability may help to determine interindividual academic abilities and help to evaluate how academic deficits are related to or caused by deficits in basic cognitive processes.** True or False?

9. **Although the samples of students with reading, mathematics, and writing disabilities reported in this chapter were not homogeneous groups, the results from the WIAT-II and KTEA-II studies showed that very distinct patterns of academic achievement clearly distinguish the SLD samples from one another.** True or False?

10. **In samples of children with reading disorders, on which achievement domain did these samples consistently score the highest for both the WIAT-II and KTEA-II?** oral langeage

Answers: 1. True; 2. a; 3. c; 4. The Arithmetic subtest is a measure of working memory and research demonstrates that there is a close relationship between working memory and the acquisition of reading skills. 5. d; 6. d; 7. a, c, & d; 8. True; 9. False; 10. Oral Language

Five

ILLUSTRATIVE CASE REPORTS

This chapter presents case studies of four children who were referred for psychoeducational evaluation. Each child was administered a complete battery of tests; two include the KTEA-II and the other two the WIAT-II. The first case report is of Keenan F., age 9, who was referred for a psychoeducational evaluation because of his difficulties in reading and spelling. Keenan's test battery includes the KTEA-II and KABC-II, as well as supplemental measures of his memory ability. The second case report is of Ryan P., age 12, who was referred for an assessment to evaluate concerns regarding his attentional difficulties, along with his receptive and expressive language problems. Ryan's test battery includes the KTEA-II and KABC-II, as well as measures of his neuropsychological and behavioral functioning. The third case report is of Eduardo R., age 8, whose parents requested an evaluation in order to determine if Eduardo has an underlying cognitive or emotional difficulty that may be contributing to his academic and attentional difficulties. Eduardo's test battery includes the WIAT-II and WISC-IV, as well as other measures of his neuropsychological and emotional functioning. The final case report is of Johnny S., a 14-year-old previously diagnosed with ADHD. Johnny's parents requested his evaluation due to their concerns regarding his learning problems in school. His test battery includes the WIAT-II and WISC-IV-Integrated, as well as supplemental measures of his behavioral functioning.

The goals of this chapter are to bring all other facets of this book together to demonstrate how the WIAT-II and KTEA-II may be used as part of a comprehensive battery, and to demonstrate the cross-validation of hypotheses with behavioral observations, background information, and supplemental test scores. The basic outline for each report includes the following: reason for referral, background information, appearance of client and behavioral observations, tests administered, test results and interpretation, summary diagnostic impression, and recommendations. All of the test data are presented in a psychometric summary at the end of each report.

As in all illustrative cases presented throughout this book, the identifying data of the clients have been changed to protect their confidentiality.

CASE REPORT I

Name: Keenan F.
Age: 9:2
Grade: 3rd

Referral and Background Information

Keenan, a 9-year-old boy, was referred for evaluation by his parents, Mr. and Mrs. F., to better understand their son's difficulty with reading and spelling at school. Furthermore, they are concerned that his current school may not be the most appropriate school environment for him. Mr. and Mrs. F. described Keenan as a "hard worker with a positive outlook about school, even though he has difficulty with assignments involving reading."

Keenan is an only child who lives at home with his father, who is a banker, and his mother, who is currently a homemaker. Mr. and Mrs. F. have been married for 15 years. Mrs. F. had a normal pregnancy and birth with Keenan, who was born weighing approximately 6 pounds, 6 ounces. Mr. and Mrs. F. described their son's developmental history as unremarkable, with the exception of some difficulties with articulation requiring speech therapy. He attended speech therapy for 18 months from ages 5:6 to 7 years. Currently, his parents stated that his articulation is quite good.

Keenan's academic history began when he was 2 years old with his first attendance at preschool 2 days a week. Reportedly, Keenan enjoyed his preschool experience and attended until he was 5 years old, when he entered kindergarten. Mr. and Mrs. F. said they first noticed Keenan's problem with reading in kindergarten. He could not recognize words. He has been seeing a tutor twice a week for the past year to help with his reading. His tutor and the program director at the tutoring center were interviewed. They stated that his current areas of most difficulty include word attack skills, irregular vowels, vocabulary and comprehension, and reading directions independently. They also said that Keenan guesses or misreads sight words. They reported that Keenan is currently reading at the beginning 3rd grade level, and that the reading done at his school is too difficult for him. His tutor mentioned that Keenan finds writing difficult and that if he can say his response orally, he can often answer questions correctly. His tutor stated that Keenan's confidence is increasing, which is important in helping him to do his work independently. Currently, he needs a lot of structure to complete assignments with her. His tutor also stated that Keenan "is a pleasure to work with."

Keenan is a third grader at a local private elementary school where he is receiving grades of mostly C's. Additionally, results of the most recent group of standardized testing (Iowa Tests of Basic Skills) conducted in the beginning of the current school year at his school placed Keenan in the average to low average range. Specifically, he showed a personal weakness in reading comprehension (15th percentile), and personal strengths in problem solving and data interpretation (60th percentile) and science (48th percentile). His current teacher was interviewed and stated that Keenan doesn't read questions properly and that he decodes words incorrectly. He is good about asking for help if he doesn't know words, but he forgets what the teacher says by the time he returns to his seat. She stated that Keenan has problems in reading, spelling, and math (with directions). His teacher reported that Keenan does not appear to have attention problems; rather, he pays attention well. She said that he sits in front and knows that she will call on him, so he pays attention. His teacher described Keenan as very concerned with making mistakes, and that he seems "afraid to do something wrong." She also described Keenan's strengths as being helpful, a great friend, and having a positive attitude.

When Keenan was asked about his experience at school he reported that his favorite subjects are recess, science, computers, PE, and math. He said his least favorite subject is Spanish. He said he liked his current teacher and seemed to have a positive view of his school. When asked about friends at school, Keenan reported that his best friend is Kyle and that they like to play kick ball.

When not in school, Keenan has participated in many sports, including lacrosse, soccer, basketball, swimming, and surfing. He said his favorite sport is lacrosse. Keenan also loves to ride his go-ped and to go on his dirt bike with his dad. Keenan said he has a close friend in the neighborhood, James, with whom he likes to play video games. Socially, Keenan's parents described him as getting along well with others, both peers and teachers. In fact, they stated that he easily makes friends and has always succeeded in the social realm.

Keenan's parents stated that he is in good health and has no significant history of illnesses, injuries, or hospitalizations. They said he does have 20/35 vision and astigmatism, but does not wear corrective lenses. There is no significant family history of academic, behavioral, or medical problems.

Behavioral Observations

Keenan is a cute boy with short brown hair who was dressed casually, wearing a T-shirt and long shorts or pants during each session of the evaluation. Keenan made good eye contact with the examiner and appeared quite comfortable conversing with the examiner, making rapport easy to establish and maintain. In fact, he noticed things around the room, such as a conch shell and a scenic painting, and used them to initiate conversation and engage the examiner, showing his adept social skills.

From the start, Keenan appeared motivated to perform well. He was concerned with his testing performance, asking if his responses were correct and sometimes asking if younger children could do some of the items he was doing. He also seemed to want to please the examiner, as evidenced by his helping the examiner put away test materials as well as his willingness to guess on items he did not know only after the examiner encouraged him to do so. Keenan frequently asked for clarification about directions, indicating his desire for structure and his difficulty understanding complex verbal instructions. For example, on a task in which he was to move a toy dog to a bone on a checkerboard-like grid containing obstacles, and to find the "quickest" path (the fewest number of moves), he asked many questions about the stated rules, such as "can you jump over all of them?" He also counted his starting point repeatedly, and had to be reminded several times not to do so. Furthermore, when reading passages and answering questions about the passages, he continually asked questions, trying to obtain more specific information about how to answer the questions. On a test of written expression in which he was to write a story that he had heard and about which he had answered questions, he responded by saying, "I don't get it. The whole story? All the details?"

Keenan was cooperative throughout the evaluation and showed a good tolerance for frustration. For those tasks that were increasingly difficult and frustrating for him, such as a task in which he was to count the exact number of blocks in various pictures of stacks of blocks, some of which are hidden, or a task in which the examiner teaches the child the nonsense names for fanciful pictures of fish, plants, and shells, Keenan would ask if we were done yet, or how many more items there were. He would also ask for a snack break or even try to start a conversation during the task to stall the testing. However, despite his noted frustration with certain tasks, he was easily brought back to the task at hand with minimal verbal encouragement. It should also be noted that Keenan appeared to tire easily. On all three testing sessions, Keenan would rub his eyes and yawn as the testing progressed, and even state that he was tired.

Keenan exhibited some fidgety behaviors and distractibility. For instance, Keenan would notice outside noises during the evaluation, such as a car spinning out, a siren, and a dog barking. He would look up and comment on the noise, sometimes using it to avoid the task at hand. However, Keenan's level of distractibility was normal for a child his age. His fidgety behaviors consisted mainly of taking his watch on and off and playing with the buckle during verbal tasks or in between items of nonverbal tasks. His behavior was not disruptive to the testing and was indicative of mild anxiety to the testing situation, as he only exhibited this fidgety behavior in the first of the three testing sessions.

Keenan struggled with writing tasks. When asked to fill in missing words, complete sentences, add punctuation and capitalization, and combine sentences, he worked very slowly. He erased frequently, changing his answers several times. He made an abundance of spelling errors and the examiner had to ask him what he had intended to write with many of his misspelled words. However, he was told that spelling did not matter on that task. Additionally, Keenan tended to misspell the same words in different ways throughout his work. For instance, in writing the word "king," he spelled it "king" and "kin" and in writing the word "dragon," he spelled it "dragn," "dragen," "dargen," "dagn," and "dargun," even when the word was written on the page in another section.

Keenan used several different types of strategies to help him solve problems. On a task in which he was to fill in the missing pictures of an incomplete story, he talked his way through the stories, indicating his use of verbal mediation. Additionally, he demonstrated a reflective problem-solving style in that he looked carefully at each picture in the story and in the picture set before placing the pictures. He was also reflective on other nonverbal tasks (e.g., when assembling colored triangles to match an abstract picture and when completing a pattern by selecting the correct picture stimulus from an array of options) as well as on verbal tasks (e.g., when told several characteristics of a concept and asked to name the concept, and when selecting from an array of pictures the one that corresponds to a vocabulary word or information question). His slower approach also carried over into his reading, in which he tended to read very slowly, and into his writing (as mentioned above). However, when he heard a story and was asked to repeat the story verbally, he spoke quickly and without much hesitation, indicating it is easier for him to express himself orally than in writing.

As was stated previously, Keenan appeared to put forth great effort and he was cooperative. Thus, the results of this assessment are deemed a valid reflection of his current cognitive and academic abilities.

Assessment Procedures

- Children's Memory Scale—selected subtests
- Clinical Interview with Keenan's parents
- Clinical Interview with schoolteacher

- Clinical Interview with tutor and program director of tutoring center
- Kaufman Assessment Battery for Children, Second Edition (KABC-II)
- Kaufman Test of Educational Achievement, Second Edition (KTEA-II), Comprehensive Form A

Test Results and Interpretation

Assessment of Cognitive Abilities

Keenan was administered the KABC-II to obtain a comprehensive picture of his mental processing and cognitive abilities. The KABC-II is based on a double theoretical foundation—Luria's neuropsychological model and the CHC psychometric theory. It offers five scales, each given a label that reflects both theoretical models: Sequential/*Gsm,* Simultaneous/*Gv,* Learning/*Glr,* Planning/*Gf,* and Knowledge/*Gc.* (From the perspective of CHC theory, *Gsm* = short-term memory; *Gv* = visual processing; *Glr* = long-term storage and retrieval; *Gf* = fluid reasoning; and *Gc* = crystallized ability.)

Examiners are given the option of selecting either the Luria model or the CHC model of the KABC-II, based on the child's background and the reason for referral. (Knowledge/*Gc* is excluded from the Luria model because measures of language ability and acquired knowledge may not provide fair assessment of some children's cognitive abilities—e.g., those from bilingual or nonmainstream backgrounds.) Keenan's primary language is English. This fact, coupled with Keenan's referral reason (that he may have a reading disability) led the examiner to select the CHC model of the KABC-II, which yields the Fluid Crystallized Index (FCI) as the global measure of general cognitive ability.

Keenan earned a KABC-II FCI of 87, ranking him at the 19th percentile and classifying his overall mental processing ability as falling within the Average to Below Average range. The chances are 90 percent that his true FCI is between 82 and 92. However, he displayed considerable variability in his standard scores on the five theory-based scales that compose the FCI, with indexes ranging from 108 on Knowledge/*Gc* to 77 on Sequential/*Gsm.* This 31-point discrepancy renders his FCI meaningless as an estimate of global ability; it is merely the midpoint of greatly varying abilities. Unlike the FCI, four out of five of Keenan's scale indexes were interpretable, as he performed consistently on the tasks that compose each separate scale (with the exception of Simultaneous/*Gv*).

Keenan functions consistently within the Average to slightly Below Average range in his ability to learn new material and to solve novel problems using fluid reasoning. These abilities were noted in his scores on the Learning/*Glr* scale (standard score = 86; 18th percentile) and the Planning/*Gf* scale (standard score

= 90; 25th percentile). Keenan's performance on the Supplementary Delayed Recall scale (16th percentile) was consistent with his initial performance, indicating that he was able to retain the newly learned paired associates (taught by the examiner during the administration of the Learning/*Glr* subtests) after an interval of about 20 minutes—despite participating in other cognitive tasks and without advance warning that he would be retested.

Although most of Keenan's abilities fall within the Average to Below Average range, he did show a significant weakness in his short-term memory, as measured by his score on the Sequential/*Gsm* scale (standard score = 77; 6th percentile). In fact, his short-term memory is both a normative weakness (compared to other children his age) and a personal weakness for him. Keenan appeared to do better with meaningful versus abstract stimuli, but meaningfulness appeared more important for Keenan in remembering verbal information than visual stimuli. To further assess Keenan's memory, his visual and auditory memory was assessed using selected subtests of the Children's Memory Scale. Keenan's memory skills did not appear to be dependent on whether the modality was visual versus auditory nor whether the stimuli were meaningful or abstract. Within the visual memory domain, he showed a strong ability to process, learn, and recall the spatial location of a dot pattern (84th percentile); however, he did poorly in his ability to recall human faces presented in a sequential format (2nd percentile). Conversely, within the verbal domain, he did well in his ability to process and recall verbally presented stories (63rd percentile), but less well in his associative memory (his ability to process, learn, and recall a list of word pairs; 16th percentile). His performance on the paired word associative memory task is consistent with his performance on the task of associative memory from the KABC-II, indicating that even though the latter task has contextual clues (the student can "read" the symbols as a sentence), Keenan did not use these clues. It is important to mention that Keenan noticed when the symbols were combined they formed sentences, as he said "Oh, like a sentence," although he still did not use this information to help him correctly identify the symbols.

Keenan's acquired knowledge of words and facts (crystallized ability) is a relative strength for him. Although his score on the Knowledge/*Gc* Index of 108 (70th percentile) is in the Average range compared to children his age, he performed significantly better on this index than his overall level of cognitive performance. During the administration of the Knowledge/*Gc* subtests, Keenan's reflective problem-solving style was observed. He took his time to look at all the options when he was to select from an array of pictures. He even willingly guessed, with the examiner's encouragement, often in an educated manner in that he would cross out with his fingers the choices that he knew were not correct.

Furthermore, on a task in which he was only given verbal information, he appropriately asked on several occasions for the question to be repeated. Of particular interest is the fact that Keenan showed significantly stronger performance on the Knowledge/*Gc* index than on his Learning/*Glr* index, indicating that despite it being more difficult for him to learn new material, he is learning verbal facts and concepts over time at home and in school. One reason for his weaker performance on the Learning/*Glr* index may be related to his difficulties with memory. However, Keenan's positive attitude combined with the additional effort he puts into his work likely contributes to his relative area of strength.

Keenan's Simultaneous/*Gv* Index of 90 (Average range) was not interpretable due to the variability he showed in his performance on both the two core tasks that comprise this scale and the two supplementary tasks. His performance ranged from the 84th percentile on a visualization task requiring him to count blocks, including those that are hidden from view, to the 9th percentile on a task in which he was to mentally fill in the gaps of an incomplete inkblot drawing to determine the object. In addition, he performed at the 5th percentile on a task in which he was to assemble foam triangles to match an abstract picture. However, his slow speed of problem solving negatively impacted his score, as evidenced by the fact that he assembled harder items correctly, but not within the time limits. The variability in Keenan's performance on these tasks demonstrates that Keenan's reasoning and problem-solving skills that depend on spatial visualization and simultaneous processing of information fluctuate without any discernible pattern.

Assessment of Academic Abilities

To assess Keenan's academic achievement in reading, math, written language and oral language, he was administered the KTEA-II Comprehensive Form, which is an individually administered set of academic achievement measures. Keenan's standard scores on the main KTEA-II Comprehensive Form Composites (based on grade norms) were all within the Average to Below Average range: Reading (98 ± 4; 45th percentile), Mathematics (102 ± 4; 55th percentile), Oral Language (97 ± 9; 42nd percentile), and Written Language (88 ± 6; 21st percentile), Comprehensive Achievement (96 ± 4; 39th percentile).

Keenan's reading skills were mostly in the Average range compared to other children his age, whether he was reading words (32nd percentile on Letter and Word Recognition), sounding out nonsense words using phonics skills (21st percentile on Nonsense Word Decoding), or demonstrating understanding of what he reads (61st percentile on Reading Comprehension). However, when asked to rapidly decode real words and nonsense words, his performance was in the Below Average range (Reading Fluency Composite = 84 ± 6; 14th percentile), indicating his speed of isolated word recognition and decoding is slower than that of his peers.

When reading real words, Keenan appeared to use a whole word approach, rarely phonetically sounding out the words, unless he clearly did not recognize the word. Using the whole word or sight approach, he often did not notice small differences in a word and would incorrectly identify it. For example, he said "quite" for "quiet," "blossom" for "blossomed," "meat" for "meant," and "swamp" for "swap." When he did not recognize the word by sight, he tried to sound it out phonetically, but had much difficulty, and often sounded it out by chunking it into smaller pieces, such as "el ee ven" for "eleven" or "untild" for "united." In reading nonsense words, Keenan often left out or changed a letter, which made him mispronounce the word, such as saying "plex" for "plux," "fape" for "fap," and "skreet" for "shreed." His performance on these reading tasks is consistent with his teacher's report that Keenan "doesn't decode properly and comes up with something different." During Reading Comprehension, he read the passages aloud, even though he was told he could read them silently. He read very slowly and with numerous whole word mistakes that changed the meaning of the passage. In fact, for the last passage, he said "worse" for "world," "Israel" for "Inca," "rings" for "ruins," and "experienced" for "entered." Despite his misreading several of the words, when asked questions about the passage he was able to use the questions to help correct himself and review the passage to find the answer.

Keenan's responses on several KTEA-II subtests were further examined by error analysis to identify specific areas of academic skill strength or weakness. He showed a significant number of specific skill weaknesses across academic areas related to reading. Keenan demonstrated difficulties with short vowels, as evidenced by his pronunciation of the word "eleven," which he pronounced "el ee ven"; for the nonsense word "mab" he said "made." Keenan also had difficulty spelling silent letters, writing "hom" for "home" and "whent" for "went." However, of particular interest is his pattern of fluctuating performance or making different kinds of errors throughout. Thus, he showed a significant number of whole word errors in that he either misread some or most of the word by omitting or inserting letters in the middle or end of the word. The absence of a pattern to Keenan's errors is consistent with what his reading tutor describes, in that Keenan often misreads sight words, but he will also sometimes skip letters, other times substitute letters, and yet other times he guesses.

Because one of Keenan's presenting concerns was his difficulties with spelling, his written language was assessed. Keenan earned a Written Language Composite standard score of 88 (21st percentile), indicating his ability to express his ideas in writing and his spelling (standard scores of 89 on each; 23rd percentile) are both in the Average to Low Average range. On the Written Expression subtest, error analysis revealed weaknesses for Keenan in capitalization and punctuation. It should be noted that Keenan was not penalized for misspelling on the Written Expression subtest, but Keenan misspelled so many words, often the same word in several different ways, that it made it difficult to discern what he was trying to communicate. However, Keenan's teacher said that despite his misspelling, she usually understands what he is trying to say.

Keenan's oral expression was also assessed, so that a comparison of his ability to understand information via reading versus listening could be made. On the Oral Language composite, Keenan performed in the Average range (standard score of 97; 42nd percentile). He performed equally well in his listening comprehension (37th percentile) as he did in his oral expression (53rd percentile). Furthermore, his ability to comprehend information from reading did not differ from his listening comprehension.

Keenan's performance in mathematics reveals consistently Average functioning in the basic skills of computation (42nd percentile) and the application of mathematical principles to solve word problems (68th percentile). Thus, his Mathematics Composite standard score of 102 (55th percentile) provides a good overview of his mathematics skills. Error analysis revealed no specific strengths or weaknesses in Keenan's math skills. However, he did exhibit a significant weakness in careless types of errors, such as using the wrong operation (adding when he was supposed to subtract), subtracting the smaller number from the larger number, and computational errors. In solving math problems, Keenan asked if he could use his fingers rather than using scratch paper. Also, he pointed to division problems and stated that he did not know how to do them.

Integration of Ability and Achievement

In evaluating the consistency of Keenan's cognitive and achievement scores, it is clear that cognitively his overall functioning is in the Average to slightly Below Average range in most areas, with significant weaknesses in his short-term memory span. His academic achievement is consistently in the Average range, with the exception of his reading fluency, which is Below Average. Thus, Keenan is currently achieving at his ability level. In fact, despite his specific skill weaknesses in decoding fluency and phonetic decoding of certain irregular patterns, his reading is still in the average range when compared to children of the same grade. Given that there are no significant discrepancies between Keenan's ability and what he is achieving, he does not meet the criteria necessary to diagnose any specific learning disorders.

Summary and Diagnostic Impressions

Keenan is a 9-year-old boy who was referred for an evaluation to determine if his difficulties in reading and spelling are indicative of a learning disability and to determine the best educational environment for him.

Keenan was friendly and responsive to the examiner throughout the testing. His positive attitude and social adeptness were evident from the start and made it a pleasure to work with him. He did show some mild distractibility and fidgety behavior; nothing of clinical significance, but it will be discussed in the recommendations.

Although Keenan does not have a learning disability, reading is an enormous struggle for him. He has vague short-term memory deficits that likely impact his ability to process and encode verbal information that has no prior meaning to him (such as single words, phonics rules). Furthermore, his reading fluency is very slow. Thus, even when he does recognize words accurately, he does so at a rate of speed that adversely affects his comprehension. This slow reading fluency, coupled with difficulties with phonetic decoding, prevent Keenan's reading process from becoming automatic. Because Keenan's decoding is not automatic, he has to devote more attention to decoding the words than to the meaning of what is being read. It is likely that Keenan will have similar difficulties with spelling and writing as he does with decoding and reading comprehension because spelling ability contributes to writing ability in a similar way. Good spelling ability reduces the amount of effort the student must devote to producing individual words. Keenan's attention to detail fluctuates such that he makes careless errors in his work (such as adding when he is supposed to be subtracting, or omitting or adding letters when reading words). Thus, he shows no true pattern to his errors.

As was stated by Keenan's parents, his strengths are in the social domain. Keenan's teacher, his tutor, and this examiner all experience Keenan as a hard worker who is eager to please and is sincerely a pleasure to work with. This positive attitude and work ethic, coupled with his ability to endear himself to others, will help him greatly in his academic environment, because he makes teachers and tutors want to help him succeed. Furthermore, they see him making an extra effort and they, in turn, are willing to give him additional support.

Recommendations

- Keenan does not meet the criteria for any specific learning disabilities. Thus, if he attends public school he will not be eligible for any special education services. However, the decision about where Keenan should attend school remains important. Keenan's current private school functions at an accelerated level for all of its students. Specifically in reading, the "open court" style of reading appears to be overly difficult for Keenan, in that he cannot complete the work without help from his tutor or parents. If his school and teacher are open to making accommodations for Keenan for his in-class and homework assignments, he may benefit from the challenge. However, Keenan's parents should discuss with his teacher how the curriculum will change and increase in difficulty for following years, to determine if this accelerated program will be such a struggle that it will impact his self-esteem and positive attitude. Furthermore, they should meet with school officials at the public school that Keenan would attend and find out how the curriculum may differ.

- Keenan should continue to work with his tutor in word attack skills (decoding), vocabulary, and comprehension. Often the phonics programs for reading decoding will focus on the same set of word skills that is needed for spelling. This will be helpful as writing becomes increasingly important in Keenan's academic workload.

- Keenan has difficulty performing tasks quickly under pressure. The emphasis on his work should be on accuracy rather than speed. Therefore, he should be provided with ample time to complete his work or his assignments should be shortened so that they can be accomplished within the period. When he is allowed extra time, do so in a way that does not bring negative attention to him.

- If Keenan's homework is taking him an excessive amount of time, reduce the amount of homework he is required to do in each area so that he can complete his assignment in approximately the same amount of time as other students. Examples of modified assignments are: solving the odd-numbered math problems instead of all the items, studying 10 spelling words instead of 20, and writing a half-page report instead of a whole page.

- Given that Keenan showed signs of distractibility and that it takes him longer to complete his work, Keenan should have a place free from distractions to do his homework (in his bedroom at a desk, rather than at the kitchen table while dinner is being made or the television is on). Additionally, if he has difficulty sustaining his attention, he should work in short intervals, with planned short breaks (e.g., work for 20 or 30 minutes, then break for 5 minutes). Also, his seating placement in the front of the classroom near the teacher is an excellent place to maximize his attention and minimize distraction from other students.

- Because Keenan has difficulty with tasks involving memory, reduce the amount of information that he is required to memorize.

- Provide intensive repetition, practice, and review in learning activities.

To promote retention, provide activities to reinforce the skills or content at frequent and regular intervals, gradually increasing the intervals to less frequent and intermittent. Additionally, when teaching Keenan new information, provide facts in small increments so that he doesn't get lost, and be sure to relate new information to information he already knows in a meaningful way.

- Ensure that Keenan understands the concept underlying any new information or skill, as well as how each aspect of the new information is related to every other part. To this end, as much as possible, present all types of verbal information accompanied by visual stimuli that clearly illustrate the concept being taught. Examples are: pictures, charts, graphs, semantic maps, and videotapes.

- Directions for homework assignments should be concisely written down for Keenan, using easy vocabulary words and pictures to help.

- Keenan tends to make careless errors in his work—for instance, not noticing the computation symbols for math problems. Therefore, he should highlight the process signs. Help him decide on colors for each of the four signs and consistently highlight each in its own color.

- After completing math problems, Keenan should use a calculator to check calculations and then rework any incorrect solutions.

- Keenan should be encouraged to continue to ask questions about his in-class assignments as they arise, as he does better with increased structure as to what is expected of him. To this end, it would be helpful if he could have written instructions, using easy vocabulary words and even pictorial stimuli to convey the directions. When Keenan asks questions about his assignments, the teacher should write down her answer for him so he can refer to the instructions while completing his assignment.

- The following books will provide useful suggestions for educational interventions that will take into account Keenan's weakness in short-term memory and speed of processing: (1) J. A. Naglieri and E. B. Pickering, 2003, *Helping Children Learn: Intervention Handouts for Use in School and Home,* Baltimore: Paul H. Brookes, and (2) N. Mather and L. Jaffe, 2002, *Woodcock-Johnson III: Recommendations, Reports, and Strategies,* New York: Wiley.

Debra Y. Broadbooks, PhD
Clinical Psychologist

Psychometric Summary for Keenan F.

Kaufman Assessment Battery for Children–Second Edition (KABC-II), CHC Model

Scale/Subtest	Standard Score (mean = 100; SD = 15)	90% Confidence Interval	Percentile Rank
Sequential/*Gsm*	**77**	**70–86**	**6**
Number Recall	6		9
Word Order	6		9
Simultaneous/*Gv*	**90**	**82–100**	**25**
Rover	12		75
Triangles	5		5
Gestalt Closure	*6*		*9*
Block Counting	*13*		*84*
Learning/*Glr*	**86**	**80–94**	**18**
Atlantis	8		25
Rebus	7		16
Planning/*Gf*	**90**	**83–97**	**25**
Story Completion	10		50
Pattern Reasoning	7		16
Knowledge/*Gc*	**108**	**101–115**	**70**
Verbal Knowledge	12		75
Riddles	11		63
Fluid-Crystallized Index (FCI)	**87**	**82–92**	**19**
Supplementary Scale			
Delayed Recall	**85**		**16**
Atlantis Delayed	*10*		*50*
Rebus Delayed	*5*		*5*

Note: Italicized subtests are Supplementary and not included in the calculation of the indexes.

Psychometric Summary for Keenan F. (Continued)

Kaufman Test of Educational Achievement–Second Edition (KTEA-II) Comprehensive Form (Form A)

Composite/Subtest	Standard Score (grade-based)	90% Confidence Interval	Percentile Rank
Reading Composite	98	94–102	45
Letter and Word Recognition	93	88–98	32
Reading Comprehension	104	98–110	61
Decoding Composite[a]	91	87–95	27
Nonsense Word Decoding	88	82–94	21
Mathematics Composite	102	96–108	55
Math Concepts and Applications	107	99–115	68
Math Computation	97	89–105	42
Oral Language Composite	97	88–106	42
Listening Comprehension	95	85–105	37
Oral Expression	101	89–113	53
Written Language Composite	88	82–94	21
Written Expression	89	80–98	23
Spelling	89	84–94	23
Reading Fluency Composite	84	78–90	14
Word Recognition Fluency	89	81–97	23
Decoding Fluency	80	73–87	9
Comprehensive Achievement Composite	96	92–100	39

Note: Italicized subtests are Supplementary.

[a]The Decoding Composite includes Nonsense Word Decoding and Letter and Word Recognition.

Psychometric Summary for Keenan F. (Continued)

Children's Memory Scale—selected subtests

Index/Subtest	Standard Score	Percentile Rank
Dot Locations		
Learning	11	63
Total Score	13	84
Stories		
Immediate	11	63
Faces		
Immediate	4	2
Word Pairs		
Learning	6	9
Total Score	7	16
Visual Immediate	91 ± 13	27
Verbal Immediate	94 ± 9	34
Learning	91 ± 11	27

Note: Mean of index standard scores = 100 (SD = 15); mean of subtest scaled scores = 10 (SD = 3).

KTEA-II ERROR ANALYSIS

Keenan's responses on several KTEA-II Comprehensive Form subtests were further examined to identify possible specific strengths and weaknesses. First, his errors on each subtest were totaled according to skill categories. Then the number of errors Keenan made in each skill category was compared to the average number of errors made by the standardization sample students, similar in age, who attempted the same items. As a result, Keenan's performance in each skill category could be rated as strong, average, or weak. Keenan exhibited no strong areas of skill compared to his peers, but did have several skills that were rated in the average level or that were determined to be weak. The diagnostic information obtained from Keenan's error analysis follows (only his weak skill areas are summarized):

KTEA-II Error Analysis for Keenan F.—weak skill areas

KTEA-II Subtests	Skill Category	Definition	Example
Nonsense Word Decoding & Spelling	Single/Double Consonant	Consonants that make a single sound.	apple, <u>m</u>ab, dressing
Nonsense Word Decoding	Initial Blend	Two or three consonants whose sounds blend together at the beginning of a word.	brother, <u>pl</u>ewness, <u>spl</u>itting
Nonsense Word Decoding	Medial/Final Blend	Two or three consonants whose sounds blend together in the middle or at the end of a word.	behin<u>d</u>, hapt, roas<u>t</u>ed
Letter and Word Recognition and Nonsense Word Decoding	Short Vowel	A vowel in a closed syllable that makes the short vowel sound.	it, d<u>o</u>mpest, w<u>e</u>nt
Nonsense Word Decoding	Vowel Team/ Diphthong	Vowel team: a pair of vowels that make one sound. Diphthong: *oi/oy* or *ou/ow*	pl<u>ea</u>se, sw<u>ai</u>ning, t<u>oa</u>sted disappoint, adr<u>ou</u>nded, sp<u>oil</u>
Letter and Word Recognition and Spelling	Silent Letter	The final e is not voiced. One of a pair of consonants is not voiced.	lat<u>e</u>, brome, shad<u>e</u> <u>k</u>neel, sulfem<u>n</u>, <u>g</u>nawed
Letter and Word Recognition and Spelling	Suffix/Inflection	Common suffixes Inflections: -ed, -s, and –ing	relatioat<u>ion</u>, norpes<u>ious</u>, extens<u>ion</u> shoe<u>s</u>, phopp<u>ed</u>, smell<u>ing</u>
Letter and Word Recognition and Nonsense Word Decoding	Insertion/Omission	Response either omits a syllable from or adds a syllable to the stimulus word	*dilapated* (dilap<u>i</u>dated) *domp i est* (dompest)

Category	Skill	Description	Example
Phonological Awareness	Rhyming	Words that are similar in sound, especially with respect to the last syllable.	hat—cat clock—block
Written Expression	Capitalization	Writing capital letters where appropriate.	First word of a sentence Proper nouns, days of week, months of year Titles of address Book or movie titles
Written Expression	Punctuation	Properly placing punctuation in a sentence.	End punctuation: period, question mark, exclamation mark Comma, apostrophe, and hyphen usage
Math Computation	Addition	Whole number addition.	$15 + 9 =$ ___
Math Computation	Subtraction	Whole number subtraction.	$21 - 7 =$ ___
Math Computation	Wrong Operation	Performing the wrong numeric operation.	Adding when a subtraction sign is present. $6 - 5 = 11$
Math Computation	Fact or Computation	Making an error in a basic fact such as adding, subtracting, multiplying, or dividing whole numbers.	$2 + 2 = 5$ $6 \times 2 = 14$
Math Computation	Subtract Smaller from Larger	Faced with a problem requiring subtracting a larger digit from a smaller one, the student simply subtracts the smaller from the larger. This is a special case of failing to regroup in subtraction.	$\begin{array}{r} 58 \\ -39 \\ \hline 21 \end{array}$ $\begin{array}{r} 533 \\ -67 \\ \hline 534 \end{array}$

CASE REPORT 2

Name: Ryan P.
Age: 12:2
Grade: 6th

Reason For Evaluation

Ryan P. is a 12-year-old boy who attends the Hillside Elementary School. Ryan lives at home with his parents, his 10-year-old brother, and his 8-year-old sister. This evaluation was initiated at his parents' request due to their concerns regarding Ryan's attentional difficulties, along with some receptive and expressive language problems identified on speech and language testing. Ryan has had some partial assessments done in the past; however, he has never had a full, comprehensive neuropsychological evaluation. He has been diagnosed with a Mood Disorder and he is currently on Trileptal and Seroquel. His parents are eager for information regarding any specific neurocognitive deficit that Ryan may be displaying, and what can be done to help him in this regard. This assessment will evaluate Ryan's cognitive status as well as assess any specific academic and emotional difficulties.

Background Information

Developmental History and Health

According to Mr. and Ms. P., Ryan is the product of a normal, full-term pregnancy, and a normal labor and delivery. He weighed 8 lbs. 11 oz. at birth. Ryan was described as a very fussy, colicky baby who did not eat or sleep well, and who suffered from "stomach problems." His mother indicated that he was nursed for 6 months. Ryan suffered from frequent ear infections until age two. No other health problems or behavior difficulties were noted as an infant. According to Ryan's parents, he reached all his developmental milestones on time. No significant deficits in self-help skills or adaptive behavior were reported.

As noted above, Ryan is currently on Trileptal and Seroquel, which were prescribed for his Mood Disorder. He has had no head injuries or concussions. Ryan complains of frequent stomachaches, nausea, and frequent bowel movements. His parents indicated that these complaints are related to anxiety. Ryan's parents indicated that he displays irregular sleeping patterns, and he has asked his mother for Benadryl to help him fall asleep at night. Although he has difficulty falling asleep at night, once he is asleep, he sleeps deeply. However, he has trouble staying awake in the classroom, and constantly falls asleep during class. His parents voiced concerns about Ryan's difficulty following auditory instruction, although they do not suspect a hearing loss, and his hearing was recently checked at school. Ryan displays a moderate impairment in articulation.

Ryan's parents described him as a talented athlete with good gross and fine coordination skills. He participates in several sports, including soccer, football, and skating, and he excels in these areas. Ryan demonstrates some significant sensory sensitivities. He cannot tolerate tags in his clothes, and he insists on wearing a specific type of sock. He also displays some motor tics, including twitching his shoulder and eye blinking.

Ryan's family history has notable instances of psychological problems. His mother reported that she is currently medicated for depression as well as possible ADHD. She also indicated that Ryan's maternal grandmother has a history of depression and suicide attempts. Ryan's father reported symptoms of high anxiety, some inattention, as well as processing problems. He noted that Ryan's paternal grandfather suffered from mood swings and anger control difficulties.

Academic History

Ryan began preschool at age 3:6 and kindergarten at age 5. He reportedly had some mild difficulty learning his letters and numbers, but his teachers reported that he was functioning at appropriate levels for his age. Ryan began attending Hillside Elementary School at first grade. His parents noted that no behavior difficulties were reported, aside from some overactivity in the lunch line and a tendency to blurt out answers in class. Through second grade he reportedly did well academically, and his grades were consistently As and Bs.

However, in third grade, Ryan's parents noted the demands of his very performance-oriented school increased, and they indicated that Ryan demonstrated some academic difficulty and organizational problems. He forgot his assignments, he did not complete homework, and he appeared to cover up his embarrassment about not understanding the work by hiding assignments in his desk. Ryan expressed significant anxiety to his parents in relation to the statewide group standardized tests, although his overall results were average for his age. His fourth grade teacher told Mr. and Ms. P. that movement and sounds in the classroom easily distracted Ryan, and that "even things on the wall distract him." As a result, Ryan was tested by the school district at the beginning of fifth grade. These results indicated that Ryan's intellectual functioning was in the Low Average range (Full Scale IQ = 83), and receptive language difficulties and articulation problems were reported. As a result of this testing, Ryan received speech pathology services at school until the end of the school year.

Ryan apparently has done better academically during his sixth-grade year. However, his parents reported that he continues to struggle to complete his homework assignments, and that he is extremely disorganized. He typically does his homework at the kitchen table, where there are numerous distractions from his younger sister. His father noted that there are many unnecessary materials on the table at this time, and that it is a very disorganized environment. Ms. P. voiced her concern about both Ryan and her own organizational difficulties, and she expressed eagerness for any assistance in this regard. In an interview with Ryan's sixth-grade teacher, she noted that her greatest concerns about Ryan were his inability to focus, his poor study and organizational skills, and his sleepiness. She noted that he is unable to stay awake between 9 A.M. to 10:30 A.M. when the class is working on reading, and that she finds it very unusual for a student to be sleepy at this time. She indicated that Ryan "is wired" after lunch and is fidgety and more distractible. She reported that Ryan is strong in math and spelling skills, but that he is "overwhelmed" by writing tasks, and is unable to complete these tasks in the classroom. She described Ryan as having a pleasant and sweet personality, a good sense of humor, and a willingness to participate in new things, and she noted that he is very popular among his peers. According to his teacher, Ryan is never uncooperative or defiant in class, and aside from some aggressive behavior on the playground, she has not noted any inappropriate conduct from him.

In an interview with Ryan, he expressed an acute awareness about his difficulty remaining awake at school. He noted: "If I read, I won't fall asleep, but if they read I get tired." When asked if he can anticipate himself falling asleep, he indicated that "I kind of know . . . I stay up and listen to it . . . my eyes are closed, I am half asleep, I can hear what is going on, I usually know what is going on." He also indicated that in the past he had experienced significant memory problems, but that "it is better now for a few weeks or months." He was unable to express what had changed to improve his memory abilities.

Currently, his parents described Ryan as extremely distractible and displaying poor sustained attention. However, his attention span is better if he is interested in the subject matter. His father indicated that when Ryan focuses, "he completes his work and tasks amazingly," but that he is rarely focused. His processing speed is reported to be inconsistent. His parents indicated that he has adequate problem-solving skills and intact visual-spatial ability. His expressive language is reported to be variable and deficits in his receptive language have been noted. His parents are unsure whether this reflects inattention, auditory processing difficulties, or an undetected hearing deficit. According to Mr. and Ms. P., Ryan demonstrates very concrete thought processes; he does not display the capacity for abstract reasoning, and he is very literal in his interpretation of events and expressions.

Emotional and Social Development

Mr. and Ms. P. reported that Ryan has always been a very irritable child who would lose control over small details, such as his trousers being too pressed, or the sun being in his eyes. In 3rd grade, Ryan apparently began displaying more intense temper outbursts, mood instability, and volatility. He also began having extreme difficulty with transitions. His parents indicated that at this time the family was experiencing a high level of stress due to moving home, building and selling another home, and living with Ryan's grandparents. Ryan was apparently displaying significant anger problems that were "creating rifts in the family." He was also extremely anxious, and he had significant difficulty getting organized in the morning.

Ryan began psychiatric treatment at this time. His psychiatrist recommended that a course of Trileptal and Seroquel be prescribed as his medication regime. The medication appeared to have a positive effect.

From a social point of view, Ryan is reported to be very popular and has several good friends. His mother described him as having a "very loving heart," and she reported that he likes to take care of the elderly, as well as a Down syndrome child at his school. His father noted that he is "very considerate, willing to please, quick witted, and funny." Ryan apparently gets along well with his brother, although there is reported to be some competition and friction between them at times. His parents noted that he used to "adore" his sister and was very responsible with her. However, he now tends to antagonize his sister as well as the family dog, and that he can be very aggressive in this regard. His parents wondered whether this could be a means for Ryan to release his frustration after a day at school.

Behavioral Observations

Ryan presented himself as a cute and friendly 12-year-old boy. Rapport was easily established and Ryan cooperated and worked diligently. He made no complaints about the length of testing, and he did not request additional breaks beyond those suggested by the examiner. However, on the first day of testing Ryan reported being very tired when he arrived, which he attributed to having had a late night the evening before. On this day he was noted to be fairly fidgety, and he frequently played with his watch, which he reported was new and needed to be reset. However, these behaviors were not evident during the second testing session. In general, Ryan's performances were extremely slow. He did not appear to rush through any task or to feel pressured on timed tests.

During the first day of testing, although Ryan gave the appearance of being attentive on many tasks, he demonstrated some significant difficulty remaining alert. On several occasions he would become completely unresponsive while completing a task, and he would sit staring ahead and blinking repetitively. On one occasion Ryan appeared to fall asleep right after this episode. He was unable to explain what he had been experiencing, merely stating that he was unable to think of any further responses to the task at hand. He did not appear to be confused and he was alert immediately after the episode. Although he was unable to complete the task he had been working on, he was able to respond to a new task. This was most noticeable on language-based tasks, and on tasks that did not require him to make extensive verbal or motor responses, but rather to focus on verbal information presented by the examiner. These episodes lasted a few seconds to a minute. With the exception of these incidents, Ryan did appear to be attentive and focused during the testing. In contrast, Ryan appeared to be completely alert during the second day of testing, and none of the episodes described earlier were observed. It should be noted that Ryan did not take his dose of Trileptal on the second day, and his dose of Seroquel had been increased at that time. In addition, he reported going to sleep earlier the night before, and he certainly appeared more vigilant and attentive. In addition, Ryan chewed gum during his second day of testing, and he reported that this helped him remain alert.

Ryan appeared to put forward his best effort at all times. On the basis of these behavioral observations, this assessment appears to be a valid measure of Ryan's neuropsychological functioning at this time.

Assessment Procedures and Tests Administered

- Clinical interview with Mr. and Ms. P.
- Clinical interview with Ryan
- Kaufman Assessment Battery for Children–Second Edition (KABC-II)
- A Developmental Neuropsychological Assessment (NEPSY): Selected Subtests
- Kaufman Test of Educational Achievement–Second Edition (KTEA-II)
- IVA Continuous Performance Test (IVA)
- Children's Depression Inventory (CDI)
- Piers-Harris Children's Self-Concept Scale 2 (PHSCS2)
- Revised Children's Manifest Anxiety Scale (RCMAS)
- Rorschach
- Sensory Profile

- Achenbach Child Behavior Checklist/6–18 (CBCL)
- Achenbach Teacher's Report Form/6–18 (TRF)
- Conners' Parent Rating Scale–Revised: Long Version
- Conners' Teacher Rating Scale–Revised: Long Version

Test Results

Intellectual Abilities

In order to assess Ryan's intellectual ability, he was administered the Kaufman Assessment Battery for Children, Second Edition (KABC-II) which is an individually administered test of a child's intellectual ability and cognitive strengths and weaknesses. One of the objectives of this test is to provide a more fair assessment of the processing abilities of children with receptive language disorders. There are four scales that are administered to such children: Sequential/Short-term Memory (Gsm), Simultaneous/Visual Processing (Gv), Learning/Long-term Retrieval (Glr), and Planning/Fluid Reasoning (Gf). The Mental Processing Index (MPI) is the global scale that is considered the most representative estimate of global intellectual functioning when administered to children with language processing problems. Ryan's general cognitive ability is within the Average range of intellectual functioning, as measured by an MPI of 89 (90 percent confidence interval = 84–94). His overall thinking and reasoning abilities exceed those of approximately 23 percent of children his age. This score is consistent with the results of the assessment conducted 2 years ago, which yielded a WISC-III Full Scale IQ of 83 (90 percent confidence interval = 79–88). In addition, additional subtests of the KABC-II were administered in order to calculate a Nonverbal Index (NVI). He scored a global IQ score of 80 on this scale (9th percentile), which is in the Low Average range. Therefore, even with the minimization of language factors on the KABC-II, Ryan's intellectual functioning is consistently in the Low Average to Average range.

Ryan's sequential processing abilities, as measured by the Sequential/Gsm scale, are in the Average range, at the 50th percentile (Standard Score = 100). This scale is designed to measure the ability to process information in a serial or temporal order, to hold information in immediate awareness, and then use that information before it is forgotten. Ryan's scores on the subtests contributing to the Sequential/Gsm scale are extremely variable. His performance was intact when required to repeat a series of numbers in the same sequence as the examiner said them (63rd percentile), as well as on a subtest assessing his ability to touch a series of silhouettes in the same order as the examiner said their names (37th percentile). He had significantly more difficulty on a task requiring him to copy a sequence of hand movements made by the examiner (5th percentile). Although no overt signs of inattention were evident on this subtest, Ryan had great difficulty remembering the examiner's hand movements, and he was only able to complete some very basic items on this subtest. This reflects notable problems with sequential processing and short-term memory in the visual-motor channel.

Ryan's simultaneous processing abilities as measured by the Simultaneous/*Gv* scale are in the Average range, at the 16th percentile (Standard Score = 85). This scale is designed to measure the visual processing of information, spatial manipulation of visual stimuli, and nonverbal reasoning. Ryan had no difficulty on a task of spatial scanning that assessed his ability to plan the quickest route for a dog to take to get to a bone (50th percentile). However, he struggled on a measure of spatial visualization in which he was required to assemble several triangles together to match a picture of an abstract design (5th percentile). His responses on this task appeared to be somewhat random, and he displayed considerable difficulty manipulating the triangles and matching the colors on the triangles with the target design. He had further difficulty on another subtest of visual orientation with regard to spatial relationships, in which he was required to count the number of blocks in a stack in which some blocks were hidden from view (5th percentile). This reflects problems with the spatial management of visual stimuli, difficulties mentally organizing visual information presented spatially, and difficulties analyzing part-whole relationships within spatial information.

Ryan demonstrated a significant weakness on the Learning/*Glr* Scale (Standard Score = 84, 14th percentile). He struggled on a task measuring his ability to learn nonsense names for pictures of fish, plants, and shells (16th percentile). He had similar difficulty on a task assessing his ability to learn words associated with particular drawings, and to read aloud sentences composed of these drawings (16th percentile). His recall of these names and words after a delay was also impaired (16th and 5th percentiles, respectively). This is indicative of considerable problems storing information in long-term memory and retrieving this information in an efficient manner, both after an initial presentation of the information as well as after a delay.

On the Planning/*Gf* scale, Ryan demonstrated an intact ability to solve novel problems with flexibility, to draw inferences and understand implications, to apply inductive or deductive reasoning, and to plan his course of action (Standard Score = 99, 47th percentile). He displayed Average ability on a subset requiring him to select, from a set of pictures, those that are needed to complete a story, and to place the missing pictures in their correct locations (37th percentile). His performance was also intact on a subtest of abstract categorical reasoning ability requiring him to complete a pattern by selecting the correct stimulus from an array

(63rd percentile). He worked slowly on these tasks, he did not display any impulsivity, and he appeared to plan his responses carefully.

Attention and Executive Functions

In order to assess his attention, Ryan was administered selected subtests from the NEPSY and the Delis-Kaplan Executive Function System (D-KEFS). Ryan demonstrated variable performances on these subtests of attention and executive functioning. His performance was Average (50th percentile) on a subtest assessing his nonverbal planning and problem-solving abilities. On this task, Ryan was required to move three colored balls to target positions on three pegs in a prescribed number of moves. He was able to complete some very difficult problems on this subtest, yet he struggled on some easier ones.

On a NEPSY subtest of selective auditory attention, Ryan's performance was also in the Average range (63rd percentile). This task required Ryan to maintain selective auditory attention and to regulate his responses to conflicting stimuli. The first phase of this task required him to maintain auditory vigilance to words presented on a tape and then place the target object in a box when its name was called out. On the next phase, he had to do the same, but with three target objects. In addition, on two of the three objects, Ryan was required to do the opposite of what he was told (i.e., put the red chip in the box to the command "yellow"). Ryan demonstrated a very strong performance on the initial phase of this task, and he was attentive and focused throughout this phase. He had slightly more difficulty on the second phase of the task, although his performance was still within the Average range. His performance on this subtest reflected no problems with inattention or impulsivity, as evident by his very low number of omission and commission errors.

In contrast to these strong performances, Ryan demonstrated great difficulty on a test of selective visual attention assessing his ability to attend to a visual stimulus and locate target pictures quickly in an array (9th percentile). Although Ryan worked accurately both when required to detect one target stimulus and when searching for two target stimuli, his speed was much slower than expected. Ryan's slow processing speed was noted consistently throughout the testing.

Ryan's motor inhibition was Average as evident by his performance on a subtest assessing self-regulation and inhibition (26–75th percentile). His impulse control and inhibition were Low Average (11–25th percentile) on a subtest assessing his ability to sustain a position over a 75-second interval. Ryan displayed some difficulty inhibiting the impulse to respond to auditory distraction on this task.

On the D-KEFS, Ryan demonstrated some significant problems with cognitive flexibility. This is indicative of some rigid and concrete thinking, and was identified by Ms. P. when she noted that Ryan tends to be very literal and to lack the capacity for abstract thinking. This was noted particularly on sequencing trail-making tasks, but was also evident on an executive functions test of verbal interference assessing inhibition of verbal response and cognitive flexibility. Despite his difficulties, Ryan demonstrated the ability to monitor and modify his behaviors in order to produce correct responses. He did not demonstrate an impulsive response style or any visual scanning difficulties, and there were no problems noted in maintaining cognitive set.

Ryan's performance was extremely impaired on the IVA Continuous Performance Test (IVA). This task is intended to be mildly boring and demanding of sustained attention over a 13-minute period of time. On this task Ryan was required to respond to target stimuli (the number 1 presented either auditorily or visually on the computer) and refrain from responding to nontarget stimuli (the number 2 presented in the same formats). During the administration of this test, Ryan's back was to the examiner, and she was therefore unable to determine his level of alertness throughout the task. A diagnosis of Attention-Deficit/Hyperactivity Disorder, Combined Type was indicated by his performance on the IVA. Ryan was unable to validly respond to visual stimuli, and therefore his response pattern to visual stimuli could not be analyzed or interpreted. This reflects significant problems with Ryan's visual attention span. Ryan also displayed problems with his general auditory attentional functioning, and he demonstrated an impaired ability to accurately and quickly respond in a reliable manner to auditory stimuli. He had significant difficulty remaining vigilant to auditory stimuli, and he also demonstrated problems with impulse control in response to auditory stimuli. This indicates that Ryan most likely is overreactive to and distracted by auditory stimuli in his environment. His pattern of responding indicates that Ryan experiences periods of random, idiopathic, impulsive responses to nontarget auditory stimuli. The impact of this deficit is likely to be significant, manifesting as impulsive responses to auditory stimuli in his home and school environments. He also demonstrated poor Fine Motor Regulation, indicating problems with self-control. Ryan demonstrated some lapses in his auditory attention, along with very poor auditory processing speed. His performance on this task indicates a tendency to make unusual, careless errors, problems remembering rules, and a likelihood that he engages in behaviors that are distracting and annoying to others.

Further measures of Ryan's attentional functioning were obtained by the Conners' Parent Rating Scale–Revised, the Conners' Teacher Rating Scale–Revised, the Achenbach Child Behavior Checklist/6–18 (CBCL), and the Achenbach

Teacher's Report Form/6–18 (TRF). On the Conners' Parent Rating Scale–Revised, the profiles generated by Mr. and Ms. P.'s reports were almost identical, reflecting a high level of consistency in the way in which they view Ryan. Both parents expressed concerns regarding Ryan's level of inattention, organizational problems, and difficulty completing tasks. They also reported a significant level of hyperactivity, restlessness, and impulsiveness, and they identified Ryan as meeting the diagnostic criteria for ADHD, Combined Type. These concerns were also noted on the CBCL. Ryan's teacher was asked to complete the Conners' Teacher Rating Scale–Revised and the TRF. The profile generated by his teacher on the Conners' scale was indicative of some inattention and a significant level of restlessness and impulsiveness. She identified Ryan as being "at risk" for ADHD, Combined Type. These Conners' profiles were compared to the Conners' profiles generated by Ryan's mother and his third grade teacher from a previous assessment. The profiles were extremely consistent, although it appears that Ms. P. is currently noting more significant problems with hyperactivity than she did a year ago.

Overall, Ryan's attention span on structured neuropsychological tests is extremely variable. Although his behaviors were not indicative of a high level of inattention or impulsivity, he clearly demonstrated variable ability to stay on task, due to significant problems remaining alert. It is very likely that his level of alertness impacts his performances and confounds the diagnosis of attention difficulties. It is essential to determine whether any neurological or medical factors are responsible for the level of inattention noted by Ryan's parents, as well as the variability in his test results.

Language

Ryan's language skills have been previously identified as an area of weakness. On the NEPSY he had some significant difficulties in these areas. His comprehension of verbal instructions was significantly impaired on a subtest assessing his ability to process and respond quickly to verbal instructions of increasing complexity (2nd percentile). Ryan was only able to complete some very basic items on this subtest. On multistep instructions, Ryan was able to follow the first part of the instruction, but he was unable to complete the entire sequence of instructions. As the instructions became more complex, Ryan failed to make any response at all. He had somewhat less difficulty, performing in the Low Average range, on a subtest of phonological processing (25th percentile), as well as on a subtest assessing his ability to access and produce familiar words in alternative patterns rapidly (16th percentile). Although he was able to name the words accurately with little difficulty, his performance was fairly slow, which is indicative of his slow processing speed.

Sensorimotor

Ryan's performances were Low Average to Average on most subtests of sensorimotor functioning. He demonstrated some problems on measures of finger dexterity and on measures requiring him to imitate hand and finger positions (25th percentile on both). He had even greater difficulty on a subtest assessing his ability to imitate a series of rhythmic movement sequences using one or both hands (3–10th percentile). In contrast, his performance was Average on a task requiring him to remain inside a curved track while drawing a line between these tracks (50th percentile). His speed was surprisingly fast on this subtest, although he had some difficulty remaining inside the lines as the track became more narrow. Overall, these results are consistent with Ryan's Low Average to Average cognitive abilities, and do not appear to reflect significant problems with fine-motor coordination or difficulty monitoring motor output.

In order to further examine Ryan's sensory processing abilities, his mother was asked to complete the Short Sensory Profile. Results indicated that Ryan demonstrates a high number of sensation-seeking behaviors. He frequently seeks to add sensory input in his daily experiences, which may reflect an overreactive neural system that may make Ryan aware of every stimulus that is available, along with an inability to habituate to these stimuli. Results further indicated some inconsistencies in Ryan's ability to screen out sounds in daily life. While his mother indicated a high sensitivity to sounds, she also noted some hyporesponsiveness to sounds, reflecting a difficulty in paying attention to relevant auditory input.

Visuospatial

Ryan consistently demonstrated relative difficulties on measures of his visuospatial functions. He scored at the 9th percentile on a task requiring him to copy two-dimensional geometric figures of increasing complexity, and at the 25th percentile on a task assessing his ability to judge line orientation. His difficulties in these areas were further noted previously on the KABC-II, on which he had great difficulty mentally organizing visual information presented spatially. It should be noted that the KABC-II subtests were presented on the first testing session, during which Ryan had great difficulty remaining alert. However, even during the second day of testing, Ryan consistently struggled on tests of visuospatial skills, reflecting some relative difficulties in these areas.

Memory

Ryan demonstrated impaired memory functions in all areas with the exception of recognition memory. While he excelled on a task assessing his memory for faces (75th percentile), he had significant difficulties on subtests measuring his memory for names (16th percentile), narrative memory (5th percentile), and verbal memory span (16th and 5th percentiles). His performances indicate a poor recall of verbal labels, difficulties in his ability to organize and retrieve details from prose, impaired auditory short-term memory for language, and an impaired ability to learn over a series of trials. However, Ryan consistently demonstrated a significantly stronger performance on delayed memory than initial memory. This was noted on tasks of recognition memory as well as verbal recall, and is a very unusual memory pattern. This appears to indicate that Ryan has some significant difficulties encoding new information.

Assessment of Academic Abilities

Ryan was administered the Kaufman Test of Academic Achievement–Second Edition (KTEA-II) in order to assess his academic skills. He demonstrated a significant discrepancy between his performance on KTEA-II tests of Oral Expression and his cognitive ability, as measured by his KABC-II MPI of 89. This is indicative of an Expressive Language Disorder. He also demonstrated significant difficulties on tasks of Listening Comprehension, reflecting signs of a Mixed Receptive-Expressive Language Disorder. Although Ryan's performances on other subtests of academic achievement did not differ significantly from his ability, Ryan's performances were frequently below grade expectancy.

Reading

Ryan's performances on all subtests of reading were consistent with his cognitive ability. He performed comparably on tasks that required him to correctly read a series of printed words (47th percentile), read sentences and paragraphs and answer questions about what was read (39th percentile), and correctly apply phonetic decoding rules when reading a series of nonsense words (47th percentile). However, he demonstrated a need for frequent repetition of questions on the reading comprehension task, and he had great difficulty remaining alert during this subtest. His passage reading speed was significantly below expected levels.

Mathematics

Ryan's skills in mathematics are diverse and may not be adequately summarized by a single number. He performed much better on tasks that evaluated his ability to add and subtract one- to three-digit numbers and multiply and divide two-digit numbers (86th percentile) than on tasks that required him to understand number, consumer math concepts, geometric measurement, basic graphs, or solve one-step word problems (34th percentile). His skills in the area of mathematical calculations are a personal strength for him, and a normative strength compared to other children his age. However, it is clear that Ryan resists performing calculations with a paper and pencil; he prefers to do mental math. As a result, he is not always accurate and he makes careless errors. Ryan's lower score on the Math Concepts and Applications subtest resulted from his difficulty comprehending auditorally presented word problems, and he requested frequent repetition of these items. This is consistent with his problems with receptive language processing.

Oral Language

Ryan performed in the Below Average to Lower Extreme range in overall language skills, and his skills in this area exceed those of only 2 percent of students his age. He struggled on tasks assessing his expressive and receptive vocabulary, and he had great difficulty on a subtest of sentence comprehension requiring him to identify the picture that best represents an orally presented descriptor. His overall performance on these tests of Listening Comprehension was in the Low Average range (10th percentile). In addition, his performance was significantly impaired on expressive language tasks requiring him to generate words within a category, describe scenes, and give directions, and he was unable to complete several of these tasks (1st percentile). In addition, Ryan was observed to display problems remaining alert on these tasks, and his behavior was extremely concerning. As indicated earlier, Ryan's performance on the Oral Expression subtest differed significantly from his cognitive ability; this was a normative weakness, a personal weakness, and was indicative of a learning disability in this area.

Written Language

Ryan's performances on tasks of Written Expression that required him to generate sentences to describe visual cues, combine sentences, and compose an organized paragraph were in the Low Average range (12th percentile). His sentences and paragraph were not well written, several punctuation errors were noted, he omitted some essential information in his writing, and he frequently changed the meaning of the sentences when combining them to create a new sentence. His writing was poorly organized, and his use of vocabulary words was extremely elementary. Ryan was noted as having difficulty remaining alert on this subtest, particularly on a test of written word fluency. In comparison, he was alert and attentive on the Spelling subtest, and scored within the Average range (34th percentile).

Emotional Functioning

Ryan completed the Rorschach, the Piers-Harris Children's Self-concept Scale 2, the Revised Children's Manifest Anxiety Scale, and the Children's Depression Inventory. His parents each completed the Conners' and the Achenbach Child

Behavior Checklist. His teacher completed the Conners' and the Achenbach Teacher Report Form.

As noted previously, on the CBCL and the Conners' Ryan was rated by his parents as displaying a significant level of inattention and hyperactivity, and as meeting the diagnostic criteria for ADHD, Combined Type. His parents also reported some significant concerns about Ryan's high level of rule-breaking behaviors and aggression at home. They further noted that Ryan displays a high level of anxiety, frequent somatic complaints, and some social problems. In contrast, his teacher did not report noting significant oppositional behaviors, and she also did not report social concerns or anxiety to be relevant issues on the TRF. However, on the Conners' she did rate Ryan as displaying a moderate level of anxiety, characterized by a sensitivity to criticism and a high level of emotionality.

On measures of emotional functioning, Ryan demonstrated a moderate level of situational guardedness and a reluctance to be forthcoming. He appears to be purposefully avoiding self-focusing, and he is fairly unwilling to process emotional stimulation or to become engaged in affectively charged situations. He also displays some evidence of oppositional tendencies, which are likely to be associated with transient irritation and situational reactions to his responsibilities and obligations.

Although Ryan certainly does not avoid interpersonal relationships, his relationships with others tend to be distant and detached rather than close and intimate. He may avoid more involved relationships out of concern that they will make more demands on him than he can handle. Testing was also indicative of some impairment in his reality testing capacity, whereby Ryan tends to misperceive events and to form mistaken impressions of people and the significance of their actions. This adaptive liability may result in poor judgment, in which Ryan fails to anticipate the consequences of his actions and misconstrues what constitutes appropriate behavior. He demonstrates some confusion in separating reality from fantasy. This results in some inappropriate behaviors, which may lead to chronic and pervasive adjustment difficulties in life. In addition, it is evident that many of his breakdowns in reality testing are prompted by feelings of anger or resentment. Therefore, it is likely that when anger clouds his judgment, Ryan may demonstrate some confusion in separating reality from fantasy. On personality testing, Ryan tended to respond in a socially desirable direction. His responses are indicative of a lack of realistic self-appraisal and of a strong need to be viewed by others in a positive manner. He denied any problematic behaviors, he expressed confidence in his intellectual and academic abilities, he expressed a high level of satisfaction with his physical appearance, and he indicated a high level of perceived popularity. He also denied experiencing any anxiety or depression. However, as indicated earlier, his self-reports reflected a defensive denial of behavior problems, in order to mask real difficulties and a high need for social acceptance.

Summary and Recommendations

Ryan is a 12-year-old boy who was referred for an evaluation of his neuropsychological and emotional status. A primary aim of this evaluation was to determine if his Low Average intellectual ability, as determined by a previous assessment, is an accurate assessment of his cognitive functioning, or if receptive and expressive language difficulties impacted his performance on earlier testing. Ryan is being treated by a pediatric psychiatrist for a Mood Disorder. He is currently on Seroquel and Trileptal. During the first day of the evaluation Ryan demonstrated significant difficulty remaining alert and oriented to the testing. On numerous occasions he sat blinking, staring straight ahead blankly, and was unresponsive to questions. After a few seconds, he was able to resume testing. On one occasion Ryan appeared to fall asleep right after this episode. However, these behaviors were not noticeable during the second testing session, during which Ryan was attentive and alert. There had been a change to his medication regime before this second testing session, and Ryan also indicated that he had had more sleep the night before. He also chewed gum during this session, which he indicated increased his alertness.

The results of this assessment indicate that Ryan's intellectual ability is consistently in the Low Average to Average range, even when tested with instruments designed to minimize the impact of language abilities. His KABC-II MPI of 89 does not differ significantly from his previously measured WISC-III FSIQ of 83, indicating other factors, aside from language, impact his performance on cognitive testing. Ryan demonstrated significant difficulty organizing visual information presented spatially. He also had struggled on measures of learning ability and memory. In fact, Ryan's short-term memory in the visual-motor and verbal channels was consistently impaired. However, his recognition memory was intact, and his delayed memory was an area of relative strength. Ryan displayed intact planning ability, although some deficits were noted in his cognitive flexibility. He demonstrated variability on measures of attention that appeared to be highly dependent on his level of alertness at the time of testing, rather than on an inconsistent attention span. Further difficulties were noted on measures of receptive and expressive language ability. Ryan meets the criteria for an Expressive Language Disorder and displays numerous indications of a Mixed Receptive-Expressive Language Disorder. No other learning disabilities were noted in any academic area; his written expression ability was in the Below Average range.

On personality testing, Ryan tended to display a high level of situational guardedness and to deny any problematic behaviors. He demonstrated a reluctance to process emotional content, and he also displayed evidence of some situational-based oppositional tendencies. Testing also indicated some reality testing difficulties, whereby Ryan forms mistaken impressions of others. This is more apparent in situations that trigger Ryan's anger or oppositionality, and appears to significantly impact his coping skills.

Recommendations

On the basis of these findings, the following recommendations are made.

Neurological and Medical Evaluation

It is imperative that Ryan's neurological status be thoroughly evaluated to determine whether his current functioning is being impacted by any undetected neurological factors. His difficulties remaining alert are extremely unusual and are of concern to his parents, his teacher, and to the examiner. It is recommended that Mr. and Ms. P. contact a neurologist who would be able to rule out any contributing neurological condition. In addition, it is essential that his parents ensure that the vision and hearing assessments conducted by his school adequately assess any difficulties in this regard. A thorough medical evaluation is strongly recommended to rule out any possibility of sleep apnea.

Ongoing Psychotherapy

Ongoing psychotherapy sessions are strongly recommended. Intervention focused on anger resolution may play an important role in improving Ryan's reality testing. In addition, the development of coping skills and stress management may be extremely beneficial.

Ongoing Pharmacological Intervention

Ryan appears to be benefiting from his current medication regime. However, it is essential to determine whether these medications could be impacting his level of alertness, creating further difficulties for him in the classroom. It is strongly recommended that his psychiatrist be informed about the results of any neurological evaluation and that she continue to modify and monitor Ryan's medications as needed.

Biofeedback

Biofeedback training may be useful for Ryan in teaching him effective ways to control his difficulties remaining alert and attentive. EEG biofeedback is a way to train those areas of the brain involved in arousal and focus. In EEG biofeedback training, Ryan will develop an understanding about the connection between what is happening in his cortex and what is recorded on the EEG. He will then learn how to gain control over his brain waves and therefore to regulate his behavior. A psychologist specializing in biofeedback will be able to further assist Ryan in this regard should it be determined that this intervention is appropriate after assessing his neurological status.

Educational Therapy

Ryan would benefit from ongoing assistance with his organizational and study skills. He needs help to meaningfully organize his study time, study materials, and the information that is to be learned. An educational therapist would be useful in helping Ryan learn to maintain his planner to keep track of his assignments and to schedule daily study periods. Assistance with memory strategies would also be extremely beneficial. His teacher has indicated that there is an educational therapist at Ryan's school whose services are available for an additional charge. Alternatively, there are a number of educational therapists who would be appropriate to work with Ryan in this regard, several of whom can meet with Ryan at his home or school. I would be happy to make this referral at the request of Mr. and Ms. P.

Speech Pathology Services

It is recommended that Mr. and Ms. P. consult with Ryan's speech pathologist, to determine recommendations on oral language development and effective teaching approaches for Ryan. Based on his test results, it appears that he would benefit from ongoing language therapy, and the speech pathologist may be able to offer further advice to his teacher regarding classroom modifications for language disabled students.

Classroom Recommendations

Ryan's Expressive Language Disability qualifies him for special educational services. In addition, his significant difficulties remaining alert, his inconsistent attentional abilities, his impaired short-term memory, and his extremely slow processing speed will make it particularly difficult for him to keep up with the pace of information being presented in a normal classroom setting. Children with Ryan's learning difficulties usually benefit from a learning environment that is carefully planned and consistently implemented in terms of the physical arrangement, schedule of activities, and expected behaviors. Consequently, it is recommended that Ryan receive classroom accommodations that include the following.

- Placement in a small classroom setting where he can receive more immediate and individual attention and consistent monitoring of his behavior is strongly recommended.

- He will learn much more effectively in a slower-paced classroom, which will allow him to acquire knowledge in a much more repetitive and less pressured environment.
- Ryan will benefit from preferential seating in the front of the classroom where his teacher can monitor him.
- Whenever possible, minimize distractions in Ryan's study area. For example, place Ryan's desk near the teacher, facing a wall, or in an area with minimal classroom traffic.
- His teacher should be informed about the nature of Ryan's language difficulties and how it affects his academic functioning. She should be encouraged to provide Ryan with both written and oral instruction whenever possible. He may often need to have instructions repeated. Thus, encourage Ryan to ask for such repetition if he initially has difficulty understanding. In instances of more elaborate instruction, allow Ryan to record the information to permit relistening at a later stage. Nonverbal input and visual reinforcement such as gestures, drawings, and modeling is essential. When giving directions, make frequent eye contact and stop at various points to ensure that Ryan understands. It would be useful to discuss task requirements with Ryan to ensure that he has an accurate interpretation of what is expected of him. Make sure that Ryan feels comfortable to ask for clarification and repetition of instructions. Provide him with visual guidelines such as checklists to help him understand the specific steps he must take to complete assignments and other classroom tasks. Ryan will benefit from having most books on tape as well as recordings from more lecture-oriented courses. Ryan could also be provided with a copy of the notes of a student who is a good note taker to supplement his own notes.
- Due to Ryan's slow processing speed, he certainly would benefit from untimed or extended time on tests. He would also benefit from having his assignments reduced in length so that he can complete his work in class rather than taking assignments home.
- Ryan would benefit from being taught strategies to improve his memory functioning. Discuss with him what strategies he uses to recall information and help him identify and learn other strategies to enhance recall. Teach him a strategy for active listening by having him learn to attend to keywords that signal that important information is about to be given, such as "first," "most important," or "in summary." When Ryan is required to learn information for a test, direct his attention to the information to be remembered, and indicate the importance of this

information. Discuss with him ways in which he would be most likely to learn and remember this information. Do not require a rapid recall of facts until Ryan understands and is able to demonstrate the underlying concepts. Before teaching new information, review previous information from the last lesson and check for mastery. When teaching Ryan factual information, provide as much review and repetition as possible, and provide frequent opportunities for practice.

- Continue consistent contact between teachers and parents via a homebook. Encourage Ryan to highlight important material (e.g., key words, instructions, main ideas) in texts or handouts. Help him establish a regular time for him to do homework. During this time family members should be available to provide assistance while limiting distracting behaviors.

- Ryan's impaired visuospatial abilities will interfere with his ability to learn more complex, nonverbal ideas, such as geometry. Also, he may have difficulty reading nonverbal communication cues, such as body language and vocal intonation, resulting in his failing to respond to salient social cues in his environment. He may therefore require additional assistance in this regard.

Michelle Lurie, PsyD
Clinical Psychologist

Psychometric Summary for Ryan P.

Kaufman Assessment Battery for Children–Second Edition (KABC-II)

Scale/Subtest	Standard Score	90% Confidence Interval	Percentile Rank	Descriptive Category
Sequential/*Gsm*	**100**	**92–108**	**50**	**Average**
Number Recall	11		63	
Word Order	9		37	
Hand Movements	5		5	
Simultaneous/*Gv*	**85**	**78–94**	**16**	**Average**
Rover	10		50	
Triangles	5		5	
Block Counting	5		5	
Learning/*Glr*	**84**	**78–92**	**14**	**Below Average**
* Atlantis	7		16	
Rebus	7		16	
Atlantis Delayed	7		16	
Rebus Delayed	5		5	
Planning/*Gf*	**99**	**90–108**	**47**	**Average**
Story Completion	9		37	
Pattern Reasoning	11		63	
Mental Processing Index	**89**	**84–94**	**23**	**Average**

Psychometric Summary for Ryan P. (Continued)

Kaufman Test of Educational Achievement–Second Edition (KTEA-II), Comprehensive Form (Form A)

Composite/Subtest	Standard Score (Age-Based)	90% Confidence Interval	Percentile Rank
Reading	**96**	**91–101**	**39**
Letter and Word Recognition	99	93–105	47
Reading Comprehension	96	89–103	39
Decoding[a]	**99**	**95–103**	**47**
Nonsense Word Decoding	99	94–104	47
Math	**104**	**99–109**	**61**
Math Computation	116	110–122	86
Math Concepts and Applications	94	87–101	34
Written Language	**87**	**81–93**	**19**
Spelling	94	87–101	34
Written Expression	82	74–90	12
Oral Language	**70**	**60–80**	**2**
Listening Comprehension	81	70–92	10
Oral Expression	67	55–79	1
Comprehensive Achievement Composite	**92**	**88–96**	**30**

[a]The Decoding composite includes Nonsense Word Decoding and Letter and Word Recognition.

Psychometric Summary for Ryan P. (Continued)

A Developmental Neuropsychological Assessment (NEPSY)

Subtest	Standard Score	Percentile Rank
Attention/Executive		
Tower	10	50
Auditory Attention and Response Set	11	63
Visual Attention	6	9
Statue		11–25
Knock and Tap		26–75
Language		
Phonological Processing	8	25
Speeded Naming	7	16
Comprehension of Instructions	4	2
Sensorimotor		
Fingertip Tapping	8	25
Imitating Hand Positions	8	25
Visuomotor Precision	10	50
Manual Motor Sequences		3–10
Visuospatial		
Design Copying	6	9
Arrows	8	25
Memory		
Memory for Faces	12	75
Memory for Names	7	16
Narrative Memory	5	5
Sentence Repetition	7	16
List Learning	5	5

Psychometric Summary for Ryan P. (Continued)

Delis-Kaplan Executive Function System (D-KEFS)

Trail Making Test: Primary Measure	Scaled Score
Condition 1: Visual Scanning	10
Condition 2: Number Sequencing	11
Condition 3: Letter Sequencing	8
Condition 4: Number-Letter Switching	1
Condition 5: Motor Speed	6

Color-Word Interference Test: Primary Measures	Scaled Score
Condition 1: Color Naming	7
Condition 2: Word Reading	8
Condition 3: Inhibition	6
Condition 4: Inhibition/Switching	7

CASE REPORT 3

Name: Eduardo R.
Age: 8:6
Grade: 2nd

Reason For Evaluation

Eduardo R. is an 8-year-old boy who lives with his mother, stepfather, and 12-year-old sister. His parents are divorced and his mother is the primary custodial parent. His mother recently remarried and is pregnant. Eduardo's father also recently remarried and Eduardo, together with his sister, visits his father and stepmother every alternate weekend and every alternate Thursday night. Eduardo's mother is a homemaker and his father is a chemist.

Eduardo attends the Georgetown Elementary School. This evaluation was initiated at his parents' request due to their concerns regarding Eduardo's difficulties at school. Specifically, Eduardo has great difficulty focusing in class, he struggles to remain seated, and he appears unable to follow rules. He is reported by his father to be extremely fidgety, and he does not participate appropriately in the classroom. His mother indicated that Eduardo is disruptive in class and that he is somewhat immature. However, both parents noted that Eduardo is a very creative and talented child who has some real strengths. Dr. R. and Ms. R. therefore requested this evaluation in order to determine if Eduardo has some underlying cognitive or emotional difficulty that may be contributing to these problems, in order to ensure that Eduardo has the opportunity to reach his potential in all areas.

Background Information

Developmental History and Health

According to Dr. and Ms. R., Eduardo is the product of a normal pregnancy and an uncomplicated vaginal delivery. He weighed 7 lbs. 10 oz. at birth. No health problems or behavior difficulties were noted as an infant. According to Eduardo's parents, he was somewhat delayed in reaching his developmental milestones. He walked slightly late, and his speech was extremely delayed. His parents reported that only by age 3 was Eduardo able to put words together to make a brief sentence. Eduardo also had some difficulty with toilet training; he was fully toilet trained by age 4:6. However, his parents indicate that he demonstrates some bladder control problems, which his mother reported have exacerbated recently. No significant deficits in self-help skills or adaptive behavior were reported.

Eduardo has always been a healthy child and he has had no surgeries, head injuries, or concussions. However, he is short in stature and his mother reported that "he hasn't grown in years." He does not eat large meals, preferring to "graze" throughout the day. His parents indicated that Eduardo does not need too much sleep and that he has some difficulty falling asleep at night. Eduardo's vision and hearing are intact. His fine-motor coordination is reported to be normal, although he has some difficulty with his gross motor skills, and his father reported that "Eduardo's ability to run, throw, catch are way below average."

There is no family history of any educational problems or learning disabilities. His mother reported that she has suffered from anxiety and panic attacks since age 20. No other psychological difficulties were reported in Eduardo's family history.

Academic History

Eduardo attended a part-time child care program at age 2. According to his mother, Eduardo enjoyed this program, although he did display some separation anxiety. Eduardo was not ready to attend kindergarten at age 5. His parents indicated that he did not know his ABCs and he was unable to correctly recognize colors at this age, and he was therefore enrolled in a pre-K program. Eduardo did extremely well in this environment, and his mother noted that the small class size and the consistency of this five-day program were very beneficial for him. By the end of the school year, Eduardo had developed appropriate skills to begin kindergarten. His parents noted that he started off his kindergarten year with difficulties; however, as the school year progressed he began to do better and was able to remain in his seat and follow instructions.

Eduardo began first grade at Georgetown Elementary School. His parents indicated that his first grade teacher was a very experienced teacher who worked extremely well with him, and he apparently thrived on the one-on-one attention that she lavished on him. In an interview with his first grade teacher, she reported that Eduardo initially had difficulty transitioning to first grade, and that he would need to be close to her or "have a hug." She noted that Eduardo appeared split between his parents' two homes, and that "he wanted to be in two places at the same time. . . . When he was with his mom he missed his dad and when he was with his dad, he missed his mom . . . he always spoke about his baby brother." She indicated that her primary concerns regarding Eduardo were his problems staying seated, his tendency to talk at inappropriate times, his lack of awareness of appropriate physical boundaries and body space, and his difficulty completing his work and handing it in. She noted that she created a behavior plan to work on these issues, and that she would find positive reinforcement, such as stickers or reading aloud to the class, to be very effective in this regard. His teacher indicated that she had some concern about a possibly large split between Eduardo's math skills and his excellent reading skills. She further noted that only when Eduardo had a book was he able to control his tendency to fidget, and that he was totally attentive when reading. She reported that although Eduardo made "funny noises" or sang aloud at inappropriate times, the other children "were surprised by him but never made fun of him," and he made some friends as the year progressed. When questioned about Eduardo's learning style, she indicated that he tended to learn by doing, and that he is "hands on." She noted that Eduardo did have some difficulty understanding directions, and that he often needed instructions to be repeated or rephrased differently. He did better in a small group than a large class, where he tended to tap his pencil, stare off into space, or yell out answers. In this first grade classroom, Eduardo was seated away from other children, but close to his teacher. She indicated that he always needed to be near an adult, and that this seemed to give him comfort and reassurance. She described Eduardo as "emotionally way beyond his years" and indicated that "music and art and theatrical areas seemed to be a way for him to express himself best."

Eduardo is having great difficulties in second grade. In particular, he is reported to be disruptive and talkative in class, and he demonstrates a great deal of fidgetiness and restlessness. He often forgets to bring his homework home and he also does not turn in his homework assignments. His parents noted that they have concerns about the manner in which his current teacher deals with his behaviors. They reported that Eduardo has been seated facing the wall in school, and that he has been "beat down" by his teacher. In an interview with his current teacher, she indicated that she viewed Eduardo as being extremely defiant, and that she believed his behaviors to be intentional. She indicated that he "smirks and is a smart-aleck" and that he does not follow instructions. She gave an example of how he would do three out of six problems correctly, but then do the last three incorrectly, and she indicated that she felt that this was intentional. However, when the examiner shared some of Eduardo's test results with her, she expressed great concern and surprise regarding his difficulties, as well as a willingness to attempt to accommodate his needs in the classroom.

Eduardo has always demonstrated exceptionally strong reading decoding and reading comprehension skills. His teachers have allowed him to read to the class as a reward for good behavior, and he apparently reads with a great deal of dramatization and expression and is sensitive to emotional nuances in the written material. He also demonstrates strong spelling skills; however, his math skills are reported to be weaker than his language skills.

His mother described Eduardo currently as having a good attention span only if he is interested in the subject matter, and she reported that he is not noted to be distractible. However, Dr. R. indicated that Eduardo is extremely distractible and fidgety, not only when working on schoolwork but even when watching a video. He indicated that "he drives everyone crazy" with his excess body movement and that he is unable to remain seated during dinner or during a family game. His information-processing speed is reported to be intact, as is his long-term and short-term memory functioning. His parents reported that Eduardo has difficulty following multiple instructions. His expressive language skills are reported to be excellent. Eduardo apparently has no interest in any activities which rely on his visuospatial abilities, although no problems were reported in this regard.

Emotional and Social Development

Eduardo's parents divorced when Eduardo was 3:6 years old. He has stated to his parents that he feels cheated, since he does not remember his parents together as a family. He is extremely close to his sister and apparently shares a room with her by choice, and frequently sleeps in her bed. According to Eduardo's parents, he has had a great deal of difficulty transitioning to his father's home during designated visiting days, and has demonstrated significant separation anxiety regarding his mother. His parents also indicated that Eduardo used to express intense fear that something would happen to his mother, and he worried about her when he was away from her home. However, these difficulties have apparently declined, and Eduardo is able to better transition between the two homes. In addition, his mother noted that since she remarried and became pregnant, he has demonstrated less need to protect her, and he is at times even slightly distanced from her. He is reported to be very attached to his half-brother and his parents agreed that he "gets along well with everyone" in both families.

From a social point of view, Eduardo has few friends, and he tends to isolate those he has. He tends to be friendly with children much younger or older than himself. His parents describe him as an extremely empathic child, but indicate that he is very immature. At age 5, Eduardo indicated to his parents that "he wished he was born a girl," and up until the age of 6, Eduardo was reported by his parents to demonstrate "effeminate behaviors" which included dressing up in cheerleading clothes and doing cheers, dressing up in female clothes, and playing with "girl toys." He was obsessed with Britney Spears and is now infatuated with Cher. Eduardo reported to the examiner that "I used to like Britney Spears, I like Cher now. . . . I've known Cher since 3 years or so." Ms. R. indicated that she believed Eduardo to be strongly influenced by the females in his life, including herself, her daughter, and a nanny. His parents expressed concern about the social implications of these behaviors, and Dr. R. indicated that he fears that Eduardo will be ridiculed by others due to these nontraditional behaviors. As a result of these concerns regarding Eduardo's atypical behaviors, Eduardo's parents had him assessed by a psychologist. The psychologist did not express concern regarding Eduardo's behaviors, and his parents have continued to address these behaviors by encouraging him to wear boy's clothes and to learn to modify his behaviors in situations that would attract negative attention.

Eduardo was reported by his parents to be an extremely talented actor with a love for singing and drama. He easily memorizes scripts from movies and enjoys acting them out. He does not always know, however, when it is appropriate to display these behaviors, and he can be very disruptive to those around him.

From an emotional point of view, Dr. R. described Eduardo as somewhat anxious and "very cautious" and he expressed concerns about Eduardo's self-esteem. His mother noted that she sees him as being preoccupied in his own world, but did not report noting any anxiety or depression. Both parents agreed that "he is just different."

Behavioral Observations

Eduardo presented himself as a very cute, small-statured 8-year-old boy with dark hair and brown eyes. He reported to the examiner that he was "nervous" at the beginning of the assessment; however, rapport was easily established and Eduardo appeared comfortable in the testing environment, and very eager to return on the second day of testing. He was willing to discuss his academic and social concerns with the examiner honestly and openly. Eduardo became extremely distraught when discussing his relationship with his current 2nd grade teacher. His eyes filled with tears when he described his classroom circumstances, and he sobbed when discussing his sense of failure and isolation in this environment.

Initially, Eduardo appeared to display a good focus of attention—he made excellent eye contact with the examiner and did not display excessive motor activity. However, as the testing progressed, Eduardo demonstrated significant distractibility, fidgetiness, hyperactivity, and inattention. He constantly swung in his chair, he did not always look at the relevant testing materials, he guessed at answers, and he had to be redirected on numerous occasions during both days of testing. He also made some slight complaints about the length of testing, and he clearly had great difficulty maintaining a consistent effort throughout the assessment. At times he acted silly, and his behavior was immature for his age. However, at no time was Eduardo defiant or uncooperative.

Eduardo demonstrated some significant difficulty following instructions. He did not always respond appropriately to task requirements, and only with repetition or demonstration from the examiner was he able to attempt some tasks. At times his difficulty was completely unexpected, given the ease with which he was able to tackle some tasks. However, when faced with even seemingly simple directions, it was evident that Eduardo was frequently unaware of what information was important, and had no idea of how to respond on many occasions. At these times, his responses were alarmingly inappropriate to the context and totally unrelated to the task at hand.

Despite these difficulties, Eduardo appeared to put forward adequate effort, and on the basis of these behavior observations, this assessment appears to be a valid measure of Eduardo's functioning at this time.

Tests Administered and Assessment Procedures

- Clinical interview with Dr. and Ms. R.
- Clinical interview with Eduardo
- Clinical interview with Eduardo's teachers and Assistant Principal
- Wechsler Intelligence Scale for Children–Fourth Edition (WISC-IV)
- A Developmental Neuropsychological Assessment (NEPSY): Selected Subtests
- Woodcock-Johnson Tests of Cognitive Ability–Third Edition (WJ-III COG): Selected Subtests
- Woodcock-Johnson Tests of Achievement–Third Edition (WJ-III ACH): Selected Subtests
- Wechsler Individual Achievement Test–Second Edition (WIAT-II)
- IVA Continuous Performance Test (IVA)
- Children's Apperception Test (CAT)
- Thematic Apperception Test (TAT)
- Child Depression Inventory (CDI)
- Piers-Harris Children's Self-Concept Scale 2 (PHSCS2)
- Revised Children's Manifest Anxiety Scale (RCMAS)
- Achenbach Child Behavior Checklist/6–18 (CBCL)
- Achenbach Teacher's Report Form/6–18 (TRF)
- Conners' Parent Rating Scale–Revised: Long Version
- Conners' Teacher Rating Scale–Revised: Long Version

Test Results:

Intellectual Abilities

In order to assess Eduardo's intellectual ability, he was administered the Wechsler Intelligence Scale for Children–Fourth Edition (WISC-IV) which is an individually administered test of a child's intellectual ability and cognitive strengths and weaknesses. This test has five composite scores: Verbal Comprehension Index, Perceptual Reasoning Index, Working Memory Index, Processing Speed Index, and Full Scale IQ. Although the Full Scale IQ (FSIQ) is generally considered the most representative estimate of global intellectual functioning, Eduardo's unique set of thinking and reasoning abilities make his overall intellectual functioning difficult to summarize by a single score on the WISC-IV. His verbal reasoning abilities are much better developed than his nonverbal reasoning abilities. This means that making sense of complex verbal information and using verbal abilities to solve novel problems are a strength for Eduardo, whereas processing complex visual information by forming spatial images of part-whole relationships and/or by manipulating the parts to solve novel problems without using words is a weakness. Thus, his FSIQ of 84 (14th percentile) does not meaningfully represent his overall level of cognitive ability; rather, it reflects an average of some extremely diverse abilities. Therefore, Eduardo's intelligence is best understood by his performance on the separate WISC-IV indexes, namely, Verbal Comprehension, Perceptual Reasoning, Working Memory, and Processing Speed.

Eduardo's verbal reasoning abilities as measured by the Verbal Comprehension Index are in the Average range (VCI = 102; 55th percentile). The Verbal Comprehension Index is designed to measure verbal reasoning and concept formation. Eduardo's performance on the verbal subtests presents a diverse set of verbal abilities, performing much better on some verbal skills than others. Eduardo demonstrated a strong ability to abstract meaningful concepts and relationships from verbally presented material (63rd percentile), and he also displayed good comprehension of social situations and knowledge of conventional standards of social behavior (84th percentile). Eduardo had more difficulty on a subtest assessing his knowledge of vocabulary words (25th percentile). On this subtest he demonstrated a great deal of variability in his performance. He was able to define some higher-level words, yet struggled on some easier ones. The degree of inter- and intra-subtest variability is unusual for a child his age and may be noticeable to adults who know him well.

In contrast to Eduardo's Average verbal abilities, his nonverbal reasoning abilities as measured by the Perceptual Reasoning Index are in the Borderline range (PRI = 79; 8th percentile). The Perceptual Reasoning Index is designed to measure fluid reasoning in the perceptual domain, with tasks that primarily assess nonverbal fluid reasoning and perceptual organization abilities. Eduardo's performance on the perceptual reasoning subtests contributing to the PRI is somewhat variable. He achieved his best performance among the nonverbal reasoning tasks on a measure of abstract categorical reasoning ability (37th percentile). He demonstrated excellent attention on this task, and no excess motor movement was noted. On this subtest, Eduardo was able to use his strong verbal reasoning skills to solve the problems, and this clearly strengthened his performance. He had significantly more difficulty on a subtest that required him to use two-color cubes to construct replicas of two-dimensional, geometric patterns. Eduardo's performance on this subtest was below that of most children his age (5th percentile). This reflects a weakness in Eduardo's ability to analyze part-whole relationships when information is presented spatially. His responses were very unusual; for example, when asked to copy a design using four blocks to make a square, he made an L-shaped design that had no resemblance to the original design. This indicates significant problems with visual-spatial perception, fine motor coordination, and planning ability.

Eduardo's ability to sustain attention, concentrate, and exert mental control is in the Low Average range (Working Memory Index = 83; 13th percentile). His performances on this index indicate that his attentional functioning is a weakness relative to his verbal reasoning abilities. This may make the processing of complex information more time-consuming for Eduardo, draining his mental energies more quickly as compared to other children his age, and resulting in more frequent errors. He demonstrated Low Average performances on a task requiring him to repeat digits forward and backward, as well as on a task in which he was required to sequence a series of digits and numbers as stated by the examiner (16th percentile on both). This reflects a difficulty in his ability to hold information in immediate awareness while performing a mental operation on the information. Eduardo seemed to be aware of his difficulty in this regard, and covered his eyes with his hand in an attempt to increase his focus of attention. Eduardo's performance on the Letter-Number Sequence Subtest was so impaired and inconsistent that it appeared that he may never really have understood the task requirements.

Eduardo's skill in processing simple or routine visual material without making errors is in the Low Average range when compared to his peers (Processing Speed Index = 80; 9th percentile). His performance on the subtests that comprise the PSI is quite variable; therefore, the PSI score should be interpreted with caution. Eduardo's performance was intact on a visual scanning task which is demanding of attention to detail and mental control (37th percentile). He had more difficulty on a visual-motor task of copying simple symbols and pairing them with numbers (2nd percentile), which is demanding of fine-motor skills, short-term memory, and learning. Therefore, this apparent weakness in processing speed appears to reflect a deficit in Eduardo's visual-motor abilities, rather than the rapidity with which Eduardo can mentally process simple or routine information without making errors.

Attention Testing

In order to assess his attention, Eduardo was administered selected subtests from the NEPSY. Eduardo demonstrated significant variability in his performances on these subtests of attention and executive functioning, with his greatest difficulty noted on tests of self-monitoring and impulse control. On a subtest assessing Eduardo's nonverbal planning and problem-solving abilities, his performance was extremely impaired (2nd percentile). On this task, Eduardo was required to move three colored balls to target positions on three pegs in a prescribed number of moves. He demonstrated significant difficulty remembering the rules of this task, and he displayed ongoing rule violations, despite being constantly reminded of these rules. He was unable to complete some very basic problems, and his performance was indicative of a considerable impairment in his problem-solving abilities. This reflects a significant weakness in Eduardo's capacity to speculate and generate new solutions to problems, and to plan and self-monitor his performance.

Eduardo's performance was Low Average on a subtest of selective auditory attention (25th percentile). This task required Eduardo to maintain selective auditory attention and to regulate his responses to conflicting stimuli. The first phase of this task required him to maintain auditory vigilance to words presented on a tape and then place the target object in a box when its name was called out. Eduardo scored in the Average range on this first phase and he appeared to display intact attention overall. On the next phase, he had to do the same, but with three target objects. In addition, on two of the three objects, Eduardo was required to do the opposite of what he was told (e.g., put the red chip in the box to the command "yellow"). Eduardo had significantly more difficulty on this phase of the task, and he scored in the Borderline range. He made a high number of omission errors (failing to respond to target stimuli) as well as commission errors (responding inappropriately to non-target stimuli), reflecting both inattention and impulsivity. These scores are consistent with those obtained on the WMI of the WISC-IV, and indicate problems in shifting and maintaining a complex set in working memory.

Eduardo demonstrated Average performance on a test of selective visual attention (50th percentile) which assessed his ability to attend to a visual stimulus and locate target pictures quickly in an array. Eduardo's speed on this task was intact; however, he demonstrated a high level of impulsivity, making numerous commission errors.

Eduardo's motor inhibition was Borderline, as evident by his performance on a subtest of the NEPSY (11–25th percentile). He demonstrated an impaired ability to self-regulate and monitor his behaviors and to inhibit his responses on this task. This is consistent with the high level of impulsivity noted earlier.

Eduardo's attention and executive functioning was further assessed with subtests of the WJ-III. He performed in the Average range (43rd percentile) on a WJ-III COG subtest assessing his selective auditory attention, specifically his ability to overcome the effects of auditory distortion in understanding oral language. However, on an executive processing subtest of the WJ-III COG requiring him to trace a pattern without removing his pencil from the paper or retracing any lines, Eduardo demonstrated great difficulty, and his performance was significantly below age expectancy (27th percentile). He was extremely impulsive and he needed frequent redirection and repetition of the rules of this task. His performance reflects impaired ability to determine, select, and apply solutions to problems using forethought.

Eduardo had significant difficulty on the IVA Continuous Performance Test (IVA). On this task Eduardo was required to respond to target stimuli (the number 1 presented either auditorily or visually on the computer) and refrain from responding to nontarget stimuli (the number 2 presented in the same formats). Eduardo had extreme difficulty on the visual component of this test, indicating significant inattention to visual stimuli, and random, impulsive responding. In addition to these difficulties, Eduardo was unable to maintain adequate vigilance for auditory target stimuli, although his response inhibition for auditory target stimuli was intact. He also displayed some difficulty staying on task when responding to auditory targets. In addition, he displayed attention processing problems related to slow discriminatory mental processing for both auditory and visual target stimuli. His performance on the IVA was indicative of Attention-Deficit/Hyperactivity Disorder, Combined Type.

Further measures of Eduardo's attentional functioning were obtained by the Conners' Parent Rating Scale–Revised, and the Conners' Teacher Rating Scale–Revised. On the Conners' Parent Rating Scale–Revised, Eduardo was rated by his father as displaying a moderate level of inattention, organizational problems, and difficulty completing tasks. He further identified Eduardo as displaying restlessness and impulsivity. His rating of Eduardo identified him as a child significantly at risk for ADHD, Combined Type. In comparison to Dr. R., Eduardo's mother's report reflected significantly less severe concerns about Eduardo's attentional functioning, and her descriptions of Eduardo's ability to focus and attend were within normal limits. Two of Eduardo's teachers were asked to complete the Conners' Teacher Rating Scale–Revised. Both teachers indicated moderate problems with inattention, and one teacher also reported some difficulties with hyperactivity. The profiles generated by both teachers identified Eduardo as having ADHD, with one teacher's report indicating Combined Type, and the other teacher expressing more concerns about inattentiveness than impulsivity/hyperactivity.

Overall, Eduardo's scores on tests of attention demonstrate evidence of a high level of inattention along with impulsivity. He clearly meets diagnostic criteria for ADHD, Combined Type.

Language Abilities

As evident on the WISC-IV, Eduardo's language abilities are a relative strength for him. However, results of the NEPSY indicated some variability in these skills. Eduardo demonstrated Average ability, consistent with his VCI on the WISC-IV, on subtests assessing his phonemic awareness (63rd percentile) and his ability to access words rapidly (50th percentile). However, in contrast to these intact performances, Eduardo demonstrated significant impairment in his comprehension of verbal instructions. This was noted on a NEPSY subtest assessing his ability to process and respond quickly to verbal instructions of increasing complexity (9th percentile). Eduardo had difficulty understanding the instructions presented on the items, and he often omitted part of the instructions or confused their order. In order to further assess this difficulty understanding directions, Eduardo was administered a subtest from the WJ-III ACH. His performance on this subtest was also impaired (7th percentile) and is indicative of a significant deficit in his ability to respond appropriately to auditory directions.

Sensorimotor Abilities

Eduardo's sensorimotor deficits were evident on the Coding subtest of the WISC-IV (2nd percentile). In addition, he demonstrated extreme difficulty on measures of sensorimotor abilities on the NEPSY. He was unable to complete a subtest of finger dexterity due to his significant difficulty sequencing, coordinating, and monitoring rapid and accurate fine finger movements, and his performance could not be validly scored. However, Eduardo did not express frustration with this task; rather, he giggled inappropriately, acted silly, and complained of his hand hurting. These behaviors are similar to those noted in his current class environment. Eduardo had further difficulty on a subtest requiring him to imitate hand and finger positions (1st percentile) and on a task requiring him to remain inside a curved track while drawing a line between these tracks (0.5 percentile). Although he completed this task quickly, he made a significant number of errors; far more than would be expected for his age. Similarly, Eduardo displayed impaired performance on a subtest designed to assess the ability to identify fingers using only tactile information (3–10th percentile on each hand). His performance on this task indicate that his sensitivity to tactile information is impaired in both hands. Eduardo also had significant difficulty on a task assessing his ability to imitate a series of rhythmic movement sequences using one or both hands (below 2nd percentile), reflecting a weakness in his ability to regulate his motor movements.

These results are indicative of significant difficulties with fine-motor coordination, inefficiencies processing tactile information, and difficulty planning and monitoring motor output. These difficulties often co-occur with the attentional problems and impulsivity discussed earlier.

Visuospatial Abilities

On neuropsychological testing, Eduardo demonstrated Low Average to Borderline performances on measures of his visuospatial functions. He scored at the 9th percentile on a task requiring him to copy two-dimensional geometric figures of increasing complexity, and at the 16th percentile on a task assessing his ability to judge line orientation. This reflects poor visual-motor integration, along with a difficulty visualizing spatial relationships.

Memory Abilities

Eduardo demonstrated significant inconsistencies in his memory functions on the NEPSY. He excelled on a task assessing his memory for faces (91st percentile), which reflects strong recognition memory. He also demonstrated strong performance on a sentence repetition task of verbal memory span and short-term memory (75th percentile). In contrast, his performance was Low Average on a subtest measuring his memory for names (25th percentile). This subtest is strongly impacted by attentional difficulties. On a subtest of narrative memory, a significant deficit was evident in Eduardo's ability to listen attentively to a story, to encode and comprehend the details, and to retrieve this information from memory (0.5 percentile). His performance is indicative of poor comprehension, inattention, auditory-verbal processing problems, and information overload when faced with detailed auditory information. When listening to the story, Eduardo appeared distracted and disinterested, and he was unable to recall many details, under both free and cued recall conditions.

These results indicate that Eduardo's recognition memory is reliable, as is his short-term verbal memory span for simple information. However, when information is more detailed and demanding of attention, Eduardo demonstrates erratic memory abilities. This is most likely evident in an academic environment and is almost certainly frustrating to both Eduardo and his teachers.

Academic Abilities

Eduardo was administered the Wechsler Individual Achievement Test–2nd Edition (WIAT-II) in order to assess his academic skills. The WIAT-II assesses academic abilities in four domains: reading, mathematics, written language, and oral language. Eduardo's academic abilities were variable both within academic domains and across different academic domains.

Reading

Eduardo presents a diverse set of skills on different aspects of reading. He demonstrated Superior ability on tasks that assessed his capability to correctly apply phonetic decoding rules when reading a series of nonsense words (97th percentile) and on tasks that required him to identify and generate letter sounds and rhyming words, and match and read a series of printed words (91st percentile). In contrast, Eduardo demonstrated Average ability to read sentences and paragraphs and answer questions about what was read (61st percentile). His performances confirm the reports of his teachers and parents—reading is an area of considerable strength for Eduardo. However, it appears that his relative difficulty understanding written material (compared to his Superior reading decoding skills) has not been fully recognized by those around him. Although Eduardo's reading comprehension skills are above grade level, they are significantly lower than his basic reading skills. Eduardo often did not understand the questions on these tasks and had to have them repeated. He also missed important details from the passages, and at times his responses lacked relevant details.

Mathematics

Eduardo scored much lower on subtests of mathematics than expected for a child with his general cognitive ability. The difference between his actual and predicted scores is significant and highly unusual; his skills in this area exceed that of only approximately 3 percent of students his age. Eduardo's performance on tasks that required him to add and subtract numbers up to three digits (6th percentile) is comparable to his performance on tasks that required him to understand basic number concepts, including unit and geometric measurement, and solve one-step word problems (3rd percentile). Thus, Eduardo may experience great difficulty keeping up with other students when these skills are needed. Eduardo was unable to solve problems involving addition of multiple one-digit numbers, as well as problems involving two-digit addition and subtraction. The significant discrepancies between his cognitive ability and his level of achievement on subtests of mathematics indicates a learning disability in the area of mathematics.

Oral Language

Eduardo performed in the Average range in overall oral language skills. He performed comparably on tasks that required him to identify the picture that best represents an orally presented descriptor or generate a word that matches the picture (50th percentile) and to repeat sentences, generate words within a category, describe scenes, and give directions (81st percentile). Despite Eduardo's strength in this area, he did demonstrate some difficulty understanding task requirements, and additional assistance and redirection was necessary. He also displayed a high level of motor activity on these tasks, such as moving in his chair and fidgeting constantly.

Written Language

Eduardo performed much higher on tasks that evaluated his ability to correctly spell verbally presented words (99th percentile; Superior ability) than on written expression tasks that required him to write the alphabet from memory, generate words within a category, generate sentences to describe visual cues, and combine sentences (32nd percentile; Average ability). Spelling is an area of significant strength for Eduardo, and he was able to spell some higher-level words with little difficulty. In contrast, his written expression skills were impacted by a significant difficulty understanding the task requirements and responding appropriately. For example, when asked to generate a list of "things that are round," Eduardo wrote "pizza, circle, triangle" and despite ongoing encouragement from the examiner, he was unable to complete the task.

Emotional Functioning

Eduardo completed the Piers-Harris Children's Self-Concept Scale 2, the Revised Children's Manifest Anxiety Scale, the Children's Depression Inventory, and the selected cards from the Children's Apperception Test (CAT) and the Thematic Apperception Test (TAT). His parents each completed the Achenbach Child Behavior Checklist and the Conners' Parent Rating Scale–Revised, and his teachers completed the Achenbach Teacher Report Form and the Conners' Teacher Rating Scale–Revised.

Eduardo's test results were not indicative of any current problems with depression, although he did report instances of feeling sad, feeling like crying, and being bothered by his life circumstances. However, his responses on personality testing reflected a child with a great deal of anxiety and emotional oversensitivity to environmental pressures. He expressed feelings of being ineffective and less capable than his peers. He indicated that "others seem to do things easier than I can," "I feel that others do not like the way I do things," "I worry about what other people think about me," "I worry about what is going to happen," and "I feel that someone will tell me I do things the wrong way." When asked about these concerns, he indicated that he is nervous at school and that "when my desk is not clean enough, my teacher will dump the tray with my books and journals and the other kids will watch." He further noted that "I worry what the kids will think when I do wrong on a paper or if my teacher moves my desk. . . . She moves my desk everywhere, I want to sit with friends."

Eduardo expressed some specific fears about his future, indicating that "I often worry about something bad happening to me," "I think bad thoughts," and "nothing will ever work out for me." When asked about this, he reported that "my mom has married and I don't want her to get divorced again. Sometimes I think that she will get divorced again. I want a stepdad at my mom's house and I'd have to find a new stepdad." He also expressed specific fears about being picked on in class by his teacher. He expressed extreme distress regarding his teacher's attitude toward him, reporting fear of her, as well as bewilderment with regards to her apparent dislike of him. Eduardo cried when discussing his current school situation, and indicated that he has to sit alone in class whereas the other children sit with their peers, despite the fact that he views himself as doing his best in class. It is very likely that this anxiety may interfere with Eduardo's ability to concentrate and perform adequately on school-related tasks.

Test results were also indicative of some impairment in Eduardo's self-esteem. He is clearly lacking in confidence in terms of his social functioning. He expressed dissatisfaction about his friendships, along with feelings of being socially isolated and made fun of by his peers. He indicated that he is unpopular with both boys and girls, that people pick on him, and that he is one of the last to be chosen for games and sports. He reported that "I hate school," "I feel left out of things," "my classmates make fun of me," and "it is hard for me to make friends." He elaborated by explaining that he is frequently teased by his classmates: "they say that I am five or six, or even four because I am short. . . . They talk mean to me about stuff. . . . They make fun of me." However, he reported that he does have a best friend who "is funny and tells funny stories and jokes."

When asked his feelings about his family and the divorce, Eduardo indicated that divorce is "kind of sad" because his parents "talk and get into fights" and he indicated that "I miss my mom when I am at my dad's and I kind of miss dad at mom's." He expressed affection for his stepparents, but indicated that he is occasionally "spanked" at his father's home by his father and stepmother for "horsing around the house . . . or even if I am not doing something and they think I did it." He indicated that his stepfather "yells a bit . . . but he is nice, I like Chip." He also expressed love for his half-brother and excitement about his mother's pregnancy.

On the CAT and TAT, Eduardo was asked to generate stories in response to picture stimuli. His stories were reflective of having his needs met by both a paternal and a maternal figure; however, they also were indicative of feelings of instability with regards to uncertainty in his living circumstances. He told a story of a rabbit who "moved and had a hard time, she missed her old bed and her old house, she was sad and finally got over it. Her new room didn't look the same, so she was not that used to it." In particular, he expressed insecurity that "at dad's I keep on getting my room taken away" and he described how he had to relocate rooms on several occasions to make room for his siblings. He made frequent references to feeling as if all the members of his father's household "have more stuff than me," and indicated that "I am the only one who has a little room at dad's," and he expressed both sadness and jealousy in this regard.

It should be noted that Eduardo did not express specific dissatisfaction with his gender, or any ideation of the female gender. He responded "no" to the items on the PHSCS "I wish I were different" and "My looks bother me," although on a later item he also replied "no" to "I like being the way I am." Eduardo did indicate, however, that he preferred "girl toys," although he did express some interest in more traditional "boy toys" such as cars and BB guns.

Dr. and Ms. R.'s responses to both the Achenbach Child Behavior Checklist and the Conners' Parent Rating Scale–Revised differed significantly, and the profiles generated from these responses indicated a great discrepancy in the manner in which Eduardo is perceived by his parents. Whereas Ms. R. indicated that Eduardo does not demonstrate any difficulties with oppositional behavior, inattention, hyperactivity, anxiety, depression, or psychosomatic complaints, Dr. R. noted problems in many of these areas, with particular concern noted regarding Eduardo's difficulties attending and his high anxiety level. However, both parents reported extreme concern regarding Eduardo's social adjustment. They expressed their concern that Eduardo demonstrates an inability to get along with others, that he is not being liked by other children, and that he is teased by his peers. Dr. R. noted that Eduardo has no friends, does not know how to make friends, and is somewhat timid. Ms. R. agreed that Eduardo does not get invited over to friends' homes, is afraid of new situations, and loses friends easily.

On the Teacher's Report Form and the Conners' Rating Scale, his first grade teacher expressed some significant concerns regarding Eduardo's level of anxiety and depression, his emotional lability, his numerous somatic complaints, as well as his attentional functioning. His second grade teacher indicated that she also views Eduardo as having problems with attention; however, in contrast to his first grade teacher and Eduardo's parents, his current teacher described Eduardo as a child with significant behavioral problems. She indicated that she views Eduardo as being uncooperative, argumentative, destructive of property, mean, demanding of attention, disobedient, explosive, stubborn, suspicious, and irresponsible. She further noted that Eduardo tends to lie or cheat, that he is not liked by other students, that he is teased a lot, and that he has strange behavior in that "he acts like a girl" and has "girl ideas." The profile generated by his current teacher differed from that generated by the other adults involved with Eduardo, and painted a picture of a child with numerous defiant and oppositional behaviors.

Summary and Diagnostic Impressions

Eduardo is an 8-year-old boy who was referred for an evaluation of his neuro-psychological and emotional status due to his parents' concerns regarding his academic and behavioral difficulties in class. Eduardo has difficulty following instructions in the classroom, he appears to be distractible, inattentive, and impulsive, and his performance is often immature and inappropriate. These problems have been more evident since Eduardo began second grade.

During his neuropsychological evaluation, Eduardo's attention appeared intact at the beginning of testing, but significant problems with inattention and excess body movement were noted as the testing progressed. Eduardo also displayed tremendous difficulty responding appropriately to instructions, and at times his responses were totally unrelated to the task at hand, reflecting impaired receptive language functions and inattention. These difficulties did not appear to be intentional in any way, and, despite acting silly at times, Eduardo seemed to put forward his best effort throughout the assessment.

The results of this assessment indicate significant unevenness in Eduardo's cognitive ability structure, along with scatter in almost all of Eduardo's neuropsychological functions. His verbal reasoning abilities are a relative strength for him, in the Average range, whereas his nonverbal reasoning and concept formation abilities are well below that of most children his age (Borderline range). This variability makes his FSIQ score of 84 meaningless to interpret; a greater understanding of his skills is gleaned from his individual index scores and supplemental neuropsychological testing. Despite his strong language skills, Eduardo demonstrates significant difficulty understanding and following directions. Neuropsychological testing also reflected impaired executive functions and a high level of inattention. It is clear that Eduardo meets the diagnostic criteria for Attention-Deficit/Hyperactivity Disorder, Combined Type. Eduardo also demonstrated significant impairment on measures of sensorimotor and visuospatial abilities, along with variable memory functions. Whereas Eduardo displays Superior reading decoding skills, his reading comprehension skills are in the Average range and reflect some relative difficulty understanding and recalling written material. In addition, he demonstrated significant problems in all areas of mathematics. Overall, Eduardo's neuropsychological profile is indicative of dyscalculia. He consistently demonstrated impairment in his right cerebral hemisphere functions, as seen by his sensorimotor and visual-spatial deficits. In children with math disorders, right hemisphere functions are often impaired; this is noted in poor spatial abilities, problems in performing quick mental calculations and abstract conceptualization, impaired motoric functions and tactile sensory discriminations, and difficulty with the visual discrimination of written mathematical symbols, which are important in routine calculations and geometry.

In addition to these neuropsychological deficits, results of personality testing indicated moderate problems with anxiety, fears about his future, impaired self-esteem, and a lack of confidence in his social functioning. In particular, Eduardo expressed significant school-related anxiety, fear of his teacher, and apprehension about being picked on in front of his peers or isolated from the rest of his class. He expressed significant doubts about his own self-worth, and expressed a lack of belief in a positive and productive future. However, he did not indicate significant family-related concerns, and he appears to have maintained an intact relationship with both parents and his siblings.

Recommendations

Eduardo's neuropsychological and emotional difficulties have undoubtedly affected his ability to succeed academically and socially. It is most likely that Eduardo's cognitive, social, and emotional functioning will continue to deteriorate if these problems are not adequately and immediately addressed. It is therefore critical that appropriate interventions be made in order to maximize Eduardo's development at this important time of his life.

Classroom Recommendations

Eduardo's ADHD qualifies him for special educational services under the Other Health Impaired classification under state law. In addition, his learning disability in the area of mathematics further qualifies him for eligibility for special educational services under the Learning Disabled classification. Eduardo's attention problems and his difficulty following instruction, along with his poor spatial abilities, will make it particularly difficult for him to keep up with the pace of information being presented in a normal classroom setting. However, Eduardo has some remarkable strengths in the area of language, and these should be drawn on in planning his academic environment. Children with Eduardo's learning difficulties usually benefit from a well-structured learning environment that is carefully planned and consistently implemented in terms of the physical arrangement, schedule of activities, and expected behaviors. It is essential that school professionals recognize Eduardo's academic needs, and do not assume that his cognitive functioning is intact based upon his strong reading decoding skills. Consequently, it is recommended that Eduardo receive classroom accommodations that include the following:

- Placement in a smaller classroom, where he can receive more immediate and individual attention, and consistent monitoring of his behavior is likely to enhance his learning success. He will also learn much more effectively in a slower-paced classroom, which will allow him to acquire knowledge in a much more repetitive and less pressured environment.
- Eduardo will benefit from preferential seating in the front of the classroom, where his teacher can monitor him. Whenever possible, minimize distractions in Eduardo's study area. For example, place Eduardo's desk near the teacher or in an area with minimal classroom traffic.
- Provide Eduardo with both written and oral instruction whenever possible. He may often need to have instructions repeated. Thus, encourage Eduardo to ask for such repetition if he initially has difficulty understanding. In instances of more elaborate instruction, allow Eduardo to tape record the information to permit relistening at a later stage. Provide Eduardo with visual guidelines such as checklists to help him internalize the specific steps he must take to complete assignments and other classroom tasks. Review these guidelines with him to ensure that he has an accurate understanding of them. All new information should be presented in short increments in a multisensory format (charts, graphs, videotapes, etc.). He would also benefit from new information being presented in a meaningful context so that he is able to relate it to his everyday life, and hopefully better retain it.
- Eduardo will benefit from individualized, multisensory instruction in mathematics utilizing base 10 blocks, math tiles, Cuisenaire Rods, and other manipulatives. For specific suggestions for teaching mathematics to children with learning disabilities, the teacher is referred to *Teaching Mathematics to the Learning Disabled* (Bley & Thornton, 1989). Do not require Eduardo to memorize math facts until his understanding of the processes are firmly established. At home, help Eduardo develop an awareness of how math skills are used in everyday life by incorporating counting skills into daily activities. Play games that build on these math skills. These games are available at teacher supply stores. Some examples of useful games include SMath, Count Dinos Number Marathon, and Let's Go Shopping.
- Because of Eduardo's difficulties with visual-motor coordination, encourage teachers not to penalize him for poor handwriting in subjects other than writing. Encourage Eduardo to learn to use a computer to assist with written language assignments. Allow Eduardo to dictate written classroom assignments.

- Eduardo needs to be taught by a professional who has had experience working with children with significant learning disabilities, along with the other difficulties that Eduardo displays. It is strongly recommended that Eduardo receive services from a resource specialist at assigned periods each day. In that way, he would not be pulled out of class when he struggles on assignments, which he may view as punitive and damaging to his self-esteem. Rather, he would be assigned work by his resource teacher, who would provide him with the appropriate modifications from the onset, rather than having him fail in the regular classroom before being sent to the resource room.
- Eduardo's assignments need to be broken down into manageable portions. Since Eduardo may be considerably distracted by other problems on his page, he should be presented with only one item at a time to focus on. For example, if Eduardo is required to write five sentences about a topic, he could be provided with an outline or visual aid to help him write one sentence on a page. Once he manages to complete this task, he could then be provided with a second similar page to write his second sentence, and so on. This would also be useful on math tasks, where Eduardo is most likely overwhelmed by numerous task requirements.
- Model for Eduardo the way in which to respond appropriately to a classroom or homework assignment. Provide him with examples of satisfactory responses along with pictures or keywords that may spark his imagination. Before working on an assignment, brainstorm with Eduardo all the words or phrases that he thinks may be important to the topic. Eduardo should be given a great deal of practice generating ideas and organizing his ideas into a visual outline prior to writing. Graphic organizers and semantic mapping are useful in helping Eduardo organize his ideas and clarify the relationships among ideas prior to working on assignments.
- Eduardo will also benefit from untimed exams or extended time on tests. Consider allowing Eduardo to dictate responses rather than write them during testing. Make sure that this is provided in a way that does not bring negative attention to him. Alternatively, the assignment can be shortened so that Eduardo can accomplish the task within the allotted time period.
- Eduardo may benefit from a buddy system, in which he is seated next to a responsible peer who will review directions with him and answer any questions that he has. He may also benefit from using active listen-

ing strategies. This involves attending to keywords that signal important information is about to be given, such as: "first," "more important," or "in summary."

- Eduardo should be provided with clear expectations and rules for behavior in class. He should be encouraged to self-monitor his responses in the classroom, and, when necessary, Eduardo should be provided with a break from the classroom environment and no penalties should be imposed at those times. Eduardo would benefit from frequent teacher feedback and redirection. Nonverbal cues may be useful to get his attention.

- Eduardo may be provided with a reward for the completion of an agreed upon amount of work. He could be given a token for each assignment appropriately completed, with the agreement that when he has a certain number of tokens, he will obtain his reward. This could be worked out between his parents and teachers, and together they could encourage Eduardo to strive toward reaching this goal on each assignment. It is essential that this not involve losing a privilege (such as TV time, "Fun Friday," or recess), but rather rewarding Eduardo with something that he desires (such as reading aloud to the class).

- Eduardo will benefit from ongoing assistance with his organizational and study skills. He needs help to meaningfully organize his study time, study materials, and the information that is to be learned. As he progresses in school, encourage him to maintain his planner to keep track of his assignments and to schedule daily study periods. Continue consistent contact between teachers and parents via a homebook. Encourage Eduardo to highlight important material (for example, key words, instructions, main ideas) in texts or handouts. It will be essential that his parents maintain clear communication with his teachers so that they are aware of test dates, assignment requirements, and upcoming projects. In higher grades, as Eduardo is required to work more independently, he will most likely require continued monitoring of his study skills and help organizing his materials.

- If these recommendations are not effective, it is strongly suggested that Eduardo's parents consider placing him in a private school, providing individualized, multisensory programs for students with learning differences in a small classroom setting. There are numerous special-needs schools in the area and I would be happy to explore these options with Dr. and Ms. R. and make appropriate recommendations at any point in Eduardo's academic career.

Occupational Therapy

Eduardo's impaired sensorimotor and spatial skills impact his day-to-day functioning and create further challenges for him in the classroom. Occupational therapy services are therefore recommended to help develop Eduardo's motor skills, fine-motor coordination, motor planning (dyspraxia), handwriting, and poor sensory functions. I would be happy to make an appropriate referral in this regard.

Pharmacological Intervention

Eduardo presents with symptoms of ADHD, Combined Type. It is strongly recommended that he be evaluated by a pediatric psychiatrist in order to assess his candidacy for stimulant medication to address these problems. In addition, medication may be effective in treating his moderate level of anxiety. I would be happy to make an appropriate recommendation to a pediatric psychiatrist.

Social Skills Group

Eduardo would benefit from direct instruction in social skills in a group led by trained professionals. These groups provide direct instruction through a variety of teaching techniques that include modeling, role-play activities, videos, coaching, and games. It is recommended that Dr. and Ms. R. contact a professional who would be able to place him in an appropriate group on a weekly basis.

Psychotherapy

Eduardo is clearly experiencing a high level of anxiety, which is impacting his performance academically and socially. It is essential that he be provided with the opportunity to discuss his concerns and to develop compensating techniques in a therapeutic environment on a consistent, weekly basis. In addition, it may be beneficial if family members participate in this therapy as deemed necessary by the therapist. I would be happy to make an appropriate referral in this regard.

Educational Therapy

Eduardo would clearly benefit from intensive, individualized, and multisensory instruction to improve his math skills, to strengthen his organizational skills, and to help him learn to control his anxiety in relation to school. The goal of this educational therapy would be to prevent the gaps in Eduardo's academic skills from widening and to allow for more evenly developed academic functioning. I would be happy to discuss appropriate referrals regarding this recommendation.

Michelle Lurie, PsyD
Clinical Psychologist

Psychometric Summary for Eduardo R.

Wechsler Intelligence Scale for Children–Fourth Edition (WISC-IV)

Scale/Subtest	Standard Score	Percentile Rank	Confidence Interval	Qualitative Description
Verbal Comprehension (VCI)	**102**	**55**	**95–109**	**Average**
Similarities	11	63		
Vocabulary	8	25		
Comprehension	13	84		
Perceptual Reasoning (PRI)	**79**	**8**	**73–88**	**Borderline**
Block Design	5	5		
Picture Concepts	9	37		
Matrix Reasoning	6	9		
Working Memory (WMI)	**83**	**13**	**77–92**	**Low Average**
Digit Span	7	16		
Letter-Number Sequencing	7	16		
Processing Speed (PSI)	**80**	**9**	**73–91**	**Low Average**
Coding	4	2		
Symbol Search	9	37		
Full Scale (FSIQ)	**84**	**14**	**80–89**	**Low Average**

Woodcock Johnson–Third Edition (WJ-III) Tests of Cognitive Abilities

Subtest	Standard Score	Percentile Rank	Age Equivalent	Grade Equivalent
Auditory Attention	97	43	8-0	2.1
Planning	91	27	6-6	1.4

Woodcock Johnson–Third Edition (WJ-III) Tests of Achievement

Subtest	Standard Score	Percentile Rank	Age Equivalent	Grade Equivalent
Understanding Directions	78	7	6-1	K.2

Psychometric Summary for Eduardo R. (Continued)

Wechsler Individual Achievement Test–Second Edition (WIAT-II)
Subtest Scores

Composite/Subtest	Standard Score	95% Confidence Interval	Percentile	Qualitative Description
Reading Composite	**122**	**119–125**	**93**	**Superior**
Word Reading	120	116–124	91	
Reading Comprehension	104	97–111	61	
Pseudoword Decoding	128	124–132	97	
Mathematics Composite	**72**	**65–79**	**3**	**Borderline**
Numerical Operations	77	68–86	6	
Math Reasoning	71	63–79	3	
Written Language Composite	**118**	**111–125**	**88**	**High Average**
Spelling	137	129–145	99	
Written Expression	93	82–104	32	
Oral Language Composite	**107**	**98–116**	**68**	**Average**
Listening Comprehension	100	88–112	50	
Oral Expression	113	103–123	81	
Total Achievement Composite	**104**	**100–108**	**61**	**Average**

Psychometric Summary for Eduardo R. (Continued)

A Developmental Neuropsychological Assessment (NEPSY)

Subtest	Standard Score	Percentile Rank
Attention/Executive		
Tower	4	2
Auditory Attention and Response Set	8	25
Visual Attention	10	50
Knock and Tap		≤ 2
Language		
Phonological Processing	11	63
Speeded Naming	10	50
Comprehension of Instructions	6	9
Sensorimotor		
Fingertip Tapping	Invalid	Invalid
Imitating Hand Positions	3	1
Visuomotor Precision	2	0.5
Manual Motor Sequences		≤ 2
Finger Discrimination (Pref)		3–10
Finger Discrimination (Non-Pref)		3–10
Visuospatial		
Design Copying	6	9
Arrows	7	16
Memory		
Memory for Faces	14	91
Memory for Names	8	25
Narrative Memory	2	0.5
Sentence Repetition	12	75

CASE REPORT 4

Name: Johnny S.
Age: 14:10
Grade: 8th

Reason for Evaluation

Johnny attends Central Middle School. This evaluation was initiated at his parents' request due to their concerns regarding Johnny's learning problems in school. Johnny was diagnosed with Attention-Deficit/Hyperactivity Disorder—Combined Type (ADHD) when in third grade and was prescribed stimulant medication. At Johnny's request, medication was discontinued after seventh grade. Specifically, he has great difficulty participating appropriately in class and in initiating tasks, and is easily bored and distracted. His parents report that Johnny is well-liked by peers and teachers, and puts forth considerable effort to do his schoolwork. Nonetheless, he is at risk for retention. Both parents noted that Johnny enjoys music and playing basketball, but he will not be able to continue on the school basketball team if he fails his courses this term. Even though school has been a struggle for him since the early grades, Johnny has never had a comprehensive psychoeducational evaluation for a possible learning disability. Mr. and Mrs. S. therefore requested this evaluation in order to determine if Johnny has some underlying cognitive or learning difficulty that may be contributing to his academic failure in school.

Background and Educational History

Johnny is a 14-year-old adolescent who lives with both parents. His mother is a fulltime homemaker and his father is an electrician. He has four older siblings, including two brothers who live at home. The family has lived in the same neighborhood for the past 6 years, and Johnny has been educated in the Bigtown School District since second grade. Johnny began kindergarten at age 5. Mrs. S. reported that his early school experience was good and that he enjoyed the half-day kindergarten and first grade program in a small private school. Moving into second grade in public school was more difficult for him, and he began to struggle with reading at that time. He attended summer school between second and third grades, and was promoted to grade 3. Johnny's problems with reading continued, and he began to experience difficulties related to offtask, inattentive, and disruptive behaviors. At his teacher's suggestion his parents had him evaluated by a developmental pediatrician, who diagnosed ADHD and placed him on Ritalin.

In spite of the noticeable benefit of medication, Johnny continued to struggle in the intermediate grades. Mr. and Mrs. S. reported that 2 to 3 hours were spent most nights helping Johnny with his homework. They also hired a private tutor, who worked primarily on reading with him through fifth and sixth grades. Improvement was noted in his ability to recognize words, but his difficulty with oral reading and understanding of what he had read persisted. He also began to have problems with math. His previous grades of Bs in math dropped to Cs and Ds in fifth grade. Johnny attended summer school again between fifth and sixth and between sixth and seventh grades, and was not retained. During the intermediate grades, Johnny's behavior seemed to have improved at school, and there were few disciplinary reports.

Johnny began middle school in seventh grade. During that school year, he had multiple teachers, and each reported some degree of academic difficulty. His greatest challenges occurred in his Language Arts course, where he continued to struggle with reading tasks and demonstrated increasing difficulty with writing. His problems in math class also began to escalate as the reading and reasoning demands of the course increased. Johnny reported that he especially enjoyed his science class because his teacher did many experiments and hands-on activities. His best grades for the year were in physical education and his elective drama course. He also began to play on the school basketball team, where he experienced success. At the end of the school year he passed to eighth grade with As in physical education and drama, a C in science, and Ds in language arts, social studies, and math. He worked with a tutor for 2 hours per week through the summer. Ritalin was discontinued in midsummer.

Eighth grade has been very difficult for Johnny. At the end of the first reporting period, he was barely passing English, math, social studies, and science classes with Ds. During the current reporting period, many of those grades are now failing. Johnny expressed concern that he will not be able to play on the basketball team if he fails a course. His parents also stated that they are concerned that in spite of many efforts to provide him with additional educational support, his school performance has continued to decline over the years, and he is now in danger of academic failure. They are also concerned about his lack of self-esteem and his growing frustration with school. Mr. and Mrs. S. would like to see him back on medication, but Johnny is unwilling to comply with their request. His teachers report concerns about his poor study habits, his difficulty working with groups of students, and what appears to be his lack of motivation to do his best in class.

Observations and Test Behavior

Johnny is a lanky young man who was casually dressed for the evaluation, and readily entered into the testing environment. He was a cooperative and diligent worker who was willing to attempt all tasks. However, his efforts were impacted by his difficulty staying focused on task, dealing with task frustration, and attending to detail. At times, Johnny was highly self critical when working on academic tasks and when describing his academic performance at school. Nonetheless, his attitude and effort were good throughout the assessment. These results are viewed as a valid and reliable measure of his current functioning levels.

Tests Administered

- Clinical interview with Mr. & Mrs. S.
- Clinical interview with Johnny
- Clinical interview with Johnny's teachers
- Wechsler Intelligence Scale for Children–Fourth Edition Integrated (WISC-IV Integrated)
- Wechsler Individual Achievement Test–Second Edition (WIAT-II)
- Academic Competence Evaluation Scales (ACES): Teacher forms from Mrs. Winter (English) and Mr. Mitchell (Math)
- Brown Attention Deficit Disorder Scales (Brown ADD): Self report and Parent reports

Test Results

Cognitive Abilities

As part of a complete psychoeducational assessment, Johnny was administered the core and select supplemental subtests of the Wechsler Intelligence Scale for Children–Fourth Edition Integrated (WISC-IV) which is an individually administered test of a child's intellectual ability and cognitive strengths and weaknesses. The WISC-IV yields five composite scores: Verbal Comprehension Index (VCI), Perceptual Reasoning Index (PRI), Working Memory Index (WMI), Processing Speed Index (PSI), and Full Scale IQ. The Full Scale IQ (FSIQ) is an aggregate score that summarizes Johnny's performance across multiple cognitive abilities in a single number. Johnny's FSIQ of 98 (45th percentile) is within the Average range. However, there are significant discrepancies in how Johnny performs on tasks requiring verbal or perceptual ability and on tasks requiring working memory and speed of processing, which reduces the meaningfulness of the FSIQ as a representation of his overall cognitive ability.

These discrepancies in Johnny's abilities are evident when comparing his per-formances across the four WISC-IV indexes. Both his VCI of 108 and his PRI of 110 are significantly higher than his WMI of 77. In fact, fewer than 2 percent of students his age show such a large difference between verbal and perceptual rea-soning when compared to working memory abilities. Similarly, his PSI of 85 is also significantly lower than his VCI and PRI, such that fewer than 8 percent of his age peers demonstrate that large of a discrepancy between processing speed and ver-bal and perceptual reasoning. Students with attention and/or learning disorders often have lower WMI and PSI scores, which can lead to a lowered FSIQ. How-ever, it is possible to examine Johnny's overall cognitive abilities with another score that removes the influence of working memory and processing speed. Unlike the FSIQ, which is derived from all four WISC-IV indexes, the General Ability Index (GAI) is a composite of only the VCI and PRI scores. Johnny's GAI score is 111 (77th percentile), which falls in the High Average range. There is a 13-point dis-crepancy between his GAI and FSIQ, which occurs in less than 1 percent of chil-dren his age. The use of GAI does not negate the importance of WMI and PSI, but provides an additional perspective on his general abilities, and should be taken into account when comparing his ability to his achievement.

Johnny's verbal reasoning abilities are measured by the Verbal Comprehension Index, and are in the average range (VCI = 108; 70th percentile). His perfor-mance was consistent across tasks that require verbal reasoning and concept for-mation. For example, his verbal reasoning and concept formation abilities allow him to distinguish between nonessential and essential features and use his ex-pressive language skills to explain abstract relationships (75th percentile). He was able to define words, which requires that he call upon his fund of knowledge, learning ability, long-term memory, and language ability, at a high average level (75th percentile). He displayed good understanding of conventional standards of social behavior (63rd percentile), and, overall, demonstrated adequate verbal abilities to support at least average achievement in school.

Johnny's verbal abilities and his perceptual abilities (PRI = 110; 75th per-centile) are equally well-developed. The Perceptual Reasoning Index is a measure of nonverbal concept formation and includes tasks that require him to use visual perception and organization, simultaneous processing, visual-motor coordina-tion, and the ability to separate figure and ground to manipulate blocks to copy a picture of a design (63rd percentile); to look at rows of pictures and choose one picture from each row to form a group with a common feature (63rd percentile); and to use fluid reasoning (the ability to manipulate abstractions, rules, general-izations, and logical relationships) to select from five choices, the missing part of an incomplete matrix (84th percentile). Johnny performed comparably on the perceptual reasoning subtests contributing to the PRI, suggesting that his visual-spatial reasoning and perceptual-organizational skills are similarly developed. Overall, Johnny's perceptual abilities and nonverbal reasoning are considered a significant strength compared to his abilities in other areas. In fact, the difference between his perceptual reasoning abilities and his abilities in other areas is so large that it is not commonly achieved by children his age in the normal population. His Average to High Average abilities in perceptual reasoning may therefore play an essential role in developing educational interventions.

In contrast to his strong perceptual reasoning abilities, Johnny's ability to sustain attention, concentrate, and exert mental control is in the Borderline range (WMI = 77; 6th percentile), and is considered a significant weakness as compared to other individuals his age in the normal population. In addition, his ability in this area is significantly lower than his abilities in other areas. In fact, the difference between his working memory and his abilities in other areas such as nonverbal and verbal reasoning is so large that it is not commonly found in the normal population. His deficits in working memory suggest that he has a disorder in this basic psychological process, a finding that should play an essential role in developing educational interventions. His weakness in working memory and mental control may make the processing of complex information more time-consuming for Johnny, draining his mental energies more quickly as compared to other children his age, and perhaps result in more frequent errors on a variety of learning tasks.

In order to further investigate Johnny's working memory skills, he was administered three process-oriented, working memory subtests. Johnny's ability to recall digits that were presented to him verbally is at the lower limit of the Average range (Digit Span Forward = 25th percentile). This score represents his ability to listen and recall increasingly long strings of numbers and repeat them verbatim. His performance suggests that he has developed an age-appropriate capacity for aural information. Although he performed somewhat better on visually presented digits (Visual Digit Span = 50th percentile) than aural, the difference is not especially uncommon. His performance suggests that he has also developed an age-appropriate capacity for visual information. Johnny's capacity for visual-spatial registration is comparable to his peers (Spatial Span Forward = 63rd percentile). This task required Johnny to track, store, mentally rehearse, and execute a sequence of spatial locations. His performance suggests that he has developed an age-appropriate ability for registration of visual-spatial information, sequencing, attention, visual scanning, and accurate execution of motor responses. Although he performed somewhat better on visual-spatial locations than aurally presented digits (Digit Span), the difference is not especially uncommon.

Johnny's capacity for visual-spatial registration with mental manipulation is comparable to his peers (Spatial Span Backward = 25th percentile). This task required Johnny to track, store, mentally rehearse, and execute in reverse order a sequence of spatial locations. His performance suggests that he has developed an age-appropriate ability for registration with mental manipulation of visual-spatial information, sequencing, attention, visual scanning, and accurate execution of motor responses. Although he performed somewhat better on reversing visual-spatial locations than aurally presented digits (Digit Span Backward = 5th percentile), the difference is not especially uncommon.

Johnny's performance on the Written Arithmetic subtest, designed to assess knowledge of numbers, mathematical symbols, and the proper sequence of performing mathematical operations, is comparable to his peers (Written Arithmetic = 84th percentile). When compared to Arithmetic (Arithmetic = 9th percentile), Johnny performed much better on Written Arithmetic, suggesting that his difficulty on the Arithmetic subtest is more likely due to working memory deficits than underdeveloped math skills.

Johnny's ability in processing simple or routine visual material quickly without making errors is in the Low Average range when compared to his peers. He performed better than approximately 16 percent of his peers on the processing speed tasks (Processing Speed Index = 85), and poorly as compared to his verbal and nonverbal reasoning ability. Processing speed is an indication of the rapidity with which Johnny can mentally process simple or routine information without making errors. His slower performance on the Coding subtest (9th percentile) occurred in part because he did not readily learn the paired association between a number and a symbol. His score on the Symbol Search subtest (37th percentile) reflected several errors. Because learning often involves a combination of routine information processing (such as reading) and complex information processing (such as reasoning), a weakness in the speed of processing routine information may make the task of comprehending novel information more time-consuming and difficult for Johnny. Thus, this weakness in simple visual scanning and tracking may leave him less time and mental energy for the complex task of understanding new material.

Academic Achievement

Johnny was administered the Wechsler Individual Achievement Test–Second Edition (WIAT-II) to assess his academic achievement. The WIAT-II yields both subtest and composite scores in the areas of reading, mathematics, written language, and oral language.

Reading

Johnny presents a diverse set of skills on different aspects of reading; therefore, the Reading composite score from WIAT-II does not meaningfully represent his global reading abilities, and the individual reading subtest scores should be investigated instead. He performed much better on tasks that assessed his capability to correctly apply phonetic decoding rules when reading a series of nonsense words (Pseudoword Decoding; 16th percentile) and correctly reading a series of printed words (Word Reading; 21st percentile) than on tasks that required him to read sentences and paragraphs and answer questions about what was read (Reading Comprehension; 1st percentile). Although decoding is weak in comparison to his peers, he demonstrates stronger performance on reading at the word level than reading text. His relatively stronger word reading is more than likely the result of the code-based instruction he has received in school and through several years of one-to-one tutoring. It can be noted that his ability to encode words (spelling) is commensurate with his ability to decode words. His slow reading rate (1st quartile), his lack of automaticity when reading single words, and his dysfluent oral reading of sentences are indicative of a reading fluency problem. Lack of fluency can impair his ability to understand what has been read and can make reading a tedious, time-consuming activity.

In contrast to Johnny's reading comprehension, his verbal reasoning and verbal comprehension abilities, as measured by the WISC-IV VCI of 108, indicate that he has the language skills to support reading comprehension, but he may lack comprehension strategies to increase understanding. In fact, when a skills analysis was conducted of WIAT-II Reading subtests, he demonstrates several high-order comprehension problems related to recognizing implied detail, predicting events and outcomes, drawing conclusions, and making inferences.

In summary, Reading Comprehension is a significant weakness for Johnny. His score is significantly less than his mean score for all WIAT-II subtests, indicating that this is an area of weakness relative to his skills in other academic areas. He performed better than only approximately 1 percent of his peers on this subtest. Thus, Johnny may experience great difficulty in keeping up with his schoolmates in this skill area. Because reading comprehension is critical to learning new information especially at the secondary school level, this deficit can significantly impact learning in several subject areas (i.e., history, literature, math, and science courses).

Mathematics

Johnny's skills in mathematics are also diverse and may not be adequately summarized by a single composite score. He performed much higher on tasks that evaluated his ability to add, subtract, multiply, and divide one- to three-digit numbers, fractions, and decimals (Numerical Operations; 55th percentile) than on tasks that required him to solve single-step and multistep word problems (Math Reasoning; 19th percentile). Because of this variability in his performance, the Mathematics Composite score (32nd percentile) does not meaningfully summarize his overall skills in mathematics, and individual subtest scores should be considered. Johnny's math calculation skills are in the Average range; a skills analysis of his Mathematics subtests indicated that he has grade-level skills, but was unable to calculate square root or percent, divide simple fractions, or solve simple algebraic equations. His lower score on the Math Reasoning subtest was the result of his inability to use fractions and decimals to solve problems, and his difficulty on multistep problem solutions. Frequently, Johnny would perform the first step on a multistep solution correctly, but would either discontinue solution at that point or would omit a critical step. He did not self-monitor by considering if his answer was logical. He also did not interpret visual information, such as graphs or grids, correctly as an aid to problem solution. The majority of his errors were on problems that required the use of fractions or decimals. He chose to use paper and pencil to solve most problems, but he appeared to lack problem-solving strategies.

Oral Language

Johnny performed in the Average range in overall language skills, as indicated by his Oral Language Composite of 109; his skills in this area exceed those of approximately 73 percent of students his age. Johnny performed comparably on tasks that required him to identify the picture that best represents an oral description or generate a word that matches the picture (Listening Comprehension; 53rd percentile) and generate words within a category, describe scenes, and give directions (Oral Expression; 84th percentile).

Compared to Johnny's mean score for all WIAT-II subtests, his performance is significantly better in Oral Expression, indicating that this is an area of relative strength for him. His skills in this area are also considered strengths in relation to those of other students his age. Johnny performed better than approximately 84 percent of his peers on this task. His oral language performance was consistent with his Verbal Comprehension Index on the WISC-IV (70th percentile), and suggests that he has age-appropriate language abilities and can use language effectively to express himself. This relative strength in oral language can be used to help Johnny verbally mediate problem solving to demonstrate what he has learned in school.

Written Language

In overall written language skills, Johnny performed in the Low Average range, as indicated by his Written Language Composite score of 85 (16th percentile). His performance was fairly consistent across the two written language subtests; therefore, the Written Language Composite is an appropriate estimate of his writing abilities. Johnny's performance on tasks that required him to generate words within a category, generate sentences to describe visual cues, combine sentences, and compose an organized, persuasive essay on a named topic (Written Expression; 13th percentile) is comparable to his performance on tasks that required him to correctly spell verbally presented words in the context of a sentence (Spelling; 23rd percentile). On the Spelling subtest, Johnny made several spelling errors on homonyms, indicating his difficulty associating word meaning to word spelling. He frequently wrote a word two or three times before deciding on a spelling, while commenting, "That doesn't look right." He demonstrated strong word fluency, as he was able to verbally generate words within a category and write words within a category better than most students his age. He was not penalized for spelling on the written fluency task, but numerous spelling errors were noted. He was able to combine sentences demonstrating an ability to revise another's writing. Johnny's greatest difficulty on the writing subtest was in composing a persuasive essay. Most students his age write much longer essays (i.e., Johnny's word count was fewer than 75% of his peers). His essay contained numerous spelling, punctuation, and grammatical errors. His essay lacked organization, and his sentence structure, as well as his use of topic sentences, linking words or phrases, introductory and concluding sentences, and use of organization to persuade were weak or missing. In addition, he was unable to convey and support a position with evidence and counterarguments. His vocabulary lacked originality and was ineffective in communicating his ideas. Just as he demonstrated reading competence at the word level but deficits at the text level, Johnny demonstrated word and sentence level writing ability, but significant problems writing text.

Ability-Achievement Discrepancy Analysis

Johnny's scores on the WIAT-II were compared to the levels of achievement predicted for a student with his general cognitive ability, as indicated by his General Ability Index score of 111 on the WISC-IV. His GAI was used in the ability-achievement discrepancy calculations as the measure of his global cognitive ability rather than his FSIQ because his disorder in the basic psychological processes involved in working memory lessened the meaningfulness of the FSIQ. Significant differences between actual and predicted achievement scores are reported in this section.

Johnny performed particularly well on tasks involving Oral Expression. He achieved a score on this subtest (actual score = 115) that was comparable to what was expected, based on his overall global cognitive ability (GAI predicted score

= 106). This level of performance indicates he is able to use his verbal comprehension and verbal reasoning skills well in tasks that require him to generate words within a category, describe scenes, and give directions.

In contrast, Johnny displays significant difficulty with achievement in reading. He scored much lower on the Reading Composite (actual score = 77) than expected for a teenager with his general cognitive ability (predicted score based on GAI = 108). The difference between his actual and predicted scores is significant and highly unusual. Thus, this is an area in which Johnny may benefit from assistance in helping him further develop his skills. To specifically determine the kind of assistance that might be of benefit, a closer look at the reading subtests is warranted. Reading Comprehension (actual standard score = 65), Pseudoword Decoding (actual standard score = 85) and Word Reading (actual standard score = 88) are all deficit areas for Johnny. The difference between Johnny's actual and predicted scores on the Reading Comprehension subtest (using GAI it is a 43 point discrepancy) is both significant and highly unusual. In fact, a discrepancy of this magnitude occurs in only about 1 percent of students his age. The discrepancy between his actual and predicted scores for Pseudoword Decoding (22 points lower than predicted) and for Word Reading (20 points lower than predicted) is also significant, suggesting a specific weakness in tasks that required Johnny to correctly apply phonetic decoding rules when reading a series of nonsense words, and to correctly read a series of printed words. Johnny needs assistance both in learning to decode words more efficiently (i.e., automatically) and in becoming a more fluent, strategic reader.

Written Expression is another area of difficulty for Johnny. Specifically, there is a noteworthy difference between his Written Expression subtest score (83) and the level of achievement anticipated for a student with his cognitive ability (using GAI predicted score of 107 yields a difference of 24 points). This significant and highly unusual difference indicates a specific weakness on tasks that required him to generate words within a category, generate sentences to describe visual cues, combine sentences, and compose an organized, persuasive essay on a named topic.

There is also a significant and unusual discrepancy between Johnny's math reasoning skills (87) and expected achievement based on his cognitive ability as represented by GAI (a difference of 21 points). Although his ability to complete basic mathematic calculations is at a level that one would expect based on his global cognitive ability, he struggles with applying his basic computational knowledge to reason out the answers to higher-level multi-step problems.

Teacher Ratings of Behavior and Academic Skill
The teacher rating scales for the Academic Competence Evaluation Scales (ACES) were completed by Johnny's math teacher, Mr. Mitchell, and Mrs. Win-

ter, his English teacher. Their responses are generally consistent with Johnny's performance on both cognitive and achievement tests. Mr. Mitchell noted Johnny's below-grade-level achievement in mental math, using numbers to solve daily problems, breaking down complex problems, developing solutions, analyzing errors, and testing hypotheses. He noted that Johnny had strong calculation skills. He also expressed concerns related to Johnny's interpersonal, engagement, motivation, and study skills in class. Specifically, he reported that Johnny had trouble working in large groups, listening to others, asking questions, volunteering answers, producing high-quality work, showing persistence, staying on task, and completing assignments correctly in a timely fashion.

Mrs. Winter described Johnny as having some of the same problems in her class. Namely, she identified his difficulty in working in groups, not being goal oriented, and failing to turn in assignments on time, to ask questions or volunteer answers in class, to prepare for class and tests, and to take notes. She noted however, that Johnny was willing to correct his behavior when asked, and that he did participate in class discussions. Academically she was concerned about his below-grade-level reading comprehension, written communication, and higher-order problem-solving abilities.

Many of the skills noted by Johnny's teachers require executive functions, working memory, and processing speed, which have been identified as problematic on the WISC-IV. His achievement in school parallels his performance on WIAT-II.

Parent and Student Behavior Ratings

Johnny and each of his parents completed the Brown Attention Deficit Disorder Scales. On the student self-report, Johnny identified significant concerns related to organizing, prioritizing, and activating to work (Cluster 1); focusing, sustaining, and shifting attention to tasks (Cluster 2); and utilizing working memory and accessing recall (Cluster 5). Johnny's self-report is very similar to his mother's parent report. She also identified problems in Clusters 1 and 2 as well as concerns with Cluster 4: managing frustration and modulating emotions. Mr. S. identified Cluster 2 as being problematic.

Johnny's scores on the Brown ADD Scales are similar to those obtained by adolescents identified with ADHD.

Summary

Johnny is a 14-year-old who completed a battery of tests that evaluated his cognitive abilities and academic achievement. His parents and teachers, as well as Johnny, completed rating scales related to his school performance and behavior.

Scores are consistent across the assessment, and are considered valid and reliable. His general cognitive ability, as estimated by the WISC-IV GAI (111), is in the Average to High Average range. Johnny's general verbal comprehension and general perceptual reasoning abilities were also in the Average to High Average range (VCI = 108; PRI = 110). However, Johnny's general working memory abilities are in the Borderline range (WMI = 77), and general processing speed abilities are in the Low Average range (PSI = 85). Johnny's abilities to sustain attention, concentrate, and exert mental control are a significant weakness relative to his nonverbal and verbal reasoning abilities, and are indicative of a disorder in this basic psychological process. In contrast, Johnny's perceptual reasoning and perceptual organizational skills are an area of significant strength for him.

Johnny demonstrated academic deficiencies in the areas of reading, math reasoning, and writing. However, his oral language abilities were intact and he showed no evidence of deficit in this area. His math calculation skills are much better developed than his math reasoning skills. In general, he has more difficulty with reading and writing at the text level, although word level skills are somewhat limited as well. There is a significant and unusual discrepancy between his ability and his achievement in reading, math reasoning, and written language.

Further, according to teacher, parent, and self-report, Johnny demonstrates many of the behavioral and academic difficulties found in adolescents with ADHD. Educational need is noted in the areas of activation, attention, emotion, and memory. Teachers are also concerned with classroom performance in the areas of interpersonal skills, engagement, motivation, and study skills.

When Johnny's academic achievement is considered in comparison to what might be expected based on his overall intellectual abilities, there is evidence of a specific learning disability in reading, math reasoning, and writing. At this time, it is difficult to determine the effect that his ADHD has on his achievement, particularly since he is currently unmedicated. It is likely that the working memory and processing speed deficits observed on his WISC-IV reflect both the executive function problems related to ADHD and the underlying processing deficits of a specific learning disability.

Recommendations

Johnny meets the criteria for a specific learning disability in reading, math reasoning, and written language, in that there is a statistically significant and unusual discrepancy between his ability and his achievement. There is evidence of underlying processing deficits, specifically in working memory and processing speed, and there is an educational need for intervention. He also has an established history of ADHD, even though he is no longer taking medication.

It is strongly suggested that Johnny and his parents meet with his physician to discuss whether medication is warranted. There appears to be a significant change in his school behaviors and academic achievement since he discontinued medication. It should be understood however, that both ADHD and a learning disability contribute to his academic and behavior difficulties in school.

Johnny would benefit from classroom accommodations to address behavioral concerns that include

- Preferential seating: He should sit where he can easily access visually-presented instructional information. Further, he should not sit in high-traffic areas of the classroom (including next to the teacher's desk, if students frequently have conferences with the teacher at her or his desk). He should sit close to students who model appropriate classroom behaviors rather than those who are disruptive or frequently off task.
- Structure and predictability: Johnny will be more successful in a consistent, structured, and predictable environment. He may benefit from time limit warnings ("In 5 minutes you will need to turn in your papers"), keeping an assignment sheet that is signed off routinely by both teachers and parents, having notice prior to changes in the daily schedule or routine (e.g., knowing when a substitute teacher will be coming or when there will be an assembly that changes his lunchtime), and written reminders or To Do lists.
- Physical proximity: Adults can use close proximity to help Johnny modify classroom behaviors such as not starting or staying on task. When inappropriate behavior occurs, the teacher can move close to Johnny, establish brief contact (e.g., a touch on the shoulder), and say nothing. If the behavior does not change, establish eye contact, and communicate clearly, in a calm, quiet voice, what he needs to do. Reward appropriate changes in behavior in verbal as well as non-verbal (e.g., a smile, a pat on the back, a thumbs up) ways.
- Response cost: Another effective behavioral strategy is to use response cost, where Johnny is rewarded for positive behavior with a point system but loses points when undesirable behaviors occur. If this is implemented at school, it should be done in such a way as to not draw attention to or embarrass Johnny. Parents may wish to implement a response-cost system at home so that his appropriate behavior at school (e.g., turning in homework on time) can earn him something that he desires.
- Self-management: The ultimate goal is for Johnny to take responsibility for his own learning and behavior. Research has shown that self-

management can increase self-esteem and reduce demands on the teacher's time. Self-management strategies include the use of a cuing system between a teacher and student to indicate that behaviors are being monitored and corrective feedback will be given, and the use of teacher-student contracts. Suggestions with step-by-step directions can be found in *Attention Deficit Disorder: Strategies for School-Age Children* by Clare B. Jones (1994; The Psychological Corporation).

- Computer access: Handwriting is a tedious task for Johnny and it interferes with his ability and willingness to communicate in written form. Although he still needs assistance in improving his composition skills, the use of a word processor for some written assignments might motivate him to participate.

Johnny would benefit from educational interventions to address academic concerns that include

- Remediation: Johnny needs to improve his ability to decode and encode words for purposes of reading and writing. As long as he is focusing on the low-level skill of decoding/encoding, he does not have the mental capacity to focus on comprehension/composing. It is recommended that a survey of his phonological and morphological skills be conducted by the school reading specialist to identify specific skill deficits. Explicit, systematic instruction should be provided to remedy identified deficits. At the same time, remediation should be offered in the context of real reading and writing by giving Johnny the opportunity to apply new skills as they develop.

- Strategy instruction: In the areas of reading comprehension and math problem solving, Johnny would benefit from learning effective strategies. For example, reading with a purpose (what are the questions that will need to be answered at the end of the passage?), learning to read with a pencil (where he underlines important information or takes notes in the margin), making semantic or story maps, or post-reading strategies, where he summarizes and reviews what has been read can help Johnny obtain meaning from reading. Elliott, DiPerna and Shapiro offer many strategies to improve comprehension and problem solving in *Academic Intervention Monitoring System* ([AIMS] 2001; The Psychological Corporation). In math, Johnny might benefit from schema-based learning, where an organizational framework is used for depicting the numerical relationships expressed in a word problem (see *AIMS*, pp. 110–111).

- Building fluency: Improvement in decoding/encoding will help improve fluency, but Johnny may also need additional practice in reading to build fluency. Fluency can be increased by such techniques as "folding-in," where material that must be learned is interspersed with material that is already known, repeated reading of short passages where reading is timed and accuracy is checked after each reading (can be effective in a peer-tutoring arrangement), and previewing, where a student reads material prior to its actually being taught by the teacher.
- Homework plan: Johnny and his parents and teachers need to work together to develop a homework plan. For example, there needs to be a place and time for homework. Materials need to be kept in the study area (which should be out of the traffic flow) so that time is not wasted looking for them. Noise should be kept at a minimum. Homework may need to be broken into manageable chunks of time with short breaks. Assignment sheets between home and school may help Johnny get back and forth with assignments. Using a calendar and a To Do list can be helpful in tracking long-term projects, tests, and assignments. Rewarding behavioral change and achievements can reinforce Johnny's progress.
- Study Skills instruction: Johnny also needs explicit instruction in study skills. Teaching him to use reading comprehension strategies such as SQ3R (Survey, Question, Read, Recite, Review), prior knowledge activation, visual imagery, self-questioning, and mapping or word pictures can help him understand and remember what he has read. He could also benefit from learning mnemonic strategies to improve memory and recall, from metacognition strategies that help him better understand his own learning style, and from test-taking and note-taking strategies.
- Accommodations: Classroom accommodations such as extended time for short reading and writing tasks, assistance in breaking long-term tasks into manageable steps with frequent feedback, occasional oral testing (when knowledge acquisition needs to be assessed), providing more visual cues and hands-on learning opportunities, and finding ways for Johnny to participate appropriately in class can enhance his learning. Preselect his group when assigning him a group project by including students who model on-task, goal-directed behaviors. If appropriate, allow him to work with a supportive study partner on tasks, so that he has cooperative learning experiences that are not compromised by

the size of the group. In this setting he can also think aloud and work through problem solving using his strong oral language abilities.

Johnny and his family might also benefit from short-term counseling to help them implement and evaluate the effectiveness of some of the intervention strategies at home, to help build Johnny's self esteem, and to engage in long-term planning for his future.

John Washington, PhD
School Psychologist

Psychometric Summary for Johnny S.

Wechsler Intelligence Scale for Children–Fourth Edition Integrated (WISC-IV I)

Scale/Subtest	Standard Score	Percentile Rank	Confidence Interval	Qualitative Description
Verbal Comprehension (VCI)	**108**	**70**	**101–114**	**Average**
Similarities	12	75		
Vocabulary	12	75		
Comprehension	11	63		
Perceptual Reasoning (PRI)	**110**	**75**	**102–117**	**High Average**
Block Design	11	63		
Picture Concepts	11	63		
Matrix Reasoning	13	84		
Working Memory (WMI)	**77**	**6**	**71–86**	**Borderline**
Digit Span	6	9		
Letter-Number Sequencing	6	9		
Arithmetic	*6*	*9*		
Processing Speed (PSI)	**85**	**16**	**78–96**	**Low Average**
Coding (CD)	6	9		
Symbol Search (SS)	9	37		
Cancellation (CA)	*8*	*25*		
Full Scale (FSIQ)	**98**	**45**	**93–103**	**Average**
General Ability Index (GAI)	**111**	**77**	**105–116**	**High Average**

Psychometric Summary for Johnny S. (Continued)

Working Memory Domain Process: Registration	Scaled Score	Percentile Rank
Digit Span Forward (DSF)	8	25
Visual Digit Span (VDS)	10	50
Spatial Span Forward (SSpF)	11	63

Working Memory Domain Process: Mental Manipulation	Scaled Score	Percentile Rank
Digit Span Backward (DSB)	5	5
Spatial Span Backward (SSpB)	8	25
Written Arithmetic (WA)	13	84

Working Memory Domain Process: Longest Span	Raw Score	Base Rate
Longest Digit Span Forward	6	73%
Longest Digit Span Backward	3	96.5%
Longest Visual Digit Span	7	61.4%
Longest Spatial Span Forward	6	64.3%
Longest Spatial Span Backward	4	94.3%

Processing Speed Domain Process Score Summary	Scaled Score	Percentile Rank
Cancellation Random (CAR)	7	16
Cancellation Structured (CAS)	8	25

Psychometric Summary for Johnny S. (Continued)

Wechsler Individual Achievement Test–Second Edition (WIAT-II)

Composite/Subtest	Standard Score	95% Confidence Interval	Percentile Rank	Qualitative Description
Reading Composite	**77**	**73–81**	**6**	**Borderline**
Word Reading	88	81–95	21	
Reading Comprehension	65	59–71	1	
Pseudoword Decoding	85	79–91	16	
Mathematics Composite	**93**	**88–98**	**32**	**Average**
Numerical Operations	102	96–108	55	
Math Reasoning	87	79–95	19	
Written Language Composite	**85**	**78–92**	**16**	**Low Average**
Spelling	89	82–96	23	
Written Expression	83	72–94	13	
Oral Language Composite	**109**	**99–119**	**73**	**Average**
Listening Comprehension	101	88–114	53	
Oral Expression	115	104–126	84	
Total Achievement Composite	**86**	**82–90**	**18**	**Low Average**

Note: WIAT-II age-based normative information was used in the calculation of subtest and composite scores.

Psychometric Summary for Johnny S. (Continued)

Ability-Achievement Discrepancy Analysis Based on WISC-IV GAI

WIAT-II Composite/Subtest	Predicted Score Based on GAI	Actual Score	Expected Difference	Critical Value	Sig. Diff. Y/N	Base Rate
Reading Composite	**108**	**77**	**31**	**7**	**Y**	**<1%**
Word Reading	108	88	20	9	Y	2–3%
Reading Comprehension	108	65	43	10	Y	<1%
Pseudoword Decoding	107	85	22	8	Y	4%
Mathematics Composite	**108**	**93**	**15**	**9**	**Y**	**5–10%**
Numerical Operations	107	102	5	11	N	
Math Reasoning	108	87	21	12	Y	2%
Written Language Composite	**108**	**85**	**23**	**14**	**Y**	**1–2%**
Spelling	108	89	19	11	Y	4–5%
Written Expression	107	83	24	15	Y	2%
Oral Language Composite	**108**	**109**	**–1**	**11**	**N**	
Listening Comprehension	109	101	8	18	N	
Oral Expression	106	115	1	15	N	
Total Achievement Composite	**109**	**86**	**23**	**8**	**Y**	**<1%**

Note: Values are calculated via a predicted difference method based upon Johnny's GAI of 111. Statistical Significance (Critical Values) at the .01 level. Base Rates are not reported when the achievement score equals or exceeds the ability score. Data obtained from *WISC-IV Technical Report #4: General Ability Index* (2005; The Psychological Corporation).

WIAT-II Subtest Error Analysis

Subtest Skill Area	% Correct
Word Reading	
Recognizing words	75%
Reading Comprehension	
Recognizing Stated Detail	75%
Recognizing Implied Detail	25%
Predicting Events and Outcomes	0%
Drawing Conclusions	33%
Using Context to Determine Word Meaning	75%
Recognizing Stated Cause and Effect	50%
Recognizing Implied Cause and Effect	50%
Identifying Main Idea	0%
Making Inferences	25%
Math Reasoning	
Identify the results of rotations and reflections	50%
Recall and apply basic addition and subtraction facts and procedures	80%
Recall and apply basic multiplication and division facts and procedures	80%
Use fraction words to name parts of a whole object or set	75%
Compare and order fractions	0%
Relate fractions to decimals	0%
Solve addition and subtraction problems using fractions and decimals	0%
Multistep problems	57%
Use grids and graphs to make comparisons, draw conclusions, or answer questions	88%
Apply calculation skills using decimals to solve problems involving money	50%
Use theoretical and experimental probability to draw conclusions, answer questions, and make predictions	50%
Numerical Operations	
Calculating square root	0%
Calculating percent	0%
Division—using simple fractions	0%
Solving simple algebraic equations	0%
Calculation of pi	0%
Listening Comprehension	
Receptive Vocabulary	75%
Sentence Comprehension	80%
Expressive Vocabulary	80%
Spelling	
Ending blend/digraph	67%
Silent letter in medial position of word	67%
"soft c or g followed by e" spelling rule	33%
Homonyms	57%
"ment" suffix	0%

Note: The Error Analysis summary lists only skill areas for which Johnny obtained less than 100% correct.

Academic Competence Evaluation Scales (ACES)

The Academic Competence Evaluation Scales (ACES) measures a student's skills, attitudes, and behaviors that contribute to academic success in the classroom. The ACES consists of two broad scales: Academic Skills and Academic Enablers. Academic Skills are the basic and complex skills (reading comprehension, computation, etc.) taught within the typical school curriculum. Academic Enablers are the skills and behaviors that allow a student to benefit from classroom instruction (completing homework, getting along with others, etc.). Both the Academic Skills and Academic Enablers scales are composed of multiple subscales. Specifically, the Academic Skills scale consists of three subscales (Reading/Language Arts, Mathematics, and Critical Thinking), and the Academic Enablers scale consists of four subscales (Interpersonal Skills, Engagement, Motivation, and Study Skills).

The first set of scores is based upon a report from Mr. Mitchell and the second is from Mrs. Winter. The following graphs display ACES scores for Johnny S., as well as 90 percent confidence intervals around these scores. These confidence intervals identify a range within which the true score would be expected to fall. Intervals that fall primarily within the Developing range represent skill areas to consider for intervention, whereas intervals that fall primarily within the Competent or Advanced ranges represent areas of strength.

ACES—Teacher Report—Single Administration
Teacher Rating: Mr. Mitchell

	Raw Score	90% CI	KEY — Developing / Competent / Advanced / Scores ±90% CI	Decile
Academic Skills			Far Below / Below / Grade Level / Above / Far Above	
Total Scale	77	±5	33 — 66 — 99 — 132 — 165 (99, 133)	3
Reading/Language Arts	22	±2	11 — 22 — 33 — 44 — 55 (33, 45)	1
Mathematics	19	±2	8 — 16 — 24 — 32 — 40 (24, 33)	3
Critical Thinking	36	±2	14 — 28 — 42 — 56 — 70 (42, 57)	3
Academic Enablers			Never / Seldom / Sometimes / Often / Almost Always	
Total Scale	92	±6	40 — 80 — 120 — 160 — 200 (108, 183)	1
Interpersonal Skills	29	±3	10 — 20 — 30 — 40 — 50 (31, 50)	2
Engagement	22	±3	8 — 16 — 24 — 32 — 40 (30, 37)	3
Motivation	18	±3	11 — 22 — 33 — 44 — 55 (25, 50)	1
Study Skills	23	±3	11 — 22 — 33 — 44 — 55 (29, 54)	1

ACES—Teacher Report—Single Administration
Teacher Rating: Mr. Mitchell

ACES Behavior Classification Scheme

Academic Skills

	Reading/Language Arts	Mathematics	Critical Thinking
Strengths Proficiency Rating = 3, 4, or 5 Importance Rating = 3		12. Computation	
Performance Problems Proficiency Rating = 2 Importance Rating = 2 or 3	1. Reading Comprehension 3. Vocabulary 4. Identify main idea 10. Oral Communication	17. Use numbers—solve daily problems 18. Break down complex problems 19. Problem solving	28. Develop solution 30. Analyze errors 33. Test hypotheses
Acquisition Problems Proficiency Rating = 1 Importance Rating = 2 or 3		16. Mental math	

Academic Enablers

	Interpersonal	Engagement	Motivation	Study Skills
Strengths Frequency Rating = 4 or 5 Importance Rating = 3				
Performance Problems Frequency Rating = 3 Importance Rating = 2 or 3	34. Follow class rules 35. Correct behavior 37. Accept suggestions 42. Work in small group 43. Interact with students	46. Class discussions 48. Assumes leadership in group 51. Asks questions when confused	56. Attempts to improve	69. Care of materials
Acquisition Problems Frequency Rating = 1 or 2 Importance Rating = 2 or 3	36. Express dissatisfaction 38. Work in large group 40. Listen to others	45. Questions tests/projects 47. Volunteers answers	52. Motivated to learn 53. Prefers challenges 54. High quality-work 55. Critical evaluation of own work 57. Makes most of learning experiences 58. Persists with difficult tasks 59. Academically challenges self 60. Responsible for learning 61. Goal oriented 62. Stays on task	63. Completes homework 64. Corrects own work 65. Finishes classwork on time 66. Prepares for tests 67. Prepares for class 68. Timely homework 70. Pays attention 71. Completes assignments 73. Reviews materials

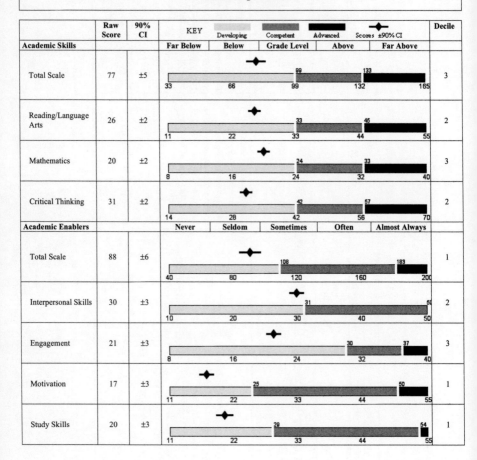

ACES—Teacher Report—Single Administration
Teacher Rating: Mrs. Winter

	Raw Score	90% CI	KEY Developing / Competent / Advanced / Scores ±90% CI	Decile
Academic Skills			Far Below / Below / Grade Level / Above / Far Above	
Total Scale	77	±5	33 — 66 — 99 — 132 — 165 (99, 133)	3
Reading/Language Arts	26	±2	11 — 22 — 33 — 44 — 55 (33, 45)	2
Mathematics	20	±2	8 — 16 — 24 — 32 — 40 (24, 33)	3
Critical Thinking	31	±2	14 — 28 — 42 — 56 — 70 (42, 57)	2
Academic Enablers			Never / Seldom / Sometimes / Often / Almost Always	
Total Scale	88	±6	40 — 80 — 120 — 160 — 200 (108, 183)	1
Interpersonal Skills	30	±3	10 — 20 — 30 — 40 — 50 (31, 50)	2
Engagement	21	±3	8 — 16 — 24 — 32 — 40 (30, 37)	3
Motivation	17	±3	11 — 22 — 33 — 44 — 55 (25, 50)	1
Study Skills	20	±3	11 — 22 — 33 — 44 — 55 (29, 54)	1

ACES—Teacher Report—Single Administration
Teacher Rating: Mrs. Winter

ACES Behavior Classification Scheme

Academic Skills

	Reading/Language Arts	Mathematics	Critical Thinking
Strengths Proficiency Rating = 3, 4, or 5 Importance Rating = 3			
Performance Problems Proficiency Rating = 2 Importance Rating = 2 or 3	1. Reading Comprehension 3. Vocabulary 4. Identify main idea 5. Reading fluency 7. Punctuation 9. Written Communication 11. Conclusions from written material	17. Use numbers—solve daily problems 18. Break down complex problems 19. Problem solving	20. Synthesize related information 22. Compare similar/different among objects/ideas 24. Generalize from info/experience 26. Decide among alternate solutions 27. Investigate problem/issue 28. Develop solution 30. Analyze errors 31. Construct issue support 32. Analyze viewpoints 33. Test hypotheses
Acquisition Problems Proficiency Rating = 1 Importance Rating = 2 or 3			

(continued)

Academic Enablers

	Interpersonal	Engagement	Motivation	Study Skills
Strengths Frequency Rating = 4 or 5 Importance Rating = 3	35. Correct behavior	46. Class discussions		
Performance Problems Frequency Rating = 3 Importance Rating = 2 or 3	34. Follow class rules 37. Accept suggestions 40. Listen to others 41. Get along with people	44. Speaks in class 51. Asks questions when confused	52. Motivated to learn	69. Care of materials
Acquisition Problems Frequency Rating = 1 or 2 Importance Rating = 2 or 3	36. Express dissatisfaction 38. Work in large group 42. Work in small group	45. Questions tests/projects 47. Volunteers answers	53. Prefers challenges 54. High quality-work 55. Critical evaluation of own work 56. Attempts to improve 57. Makes most of learning experience 58. Persists with difficult tasks 60. Responsible for learning 61. Goal oriented 62. Stays on task	63. Completes homework 64. Corrects own work 65. Finishes classwork on time 66. Prepares for tests 67. Prepares for class 68. Timely homework 70. Pays attention 71. Completes assignments 72. Takes notes 73. Reviews materials

References

Adams, M. (1990). *Beginning to read: Thinking and learning about print.* Cambridge: The MIT Press.

Alexander, A., Andersen, H., Heilman, K., Voeller, K., & Torgesen, J. (1991). Phonological awareness training and remediation of analytic decoding deficits in a group of severe dyslexics. *Annals of the Orton Society, 41,* 193–206.

Altemeier, L., Jones, J., Abbot, R., & Berninger, V. (in press). Executive functions in becoming writing-readers and reading-writers: Note-taking and report writing in third and fifth graders. *Special Issue of Developmental Neuropsychology.*

American Psychological Association. *Standards for educational and psychological testing.* (1999). Washington, DC: Author.

Archer, R. P., Maruish, M., Imhof, E. A., & Piotrowski, C. (1991). Psychological test usage with adolescent clients: 1990 findings. *Professional Psychology: Research and Practice, 22,* 247–252.

Barkley, R. A. (1990). *Attention-Deficit Hyperactivity Disorder: A handbook for diagnosis and treatment.* New York: Guilford.

Barkley, R. A. (1998). *Attention-Deficit Hyperactivity Disorder: A handbook for diagnosis and treatment* (2nd ed.). New York: Guilford.

Barkley, R. A. (2003). Attention-Deficit/Hyperactivity Disorder. In E. J. Mash & R. A. Barkley (Eds.), *Child psychopathology* (2nd ed., pp. 75–143). New York: Guilford.

Barkley, R. A., DuPaul, G. J., & McMurray, M. B. (1990). A comprehensive evaluation of attention deficit disorder with and without hyperactivity. *Journal of Consulting and Clinical Psychology, 58,* 775–789.

Berninger, V. (1998). *Process Assessment of the Leaner (PAL): Guides for intervention.* San Antonio, TX: The Psychological Corporation.

Berninger, V. (1999). Coordinating transcriptions and text generation in working memory during composing: Automatized and constructive processes. *Learning Disability Quarterly, 22,* 99–112.

Berninger, V. (2001). *Process Assessment of the Learner: Test for Reading and Writing manual.* San Antonio, TX: The Psychological Corporation.

Berninger, V., & Abbott, S. (2003). *PAL research-based reading and writing lessons.* San Antonio, TX: The Psychological Corporation.

Berninger, V., & Amtmann, D. (2003). Preventing written expression disabilities through early and continuing assessment and intervention for handwriting and/or spelling problems: Research into practice. In H. L. Swanson, K. Harris, & S. Graham (Eds.), *Handbook of research on learning disabilities* (pp. 345–363). New York: Guilford.

Berninger, V., Dunn, A., & Alper, T. (2005). Integrated multilevel model of branching assessment, instructional assessment, and profile assessment. In A. Prifitera, D. Saklofske, & L. Weiss (Eds.), *WISC-IV clinical use and interpretation* (pp. 151–185). San Diego, CA: Elsevier Academic.

Berninger, V., Nagy, W., Carlisle, J., Thomson, J., Hoffer, D., Abbot, S., Abbot, R., Richards, T., & Aylward, E. (2003). Effective treatment for dyslexics in grades 4 to 6. In B. Foorman (Ed.), *Preventing and remediating reading difficulties: Bringing science to scale* (pp. 381–417). Baltimore: York Press.

Berninger, V., & O'Donnell, L. (2005). Research-supported differential diagnosis of specific learning disabilities. In A. Prifitera, D. Saklofske, & L. Weiss (Eds.), *WISC-IV clinical use and interpretation* (pp. 189–233). San Diego, CA: Elsevier Academic.

Berninger, V., Stage, S., Smith, D., & Hildebrand, D. (2001). Assessment for reading and writing intervention: A three-tier model for prevention and remediation. In J. Andrews, D. Saklofske, & H. Janzen (Eds.), *Handbook of psychoeducational assessment. Ability, achievement, and behavior in children* (pp. 195–223). New York: Academic.

Berninger, V., Vaughn, K., Abbott, R., Brooks, A., Abbott, S., Reed, E., Rogan, L., & Graham, S. (1998). Early intervention for spelling problems: Teaching spelling units of varying size within a multiple connections framework. *Journal of Educational Psychology, 90,* 587–605.

Bley, N., & Thornton, C. (1989). *Teaching mathematics to the learned disabled.* Austin, TX: Pro-Ed.

Braden, J. P., & Weiss, L. (1988). Effects of simple difference versus regression discrepancy methods: An empirical study. *Journal of School Psychology, 26,* 133–142.

Brock, S. W., & Knapp, P. K. (1996). Reading comprehension abilities of children with attention-deficit/hyperactivity disorder. *Journal of Attention Disorders, 1,* 173–186.

Bryant, D., Ugel, N., Thompson, S., & Hamff, A. (1999). Instructional strategies for content-area reading instruction. *Intervention in School and Clinic, 34,* 293–302.

Carroll, J. B. (1993). *Human cognitive abilities: A survey of factor-analytic studies.* Cambridge, UK: Cambridge University Press.

Carroll, J. B. (1997). The three-stratum theory of cognitive abilities. In D. P. Flanagan, J. L. Genshaft, & P. L. Harrison (Eds.), *Contemporary intellectual assessment: Theories, tests, and issues* (pp. 122–130). New York: Guilford.

Carrow-Woolfolk, E. (1996). *Oral and Written Language Scales.* Circle Pines, MN: American Guidance Service.

Casey, J. E., Rourke, B. P., & Del Dotto, J. E. (1996). Learning disabilities in children with attention deficit disorder with and without hyperactivity. *Child Neuropsychology, 2,* 83–98.

Cattell, R. (1943). The measurement of adult intelligence. *Psychological Bulletin, 40,* 153–193.

Cattell, R. (1963). Theory of fluid and crystallized intelligence: A critical experiment. *Journal of Educational Psychology, 54,* 1–22.

Cattell, R., & Horn, J. (1978). A check on the theory of fluid and crystallized intelligence with description of new subtest designs. *Journal of Educational Measurement, 15,* 139–164.

Clay, M. (1972). *The early detection of reading difficulties.* Auckland, New Zealand: Heinemann.

Cohen, J., Cohen, P., West, S. G., & Aiken, L. S. (2003). *Applied multiple regression/correlation analysis for the behavioral sciences.* Mahwah, NJ: Erlbaum.

Das, J. P., Naglieri, J. A., & Kirby, J. R. (1994). *Assessment of cognitive processes.* Needham Heights, MA: Allyn & Bacon.

Demaray, M. K., Schaefer, K., & Delong, K. (2003). Attention-deficit/hyperactivity disorder (ADHD): A national survey of training and current assessment practices in the schools. *Psychology in the Schools, 40,* 583–597.

DiPerna, J., & Elliott, S. (2000). *Academic Competence Evaluation Scales.* San Antonio, TX: The Psychological Corporation.

Donders, J. (1997). Sensitivity of the WISC-III to injury severity in children with traumatic head injury. *Assessment, 4,* 107–109.

Dunn, A. (2002, Fall). Partnership and problem solving to promote early intervention in literacy: Using the PAL. *CASP Today.*

Dunn, A. (in press). Los Angeles Unified School District (LAUSD) school psychology project bridging special and general education. *CASP Today.*

Dunn, L., & Dunn, L. (1997). *Peabody Picture Vocabulary Test–Third Edition.* Circle Pines, MN: American Guidance Service.

Ehri, L. C., Nunes, S. R., Stahl, S. A., & Willows, D. M. (2001). Systematic phonics instruction helps students learn to read: Evidence from the National Reading Panel's meta-analysis. *Review of Educational Research, 71,* 393–447.

Elliott, C. (1990). *Differential Ability Scales.* San Antonio, TX: The Psychological Corporation.

Elliott, S., DiPerna, J., & Shapiro, E. (2001). *Academic Intervention Monitoring System.* San Antonio, TX: The Psychological Corporation.

Faraone, S. V., Biederman, J., Lehman, B. K., & Spencer, T. (1993). Intellectual performance and school failure in children with attention deficit hyperactivity disorder and in their siblings. *Journal of Abnormal Psychology, 102*(4), 616–623.

Flanagan, D. P., & Kaufman, A. S. (2004). *Essentials of WISC-IV assessment.* New York: Wiley.

Flanagan, D. P., McGrew, K. S., & Ortiz, S. O. (2000). *The Wechsler intelligence scales and Gf-Gc theory.* Boston: Allyn & Bacon.

Flanagan, D. P., & Ortiz, S. O. (2001). *Essentials of cross-battery assessment.* New York: Wiley.

Flanagan, D. P., Ortiz, S. O., Alfonso, V. C., & Mascolo, J. (2002). *The achievement test desk reference (ATDR): Comprehensive assessment and learning disabilities.* Boston: Allyn & Bacon.

Frick, P. J., Kamphaus, R. W., Lahey, B. B., Loeber, R., Christ, M. A. G., Hart, E. L., & Tannenbaum, L. E. (1991). Academic underachievement and the disruptive behavior disorders. *Journal of Consulting and Clinical Psychology, 59,* 289–294.

Fry, A., & Hale, S. (1996). Processing speed, working memory, and fluid intelligence: Evidence for a developmental cascade. *Psychological Science, 7,* 237–241.

Gathercole, S., Pickering, S., Ambridge, B., & Wearing, H. (2004). The structure of working memory from 4 to 15 years of age. *Developmental Psychology, 40,* 177–190.

Goldberg, E., & Bougakov, D. (2000). Novel approaches to the diagnosis and treatment of frontal lobe dysfunction. In A. Christensen & B. P. Uzell (Eds.), *International handbook of neuropsychological rehabilitation* (pp. 93–112). New York: Kluwer/Plenum.

Glutting, J., Oakland, T., & Konold, T. (1994). Criterion-related bias with the guide to the assessment of test-session behavior for the WISC-III and WIAT: Possible race/ethnicity, gender, and SES effects. *Journal of School Psychology, 32,* 355–369.

Gottfredson, L. (1998). The general intelligence factor. *Scientific American,* November, 1–10. Retrieved February 5, 2002 from http://www.scientificamerican.com/specialissues/1198intelligence/1198gottfred.html

Goodman, Y., & Burke, C. (1972). *Reading miscue inventory: Procedure for diagnosis and correction.* New York: Macmillan.

Hammill, D. D., Fowler, L., Bryant, B., & Dunn, C. (1992). *A survey of test usage among speech/language pathologists.* Unpublished manuscript.

Hasbrouck, J., & Tindal, G. (1992). Curriculum based oral reading fluency norms for students in grades 2 through 5. *Teaching Exceptional Children, 24,* 41–44.

Henry, M. (2003). *Unlocking literacy. Effective decoding and spelling instruction.* Baltimore: Paul H. Brookes.

Hooper, S. R., & Hynd, G. W. (1982, October). *The differential diagnosis of developmental dyslexia with the Kaufman Assessment Battery for children.* Paper presented at the meeting of the National Academy of Neuropsychologists, Atlanta, GA.

Horn, J. (1991). Human cognitive capabilities: *Gf-Gc* theory. In D. Flanagan, J. Genshaft, & P. Harrison (Eds.), *Contemporary intellectual assessment: Theories, tests, and issues* (pp. 53–91). New York: Guilford.

Hutton, J. B., Dubes, R., & Muir, S. (1992). Assessment practices of school psychologists: Ten years later. *School Psychologist Review, 21,* 271–284.

Individuals with Disabilities Education Act Amendments of 1997, 20 U.S.C. 1400 *et seq.* (Fed. Reg. 64, 1999).

Individuals with Disabilities Education Improvement Act (IDEA) of 2004, Public Law No. 108-446.

Individuals with Disabilities Education Act–section 602 (15) (1991). Compilation of Federal Education Laws Vol. V. Washington, DC: U.S. Government Printing Office.

James, E. M., & Selz, M. (1997). Neuropsychological bases of common learning and behavior problems in children. In C. R. Reynolds & E. Fletcher-Janzen (Eds.), *The handbook of clinical child neuropsychology* (2nd ed., pp. 157–203). New York: Kluwer-Plenum.

Johnson, M., Kress, R., & Pikulski, J. (1987). *Informal reading inventories* (2nd ed.). Newark, IL: International Reading Association.

Joint Committee on Testing Practices (1988). *Code of Fair Testing Practices in Education.* Washington, DC: American Psychological Association.

Kail, R., & Salthouse, T. (1994). Processing speed as a mental capacity. *Acta Psychologica, 86,* 199–225.

Kamphaus, R. W., & Reynolds, C. R. (1987). *Clinical and research applications of the K-ABC.* Circle Pines, MN: American Guidance Service.

Kaufman, A. S., & Kaufman, N. L. (1985, 1997). *Kaufman Test of Educational Achievement.* Circle Pines, MN: American Guidance Service.

Kaufman, A. S., & Kaufman, N. L. (2001). *Specific learning disabilities and difficulties in children and adolescents.* New York: Cambridge University Press.

Kaufman, A. S., & Kaufman, N. L. (2004a). *Kaufman Test of Educational Achievement, Second Edition Comprehensive Form Manual.* Circle Pines, MN: American Guidance Service.

Kaufman, A. S., & Kaufman, N. L. (2004b). *Kaufman Assessment Battery for Children–Second Edition Manual.* Circle Pines, MN: American Guidance Service.

Kaufman, A. S., & Kaufman, N. L. (2004c). *Kaufman Brief Intelligence Test–Second Edition Manual.* Circle Pines, MN: American Guidance Service.

Kaufman, A. S., & Kaufman, N. L. (2005). *Kaufman Test of Educational Achievement–Second Edition Brief Form Manual.* Circle Pines, MN: American Guidance Service.

Kaufman, A. S., Lichtenberger, E. O., Fletcher-Janzen, E., & Kaufman, N. L. (2005). *Essentials of KABC-II assessment.* New York: Wiley.

Kirby, J. R., & Williams, N. H. (1991). *Learning problems: A cognitive approach.* Toronto: Kagan and Woo.

Kuhn, M., & Stahl, S. (2000). Fluency. *A review of developmental and remedial practices* (CIERA Report #2-0008). Ann Arbor, MI: Center for Improvement of Early Reading Achievement, University of Michigan.

Laurent, J., & Swerdlik, M. (1992, March). *Psychological test usage: A survey of internship supervisors.* Paper presented at the annual meeting of the National Association of School Psychologists, Nashville, TN.

Lennon, J., & Slesinski, C. (1999). Early intervention in reading: Results of a screening and intervention program for kindergarten students. *School Psychology Review, 28,* 353–364.

Lichtenberger, E. O. (2001). The Kaufman tests-K-ABC and KAIT. In A. S. Kaufman & N. L. Kaufman (Eds.), *Specific learning disabilities and difficulties in children and adolescents* (pp. 283–306). New York: Cambridge University Press.

Lichtenberger, E. O., Broadbooks, D. Y., & Kaufman, A. S. (2000). *Essentials of cognitive assessment with KAIT and other Kaufman measures.* New York: Wiley.

Lovett, M. (1987). A developmental approach to reading disability: Accuracy and speed criteria of normal and deficient reading skill. *Child Development, 58,* 234–260.

Luria, A. R. (1966). *Human brain: An introduction to neuropsychology.* New York: Basic Books.

Luria, A. R. (1970). The functional organization of the brain. *Scientific American, 222,* 66–78.

Luria, A. R. (1973). *The working brain: An introduction to neuro-psychology.* London: Penguin.

Lyon, G., Fletcher, J., & Barnes, T. (2003). Learning disabilities. In E. J. Mash & R. A. Barkley (Eds.), *Child psychopathology* (pp. 520–586). New York: Guilford.

Lyon, R., Shaywitz, S., & Shaywitz, B. (2003). A definition of dyslexia. *Annals of Dyslexia, 53,* 1–14.

Markwardt, F. C. (1998). *Peabody Individual Achievement Test, Revised.* Circle Pines, MN: American Guidance Service.

Masterson, J., Apel, K., & Wasowicz, J. (2002). *SPELL. Spelling Performance Evaluation for Language & Literacy: A prescriptive assessment of spelling on CD-ROM.* Evanston, IL: Learning by Design.

Mather, N., Wendling, B. J., & Woodcock, R. W. (2001). *Essentials of WJ III Tests of Achievement assessment.* New York: Wiley.

Mather, N., & Woodcock, R. W. (2001). *Woodcock-Johnson III Tests of Achievement Examiner's manual.* Itasca, IL: Riverside.

McGrew, K. S., & Flanagan, D. P. (1998). *The intelligence test desk reference (ITDR): Gf-Gc cross-battery assessment.* Boston: Allyn & Bacon.

Moats, L. C. (1995). *Spelling: Development, disabilities, and instruction.* Baltimore: York Press.

Naglieri, J. A. (2001). Using the Cognitive Assessment System (CAS) with learning disabled children. In A. S. Kaufman & N. L. Kaufman (Eds.), *Specific learning disabilities and difficulties in children and adolescents* (pp. 141–177). New York: Cambridge University Press.

National Council of Teachers of Mathematics. (2000). *Principles and Standards for School Mathematics.* Reston, VA: Author.

National Institute of Child Health and Human Development. (2000). *Report of the National Reading Panel: Teaching children to read.* Washington, DC: National Institute of Child Health and Human Development.

National Reading Panel. (2000). *Teaching children to read: An evidence-based assessment of the scientific research literature on reading and its implications for reading instruction* (NIH Publication No. 000-4754). Washington, DC: National Institute of Child Health and Human Development.

Nunnally, J. C. (1978). *Psychometric theory* (2nd ed.). New York: McGraw-Hill.

Perlow, R., Jattuso, M., & Moore, D. (1997). Role of verbal working memory in complex skill acquisition. *Human Performance, 10,* 283–302.

Psychological Corporation, The. (1992). *Wechsler Individual Achievement Test.* San Antonio, TX: Author.

Psychological Corporation, The. (1999). *Wechsler Abbreviated Test of Intelligence.* San Antonio, TX: Author.

Psychological Corporation, The. (2001). *Wechsler Individual Achievement Test–Second Edition–Abbreviated (WIAT-II-A).* San Antonio, TX: Author.

Psychological Corporation, The. (2002). *Wechsler Individual Achievement Test–Second Edition.* San Antonio, TX: Author.

Prifitera, A., Saklofske, D. H., & Weiss, L. G. (Eds.). (2005). *WISC-IV clinical use and interpretation.* New York: Elsevier Academic.

Rack, J., Snowling, M., & Olson, R. (1992). The nonword reading deficit in developmental dyslexia: A review. *Reading Research Quarterly, 27,* 28–53.

Raiford, S., Weiss, L., Rolfhus, E., & Coalson, D. (2005). *WISC-IV technical report #4: General abilities index.* San Antonio, TX: The Psychological Corporation.

Raney, G. E. (1993). Monitoring changes in cognitive load during reading: An event-related brain potential and reaction time analysis. *Journal of Experimental Psychology: Learning, Memory and Cognition, 19,* 51–69.

Reynolds, C. R., Kamphaus, R. W., Rosenthal, B. L., & Hiemenz, J. R. (1997). Applications of the Kaufman Assessment Battery for Children (K-ABC) in neuropsychological assessment. In C. R. Reynolds & E. Fletcher-Janzen (Eds.), *The handbook of clinical child neuropsychology* (2nd ed., pp. 253–269). New York: Kluwer-Plenum.

Roberts, M., Turco, T., & Shapiro, E. (1991). Differential effects of fixed instructional ratios on student's progress in reading. *Journal of Psychoeducational Assessment, 9,* 308–318.

Rourke, B. (1989). Significance of Verbal-Performance discrepancies for subtypes of children with learning disabilities: Opportunities for the WISC-II. In A. Prifitera & D. Saklofske (Eds.), *WISC-II clinical use and interpretation* (pp. 139–156). San Diego, CA: Academic Press.

Samuels, S. (1988). Decoding and automaticity: Helping poor readers become automatic at word recognition. *The Reading Teacher, 48,* 756–760.

Sattler, J. (2001). *Assessment of children: Cognitive applications.* (4th ed.). San Diego, CA: Author.

Siegel, L. S. (1999). Issues in the definition and diagnosis of learning disabilities: a perspective on Guckenberger v. Boston University. *Journal of Learning Disabilities, 32,* 304–319.

Siegal, M. (1997). *Knowing children: Experiments in conversation and cognition* (2nd ed.). Hove, England: Psychology Press.

Smith, D. K. (2001). *Essentials of individual achievement assessment.* New York: Wiley.

Spreen, O. (2001). Learning disabilities and their neurological foundations, theories, and subtypes. In A. S. Kaufman & N. L. Kaufman (Eds.), *Specific learning disabilities and difficulties in children and adolescents* (pp. 283–306). New York: Cambridge University Press.

Stanovich, K. E. (1985). Explaining the variance in reading ability in terms of psychological processes: What have we learned? *Annals of Dyslexia, 35,* 67–96.

Stanovich, K. E. (1992). Developmental reading disorder. In S. R. Hooper, G. W. Hynd, & R. E. Mattison (Eds.), *Developmental disorders: Diagnostic criteria and clinical assessment* (pp. 173–208). Hillsdale, NJ: Erlbaum.

Stanovich, K. E. (1999). The sociopsychometrics of learning disabilities. *Journal of Learning Disabilities, 32,* 350–361.

Stanovich, K. E., & Siegel, L. (1994). Phenotypic performance profile of children with reading disabilities: A regression-based test of the phonological-core variable-difference model. *Journal of Educational Psychology, 86,* 24–53.

Sternberg, R. (1995). *In search of the human mind.* Fort Worth, TX: Harcourt Brace.

Stinnett, T. A., Havey, J. M., & Oehler-Stinnett, J. (1994). Current test usage by practicing school psychologists: A national survey. *Journal of Psychoeducational Assessment, 12,* 331–350.

Swanson, H. (1996). Individual and age-related differences in children's working memory. *Memory & Cognition, 24,* 70–82.

Swanson, H., & Howell, M. (2001). Working memory, short-term memory, and speech rate as predictors of children's reading performance at different ages. *Journal of Educational Psychology, 9,* 720–734.

Teeter, P. A. (1997). Neurocognitive interventions for childhood and adolescent disorders: A transactional model. In C. R. Reynolds & E. Fletcher-Janzen (Eds.), *The handbook of clinical child neuropsychology* (2nd ed., pp. 387–417). New York: Kluwer-Plenum.

Teeter, P. A., & Semrud-Clikeman, M. (1998). *Child clinical neuropsychology: Assessment and interventions for neuropsychiatric and neurodevelopmental disorders of childhood.* Boston: Allyn & Bacon.

Torgesen, J., Wagner, R., & Rashotte, C. (1994). Longitudinal studies of phonological processing and reading. *Journal of Learning Disabilities, 27,* 276–286.

Vellutino, F. R., Scanlon, D. M., & Lyon, G. R. (2000). Differentiating between difficult-to-remediate and readily remediated poor readers: more evidence against the IQ-achievement discrepancy definition of reading disability. *Journal of Learning Disabilities, 33,* 223–238.

Wechsler, D. (1975). Intelligence defined and undefined: A relativistic appraisal. *American Psychologist, 30,* 135–139.

Wechsler, D. (1981). *Wechsler Adult Intelligence Scale–Revised.* San Antonio, TX: The Psychological Corporation.

Wechsler, D. (1989). *Wechsler Preschool and Primary Scale of Intelligence–Revised.* San Antonio, TX: The Psychological Corporation.

Wechsler, D. (1991). *Wechsler Intelligence Scale for Children–Third Edition.* San Antonio, TX: The Psychological Corporation.

Wechsler, D. (1997). *Wechsler Adult Intelligence Scale–Third Edition.* San Antonio, TX: The Psychological Corporation.

Wechsler, D. (2001). *Wechsler Individual Achievement Test, Second Edition.* San Antonio, TX: The Psychological Corporation.

Wechsler, D. (2002a). *Wechsler Individual Achievement Test–Second Edition Supplement for Adults and College Students.* San Antonio, TX: The Psychological Corporation.

Wechsler, D. (2002b). *Wechsler Preschool and Primary Scale of Intelligence–Third Edition.* San Antonio, TX: The Psychological Corporation.

Wechsler, D. (2003). *Wechsler Intelligence Scale for Children–Fourth Edition.* San Antonio, TX: The Psychological Corporation.

Wechsler, D., Kaplan, E., Fein, D., Kramer, J., Morris, R., Delis, D., & Maerlender, A. (2004). *WISC-IV integrated technical and interpretive manual.* San Antonio, TX: Harcourt Assessment.

Wilkinson, G. S. (1993). *Wide Range Achievement Test–Third Edition administration manual.* Wilmington, DE: Wide Range.

Wilson, M. S., & Reschley, D. J. (1996). Assessment in school psychology training and practice. *School Psychology Review, 21,* 9–23.

Wolf, M., & Bowers, P. (1999). The double-deficit hypothesis for the developmental dyslexias. *Journal of Educational Psychology, 91,* 415–438.

Woodcock, R., & Johnson, B. (1990). *Woodcock-Johnson Psycho-Educational Battery–Revised, Tests of Achievement.* Chicago, IL: Riverside.

Woodcock, R. W., McGrew, K. S., & Mather, N. (2001). *Woodcock-Johnson III.* Itasca, IL: Riverside.

Zachary, R. (1990). Wechsler's intelligence scales: Theoretical and practical considerations. *Journal of Psychoeducational Assessment, 8,* 276–289.

Annotated Bibliography

Berninger, V., & Richards, T. (2002). *Brain literacy for educators and psychologists.* San Diego, CA: Elsevier Science.

This comprehensive text is organized around three themes: the interplay between nature (genetics) and nurture (experience and environment), the functional systems of the brain and how they lead to reading, writing, and mathematics; and research in the field of educational neuropsychology, including the use of brain mapping in the diagnosis of reading and writing disorders.

Berninger, V., Dunn, A., & Alper, T. (2005). Integrated, multilevel model of branching assessment, instructional assessment, and profile assessment. In A. Prifitera, D. Saklofske, & L. Weiss (Eds.). *WISC-IV Clinical use and interpretation* (pp. 151–185). San Diego: Academic Press.

This chapter presents a multilevel approach to integrated assessment. It discusses methods for integrating results from achievement and cognitive measures with students' response to intervention. The final goal of the assessment approach is to provide the most useful information that is relevant to instructional planning.

Flanagan, D. P., & Kaufman, A. S. (2004). *Essentials of WISC-IV assessment.* New York: Wiley.

This book details administration, scoring, and interpretation of the WISC-IV. It provides a theory-driven approach to integrating the WIAT-II and WISC-IV in the assessment of learning disabilities. Case reports are presented that exemplify how to integrate the WIAT-II with the WISC-IV.

Flanagan, D. P., Ortiz, S. O., Alfonso, V. C., & Mascolo, J. (2002). *The achievement test desk reference (ATDR): Comprehensive assessment and learning disabilities.* Boston: Allyn & Bacon.

This book provides comprehensive information about the most important psychometric, theoretical, and qualitative characteristics of the major achievement batteries, including the WIAT-II, WJ III ACH, DAB-3, DATA-2, KTEA/NU, and PIAT-R/NU. In addition, test characteristics are summarized for brief/screening measures as well as special-purpose batteries that are used to assess specific academic skill areas such as reading, math, writing, oral language, and phonological processing. In addition, this book offers a comprehensive framework for LD determination and provides practitioners with a step-by-step decision making process in responding to learning-related referrals.

Kaufman, A. S., & Kaufman, N. L. (2001). *Specific learning disabilities and difficulties in children and adolescents.* New York: Cambridge University Press.

This book contains 13 chapters written by experts in the field of learning disabilities. History and traditions are examined along with alternative cognitive approaches to learning disabilities assessment and remediation. In addition, several chapters focus on neuropsychological assessment and remediation and the assessment of memory. A summary chapter reviews current controversies and future issues.

Kaufman, A. S., & Kaufman, N. L. (2004). *Kaufman Test of Educational Achievement–Second Edition (K-TEA-II): Comprehensive Form.* Circle Pines, MN: American Guidance Service.

The manual of this test (included in the test kit) gives detailed information about KTEA-II test development, standardization, and the test's psychometric properties. It describes all of the subtests and scales, and instructs examiners on how to score and analyze the KTEA-II data. Because the KTEA-II was conormed with the KABC-II, this manual provides a wealth of correlational data and information about how the tests are related.

Kaufman, A. S., Lichtenberger, E. O., Fletcher-Janzen, E., & Kaufman, N. L. (2005). *Essentials of KABC-II assessment*. New York: Wiley.

Covers thoroughly the administration, scoring, and interpretation of the KABC-II, including treatment of how it can be integrated with the KTEA-II. It includes sample case reports exemplifying use of the KTEA-II with the KABC-II.

Lichtenberger, E. O., Mather, N., Kaufman, N. L., & Kaufman, A. S. (2004). *Essentials of assessment report writing*. New York: Wiley.

This book reviews the essential elements and structure of well-written psychological and psychoeducational reports. It covers all aspects of preparing a written report and provides numerous illustrative examples of clear, informative reports. It includes the case reports of Xander, a 5-year-old who was administered the WPPSI-III and the WIAT-II, and of Brianna, an 18-year-old diagnosed with ADHD, who was assessed with the KABC-II and KTEA-II.

National Reading Panel. (2000). *Teaching Children to Read: An evidence-based assessment of the scientific research literature on reading and its implications for reading instruction* (NIH Publication No. 000-4754). Washington, DC: National Institute of Child Health and Human Development.

This report resulted from the work of the National Reading Panel, which was convened in 1997 in response to Congress, in consultation with the Secretary of Education, for the purpose of assessing the status of research-based knowledge, including the effectiveness of various approaches to teach children to read. The report addresses the critical role of alphabetics, fluency, and comprehension in the acquisition of reading skills and includes an assessment of teacher education and computer technology as they relate to reading instruction. The report can be a valuable tool for the clinician when writing intervention plans and in understanding the necessary components of a balanced instructional reading program.

Smith, D. K. (2001). *Essentials of individual achievement assessment*. New York: Wiley.

This book reviews several achievement tests: WIAT, WIAT-II, K-TEA/NU, PIAT-R, and WRAT3. For each test, important information on administration, scoring, and interpretation is provided. Case reports are included that exemplify how to utilize each of the achievement instruments in an assessment.

Swanson, H. L., Harris, K., & Graham, S. (Eds.). (2003). *Handbook of research on learning disabilities*. New York: Guilford.

This handbook reviews the major theoretical, methodological, and instructional advances that have occurred in the field of learning disabilities over the last 20 years. With contributions from leading researchers, the volume synthesizes a vast body of knowledge on the nature of learning disabilities, their relationship to basic psychological and brain processes, and how students with these difficulties can best be identified and treated. Findings are reviewed on ways to support student performance in specific skill areas—including language arts, math, science, and social studies—as well as general principles of effective instruction that cut across academic domains.

The Psychological Corporation. (2002). *Wechsler Individual Achievement Test–Second Edition*. San Antonio, TX: Author.

The manual of this test (included in the test kit) gives detailed information about WIAT-II test development, standardization, and the test's psychometric properties. It describes all of the subtests and scales, and instructs examiners on how to score and analyze the WIAT-II data. Because the WIAT-II was conormed with several Wechsler instruments, this manual provides a wealth of correlational data and information about how the tests are related.

Index